# Equity in Schools and Society

# Equity in Schools and Society

edited by
**Judy M. Iseke-Barnes**
and
**Njoki Nathani Wane**

Canadian Scholars' Press Inc.　　　　Toronto　　　　2000

**Equity in Schools and Society**
Edited by Judy M. Iseke-Barnes and Njoki Nathani Wane

First published in 2000 by
**Canadian Scholars' Press Inc.**
180 Bloor Street West, Suite 1202
Toronto, Ontario
M5S 2V6

We acknowledge the financial support of the Government of Canada through the Book Publishing Industry Development Programme for our publishing activities.

**Canadian Cataloguing in Publication Data**

Main entry under title:

Equity in schools and society

Includes bibliographical references.
ISBN 1-55130-167-9

1. Discrimination in education. 2. Discrimination. I. Barnes, Judith M. (Judith Marie), 1963– . II. Wane, Njoki Nathani

LC212.E64 2000          379.2'6          C00-932175-6

Page layout and cover design: Brad Horning

02 03 04 05 06          6 5 4 3 2

Printed and bound in Canada by AGMV Marquis

# Acknowledgments

We wish to acknowledge: Our families for their consistent source of inspiration, patience, love, support; Neal Barnes and Amadou Wane for believing in us, for humor at the most needed times, and for editorial help; Quinton, Tegan, and Jennice who waited for mom many hours but provided reason to complete this project; Sein for asking "is it through yet" and providing a reason for it to end; Barbara Waterfall for always being at the right place at the right time; Cecelia Reynolds whose words of advice and letter of support got the ball rolling; Kathy Bickmore whose comprehensive course packs inspired the idea of this text; The encouragement of Canadian Scholars' Press for giving us a chance to publish at this important juncture; Last but not least our grandmothers, mothers, aunties, cousins, sisters, fathers, brothers, and our ancestors whose spirits have always been there in our academic struggles.

To All My Relations, Asante

Judy Iseke-Barnes
Njoki Nathani Wane

# Publisher's Acknowledgments

**Chapter 2**: Marva N. Collins, "Why I Teach", in Gerald Taylor and Robert Runté, *Thinking About Teaching: An Introduction*, pp. 19-21. © 1995 by Harcourt Brace & Company, Canada, Ltd. All rights reserved. Reprinted by permission of Harcourt Canada, Ltd.

**Chapter 3**:"Our Schools Our Selves: The Story of a New Teacher" by Laura Ford and Lisa Beta Ford. In *Orbit* 25(4), pp. 21-22. © 1994 Orbit. Reprinted by permission of *Orbit* – OISE/UT's Magazine for Schools.

**Chapter 4**: Carl A. Grant and Kenneth M. Zeichner, "On Becoming a Reflective Teacher," in Gerald Taylor and Robert Runté, *Thinking About Teaching: An Introduction*, pp. 54-61, 63-68. © 1995 by Harcourt Brace & Company, Canada Ltd. All rights reserved. Reprinted by permission of Harcourt Canada, Ltd.

**Chapter 5**: Benjamin Levin and Jon Young, *Understanding Canadian Schools: An Introduction to Educational Administration*, pp. 2-7, 11-13, 16-18. © 1994 Harcourt Brace & Company, Canada Ltd. All rights reserved. Reprinted by permission of Harcourt Canada, Ltd.

**Chapter 6**: "On Being and Becoming a Teacher in Alberta" by Ted T. Aoki. In *Canadian Ethnicity: The Politics of Meaning* edited by T. Aoki, J.

# Contents

## PART 1
### OVERVIEW AND TEACHER'S UNDERSTANDING
### AND DEFINING OF THEIR LOCATION

## PART 2
### THE POLITICS OF MEANING

## Part 6
## Gender and Regulation of Bodies

## Part 7
## Issues of Sexuality in Schools

## Part 8
## Students at Risk: Class, Poverty, and Marginality

# Foreword

The unprecedented pace of global change with continual relocation and diversification of the population has created significant social changes in society. There is pressing need for educational organizations to reflect and respond to the diversity of the population and social change. This book offers resources for educators and students to examine the relationship of schools and society and to address the multiple equity issues produced by social change.

Today many are questioning the inadequacy of social, educational, and political practices that do not speak adequately to the variety of human experiences or to the diverse history of events and ideas that have shaped human growth and development. Examining teachers' locations, the politics of meaning in education, and issues of bias in education — including race, class, and gender — can highlight the problems associated with the institution of schooling as sites for the reproduction of societal inequalities. Theoretical and practical underpinnings of cultural studies, critical pedagogy, feminist studies, anti-racist education, and Aboriginal education are included in this collection to interrogate power inequalities and bias in educational settings and society.

This text draws together existing scholarly and critical work from diverse sources and perspectives, applies theoretical, scholarly, and critical work to issues of teachers' practices, broadening the literature about teacher roles to include discussion of equity issues. This collection draws upon critical educational theories and social theories to articulate a pedagogic discourse to understand the political organization and relationship of schools and society. It examines both reproductive theories of schooling: the structural processes that create inequitable outcomes, and the structural processes of resistance and oppositional cultures that counter the way schools function to reproduce dominant ideologies of society. The focus throughout this text on differential power relations within society and implications for education provides educators and students analyses of how schools work to maintain the status quo and discourses of resistance to prevailing cultures of dominance. A pedagogic challenge is posed to understand the politics of meaning in education, including assumptions of what is normative and what is valid knowledge as well as alternatives to the dominant discourses.

We believe there is a need to develop a more critical integrative pedagogical orientation that examines the socially constructed ways of making meanings in a racialized, gendered, and classed world. As educators we are implicated in examining and interrogating established hegemonic ways of knowing.

# Preface

This book is an excellent and welcome contribution to the field of equity in education. Judy Iseke-Barnes and Njoki Nathani Wane bring a very unique analysis to equity discourse as it addresses colonialism and Aboriginal oppression in Canada. As an Aboriginal woman I am cognizant of the fact that we will never be able to achieve equity and justice in this country until the issues of colonialism and Aboriginal oppression are addressed. I commend Judy and Njoki's efforts, as I am not aware of any other text of its kind in the current literature. The analysis presented in this book provides a broad understanding of the themes of race, ethnicity, class, gender, and sexuality as these themes intersect in the Canadian educational system. Given that this broad understanding includes Aboriginal issues, the book provides a quality of leadership in current equity discourse.

Judy and Njoki suggest that this book serves the functions of countering negative effects of oppression and addressing places and situations where critical work is needed. As an Aboriginal educator I know that a great deal of sensitivity and knowledge is required to handle the intersecting issues of equity in the classroom. To do so effectively requires that our praxis be informed by a solid framework. Without such a framework our good intentions can end up reinforcing and exacerbating the reality of inequity in the classroom. I speak from my own past practice of introducing the topic of heterosexism and homophobia into a university curriculum. Before reflecting on my practice from a critical equity perspective, I thought my efforts were sufficient. Since then I see that the mere introduction of homophobia and heterosexism did little to disrupt the taken-for-granted acceptance of homophobic and heterosexist discourse. I merely brought a "token" lesbian into the classroom as a guest speaker. I had failed to create a classroom setting where power imbalances were actively ruptured. I had also failed to create a safe space for my students to openly "come out" as two-spirited, gay, lesbian, or transgendered persons. My praxis intensified these students' feelings of isolation and being closeted among their peers. While I fully understood the implications of token gestures with respect to the inclusion of Aboriginal issues, I had failed to comprehend oppressions as intersecting. My analysis of oppression from a critical equity perspective was thus severely lacking. I have since then developed a critical, equitable pedagogy.

This book provides a solid framework for an educational equity based on systems discourse. This discourse enables us to understand power imbalances as well as the systemic and methodological impediments that hamper an equity agenda. The reading of this book enables one to engage in critical reflection. The book also goes beyond critical analysis by offering valuable suggestions for addressing and attenuating the intersecting themes of race, ethnicity, class, gender, and sexuality in the classroom. It provides both teachers and students with concrete knowledge and tools to help create an equitable educational environment. The sections in this text are well organized and raise critical questions to facilitate a space for the discussion of equity in education. They offer concrete examples and a suggested reading list for furthering understanding. This book is a valuable tool for both pre-service students and practising educators.

I highly encourage the reader to seriously reflect on this text. I also encourage all students and educators to take seriously the challenge of working toward creating equity in education. In the current political climate of budget cuts and predominant conservative discourse, the objectives of equity in education are being severely compromised. This book offers both a timely and a practical solution to the current problematic of attempting to create an equitable curriculum and classroom practice. I wish for all of us so motivated to have the courage and fortitude to rupture the dominant and prevailing oppressions that have become an everyday reality in the classroom and in society.

June 2000
Prof. Barbara Waterfall,
The Department of Native Human Services,
Laurentian University,
Sudbury, Ontario

# Introduction

The focus of this book is to examine equity issues in school and society. It draws on history, sociology, literature, cultural expressions, films, and theory. The book provides space to discuss and rethink education, its politics, and the relationships between school and society. It also explores knowledge and skills that are basic requisites to understanding and working within the Canadian context. In addition, the text explores issues and dilemmas relevant to students and teachers in order to understand how race, ethnicity, class, sexuality, and gender influence teaching and learning experiences.

## Main Objectives

The principle objectives of this text are

1. To increase critical awareness of issues concerning equity in school and society for students and teachers;
2. To discuss the complexities of both school and society as institutions and search for paradigms to highlight the dilemmas and lived experiences of teachers as they grapple with the interpretation and implementation of goals and policies and work to address students' needs;

3. To generate greater awareness of the political economy of schools and societies;
4. To increase understanding of hidden biases such as racism, classism, and sexism in order to develop practical strategies for dealing with these forms of oppression;
5. To enhance the acquisition of critical intellectual skills related to both comprehension and analysis of teaching and learning in a culturally diverse context;
6. To generate and reformulate teachers' roles in relation to the multiple demands of teaching and learning in complex environments.

## ORGANIZATION OF THE TEXT

This text is organized into eight parts, each highlighting the tensions and contentions of teaching and learning in complex environments. Each section is composed of a set of readings that emphasizes selected themes for the purposes of identifying common knowledges. The themes examine the history of how these knowledges are acquired in order to interrogate stereotypes, biases, and misrepresentations. Sections are organized to assist the reader in identifying ways of dealing with stereotypes in order to generate working knowledges of biases in schools and broader societal contexts. The text also provides a rationale for the selection of topics and resources in each section, which is summarized at the end of most chapters by a set of exercise questions for further exploration. References for further readings are also provided.

### Part 1 — Overview and Teacher's Understanding and Defining of Their Location

Part 1 begins by exploring interconnections between schools, students, and society through a systems discourse, which examines the relationships between the three institutions that are referred to as subsystems (Wane). Wane argues that "a systems discourse is a discursive framework that illustrates the functioning and relationships of subsystems within larger society. It illustrates systematic power imbalances, as well as methodical barriers that are embedded within the various sub-systems of larger society. A systems discourse enables an understanding of institutions and how they create and sustain interconnectedness and interdependency. This framework addresses the dilemmas, tensions, and fears that occupants of these institutions may experience as they come to grips with their roles in the systems discourse" (Wane).

The thought process of preparing to teach is shared in "Rethinking Teaching Using a Systems Discourse" (Wane) to highlight the importance of keeping in mind the stakeholders involved — namely students, teachers, school administrators, governments, and the community at large — when selecting topics, themes, and methodologies for teaching. Wane provides graphic representations of the systems discourse employed to summarize and highlight the important issues and relationships for discussions.

Next is an overview of teachers' understandings and defining their locations in relation to students, schools, and society. In the articles "Why I Teach" and "Our Schools Our Selves: The Story of a New Teacher," readers can contrast different ways of defining teacher roles and begin to examine personal orientations to teaching. "On Becoming a Reflective Teacher" then highlights the use of reflectivity in teaching. A list of recommended readings are provided in order to expand the scope of consideration of this topic.

## Part 2 — The Politics of Meaning

This part examines the politics of meaning, asking what the implications are for teachers' pedagogy and for education in Canada of issues of identity and understanding of self and other. It seeks to identify for whom the school system is organized and by whom it is dominated. Readers are encouraged to examine their own positions or frames of reference with respect to their power, social class, access, and privilege, and how their positions perpetuate or challenge the status quo. In the article "Making Sense of Public Schooling," Levin and Young state that "questions of 'how to' cannot be separated from questions of 'why.' Nor is it possible to detach the discussion of school organizations from a broader discussion of the purposes of schooling and its place in Canadian society." They also indicate that "the official image [of schooling] is often a pale reflection of the complexity of real classrooms and schools."

This paper will assist readers in examining orientations to public schooling. The remaining two readings in Part 2 highlight the contradictions in which teachers find themselves, especially when they are trying to deconstruct the politics of meaning. It is important to highlight the danger of engaging in these types of politics when we are not grounded with the appropriate epistemologies, thus perpetuating the status quo and objectifying the "other" rather than rupturing the existing structures of domination.

## Part 3 — Rethinking Inclusion: Representation and Stereotypes

The aim of the next two parts is to begin to envision the larger societal dynamics affecting school cultures and student learning, to begin to get beyond the initial impulse to chalk up conflict and resistance to individualized/personalized "bad attitude," and to become aware of the historical context of contemporary social relations in Canada. In particular, the readings in Part 3 help us begin to define racism, race, and ethnocentrism. This section begins by sharing common knowledges of racism, prejudice, bias, and discrimination, and how these are manifested on a daily basis. Readers initially taking up this text may wish to engage in brainstorming in order to develop a working definition of the discriminatory practices of racism, classism, sexism, elitism, etc. The text provides further insights into how these practices are produced, maintained, and perpetuated at the subconscious level. The articles "I'm Not White" and "I'm Not Racist" interrogate the denial and guilt that many students might find themselves caught in. "Talking About Race, Learning About Racism: The Application of Racial Identity Development Theory" provides an approach on how to problematize these feelings in order to engage in anti-racist education.

To help us consider what it is that teachers are facing in classrooms, we next turn to excerpts from Stuart Hall's *Representation: Cultural Representations and Signifying Practices*, which examines issues of cultural identity in relation to media and representations, and proceeds to examine types and stereotypes. In this section readers begin to see how society produces images of culture and myths about cultural groups.

This part concludes with Short's article on "Anti-racist Education and Moral Behaviour: Lessons from the Holocaust." The main argument in this article is that anti-racist educators should heed the lesson of the Holocaust and adopt measures aimed specifically at preventing bystander behaviour and conformity to peer-group pressure.

We recommend as an additional resource to this test the film called *For Angela*, which is commonly used in high schools for discussions of stereotypes, and we have provided questions in the Appendix. This film examines stereotypes of Aboriginal peoples in Canada through a scene in which a group of adolescent boys direct demeaning comments toward an Aboriginal woman and her daughter who are sitting at a bus stop and later riding the bus. On the bus, other passengers and the bus driver note the behaviour but fail to take any action. The behaviour of these teens profoundly affects the little girl, Anglea. Angela's mother takes action to aid her daughter and to begin a dialogue with these boys to counteract their stereotyping and very negative understanding of Aboriginal peoples. The adolescent behaviour portrayed in this movie is not uncommon or strange in our schools. The film challenges all educators who might encounter such behaviours and attitudes and who abdicate their responsibilities to respond to the situations. Educators are encouraged to take action to respond to the underlying structural biases perpetuated in our schools and societies to ensure that communities and diversity are respected.

## Part 4 — Rethinking Inclusion: Representation and Stereotypes

Part 4 examines representations and stereotypes while rethinking inclusion in education, and begins by taking up images of Indianness produced in colonialism. The text of *Fluffs and Feathers* is based on a museum display originally mounted in the Woodlands Cultural Centre, Brantford, Ontario, later at the Royal Ontario Museum, and finally at a travelling exhibit throughout Ontario. The exhibit examines the production of images of Indians (the term used for the images and myths produced in dominant culture about "Indians") in media and cultural productions. Readers might originally not see anything wrong with these images and representations but Doxtator's text, in addition to critiquing these representations, creates awareness and sensitizes readers to the assumptions of the dominant culture about Aboriginal peoples. Extending this text into classroom discussions are excerpts from *How to*

*Tell the Difference: A Guide for Evaluating Children's Books for Anti-Indian Bias*, which provide examples of colonial images pervasive in textbooks and initial discussion of the difficulties of these images, which will assist readers in formulating ideas about countering images of Indianness in texts. Teachers taking up images of Indianness in the classroom will need to examine materials carefully and question their use. We need to examine the troubling images of Aboriginal peoples in texts for children and positive portrayals in *How to Tell the Difference* to help in this task.

In the previous section, Stuart Hall examined ways that power "produces" new discourses, new kinds of knowledge, and new objects of knowledge, and shapes new practices and institutions. Readers are called upon to apply these knowledges in examining the "new" kind of knowledge being produced about Aboriginal peoples, what and who is the object of the knowledge, what "new" practices are carried out, what "new" institutions are created, and how these continue today.

Next we turn our attention to images in video and ways of using video in an anti-racist pedagogy. We use the ideas about representation and stereotypes developed so far and apply them to viewing films. Through reading and evaluating the TVO resources for *Anti-Racist Education*, it is possible to develop a set of guidelines for using film and video in anti-racist pedagogy. These guidelines can then be applied to films and documentaries used in teaching.

Using the guidelines developed, we can watch the video *Women in the Shadows*. This film will help further the consideration of the impact of colonialism on Aboriginal peoples in Canada as it pertains to issues of identity. Canadian Aboriginal peoples have had their identities defined for them through the Indian Act, which still makes a distinction between Indian and person. This act has served the purpose of governments who wished to deal with "the Indian problem" by eliminating Aboriginal peoples. this story helps us recognize the destructive acts and sense of loss in acts of genocide against Aboriginal peoples. Discussions questions for *Women in the Shadows* are also provided in the Appendix.

## Part 5 — Gender Equity

Part 5 examines gender equity as well as sexual harassment. In society and popular discourses about schools, the assumption that there is no need to work on these areas — that enough has been done — is evident. These are real issues in schools today, and they need definition and examination. There is a need to work toward reinvigorating discussions and activities in these areas. In particular, it is important to re-examine how schools are failing to meet the needs of all students. This section begins by asking simple questions such as how do you define gender, equity, gender equity, harassment, and sexual harassment. How can you tell that a certain act is sexual harassment? Is it everybody's responsibility to deal with issues of gender equity or only the responsibility of school administration and teachers? By addressing these questions, it will be possible to frame issues of gender and sexual harassment within school and society and to select the appropriate themes and topics for in-depth examination and discussion.

The article "Working Toward Equity" identifies the gaps in our schools, curriculum, and government policies in addressing inequalities, and challenges these structures to address the needs of all students. The *S.T.A.R.S. Equity Advisory Kit* focuses on defining sexual harassment, who is governed by sexual harassment policies, and what we can do to eliminate these negative practices.

A question for discussion of all the remaining readings in Part 5 is, How do we build a transformative culture that identifies issues of gender equity and sexual harassment? "Producing the Female Reserve Labour Force: Women and Schooling" examines the history of how schools function to reproduce gender and class discrimination. The articles in *Schoolgirls: Young Women, Self-Esteem, and the Confidence Gap* help students make connections between theory and practice and examine the structural and systematic nature of sexism particularly in regard to larger issues of power. The excerpts provide an example of privilege and inequity in classrooms and discuss the relationship between confidence and competence in mathematics; examine how school culture values particular skills and orientations based on stereotypes of females; and examine gender relations and dominance in classrooms.

## Part 6 — Gender and Regulation of Bodies
Part 6 interrogates the politics of gender, race, and "other" as well as the internalization of female beauty. Discourses about bodies are produced in society for purposes of control and regulation. They produce "the right female images," which are internalized and justified. This section enables the reader to examine the everyday practices — in newspapers, on television, in music videos, in other media — and problematize how

images are produced and reproduced. The article "Readings of Cultural Narratives of Diet, Technology, and Schooling in Multimedia Stories" examines unconstructed truths about gender produced in discourses of diet, technology, and schooling in order to show the complexity of positioning within lived and told storylines and the impossibility of enforcing or controlling the meanings that individual children make. The section concludes with Naomi Wolf's article on *The Beauty Myth*, which explores the issues of beauty as a commodified product.

## Part 7 — Issues of Sexuality in Schools

The interest of schools in sexuality is a more recent phenomenon than that of gender. It is a topic that needs to be thoroughly interrogated in the light of its politics, invisibility, subordination, and intersections of oppression. Because of its sensitivity teachers need to strategize ways of building trust and avenues to deal with this issue. A suggested pedagogical approach is to divide the class into groups, let each group deal with a segment of the text provided, and then have groups report on their discussions of the piece.

In Part 7, readers will build their knowledge of sexuality, problematize the myths, and be ready to engage in a more complex discussion of how sexuality intersects with other forms of oppression. The materials in "Safely Out: Activities for Challenging Homophobia in Schools" addresses anti-homophobia at a school board and highlights some of the principles of anti-homophobia education. Challenges and difficulties in changing the way a school system operates include, amongst others, invisibility, visibility, organized opposition, and fear of parental reaction. Definition of terms related to sexual orientation will be appropriate in order to enable readers to include them in their discussions. Facts about being lesbian, gay, or bisexual are next presented to dislodge the myth that being homosexual is a sickness. Examining the statistics about the developmental process for women and men enables the beginning teacher to understand that they are dealing with students in a vulnerable state who develop into adults still unable to live their lives as openly sexual beings.

Examination and discussion of levels of homophobia will allow readers to identify repulsion, pity, tolerance, heterosexual chauvinism, and denial. Discussions of positive attitudes toward homosexuality will assist readers in identifying passive acceptance, support, admiration, appreciation, and nurturance. By understanding these levels, students might be aided in locating themselves in the discourse of sexuality. It is important to debunk myths about homosexuality in order to understand the consequences of homophobic behaviour. Questions about homosexuality that are addressed in this text include, Who is a homosexual? How is a person's sexual orientation determined? Can a person change his or her sexual orientation? How many homosexuals are there in society? And does our society discriminate against homosexuals? Addressing these questions will enable readers to understand the broader social consequences of homophobia. This will enable discussion of the integration of gay and lesbian issues in the curriculum. Further activities are provided to aid teachers new to teaching this topic in considering how they might take up these issues in their classrooms.

"(In)visibility: Race, Sexuality, and Masculinity in the School Context" enables the reader to reflect and respond to questions, issues, and problems of sexuality from their own standpoint. The issue of sexuality can then be broadened to understanding other people's locations and responses with the purpose of building a comfort zone for an open discussion. The chapter problematizes the roles of schools and the failure of the school system to incorporate psychodynamic explanations of forms of oppression other than race. It also examines the formation of sub-cultures as responses to self-representation and ways of engaging in resistance. In addition, the paper problematizes the normalization of white heterosexuality in light of visibility of race and invisibility of homosexuality.

## Part 8 — Students at Risk: Class, Poverty, and Marginality

Poverty is manifested in our lives by those who live it and those who participate in its production or in perpetuating its cycle. The issue of poverty is addressed in this section from both macro and micro perspectives, examining both children's stories of poverty and the institutions that produce poverty. Issues of poverty are rarely a part of the curriculum, yet poverty is manifest in the lives of all students in schools. The challenge in this section is how we can incorporate an education that enables readers to identify practices that produce or maintain poverty in order to narrow the gap between those who "have" and those who "have not." Readers are asked to identify instances of poverty in their own lives and explain them. Readers need to consider in relative terms, What is poverty? How it can be understood? And how can poverty be addressed?

*A Child Is Not a Toy* provides a grounding reality of how poverty is manifested in the lives of a child and the devastating effects of poverty in the realization of a child's dreams. Children's stories demonstrate that they may not realize they are living in poverty until they go to school — that it is not everyone's experience to go hungry.

How is poverty that is manifested at a global level translated into local issues and everyday living? The importance of this question is to enable the reader to rethink how they can incorporate in their classroom practices ways of sensitizing students about issues of class, poverty, and marginality. "The Organic Goodie Simulation" addresses issues of power and poses the challenge of creating a just and united society where there is an equitable distribution of goods and services. In *Challenging Class Bias* readers will see a sample activity that can aid students in recognizing and relating social responses to poverty.

Class, poverty, and marginality are very invisible in the standard curriculum. What this section allows the educator to do is to bring consciousness and increased sensitivity to the issues. The poem "Students at Risk" is provided in order to situate poverty. The child in this poem is screaming thoughts but no one is listening. No one is seeing beyond the mask. The student is dealing with the gaze from other students, the institution, the teachers who cannot get beyond their own assumptions. The poem highlights the ways that the system produces this child's location and poverty.

## Conclusions

This book enables the reader to reflect upon and ponder the inequities in our educational system. Our existing educational systems are undergoing tremendous educational change. Some of these changes impact the lives of students in positive directions, increasing awareness of equity issues. But these changes are not widespread nor universal and some of them can have a numbing effect or reduce awareness of equity. This text works to counter these negative effects and to address situations where equity work is needed.

# Part 1

# Overview and Teacher's Understanding and Defining of Their Location

**Wane**
"Rethinking Teaching Using a Systems Discourse"

**Collins**
"Why I Teach"

**Ford and Ford**
"Our Schools Our Selves:
The Story of a New Teacher"

**Grant and Zeichner**
"On Becoming a Reflective Teacher"

## Chapter 1

# Rethinking Teaching Using Systems Discourse

## Njoki Nathani Wane

To see a child is to see possibility...
Someone in the process of becoming

Manen, *The Tact of Teaching the
Meaning of Pedagogical Thoughtfulness*

This is an exploratory discussion based on my teaching experiences. It invites readers to share the thought processes and experiences that informed my formulation of the systems discourse. This discourse is a discursive framework that illustrates the functions and relationships of the sub-systems that structure the education system. It illustrates the systematic power imbalances, as well as barriers that are embedded within the various sub-systems of the larger society. The systems discourse promotes an understanding of institutions and how they create and sustain interconnectedness and interdependency. The systems discourse also provides a framework for understanding the dilemmas, tensions, and fears that members of various institutions experience as they come to terms with their prescribed institutional roles. This paper uses the systems discourse to explore a series of questions about teachers, schools, and society: How do pre-service instructors prepare future teachers for their challenging role in society? How can teachers create a balanced curriculum that meets the needs of all students in their classroom? What are some of the critical pedagogical questions teachers should ask themselves as they prepare for each class? Is it possible to achieve a balanced and inclusive learning environment? And, how do teachers situate themselves in relation to school administrators, students, and society at large? These questions are valid and important not only for teachers, but also for everyone connected to the school system, including students, administrators, parents, and members of the larger community.

At the beginning of "Students, Schools, and Systems," a compulsory course for pre-service teachers in the faculty of education where I teach, I graphically represent the systems discourse with three interlocking circles (see Figure 1.1). The circles represent schools, students and systems, and the "T" situated at the intersection of the three circles represents teachers. Broadly defined, systems refer to the government; the ministry of education; parent organizations; religious and ethnic groups; and the business sector. In other words, systems represent everything located outside the school context. In the context of this discussion, "the system" will refer to all the intersecting groups depicted in the diagram: students, schools, systems, and teachers.

Early in the course, I encourage my students to locate themselves within the system described above. I begin by asking them to simply

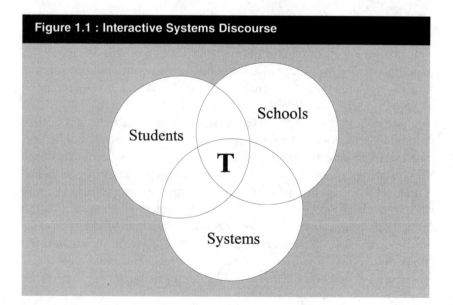

Figure 1.1 : Interactive Systems Discourse

write something inside one of the diagram's circles. At the end of this exercise, words such as coach, trainer, nurturer, educator, determinant, expert, and employee are typically found in the "T" section of the diagram. Schools are described with words such as institution, learning, training, libraries, books, processing, education, building, teachers, principals, school counsellors, fun, depressing, minds, students, and future. Inside the systems circle, one usually discovers words such as ethnicity, churches, religions, government, races, business community, industries, parents, and jobs. When I ask students to describe how they feel about the intersecting systems depicted in the diagram, many talk about their nostalgia for the school system. Others speak of their experiences of tension, frustration, fear, and hope. Some students discuss how the boundaries between the three circles interfere with learning and teaching. Others indicate that the exercise is useful in exposing the connections between the systems depicted in the diagram. Finally, while some students argue that the systems depicted can function independently, others assert that this separation is not necessary and that there can only be one system made up of related sub-systems.

The students' rich, diverse, and often contradictory responses provide a basis upon which to further explore the complexity and significance of systems discourse. When asked to write one sentence explaining how their contribution to the diagram relates to teaching, students' responses are typically just as diverse. The following excerpts represent some of the responses I have received:

> Teachers are torn between the three circles.
> It is very difficult for teachers to carry out their work without interference from the administrators, parents, or communities outside the school.
> I wonder how teachers maintain their sanity?
> As a student in high school, I did not realize the tensions that teachers go through.

The exercise enables students to recognize the complexity of systems discourse, and to begin strategizing on how to become effective agents of change in the school system.

As the students complete the intersecting circles and engage in the follow-up discussion and exercise, I also ask them to think about the ways in which they are both marginalized and privileged on the basis of their creed, race, class, sexual orientation, religion, gender and/or ability. I believe that the complexity of the systems represented in the diagram is best understood when social differences are foregrounded. Unfortunately, the diagrams cannot account for the tensions that inevitably emerge between students, teachers, schools, and systems. In order to address this concern, students are asked to complete a reflective assignment in which they are encouraged to explore these tensions in relation to their own experiences.

Grant and Zeincher (1998) suggest that in order to become reflective, teachers must constantly ask themselves how they can test guidelines to determine their suitability, effectiveness, and substance, and further question the purposes and goals toward which they are working. This process reflects what Dewey (1959) regards as "reflective action"; that is, being engaged in behaviour that involves active, persistent, and careful consideration of one's beliefs and practices in light of the grounds that support them and the consequences to which they may lead. In other words, it is important for teachers to actively reflect upon their teaching and upon the educational, social, and political contexts in which their teaching is situated (Grant and Zeincher, 1998). However, I also believe it is important that my students understand that being reflective demands an open mind, and an ability to listen to more than one side of the story, pay full attention to alternatives, and recognize human errors.

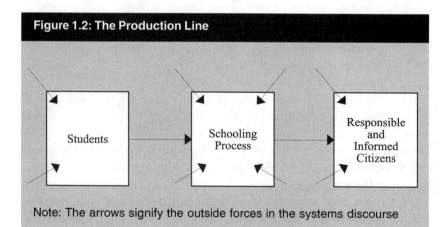

**Figure 1.2: The Production Line**

Students → Schooling Process → Responsible and Informed Citizens

Note: The arrows signify the outside forces in the systems discourse

History has demonstrated that dominant culture typically dictates the end product of the school process. In our society, the school process may be viewed as a production line where students (inputs) are schooled (processed) and transformed into educated adults (products). The above paradigm employs a result-based management approach where outcomes are measurable based on a cause-and-effect relationship. Although all players in the systems discourse have an interest in determining the outcome of the school process, it is largely determined by those people whose voices are most legitimized through the process. For example, all parties — including parents, teachers, religious groups, and government officials — would like to create and reproduce themselves through the school system. Each of these stakeholders would like to produce "informed citizens." However, the definition of an "informed citizen" varies across the system. The government's goal is to produce law-abiding citizens who conform to and maintain the political and economic status quo. But who defines what is lawful? Who is excluded from that definition? And, whose interests are being protected? Similarly, the business community seeks to produce citizens capable of participating in the production and consumption of goods and services in order to maximize their own profits. As for students, few systems ask them what they want. The assumption is that they cannot know. They are in school to be "educated" and become informed and responsible citizens, and active producers and consumers. Teachers, the education system's frontline workers, often find themselves in a "push-pull" situation as various stakeholders in the system place demands on them to reproduce their own version of the ideal citizen. However, this is precisely why educators interested in addressing the inequalities in our society need to employ curriculum materials and an instructional methodology that is capable of negotiating the competing interests found within the public education system.

While the ability to negotiate competing interests within the school system is an important goal, in reality, teachers sometimes have no choice but to comply with the school system's demands. As illustrated in Figure 1.3, this can lead to a significant imbalance within the system.

The curved "T" (as depicted above) — which situates schools at the bottom, students at the top, and systems at the far right — demonstrates how teachers are pulled in different directions. Sometimes the T curves

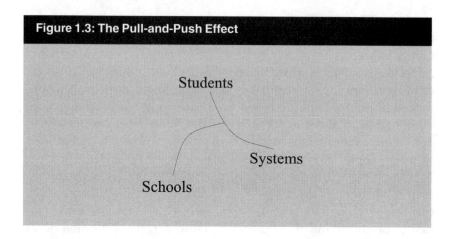

Figure 1.3: The Pull-and-Push Effect

to one side, indicating an imbalance of power within the system. More often than not, this imbalance serves the interests of systems as opposed to students and teachers, and thus works to reproduce the inequities already embedded within many classrooms and schools.

Working on the assumption that it is important for student teachers to define and understand their locations in relation to students, schools, and systems, I introduce my student teachers to systems discourse at the beginning of the year. Systems discourse, as already described, not only highlights the complexities of the systems that affect the everyday life of schools, but also draws attention to some of the challenges would-be teachers are bound to face as they prepare to commence their teaching careers. Subsequently, students are encouraged to ask themselves why they need to locate themselves in relation to the systems discourse and why it is important to become increasingly aware of the education system's tacit practices and assumptions. The exercise enables students to recognize the systemic barriers that are inherent in the system, and to explore how their class, race, gender, ability, and sexual orientation may affect their ability to negotiate the school system. Most importantly, this exercise enables students to unmask the hegemonic authorizations at work in teaching practices. As students become familiar with systems discourse they are also able to begin thinking seriously about what can be done to collapse the boundaries that keep schools, students, and systems at loggerheads, and exploring how they can address the systemic and structural barriers that limit some students' access to education.

Experience has shown that at this point students are also prepared to engage in discussions pertaining to access, equity, and educational policy. Levin and Young (1998) suggest that it is important for students to become familiar with education policies, politics, and structures. It not only enables them to participate in the implementation of school curriculum, but also to develop a responsiveness to the dynamic processes of learning and to develop their own resourcefulness, adaptability, and creativity. As a teacher educator, I believe it is imperative to help student teachers assess the goals of the education system, and to help them accept the fact that their own goals may not always reflect the system's goals.

In order to facilitate the students' exploration of the education system's goals, policies, and politics, I ask them to engage in role-play that involves parents, school administrators, students, officials from the Ministry of Education, and representatives from various community groups. As a facilitator, I usually suggest various topics or themes for the role-play. The themes range from controversial books to standardized testing to sex or religious education. Each time I facilitate the exercise, I am fascinated by the ways in which the role-plays reveal how various groups of people negotiate the school system, and demand to have their voices heard, validated, and acknowledged within its regulatory structures. At the end of the exercise, students have commented:

> It was so frustrating talking to government officials who have no notion of what happens in the classroom.
> I could not believe how difficult it is to come to a consensus.
> As a parent, my voice was silenced every time I tried to talk.
> It was quite obvious that teachers did not want to compromise especially when they feel that they know how the system discourse functions.
> I think all the interested parties should be introduced to refresher courses to keep them abreast of what is happening in our school.

The role-playing and debriefing permit students to experience the tensions, difficulties, and frustrations that all stakeholders in the school system experience. Through dialogue and debate, students become familiar with the dynamics of conflict resolution, threats, consensus, power dynamics, and power struggles. After our discussions and assessment, we engage in an exercise that explores what it means to study and work in an education system that often remains inaccessible.

Dei (1996) voices the need to have an inclusive curriculum, one that encompasses the stories, experiences, and backgrounds of all students present in the school system. He notes that a curriculum that is inclusive calls for the transformation of educational structures in Canada. Under the current restructuring process, Dei feels that an Afrocentric pedagogy would enhance other theories and pedagogies aimed at progressive forms of scholarship. But what is inclusivity or marginality, especially when the official educational mandate already states that there are equal opportunities for all students regardless of creed, sexual orientation, ethnicity, or race? Is it possible to be simultaneously inclusive and exclusive? Kirkness (1998) highlights the importance of taking other forms of knowledge into account in our teaching. She suggests that the inclusion of indigenous knowledges is necessary in order to appreciate non-European knowledge systems, including those associated with the First Nations. In addition to the recognition and inclusion of non-European knowledges, it is important to pay attention to the resources that we bring to class, including textbooks, posters, and invited guests. Allen (1996) poignantly addresses how students respond to the inclusion of inappropriate materials, such as distorted images or negative portrayals of people from other cultures. He argues that inclusion of such material can make students resist the paradigm of inclusion or restructuring. According to him, students refuse to be associated with the stereotypical images portrayed in books. However, Allen indicates that students also emphasize that inclusive representation must be supported by the transformation of educational structures.

My teaching experience has shown that discussions about policies, politics, curriculum, inclusivity, and representation in education usually make students increasingly aware of the extent to which they are unaware of the inequities embedded in the school system. As my own students have commented:

> I never realized our education system alienated certain groups of people.

> I wonder why our history is not inclusive?
> I never realized the power of imagery and how it can stop
> you from learning.

While student teachers are sometimes reluctant to criticize the system in which they are about to begin working, it is essential that they come to terms with their own cultural and class-bound perceptions of students. An understanding of the cultural, economic, and social lives of students enables educators to appreciate how students interpret their school experiences (Allen, 1996). By introducing the notion of inclusion, student teachers are better able to strategize on how to negotiate the present school curriculum, design their own strategies for "change," and respond to other systemic problems in our schools. But as my students often ask, How do we confront the systemic structural barriers inherent in our education system? Can good teaching strategies help us dismantle some of these barriers to effective teaching and learning? According to Schorr (1997), effective teaching strategies are characterized by a high degree of comprehension, flexibility, responsiveness, and preservation. In other words, effective strategies place children in the context of their families and community. Such strategies allow for a clear mission and continue to evolve over time (Fullan, 1998). Effective strategies allow educators to take changing demographics into account. In Canada, where the ethnic composition has shifted significantly since the 1970s, the ability to respond to demographic change is undoubtedly crucial.

Demographics indicate that the Canadian population is becoming increasingly racially and ethnically diverse (Magsino, 1986). This increased diversity is reflected in the student population, and poses a new set of challenges for teachers working to address student needs. A review of research on equity initiatives in our schools indicates that there is still significant work to be done on racism, sexism, and homophobia (Goldstein, 1998). Larkin's 1994 study in four Toronto high schools reveals that some female students dread going to school due to the sexual harassment they experience from their male counterparts. Moreover, despite the publication of numerous policy documents on the need to address school-based harassment and discrimination in Ontario, racial and sexual harassment, gay-bashing, and class-based streaming continue to reproduce the status quo in schools throughout the province (Curtis, 1992, Goldstein, 1998, Larkin, 1994, Allan, 1996).

In a world characterized by vast change, complexity, plurality, fragmentation, conflicts, and contradictions of beliefs, values, and faiths, the ability to understand students' experiences both within and outside the context of the school is more important than ever. In a world where young people's lives appear to be growing increasingly unstable and unpredictable, it is essential that teachers pay more attention to developing caring school environments that can accommodate a diverse range of student needs. Like Manen (1991), I believe that good pedagogy should be informed by a deep sense of responsibility, moral intuitiveness, and understanding, and be delivered with a great deal of thoughtfulness and tact.

The course described in this discussion, and the systems discourse framework upon which the course is structured, serve as points of departure for student teachers at the onset of their teaching careers. Not surprisingly, at the end of each course, many students, overwhelmed by their increasing awareness of the schools system's inherent inequities, express the need for a full-year course exploring issues related to systems discourse. Unfortunately, the structure of most one-year pre-service programmes does not allow for a full-year course exploring social and educational systems. The systems discourse provides student teachers with a tool to examine and interrogate the structures that inhibit the promotion of educational access and equity. In conclusion, I emphasize here, as I do in my course, that people should avoid viewing systems discourse simply as a theoretical tool through which to analyze the school system from a distance. Instead, I encourage the use of systems discourse as a lens through which to articulate, develop, and implement an inclusive educational praxis.

## References

Allen, A. (1996). "I don't want to read this": Students' responses to illustrations of black characters in children's picture books. In K. Brathwaite and C.E. James (eds.) *Educating African Canadians*. Toronto: James Lorimer & Company.

Cameron, L.M. (1998). A practitioner's reflections. *Orbit*, 28, 10–15.

Clarke, C. (1996). A letter to a principal. In K. Brathwaite and C.E. James (eds.) *Educating African Canadians*. Toronto: James Lorimer & Company.

Curtis, B., D. Livingstone, and H. Smaller. (1992). Streaming in the secondary school. *Our Schools/ Our Selves*, 24, 83–98.

Dei, G.J.S. (1996). The role of Afrocentricity in the inclusive curriculum in Canadian schools. *Canadian Journal of Education*, 21, 170–186.

Dewey, J. (1959). *Experience and education: The Kappa Delta Pi lecture series*, New York: Collier Books, Macmillan.

Fever, F. (1994). Who cares? Memories of childhood in care. In M. Blair and J. Holland with S. Sheldon, *Identity and diversity: Gender and the experience of education*. Buckingham: The Open University.

Fullan, M., and H. Lynne. (1998). Assessing strategies: From reform to renewal [Special issue]. *Orbit*, 29, 7–9.

Goldstein, T. (1998). Working towards equity. *Orbit*, 29, 14–16.

Grant, C.A., and K.M. Ziechner. (1998). On becoming a reflective teacher. In G. Taylor and R. Runte (eds.) *Thinking about teaching: An introduction*. Toronto: Harcourt Brace.

Kirkness, V.J. (1998). Our peoples' education: Cut the shackles, cut the crap; cut the mustard. In *Canadian Journal of Native Education*, vol. 22.1, 10–15.

Larkin, J. (1994). *Sexual harassment: High school girls speak out*, Toronto: Second Story Press.

Levin, B. and J. Young. (1998). Making sense of public schooling; The structure of Canadian schooling. In *Understanding Canadian schools: An introduction to educational administration*, Toronto: Harcourt Brace.

Livingstone, D., and D. Hart. (1998). The "crisis" of confidence in schools and the neoconservative agenda: Diverging opinions of corporate executives and the general public. *Alberta Journal of Educational Research*, XLIV, 1–19.

Livingstone, D. (1998). Public opinion. *Orbit*, 29,17–22.

Ghaill, M.. (1994). (In)visibility: Race, sexuality and masculinity in the school context. In M. Blair and J. Holland (eds.) *Identity and diversity: Gender and the experience of education*, Buckingham: Open University Press.

Magsino, R.F. (1986). Multiculturalism in schools: Is multicultural education possible and justifiable? In Sonia V. Morris (ed.) *Multiculturalism and Intercultural Education: Building Canada*, Calgary: Detselig.

Manen, van M. (1991). *The tact of teaching the meaning of pedagogical thoughtfulness*, New York: SUNY.

Manners, E. (1997). The role of the federation in secondary school reform. *Orbit*, 28, 11–13.

Pearl, S. (1995). Building school councils: The need for a balanced approach. *Orbit*, 26, 24–25.

Schorr, L. (1997). *Common purpose: Strengthening families and neighborhoods to rebuild America*, New York: Doubleday.

# Chapter 2

# Why I Teach

## Marva N. Collins

Often I am in the company of people who run billion-dollar corporations and have amassed fortunes through the expertise of selling one product or one service or another. These people seem to have all of the material things that are inherent in our idea of the American Dream. It is during these moments that I reflect again and again as to why I teach.

When I return to the classroom and see children's eyes holding wonder like a cup then I know why I teach. I hear a child say, "I love you, Mrs. Collins"; I am the recipient of many gifts such as rings that tarnish and candy that is sticky from being in a sweaty palm, although I must courageously eat it; another child says to me, "You smell good, I love you"; ... I then know why I teach.

When I see a précis written by my students filled with ideas germinated in my classroom, and when I hear ideas that I have given expanded upon with lofty thoughts of their own, I know why I teach.

I then, too, think that most human beings are as good as they are because some unknown teacher cared enough to continue polishing until a shiny luster came shining through; because some teacher cared enough to remove the previous fetid tags and labels of failure from their psyches.

I then think of how many times visitors from all over the world have come to Westside Preparatory School and replied: "It's amazing what you do here with children." I think how many times we have called the profits of a billion-dollar corporation a miracle; we expect profits; we expect success. Why then can't we expect the same success from our children?" That is why I teach.

There is Tiffany, a child considered autistic who had not spoken, who had been told by the experts that she was an unlovable and unteachable child. One day after much patience, prayers, love, and determination, Tiffany's first words to me were: "I love you, Mrs. Ollins." The consonant "C" was left off; but I realized that the tears that flowed from Tiffany's declaration made me the wealthiest woman in the world. Today, to see Tiffany writing her numerals, beginning to read single words, talking, and most of all, to see that glee in her eyes that says, "I, too, am special. I, too, can learn": this to me is worth all of the gold in Fort Knox.

I don't know much about tax shelters, balance sheets, and takeovers mentioned in big business, but the biggest business on earth to me is to see a child whose eyes proclaim you his or her heroine.

Another reason I teach is Durvile. Durvile is a student front the Cabrini-Green Housing Project. This is an area where one keeps score of the murders, rapes, and crimes that prevail in the area every minute. Yet, this lad came to our school in September with a fourth-grade level in reading and now in April he has scored at a twelfth-grade reading level. Durvile squints because he has difficulty seeing, yet despite the odds, he is the brightest lad we have ever had at our school. Durvile confuses the statisticians and the people who do all of the baleful studies as to what one can become when one is a resident of a fetid area. Right on, Durvile, one day you will show the world that all you need is an opportunity. Despite the fact that you are not a paying pupil at Westside Preparatory School, and we are always financially strapped, it is worth all of my sleepless nights wondering how I am going to balance our deficits to see the glow in your eyes that will one day light the world.

There is Takiesha, a three-year-old who is reading, knows her alphabets, and can compute with two-digit numerals and takes pride in her knowledge, proving again that young children can do more than take naps, drink milk, and go home at the end of an average school day.

These are the real reasons why I teach. To see people grow right in front of my eyes is truly God's work on earth, it is my miracle. It is the kind of miracle that one cannot see from totals on a balance sheet, from profits and takeovers. I may not be mentioned in *Fortune* magazine as one of the wealthiest women in America, but my wealth cannot be measured on a balance sheet. I do not have financial power, but I have the power to mold, to nurture, to hold, to hug, to love, to cajole, to praise, and yet criticize too, to point out pathways ... to become a part of another person's well-being. What could be more powerful?

Repeatedly I have seen myself intoxicated with the power of taking child after child written off in other systems, yet with constant nurturing that child has blossomed into seeds of fruition here ... I now do not believe that any child cannot be taught something.

To be a teacher is to become a part of a kind of creation. A creation of knowing that miracles occur because you cared, loved, and patiently kept polishing until the dark corners of a child's mind became brightened, and as you watch those former sad eyes become luminous, you then know why I teach. You know that there is no brighter light ever to shine than that which comes from a child's eyes formerly hidden in the dark.

Then, there is Kevin Ross. Kevin was a 24-year-old college athlete who had spent four years at Creighton University and came to Westside Preparatory School reading at a second-grade level. I watched Kevin's ambivalence fade away as he learned the printed word, as he learned grammar, and he learned that the light of literacy could be his domain. Today as he speaks at such places as Harvard University and can hold his own on shows like "Face the Nation," I know, too, that teaching is the greatest profession on earth.

I teach because I believe Plato was right when he said, "Education is cumulative and it affects the breed." To think that I have given a generation the torch of literacy that can be passed to their heirs is truly the denouement of living. To think that I have been a small part of a miraculous living person is truly God's work here on earth. I know that though much has been taken from most of the students that enroll at Westside Preparatory School, I believe that with tempered hopes much still abides, and I am willing to work as long as it takes until each student finds his or her rightful potentiality.

I teach because I am there when the first breath of knowledge comes shining through, and I then, too, can catch that breath of fulfillment that comes from knowing that I was a small part of that revitalization.

I teach because I do not have to worry about children thinking that I want something in return when I hug them, when I say, "I love you and right now I need a big hug." I do not have to worry that I will be called a phony because I care. Children are like the velveteen rabbit we read about in the classic story of what it's like to become real. Children are real, and they can never become unreal once they find someone who really, really loves them for what they are with a genuine respect for what they can become. That is why being real does not happen to adults, because they do not understand. Adults are too easily hurt, they are frayed at the edges, they have to be carefully kept, and, therefore, the real world is an illusive one for them. This is the reason I teach.

I teach because a withered orange given to me by a child is a gift of love, and not a bribe for my favour. To draw a happy face on a child's paper is his paycheque, and it draws a smile quicker than all of the toys that parents buy at Christmastime.

I found that teaching offers more than money. It offers love. It offers something that most people spend a lifetime unable to obtain.

I teach because of Sam, the young man put out of another school for throwing an eraser. After just four months at our school, he has won a national merit honour, and scored so high at his selected high school for September that he has been given a scholarship. I teach for Sam who will one day make a real contribution to America and the world, and to know that I have been a small part of that contribution is to me the greatest power on earth.

I teach because after being told day-by-day that I am loved, I begin to love myself more, and I find that I have even more love to give. And that is why I teach.

# Chapter 3

# Our Schools Our Selves: The Story of a New Teacher

Laura Ford
Lisa Beta Ford

... education is the most personal, the most intimate, of all
human affairs, there more than anywhere else, the sole
ultimate reliance and final source of power are in the training,
character and intelligence of the individual. But as long as a
school organization which is undemocratic in principle tends
to repel from all but the higher portions of the school system
those of independent force, of intellectual initiative, and of
inventive ability, or tends to hamper them in the work after
they find their way into the schoolroom, so long all other
reforms are compromised at their source and postponed
indefinitely for fruition.

— John Dewey, 1931

The subject of educational change and its predictable failure has been
the subject of countless books, academic journals, and articles in the
popular press. In a body of work over a lifetime, Yale professor of
psychology Seymour Sarason raises the question, "Why do schools fail
of their purposes?" and he rests his case on the system and power politics
of the public schools. Peter Drucker, professor of social science, reinforces
Sarason's conclusions in a recent article in the November issue of *The
Atlantic Monthly*. In his survey of social transformation over the past
century, Drucker sees schools as providing economic and social order.

Perhaps I have become somewhat jaundiced over the years as I read the words of restructuring for tomorrow and recall the reconceptualizing of yesterday's programs. The new directives emerging from ministries and central board offices and issued to school administrators are passed on to teachers for implementation with our students. In my view, it is the relationship between facts and perceptions among these different bodies that needs to be looked at more closely and clarified.

To address this issue of what restructuring might mean for teachers, I invited a teacher who entered the profession four years ago with enthusiasm and passion, knowledge and creativity, to join me in writing this text. This is her story.

## Becoming a Teacher

I was very philosophic about becoming a teacher. My teachers had given me so much, and I have a great love for mathematics. I knew I wanted to continue my learning. So teaching fit wonderfully. I could give back the gift of the joy of mathematics to my students as well as have a career that would give me some time to pursue my own learning. Surely in an education environment there would be respect for one's own learning.

My disillusionment and cynicism began when I entered my teacher education course. During the introductory address, we were told not to feel as if we had something to be ashamed of in the academic community, that even becoming a teacher was valid work. I wondered what made this man so defensive. There were the student introductions. 'Oh, well," were the words I was hearing, "it will give me a good living." Having worked in a large, international business organization, I knew teaching was a very modest goal if one wanted a "good living," though it does offer safety in its security. Still, I found students who were excited about what they were doing and who, like me, wanted to share a love for their subject, to share their learning and their love of life. We were the students who believed that what we were doing was important.

My math methods course was enlightening. The instructor introduced new ideas and techniques by having the class work out the problems within what appeared to be the simplest of assignments. Using blocks for counting encouraged us to come up with ideas and arguments to enrich our own understanding of math education. He modelled his own vision. It was a far different experience from sitting in a lecture hall with 400 other students and listening to an instructor list the "ten do's and don'ts" of teaching and understanding.

In my practicum, I met some very supportive teachers. I met teachers who were there to truly help the students, focusing their time and attention on what was happening in the classroom. I also met cynical teachers. And I met administrators who told us there were no gangs or gang-related problems in the schools yet they walked around with cellular phones. There was a schoolwide plan to deal with any outbreaks of violence, and a police officer spoke at a staff meeting on gangs in the community and in the school.

I met a couple of student teachers who were to become my best friends, while car pooling to our practicum school. There was much soul searching as we shared crises situations. We were always exhausted, often sick. If our sponsor teachers weren't unreasonable, our advisors were.

I was introduced to the culture of schools. It was the bells that got to me. They symbolized the expectation for *automation:* be at school well before class time and stay late (but don't expect office supplies and student-file information to be accessible). Don't expect to go to the washroom when nature calls. Expect to be on school property the entire teaching day. The 45 minutes for lunch break ensures not going out for lunch but presents the challenge of including an opportunity to do some additional preparation, set up the necessary arrangements for the sports programs, take care of any personal matters, or attend meetings.

In my first year, I taught five different courses in seven different classrooms. After the first couple of weeks, I was given a desk to work at in a corner of the computer science room. Every day I'd come home with a new wondrous story of math learning in the classroom. But I also came home in tears. Was I trained to deal with students who were afraid to go home because their fathers threatened to assault them? How was I to interact with students talking about shared social workers and their personal home concerns? When had I been taught to deal with threatening male students who refused to stay after class? How do I deal with a sports team meeting that expresses racial prejudices? And when was I to decide how to deal with all these problems? My evenings and weekends were filled with working and planning, and sleeping out of exhaustion. When?

## Becoming Disillusioned

My teaching friends and I try to find time to help each other share our stories and find our voices. We meet Friday evenings to "debrief." We share stories of attacks on teachers, student abuse, drug use, death. We share the absurd reactions we get when we try to find help for our students. Here is one story, which is not uncommon, about a meeting between a teacher and a school counsellor.

> Johnny needs help with his math basics. Can we put him in the special program?
> No. That's for problem kids and he's been clean for six months.
> But the class can really help him.
> No. We'll put him in special program #2.
> But we know there's nobody there to teach him what he needs since the last teacher cut.
> We must follow the rules.

The school administrator then reproached the teacher for interfering with the counsellor's role.

At a recent Friday meeting, a friend noticed my silence. "What's happened to you? You used to come here full of excitement about all the great things that happened in the classroom." She tried to reassure me, "Don't worry, it'll come back." But I don't think it will.

When I first started teaching, I was excited about how students came to math and how they made discoveries. How could I make their hour with me worthwhile and enjoyable? The first year, the department head was a great mentor of mine and the principal was supportive of my initiatives. But things have changed. Now I feel that all that is wanted of me is a quiet classroom, with no problems that go beyond my realm as math teacher. No one is there to hear me and to give a response outside the classroom.

During holidays I try to find time to take care of my personal life. It is difficult to get recharged in the face of the cynicism about my profession.

I get upset by the teacher-bashing articles in the news and the teacher union's latest fight with the school board.

I've been teaching for three years. Most of my teacher friends see themselves teaching for one or two more. I still love to teach math. I wish I could spend more time doing it. I wish I had more time for reflection and preparation, for research and sharing. But most of all I want more time with students and less time with forms, meetings, and marking. I want less time to defend my teaching environment, to defend it from those teachers who have already given up and lost their respect for themselves and their students, to defend myself from administrators and counsellors with their organizational concerns, from parents who neglect their children.

Students' needs are like a bottomless well. When I meet with friends we try to determine when to stop giving. We give so much with so little return.

## One Teacher's Story?

The story that is told isn't every teacher's story but it is a story that would resonate particularly for those many teachers who drop out of teaching during the first five years. It is also a story of a particular place. I am not addressing economics, nor am I addressing the government's need to solve social problems. We are talking about the teacher's role in restructuring our schools. Our schools are for both students and teachers. "If the collegial conditions do not exist wherein teachers can learn, change, and grow, they cannot create and sustain those conditions for productive learning in their students" (Sarason, 1993). Teachers bring to the students their knowledge and their skills and all that is required for teaching and learning. How teaching and learning find their meaning has to do with the expression of the people in that place.

When Edward Rosen, a psychiatrist employed by the Etobicoke Board of Education in 1968, met with teachers in meetings about the needs of those children with emotional or learning problems, he expressed his ultimate respect and overwhelming appreciation for the skillfulness, compassion, and concern with which the teachers accepted the challenges of their profession. And he counselled these teachers and aided them by saying, "Remember, you are teachers. You are not their parents nor are you the social worker. If you begin to replace these other members of society, they will not be there for their responsibilities and you will not be here to accomplish what you are asked to do." Dr. Rosen was preserving those qualities of teachers that provide the best experiences for students. As long as teachers are not supported with the appropriate personnel and physical resources, they are forced into situations that intrude on their own teaching responsibilities.

To be called teacher is a gift. If we want the gift-ed teacher to teach our children we must allow for the creation of school settings in which the participants are the creators. In the October 31, 1994 issue of *Time*, the cover story examined the grassroots revolt in education, with parents and teachers bucking bureaucracy and recognizing that the top-down reform has not worked.

The school is a place that serves the education of our society. But place is more than a physical location. It embraces the history and traditions and the stories of its people. It encompasses all the different voices and the pictures around it. Place is the landscape that tells the stories in Thomas Hardy's writings, place is the landscape of Georgia O'Keefe's paintings, and place is where teachers and students create a setting for teaching and learning.

In 1994, if those independent individuals who choose to become teachers, bringing their intellectual initiatives and inventive abilities into the schools, are not heard and are denied access to creating their settings, they will find themselves in our graduate schools or other settings where their words will be heard. And it will be the loss of our public school system and our students.

## References

Dewey, J. (1931). Democracy in education. *Progressive Education*, 8(3), 216–218.
Sarason, S. (1993). *Letters to a serious education president*, Newbury, CA: Sage.

# Chapter 4

# On Becoming
# a Reflective Teacher

## Carl A. Grant
## Kenneth M. Zeichner

If teachers today are to initiate young people into an ethical
existence, they themselves must attend more fully than they
normally have to their own lives and its requirements: they
have to break with the mechanical life, to overcome their
own submergence in the habitual, even in what they conceive
to be virtuous, and to ask the "why" with which all moral
reasoning begins.

Maxine Green, *Teacher as Stranger*

As you proceed with your professional education, you will continually
be confronted with numerous choices about the kind of teacher to become.
Recent literature in education has clearly shown that teachers differ
substantially according to their goals and priorities and to the
instructional and classroom management strategies that they employ.
These differences among teachers have usually been portrayed as
contrasting "types." For example, much has been written in recent years
about the differences between teachers who are "open or traditional,"
"child-centered or subject-centered," "direct or indirect," and
"humanistic or custodial." These dichotomies attempt to differentiate
teachers who hold different views about what is important for students
to learn, preferred instructional and management strategies, and types

of curricular materials, and about the kinds of school and classroom organizational structures within which they want to work. The kind of teacher you wish to become, the stands you take on educational issues, and the knowledge and skills you need for putting your beliefs into action all represent decisions you as a prospective teacher need to make.

Over a hundred years of educational research has yet to discover the most effective instructional methods and school and classroom organizational structure for all students, This, together with the fact that "rules for practice" cannot now and probably never will be easily derived from either college coursework or practical school experience makes your choices regarding these issues and the manner in which you determine them of great importance.

With regard to instructional strategies and methods, you will literally be bombarded in your courses and practicums with suggestions and advice regarding the numerous techniques and strategies that are now available for the instruction of children in the various content areas. For example, you will be taught various strategies for leading discussions, managing small groups, designing learning centers, administering diagnostic evaluative procedures, and teaching concepts and skills.

Furthermore, in each of the content areas there are choices to be made about the general approach or orientation to instruction over and above the choice of specific instructional techniques and procedures. You, ultimately, must make decisions about which approach or combination of approaches to employ amid competing claims by advocates that their approach offers the best solution to problems of instruction.

Undoubtedly, there is a great deal of debate in education today over how to go about teaching agreed upon content and skills and about the ways to manage classroom and children. However, the question of what to teach, and to whom, precedes the question of how to teach. The selection of content to be taught to a particular group of children and of the types of instructional materials and resources to support this process are issues of great importance, despite the fact that any school in which you are likely to work will have some set of policies. Although there are limits placed upon teachers regarding curricular content and materials, teachers usually have some latitude in the selection of specific content and materials within broad curricular guidelines.

For example, in the state of Wisconsin it is required that teachers teach the history of their state as part of the fourth-grade social studies curriculum. Within these guidelines, individual teachers usually have some degree of choice about what to teach or emphasize about Wisconsin history and about what materials to use. This holds true in most curricular areas; even where schools have adopted particular instructional approaches and programs, such as in reading and math, teachers are still permitted some degree of personal discretion in the selection of content and materials.

You will also face a set of options about the kinds of school organizational structures in which you will work, and you will need to be aware that not all structures are compatible with all positions on issues of curriculum and instruction. At the elementary school level, for example, do you prefer to work in a self-contained classroom with one group of children, or do you prefer to work closely with colleagues in a departmentalized context, such as is found in many individually guided education schools? Furthermore, you must begin to form positions about the kinds of school and classroom structures that will support the kind of teaching you want to do.

In addition to these numerous choices and issues, there is another and more basic choice facing you. This choice concerns the way in which you go about formulating positions with regard to the issues mentioned above. To what degree will you consciously direct this process of decision-making in pursuit of desired ends and in light of educational and ethical principles? On the other hand, to what degree will your decisions be mechanically directed by others; by impulse, tradition, and authority? An important distinction is made between being a reflective or an unreflective teacher, and it necessarily involves every prospective teacher no matter what your orientation and regardless of the specific positions that you eventually adopt on the issues of curriculum and instruction.

You may be wondering what we mean by being a reflective teacher. In the early part of this century, John Dewey made an important distinction between human action that is reflective and that which is routine. Much of what Dewey had to say on this matter was directed specifically to teachers and prospective teachers, and his remarks remain very relevant for those in the process of becoming teachers today.

According to Dewey (1933), *routine action* is behavior that is guided by impulse, tradition, and authority. In any social setting, and the school is no exception, there exists a taken-for-granted definition of everyday reality in which problems, goals, and the means for their solution become defined in particular ways. As long as everyday life continues without major interruption, this reality is perceived to be unproblematic. Furthermore, this dominant world view is only one of the many views of reality that would theoretically be possible, and it serves as a barrier to recongizing and experimenting with alternative viewpoints.

Teachers who are unreflective about their work uncritically accept this everyday reality in schools and concentrate their efforts on finding the most effective and efficient means to achieve ends and to solve problems that have largely been defined for them by others. These teachers lose sight of the fact that their everyday reality is only one of the may possible alternatives. They tend to forget the purposes and ends toward which they are working.

Dewey (1933) defines *reflective action*, on the other hand, as behavior that involves active, persistent, and careful consideration of any belief of practice in light of the grounds that support it and the further consequences to which it leads. According to Dewey, reflection involves a way of meeting and responding to problems. Reflective teachers actively reflect upon their teaching and upon the educational, social, and political contexts in which their teaching is embedded.

There are three attitudes that Dewey defines as prerequisites for reflective action. First, *openmindedness* refers to an active desire to listen to more sides than one, to give full attention to alternate possibilities, and to recognize the possibility of error even in the beliefs that are dearest to us. Prospective teachers who are openminded are continually examining the rationales (educational or otherwise) that underlie what is taken to be natural and right and take pains to seek out conflicting evidence on issues of educational practice.

Second, an attitude of *responsibility* involves careful consideration of the consequences to which an action leads. Responsible student teachers ask themselves why they are doing what they are doing in the classroom in a way that transcends questions of immediate utility and in light of educational purposes of which they are aware. If all that is taught in schools were imparted through the formally sanctioned academic curriculum and if all of the consequences of teachers' actions could be anticipated in advance, the problem here would be much simpler than it is in actuality. However, there is a great deal of agreement among educators of various ideological persuasions that much of what children learn in school is imparted through the covert processes of the so-called "hidden curriculum" and that many consequences of the actions of educators are unanticipated outcomes that often contradict formally stated educational goals. Given the powerful impact of the hidden curriculum on the actual outcomes of schooling and the frequently unanticipated consequences of our actions, reflection about the potential impact of our actions in the classroom is extremely important.

The third and final attitude of the reflective teacher is one of *wholeheartedness*. This refers to the fact that openmindedness and responsibility must be central components in the life of the reflective teacher and implies that prospective teachers who are reflective must take active control over their education as teachers. A great deal of research demonstrates that prospective teachers very quickly adopt beliefs and practices of those university and school instructors with whom they work. Many prospective teachers seem to become primarily concerned with meeting the oftentimes conflicting expectations of university professors and cooperating teachers, and with presenting a favorable image to them in the hope of securing favorable evaluations. This impression management is understandable and is a natural consequence of existing power relationships in teacher education, but the divided interest that results tends to divert students' attention from a critical analysis of work and the context in which it is performed. If reflectiveness is to be part of the lives of prospective teachers, students will have to seek actively to be openminded and responsible, or else the pressure of the taken-for-granted institutional realities will force them buck into routine behavior.

Possession of these attitudes of openmindedness, responsibility, and wholeheartedness, together with a command of technical skills of inquiry (for example, observation) and problem solving, define for Dewey a teacher who is reflective. Reflection, according to Dewey,

> emancipates us from merely impulsive and routine activity
> … enables us to direct our actions with foresight and to plan

> according to ends in view of purposes of which we are aware.
> It enables its to know what we are about when we act.
> (Dewey, 1933, p. 17)

On the other hand, according to Dewey, to cultivate unreflective activity is "to further enslavement, for it leaves the person at the mercy of appetite, sense and circumstance" (p. 89).

Choosing between becoming a reflective teacher or an unreflective teacher is one of the most important decisions that you will have to make. The quality of all of your decisions regarding curriculum and instruction rests upon this choice.

You are probably saying to yourself, "Of course I want to be a reflective teacher, who wouldn't. But, you need to tell me more." The following sections of the paper discuss the three characteristics of reflective thinking in relation to classroom teaching, analyze whether reflective teaching is a realistic and/or desirable goal, and offer suggestions for how you can begin to become a reflective teacher.

## Further Insight

We have pointed out that openmindedness, responsibility, and wholeheartedness are the characteristics of reflective thinking. Let us now discuss each characteristic in relation to classroom teaching.

### Openmindedness

When you begin to teach, both as a student teacher and as a licensed teacher, you will most likely be asked to accept teaching procedures and strategies that are already being used in that school or classroom. Will you accept these without question, or will you explore alternative ways of looking at existing teaching practices? For example, celebrating holidays like Thanksgiving and Columbus Day helps to affirm the prevailing historical accounts of these days as well as the customs and traditions associated with them. As a teacher, would you be willing to reevaluate what and how you teach about holidays if some of the students in your class hold a different point of view about them? Would you modify your teaching to take into account their views and beliefs? Being a reflective teacher means that you keep an open mind about the content, methods, and procedures used in your classroom. You constantly reevaluate their worth in relation to the students currently enrolled and to the circumstances. You not only ask why things are the way that they are, but also how they can be made better.

The reflective teacher understands that school practices should not be accepted just because they are clothed in tradition. If, for example, most of the boys but only a few of the girls are being assigned to Industrial Arts, you should inquire as to why this is happening. You could then begin to formulate teaching and counseling plans (for example, career opportunities, workshops) that would allow students regardless of gender to benefit from the training that is available in those courses.

## Responsibility

Teaching involves moral and responsible action. Teachers make moral choices when they make voluntary decisions to have students attain one education objective instead of another. These decisions are conscious actions that result in certain consequences. These actions can be observed when teachers develop curriculum and choose instructional materials. For example, until recently a textbook company had two basal readers in its reading series. One basal reader was somewhat racially integrated and the other had all white characters. When teachers consciously chose one basal reader over the other or did not modify the all-white reader to correct the racial bias, they made a decision that affected not only their students' racial attitudes and understanding about different groups of people, but also their attitudes about themselves. In other words, teachers can encourage ethnocentric attitudes as well as teach an unrealistic view of the world community beyond the school community by failing to provide knowledge about other groups.

As a reflective teacher you are aware of your actions and their consequences. You are aware that your teaching behavior should not be conditioned merely by the immediate utility of an action. For example, it may be much easier to have your students answer questions or work problems on conveniently prepared ditto sheets than to have them do small group projects or hold classroom debates. It may also be much easier if you use one textbook to teach a unit on the Mexican-American War than if you use multiple textbooks and other historical documents that would represent both governments' points of view. But immediate utility cannot become the sole justification for your actions and cannot excuse you from the consequences of your actions. Your actions must have a definite and responsibly selected purpose. You have an obligation to consider their consequences in relation to the lives of the students you have accepted the responsibility to teach.

## Wholeheartedness

A reflective teacher is not openminded and responsible merely when it is convenient. Openmindedness and responsibility are integral, vital dimensions of your teaching philosophy and behavior. For example, we have seen teachers publicly advocate a belief in integrating handicapped students into the regular class; however, when observing in their classrooms, we saw the handicapped students treated in isolation because the curriculum and the instructional strategies had not been modified to capitalize upon the students' strengths or to acknowledge the students' individual differences. The teachers often left handicapped students to sit in the outer boundaries of the classroom instead of changing the physical environment of the classroom — desk arrangements — to allow them to move about freely as other students would. As a reflective teacher, you do not hesitate or forget to fight for your beliefs and for a quality education for all.

The reflective teacher is dedicated and committed to teaching *all students*, not just certain students. Many of your peers say they want to teach because they love and enjoy working with kids. Are they *really* saying *any* and *all* kids, or are they saying kids that are just like them? The story of Mary Smith will help to illustrate our point. During a job interview with a rural school system, Mary Smith, a graduate from a large urban university, was composed and fluent in discussing teaching methods and curriculum. She also stressed her genuine love for and enjoyment of children and her desire to help them. Her "performance" was so compelling that she was invited to accept a teaching position. Mary Smith, we must point out, believed what she said in the interview and eagerly looked forward to her teaching assignment. Her assignment was to a six-room rural school, where the majority of the students spoke with a heavy regional dialect that she had never before heard. The students' reading and mathematics achievement according to standardized tests was three to four years below grade level. Their behavior and attitudes toward school were different from what she had been accustomed to. They regarded the schools as boring and irrelevant to their lifestyle and their future, and they demonstrated their disregard for the school and the teacher by disobeying many instructional and behavioral "requests." Mary tried diligently for three months to get the students to cooperate and follow her instructions. At the beginning of the fourth month, however, she resigned her position. In her letter of resignation, she stated that "these kids are not ready to accept what I have been trained to give them. Therefore, I will seek teaching employment where the students want to learn."

There are many teachers like Mary Smith, but the reflective teacher is not one of them. The reflective teacher is wholehearted in accepting *all* students and is willing to learn about and affirm the uniqueness of each student for whom he or she accepts responsibility. If you are a reflective teacher, your teaching behavior is a manifestation of your teaching philosophy, and you are unswerving in your desire to make certain that the two become one and the same.

## Is Reflective Teaching a Realistic and/or Desirable Goal?

Throughout this century many educators have argued that teachers need to be more reflective about their work. The argument is often made that schools and society are constantly changing and that teachers must be reflective in order to cope effectively with changing circumstances. By uncritically accepting what is customary and by engaging in fixed and patterned behaviors, teachers make it more unlikely that they will be able to change and grow as situations inevitably change. Furthermore, it is commonly accepted that no teacher education program, whatever its focus, can prepare teachers to work effectively in all kinds of classroom settings. Therefore, it becomes important for you to be reflective in order that you may intelligently apply the knowledge and skills gained in your formal preparation for teaching to situations that may be very different from those you experienced during your training.

At the same time, many questions have been raised about whether reflective teaching is a realistic or even necessary goal to set before prospective teachers. The purpose of this section is to examine briefly one of the most common objections that have been raised about the goal of reflective teaching and to demonstrate how, despite these doubts, it is still possible and desirable for teachers to work toward a more reflective orientation to both their work and their workplace.

## Is It Possible to Take the Time to Reflect?

Many have argued that the nature of teaching and the ecology of classrooms make reflective teaching unrealistic and even undesirable. For example, it is frequently pointed out that classrooms are fast-paced and unpredictable environments where teachers are often required to make spontaneous decisions in response to childrens' ongoing reactions to an instructional program. Phillip Jackson (1968) has estimated that teachers engage in approximately 1,000 interpersonal interactions on any given day, and there is no way to describe life in the classroom as anything but extremely complex.

Furthermore, institutional constraints such as high pupil-teacher ratios, the lack of released time for reflection, and pressures to cover a required curriculum with diverse groups of children who are compelled to come to school shape and limit the range of possible teacher actions. The point is made that teachers do not have the time to reflect, given the necessity of quick action and the press of institutional demands. According to this view, intuitiveness (as opposed to reflectiveness) is an adaptive response and a natural consequence of the fast-paced and unpredictable nature of classroom life and is necessary in order for teachers to be able to negotiate classroom demands.

Phillip Jackson expresses serious doubts about whether teachers could even function at all in classrooms if they spent more time reflecting about the purposes and consequences of their work.

> If teachers sought a more thorough understanding of their world, insisted on greater rationality in their actions, were completely open in their consideration of pedagogical choices and profound in their view of the human condition, they might well receive greater applause from intellectuals, but it is doubtful that they would perform with greater efficiency in the classroom. On the contrary, it is quite possible that

such paragons of virtue, if they could be found to exist, would actually have a deuce of a time coping in any sustained way with a class of third graders or a play yard full of nursery school tots. (p. 151)

While classrooms are indeed fast-paced and complex environments, it does not automatically follow that reflective teaching is incompatible with this reality and that teachers by necessity must rely primarily upon intuition and unreflective actions. Several studies (for example, see Eliott, 1976–1977) have convincingly shown that the quality of teacher deliberations *outside* of the classroom (for example, during planning periods or team meetings) affects the quality of their future actions *within* the classroom. As Dewey (1933) points out, "To reflect is to look back on what has been done to extract the meanings which are the capital stock for dealing with further experience" (p. 87). Reflection that is directed toward the improvement of classroom practice does not necessarily need to take place within the classroom to have an impact on classroom practice. Despite the fact that reflection as has been defined in this paper does not occur in many schools even when there has been time set aside for that purpose[1] the possibility still exists.

Furthermore, the fast pace of classroom life does not preclude a certain amount of reflection within its boundaries. Those who have written about reflective teaching have never argued for "complete openness of mind." On the contrary, reflective teaching involves a balance between thought and action: a balance between the arrogance that blindly rejects what is commonly accepted as truth and the servility that blindly receives this "truth." There is clearly such a thing as too much thinking, as when a person finds it difficult to reach any definite conclusion and wanders helplessly among the multitude of choices presented by a situation, but to imply that reflection necessarily paralyzes one from action is to distort the true meaning of reflective teaching.

## How to Begin

You may be asking, "How can I become reflective, especially given the fact that I haven't started teaching yet?" The suggestions that we will now offer will help you get started. Remember, becoming a reflective teacher is a continual process of growth.

Many educators have correctly pointed out that even before you enter a formal program of teacher preparation you have already been socialized to some extent by the 12 years or more you have spent as a student. You have spent literally thousands of hours assessing schools and classrooms and have by now internalized (largely unconsciously) conceptions of children, learning, the roles of teacher and student, curriculum, beliefs, and assumptions concerning almost every issue related to schooling. From our point of view, a good place to begin the process of reflective teaching is to examine these numerous predispositions that you bring with you into formal preparation for teaching. Consciously or not, these will affect how you will perceive what will be presented to you in your teacher education program and how you will interpret your own and others' actions in the classroom.

It is important for you to begin to discriminate between beliefs and assumptions that rest upon tested evidence and those that do not, and to be cautious about putting confidence into beliefs that are not well justified. Some of our ideas have, in fact, been picked up from other people merely because they are widely accepted views, not because we have examined them carefully. Because of the nature of teaching, we may often be compelled to act without full confidence in a point of view or an approach to a problem. This is unavoidable. However, if we remain tentative about our beliefs, the possibility will remain that we may revise our thinking if future evidence warrants it. On the other hand, if we are dogmatic about our beliefs and refuse to entertain the possibility that we may be in error, the avenues for further growth are closed off. There are no greater errors that prospective teachers can make than those that stem from an unbending certainly in one's beliefs.

In *Dilemmas of Schooling*, Ann Berlak and Harold Berlak (1981) propose several specific steps for proceeding with a reflective analysis of the assumptions and beliefs regarding schooling that one brings into one's teacher preparation. The first step is to begin to articulate your current beliefs regarding a host of specific issues and to examine the assumptions that underlie these beliefs. For example, what knowledge and skills should be taught to different groups of children? How much control should a teacher exert over childrens' learning and behavior? To what extent should teachers transmit a common core of values and beliefs to all children, and to what extent should the curriculum attend to the cultural knowledge and background experiences of children? The issues here are endless. The above examples are only intended as illustrations of the kinds of questions that can be considered.

The next step is to compare your own beliefs with the beliefs of others. It is important for you to seek actively to understand the beliefs of others (peers, instructors, friends,) within your formal courses and, more generally, by reading, observing, and talking to others in both professional and nonprofessional settings. Prospective teachers who are sensitive to the tentative nature of their beliefs take pains to examine any issue from more than one perspective.

Once you have begun to identify the substance of your own beliefs and have become more conscious of alternatives that exist or could be created, it is important for you to do some thinking about the origins and consequences of these beliefs. For example, how has your own biographical history (for example, unique factors in your upbringing, your school experience as a pupil) affected the way in which you currently think about issues of schooling? Which of your current beliefs have you examined carefully through weighing and then rejecting alternative points of view, and which do you hold merely because they are widely accepted by those with whom you associate? Also, which of your current beliefs are the result of outside forces over which you have no control, and which beliefs are merely rationalizations masking an unwillingness to risk the difficulties and/or the possible displeasure of others that would result from their implementation?

Along with doing this analysis of the origin of your beliefs, you should begin to consider the possible consequences for yourself and others of holding particular beliefs. For example, what meanings (intended and unintended) are children likely to take from particular beliefs if they were actually implemented in the classroom? In considering the likely consequences of various courses of action, it is important to consider more than the immediate utility of an action. The costs associated with what works in the short run to help you get through a lesson smoothly at times may outweigh the benefits to be gained.

Because of the intimate relationship that exists between the school and society, any consideration of the consequences of an educational action must inevitably take one beyond the boundaries of the classroom and even the school itself. There is no such thing as a neutral education activity. Any action that one takes in the classroom is necessarily linked to the external economic, political, and social order in either a primarily integrative or a creative fashion. Either a teaching activity serves to integrate children into the current social order or it provides children with the knowledge, attitudes, or skills to deal critically and creatively with that reality in order to improve it. In any case, all teaching is embedded in an ideological background, and one cannot fully understand the significance or consequences of an activity unless one also considers that activity in light of the more general issues of social continuity and change.

For example, what are the likely consequences for the life chances of various groups of children if you present school knowledge as certain and objective to some groups of children and stress the tentativeness of knowledge to others? In other words, if you teach some students to accept what they are told and others to question and make their own decisions, how will this affect the social roles they hold later, and which group of children will you be preparing for which social roles? This example is cited to make the point that one can at least begin to identify the connections between everyday classroom practices and issues of social continuity and change. Because of the numerous forces acting upon children over a period of many years, we can never be certain of the effect that any given course of action by one teacher has in the long run, but it is certain that, despite the complexity, linkages do exist. It is important at least to attempt to think about the consequences of our actions in a way that transcends questions of immediate utility.

Finally, once you have begun to think about the origins and consequences of the beliefs that you bring into your formal education, the issue of "craft" also needs to be considered. What knowledge and skills will you need to gain in order to implement successfully the kind of teaching that follows from your education beliefs? If you as a prospective teacher are reflective, you do not passively absorb any and all of the skills and knowledge that others have decided are necessary for your education as a teacher. The craft knowledge and skills for teaching that you will gain during your formal preparation will originate from two major sources: your university instructors and supervisors, and the teachers and administrators with whom you will work during your practicum experiences in schools. If you are reflective about your own education for teaching, you will give some direction to the craft knowledge and skills that you learn in your training.

Within the university, your socialization for teaching is much more than the learning of "appropriate" content and procedures for teaching. The knowledge and skills that will be communicated to you through your university courses are not neutral descriptions of how things are: In reality, they are *value governed selections* from a much larger universe of possibilities — selections that reflect the educational ideologies of the instructors with whom you came into contact. Some things have been selected for your pursuance while other things have been de-emphasized or even ignored. These selections reflect at least implicitly answers to normative questions about the nature of schooling, the appropriate roles for teachers and students, how to classify, arrange, and evaluate educational knowledge, and how to think about educational problems and their solutions. But just as you will find diversity in the educational perspectives of a group of teachers in any given school, within any university program different university instructors will emphasize, de-emphasize, and ignore difficult points of view. As a result, it often becomes necessary for you to make decisions about the relevance of conflicting positions on an issue and to seek out information that supports views that may have been selected out by your instructors.

Therefore, if you want to give some direction to your education and to play an active role in shaping your own occupational identity, it becomes important for you to be constantly critical and reflective about that which is presented to you and that which has been omitted. That which is presented to you may or may not be the most appropriate craft knowledge and skill to help you get where you want to go. You need to filter all that is offered to you through your own set of priorities. At the same time, identify and use the instructors' stances about educational issues as alternatives that can help you develop your own beliefs. Generally, the same critical orientation that we have encouraged you to bring to bear upon your own prior experiences and beliefs should also be applied to that which is imparted to you by university instructors. Specifically, what are the origins and consequences of the viewpoints presented, and of the alternatives that are available or could be created?

Finally, one important part of your education for teaching will be the time you spend observing and working with teachers and administrators in school practicums. When you participate in a practicum you come into a setting (someone else's classroom) after certain patterns have been established and after certain ways of organizing time, space, instruction, and so forth have become routine. Cooperating teachers, who make many of these decisions, will often not take the time to explain to you how and why these decisions have been made, partly because the routines are by then part of the taken-for-granted reality of their classrooms. Consequently, prospective teachers often fail to grasp how what they see came to be in the first place and are often incapable of creating certain structures on their own once they have their own classrooms. This is a serious lapse in an education student's learning because it is difficult to understand any setting adequately without understanding how it was produced. If you want to understand the settings in which you will work, you will need to question your teachers about the reasons underlying what exists and is presently taken for granted. The following questions illustrate the things you shall seek to understand: Why is the school day organized as it is? Why is math taught every day but science taught only once per week? How and why was it decided to teach this particular unit on pollution? How are children placed into groups for reading and what opportunities exist for movement among groups? These regularities exist for particular reasons, and it is up to you to seek an understanding of how what is, came to be.

You will also need to ask your cooperating teachers about the ways in which particular decisions are being made while you are there. Although many of the basic patterns of classrooms will be established before you arrive, others will still be developing. The basic problem here is for you to gain an understanding of the thought processes that underlie your cooperating teacher's current actions. Importantly, many researchers have discovered that unless education students initiate these kinds of discussions with their mentors, the logic behind classroom decisions is often missed by prospective teachers (Tabachnick, Popkewitz, and Zeichner, 1979–1980). Experienced teachers may take many important factors for granted, and unless you actively probe for what underlies their behavior you will miss much of what is significant about the nature of teacher decision-making.

Seymour Sarason (1971)proposes that two basic questions be asked of any educational setting. One is what is the rationale underlying the setting? And the other is what is the universe of alternatives that could be considered? We strongly feel that asking these questions is necessary in order for you to gain the maximum benefit from your practical experience in schools. If you choose not to follow our advice but to take a primarily passive role as a student teacher, your learning will be limited to that which you happen upon by chance. If you want to be a certain kind of teacher and to have a particular quality of impact on children, you will need to ensure that your education for teaching will help you get where you want to go and that where you want to go is worth the effort. As you gain more experience you may frequently change your mind about the kind of teacher you want to become, but taking an active part in your own professional preparation will at least give you some control over determining the direction in which you are headed.

We have attempted to alert you to some of the numerous issues that you will have to confront during the next few years of your education for teaching. We have argued that there is a fundamental choice for you to make: whether you will give some direction to your training or let others direct it for you. In doing so, we have argued that reflective teaching is both possible and desirable. If the teachers of tomorrow are to contribute to the revitalization and renewal of our schools, there is no alternative. However, as in all decisions, the final choice is up to you.

## ENDNOTE

1.  Frequently, discussions that occur among teachers during planning session, team meetings, etc., focus almost entirely on procedural issues (for example, *How* will we teach what has already been decided to teach?) to the neglect of curricular questions, such as "What should we be teaching and why?" See Thomas Popewitz, B. Robert Tabachnick, and Gary Wchlage. *The Myth of Educational Reform* (Madison: University of Wisconsin Press, 1982) for an example for how this occurs in exemplary "individually guided education" schools.

## References

Berlak, Ann, and Harold Berlak (1981). *Dilemmas of Schooling*, London: Methuen.

Dewey, John (1933). *How we think: A restatement of the relation of reflective thinking to the educative process*, Chicago: Henry Regnery.

Elion, John (1976–1977). Developing hypotheses about classrooms from teachers' personal constructs. *Interchange*, 7(2), 22.

Greene, Maxine (1971). *Teacher as stranger*, Belmont, CA: Wadsworth Publishing, p. 46.

Jackson, Phillip (1968). *Life in classrooms*, New York: Holt, Rinehart and Winston.

Sarason, Seymour (1971) *The culture of the school and the problem of change*, Boston: Allyn and Bacon.

Tabachnick, Robert B., Thomas Popkewitz, and Kenneth Zeichner (1979–1980). Teacher education and the professional perspectives of student teachers. *Interchange*, 10(4), pp. 12–29.

# Part 2

# The Politics
# of Meaning

**Levin and Young**
"Making Sense of Public Schooling"

**Aoki**
"On Being and Becoming
a Teacher in Alberta"

**Allen**
"'I Don't Want to Read This':
Students Responses to Illustrations
of Black Characters in
Children's Picture Books"

# Chapter 5

# Making Sense
# of Public Schooling

### Benjamin Levin
### Jon Young

## PROLOGUE: The Staff Room, 8:15 A.M.

Linda Chartrand arrived at school at her usual time: 8:15 a.m. Getting
her own children ready for school and to the neighbour's for preschool
care was hard, but she found that she needed at least half an hour before
the students arrived to review her plans for the day and make sure that
she had all the materials ready. She also used the time to chat with
colleagues in the staff room, to find out whether there had been any
important developments since yesterday, or to check on which resource
people might be in school that day.

"By the way, Linda," Pat, the office secretary, said as she came
through the staff-room door, "don't forget that your class will be going to
the auditorium at 3:00 p.m. to practise for the school concert. And could
you make sure that all the money is in for the book orders? Oh, and Mrs.
Koslowski is looking for you. She wants to ask if she could send the kids
back 10 minutes early from Phys. Ed. so she can make a meeting with the
divisional consultant. Is that OK?"

"Sure," Linda replied. As an experienced teacher at both the junior
high and elementary levels, she knew that there would be days requiring
last-minute changes in her schedule. She had intended to get into a new
unit with the class toward the end of the day, but that would have to

wait, and she would have to find something else for them to do for the half hour between 2:30 and 3:00 p.m. As she was pondering what this might be, the resource teacher, Eric Sigurdson, asked if he could take three of her students for an extra half hour that morning. "The parents I was going to meet with had to cancel, so I'd like to give your kids the time." Again, Linda agreed to the change. She didn't like the model of resource withdrawal very much, preferring a collaborative, in-class approach, but there was no doubt that Eric was a help to the students he saw; she had a hard time finding the time to give them the individual attention they needed, even in her relatively small class of 23.

Linda checked her staff mailbox and pulled out an agenda for an upcoming in-school, professional development day. At the first staff meeting of the year, the principal had asked the staff to spend the year reviewing the school's mission statement and reaffirming their collective vision and goals for the school. This was to be the focus of the day's meetings.

Linda had been through a comparable process in her previous school, and she smiled to herself as she thought of the similar reactions to the request among the two staffs. Some teachers had asked what was wrong with the existing mission statement that had been written by the previous principal when the school first opened 15 years ago. Others expressed surprise that the school *had* a mission statement, because they'd been working at the school for several years and had never seen it. A few wondered why it would take a year to do this. Surely, they argued, a small subcommittee could draft something fairly easily, working from the old statement and from a few other schools' goals. This, they maintained, would allow time for the rest of the staff to focus on some of the pressing and practical issues that needed to be dealt with, like a new conflict-resolution program for the children and the cooperative learning initiatives that the Grade 6 teachers were working on.

But the discussion that had followed had been a good one, and by the end of the meeting most of the staff were supportive of the project. The principal had emphasized that she wasn't interested in simply producing a public-relations document full of all the right phrases and current jargon. She wanted the staff to talk through their different views of the school's goals and priorities, and to come up with a statement of purpose that the staff as a whole would feel was their own, and that would relate to daily school practices as well as set a direction for future initiatives. Some teachers began talking about their dreams for — and frustrations with — the school, and how they thought it had changed over the years. Despite the differences in the concerns and ideas expressed by the teachers, when the meeting ended there was an air of excitement about the project, which had carried over into the ensuing weeks.

Now, as the bell rang for the first class of the day, Linda was still thinking about the process of developing a mission statement that would actually capture what the school was all about. She thought of the mixed group of students she had in her class. They were good kids and she liked them all, but she was always being reminded of how different they were, from her and from one another. It wasn't that their reading levels ranged from Grades 2 to 8; that was normal. It was just that there were so many other differences. The two new immigrant children were just starting to learn English, and couldn't yet speak very much to the other kids. She hardly noticed Rose's wheelchair anymore, since Rose was so much a part of the class now. But Tommy still had occasional severe outbursts of rage that were hard on her and the students, although he'd improved since the year began. The fulltime teacher aide helped, but Linda wondered how much Tommy was really learning. And there were so many others, the quiet ones for example, who raised questions in her mind about her teaching strategies and effectiveness.

Yes, she thought, it was going to be a good exercise to step back a bit from the everyday demands of the classroom and to think through what the school's priorities were, and what kind of balance it wanted to establish among what seemed to be an unending set of demands and expectations. What were the goals of the school?

## LIMITATIONS OF THE STATUS QUO

Many people may take for granted the organizational aspects of schools, assuming that schools are the way they are for good and sufficient reasons, as people do with much of the world they encounter every day. But because schools have the potential to be much better places for both teachers and students, we regard it as very important for everyone involved with education to understand the way in which our schools are organized and operated so that they can ask questions about, and propose changes to, current practices. One approach to developing this understanding is to embark on a description of the existing constitutional, legal, and administrative structures that currently exist and give direction to administrators, teachers, and students in the daily routines of school life. This has become, in a sense, the official or taken-for-granted version of school organization. It is important because no one who is to be involved in schooling can afford to ignore the power exercised through these structures and processes. As a result, this text gives considerable attention to them and attempts to demonstrate concretely how they affect, on a daily basis, the work of teachers and what it means to be a teacher.

However, this approach is not a sufficient introduction to school organization, because the context for Canadian schooling has been shifting in important ways, and from many points of view the status quo is no longer seen as adequate. Whereas 20 years ago schooling was an unquestioned positive and Canada was busy expanding its education system at all levels, today there are many questions about what schools are for and how well they are meeting their goals. Changes in policy and practice are frequently announced by governments and school districts. A variety of lobby groups press for changes of one sort or another. Newspapers and other media ask questions about whether our schools are good enough, too costly, well run, and so on.

The reasons for the current climate of uncertainty are varied, but are largely connected to changes in Canadian society generally. Changes in the nature of work, in the structure and functioning of families, in gender roles, in technology, in the age profile of the population, in the role of government — all of these affect the schools (Levin and Riffel, 1997). Practices that used to seem effective may no longer seem so, not because schools have changed, but because the practices are no longer seen as consonant with what people feel they need (Hargreaves, 1994). For example, rising unemployment may call into question the value of secondary schooling. Information technology can change how, where, and when people learn. Changing roles for women and changes in family structures mean that the traditional school day and year don't work as well as they used to. And so on.

In a climate of change, critical re-examination of school organization is essential. Rather than viewing current practice as somehow natural or obvious, we want to examine why things are the way they are, how they came to be the way they are, who benefits most from them, and how they might be otherwise.

We also believe that one must approach school organization from a moral and educational perspective as well as from a technical perspective. In other words, questions of "how to" cannot be separated from questions of "why." Nor is it possible to detach the discussion of school organization from a broader discussion of the purposes of schooling and its place in Canadian society.

Another way in which we have sought to extend the official version of school organization in this text has been to recognize the real world in which students, teachers, and administrators live and work on a daily basis. The official image is often a pale reflection of the complexity of real classrooms and schools. It is important to pay attention to the uniquely human nature of schools and to human behaviour with all of its idiosyncrasies, its intertwining of personal and professional lives, its dreams and disappointments, its friendships and hostilities, its egos and ambitions. Often all of this is underemphasized in administration texts as being too messy for neat theories, lectures, and organizational charts of the way the world ought to be. We attempt to incorporate this reality into our discussion.

School organization and administration must be seen as concerning not only those people who occupy positions termed "administrative" (e.g., policymakers, directors, superintendents, and principals), but everyone who is engaged in, and affected by, the educational process. As Baron notes, "[V]iewed in its widest sense as all that makes possible the educational process, the administration of education embraces the activities of Parliament at one end of the scale and the activities of any home with children at the other" (cited in Saxe, 1980, p. 14).

## THE PURPOSES OF EDUCATION

In everyday language, people slip easily from "education" to "schooling" as though the two words, if not synonymous, were at least mutually supportive, with schools as the formal institutions of education. This blurring of concepts is not always helpful. If we are to examine thoughtfully the organization and administration of schooling in Canada, then it is important to think about the meaning of education, the purposes of schooling, and the significance of public schooling.

Questions of what it means to educate, or to be educated, have long been the subject of intellectual debate. In the Western liberal tradition, education is inextricably bound to ideas of self-knowledge or identity, as well as to empowerment, which means "becoming more than we are." In describing the relationship between education and self-knowledge, Symons (1975) argues that to be educated means to know ourselves: who we are, where we are in time and space, where we have been and where we are going, and what our responsibilities are to ourselves and to others. Nor, he suggests, can self-knowledge be separated from an awareness of the social context in which we live our lives, the two kinds of knowledge being not merely interdependent, "but ultimately one and the same" (p. 14).

For this process of acquiring self-knowledge to be considered educative and not simply socialization into existing ways of thinking, people must play an active and critical role in creating their knowledge. It must be an active and purposeful endeavour that informs our actions and provides the understanding, skills, and dispositions that enable people to grow and to exercise more control over the ways in which they live their lives within their social, communal, and ecological contexts. This view of education, although simplified in its presentation here, would not be acceptable to everyone. Traditionalists, for example, might argue that it does not give adequate attention to absorbing the central lessons of the past and the best of our collective cultures. Furthermore, when we speak of "control" we need to pay very careful attention to the interrelated nature of our social lives, and to the global devastation that has resulted from the pursuit of control over the environment.

This definition of education is still too broad to be confined to the formal process and structure of schools. Indeed, the great bulk of what people know, believe, and can do is not learned in schools (Resnick, 1987). We learn many of the most important things in our lives before we begin our schooling, and over the course of our schooling we continue to learn many things outside of schools as a result of our experiences, our reading, and our contact with other people. Even institutional education extends well beyond the school system. Programs ranging from daycare to courses for senior citizens, and including the vast gamut of adult education activity in Canada, are also clearly educational in their focus.

At the same time, for many people there is a clear connection between these general ideas of self-knowledge and their expectations of public schools in Canada. We expect schools to be places of learning and development for students. Yet this rhetoric masks the multiple functions that have been assigned to public schools since their establishment as compulsory institutions in Canadian society. The problems and tensions facing schools can be seen by considering their official goals and their actual purposes.

## THE GOALS OF SCHOOLS

Why have formal education at all? We tend to take the goals of schooling as being relatively self-evident, but they are actually quite problematic. To understand the operation of schools, we need to go beyond formal statements of goals and ask about the functions schools actually perform. Schools have purposes that are rarely talked about in the official statements. Holmes (1986) describes six such purposes for Canadian secondary schools — allocative, custodial, intellectual-vocational, socializing, aesthetic, and physical. The allocative function has to do with determining who gets what — for example, who qualifies to go to university. Custodial refers to the childcare function of the schools. Intellectual-vocational includes what are usually thought of as school goals developing knowledge and skills. The socializing function refers to inculcating desired values and behaviours. The aesthetic purpose has to do with developing appreciation for arts, culture, and beauty. And the physical function involves the training of the body — sports, exercise, and so on. Educational philosopher Robin Barrow (1981) identifies a similar list — critical thinking, socialization, childcare, vocational preparation, physical instruction, social-role selection, education of the emotions, and development of creativity.

There are several important questions to ask about any statement of educational goals:

- Are the goals mutually compatible?
- Are the goals achievable?
- Do the goals have a commonly shared meaning?
- Do the goals affect what schools do on a day-to-day basis?

## TENSIONS AND DILEMMAS IN CANADIAN EDUCATION

One way to think of public education is in terms of a series of characterizing attributes or elements. For example:

1. *Public accessibility.* All persons of school age should have a right to free access to schooling.
2. *Equal opportunity.* All children should receive equal opportunity to benefit from schooling, regardless of factors such as their culture, gender, ability, and so on.
3. *Public funding.* The costs of schooling should be borne by government so that the quality of schooling received by a student is not related to the ability of the student or the parents to pay for that schooling.
4. *Public control.* Decisions about the nature of public schools are made through public political processes, by persons who are elected at large to carry out this responsibility.
5. *Public accountability.* Public schools act in the interests of the public and are answerable to the public for what is taught and for the quality of the experiences provided to students.

Most people would probably agree with these characteristics in principle, but what they might mean in practice is much less evident. As Canadians have struggled with them in specific situations, a number of ongoing tensions or dilemmas have arisen — areas where trying to recognize one reality leads us away from another that may be equally important. Much of the history of Canadian education can be seen as an effort to find an appropriate but always temporary balance between these competing objectives. Three tensions are particularly important: uniformity and diversity, stability and change, power and equality. This chapter discusses the first of these tensions in detail below.

## Uniformity and Diversity

The first tension is between the desire to have a common education system for all, and the recognition that students and communities are quite different from one another and may therefore have different educational needs.

In many ways, despite the variety of school systems, present-day schools in Canada are remarkably similar to one another in their internal appearance: rows or groups of classrooms full of desks or tables, generally empty hallways, libraries, gyms, administrative offices, and almost always groups of students of about the same age who are engaged in some activity that is directed and supervised by a single adult.

Students everywhere in Canada study quite similar material, which is divided into subjects. They have to learn certain material on which they are tested, and their progress through the system depends largely on how well they do on various assessment measures. Children are judged individually, and do the vast bulk of their work as individuals. Students have very little say in shaping the nature of their education, and classrooms tend to be dominated by teacher discussion, with students playing a largely passive role in the whole process. The school day is about the same length and covers about the same hours of the day almost everywhere.

While these similarities are quite consistent, even to the point of crossing national boundaries, schools are found in diverse settings. Consider a school in a very small community in the high Arctic. The community has a few hundred people. It is very isolated, and transportation in and out of the region is entirely by airplane, with limited service. There is continuous darkness for about three months each winter, and continuous sunlight for three months each summer. The school has a few dozen students, from kindergarten to Grade 9, and a couple of teachers. Most of the children are Inuit, and they come to school speaking Inuktitut, while the teachers are probably white, come from southern Canada, and often leave after three or four years. Resources for the school have to be flown in from outside, as does much of the community's food. Many of the children have never been in another community, although through satellite communications they do have access to television. Everyone in the community knows everyone else, and many of the students are related to half or more of the people in the community. They rely heavily on one another for almost everything.

Compare such a community with a school in a new suburb of Montreal. There may be 400 or 500 students and about 30 teachers in such a school. Nobody has lived in that community for more than a few years because the homes and school were built only a few years ago. Most but not all of the children speak French. Many also speak English. The school is officially Catholic, and includes religious exercises in its program. A significant number of students are members of visible minority groups. Many of the children have travelled quite extensively with their families and are used to books, libraries, museums, and all the other amenities of a large city. They also face the pressures of commercialism and isolation that inundate our cities. Many of them do not have any close relatives living in, or even near, the same community.

Or consider a third setting — an inner-city school in Winnipeg. Here, many of the children are from non–English-speaking families. Many families are Aboriginal or immigrant. Many of the families are subject to frequent unemployment and are unable to afford adequate food and housing, let alone holiday trips or the latest trend in athletic shoes. Some children move to different schools two or three times in a school year. Their parents have limited education and are intimidated by the school system. After years of unsuccessful struggle, some may feel powerless to influence their situation and live very much on a day-to-day basis.

It is clear from these limited descriptions that the conditions of learning and the job of teaching vary across settings, even though the schools themselves may be structured in quite similar ways. There can be no single right way to organize schools and schooling. Different students and communities may well require different educational approaches. There will be substantial disagreement about how best to organize and conduct schooling to meet these needs. It is also possible to conceive of ways of conducting schooling that are quite different from those in common use. Yet there is surprisingly little debate about many basic aspects of schooling that are shared by all kinds of schools and communities.

## THE MORAL NATURE OF SCHOOLS AND TEACHING

A final complication in the discussion of the goals and purposes of schooling has to do with its moral nature. Schooling is not simply a matter of teaching skills to students, although this is how it is often described. Rather, schooling is essentially concerned with introducing young people (and, increasingly, adults) to the nature of the world as we understand it, and equipping them to live in that world — what we earlier called the development of self-knowledge. In this process, moral and ethical considerations are of fundamental importance, for students learn as much from how they are taught and treated in schools as they do from what they are taught. Every day, teachers and school administrators are acting as moral examples to students and one another, and are creating a community that embodies particular concepts of ethical behaviour. If students are treated as unimportant, as people whose ideas and feelings are of no consequence, then they are more likely to see the world as one in which some people matter while others do not. If teachers embody respect for students, for one another, for their subjects, and for the development of knowledge, then students are more likely to develop and prize these qualities. According to Gary Fenstermacher,

> Teaching becomes nearly incomprehensible when disconnected from its fundamental moral purposes. These purposes are rooted in the moral development of the young ... moral qualities are learned — acquired in the course of lived experience. If there are no models for them, no obvious or even subtle pressures to adopt moral qualities ... the moral virtues may be missed, perhaps never to be acquired.
> ...
> What makes teaching a moral endeavor is that it is, quite centrally, human action undertaken in regard to other human beings. Thus, matters of what is fair, right, just, and virtuous are always present. ... The teacher's conduct, at all times and in all ways, is a moral matter. For that reason alone, teaching is a profoundly moral activity. (1990, pp. 132–33)

There are some important technical skills to be learned about teaching. Student teachers are understandably anxious about their ability to manage classes, maintain order, and create reasonable learning experiences for students. But these skills are not meaningful unless they are tied to an ethical and moral view of teaching. Think back to the teachers you had, and you will probably see that the example set by good teachers had more impact on you, and is more vivid in your memory, than the subject matter they taught.

Moral issues are not only embedded in the fabric of teaching, they are also integral to school organization and administration. Such matters as the division of schools into classes, grades, and ability levels, the assignment of work to students, or the awarding of marks and credits also have important moral dimensions.

## CONCLUSION

The inconsistencies and tensions discussed in this chapter raise important questions. How do we work in an institution whose goals are uncertain, sometimes in conflict with one another, and perhaps unachievable? How do we decide what is worth our time and effort? Even more significantly, the idea that schools might actually require some students to fail — that this is a built-in part of what schools do — is a difficult one for many teachers who see their job as helping students to succeed.

Some teachers probably don't think about these issues very much. They just go on doing their daily work, help students as much as they can, and try to avoid the contradictions in the system. Other teachers come to the conclusion that they cannot do the things they value in schools as presently constituted, and they leave teaching. Some combine their teaching with active involvement in larger educational and social issues, whether through their professional association or through other kinds of volunteer work and public service. Others make up their minds to live with the frustration and inconsistencies because they continue to believe that their work is important, and that they can make a difference, even if only in their own classroom. In taking this position, teachers are embodying a concept of schools as institutions that are based fundamentally on moral considerations. A vision of the good school is intimately connected with a vision of the good society and the good life.

## References

Barrow, R. (1981). *The philosophy of schooling*, New York: John Wiley.

Fenstermacher, G. (1990). Some more considerations on teaching as a profession. In J. Goodlad, R. Soder, and K. Sirotnik (eds.) *The moral dimensions of teaching*, San Francisco: Jossey-Bass. 130–51.

Hargreaves, A. (1994). *Changing teachers, changing times*, New York: Teachers College Press.

Holmes, M. (1986). The secondary school in contemporary western society: Constraints, imperatives, and prospects. *Curriculum Inquiry*, 15(1), 7–36.

Levin, B., and J.A. Riffel (1997). *Schools in a changing world. Struggling toward the future*, London: Falmer Press.

Resnick, L. (1987). *Education and learning to think*, Washington, DC: National Academy Press.

Saxe, R. (1980). *Educational administration today*, Berkeley, CA: McCutchan.

Symons, T.B. (1975). *To know ourselves: The report of the commission on Canadian studies*, Ottawa: Association of Universities and Colleges of Canada.

## Exercises

In a discussion of schools Levin and Young (1998, p. 5) state
> Questions of "how to" cannot be separated from questions of "why." Nor is it possible to detach the discussion of school organization from a broader discussion of the purposes of schooling and its place in Canadian society.

And they indicate that "the official image [of schooling] is often a pale reflection of the complexity of real classrooms and schools."

1. If "education" and "schooling" are not the same thing, then what are some of the possible differences?
2. "Self knowledge" and "awareness of the social context" are "two kinds of knowledge" but they are "ultimately one and the same." How are they the same?
3. Do all people in society hold the same basic attitudes and values? Whose values are taught in schools?
4. Who does the goal of uniformity serve?
5. Who does the goal of diversity serve?
6. Discuss the relative power of teachers, students, administrators, boards, parents and communities to make decisions in regard to

curriculum, teaching methods, and school policies and rules. Who does not have power?

7.  Discuss the relative position of students in a class to a general population (possibly use census data to do so).

# Chapter 6

# On Being and Becoming a Teacher in Alberta[1]

## Ted T. Aoki

I speak from the perspective of a Japanese Canadian Nisei and an evacuee. Hence, I speak from the perspective of a Nisei who experienced the evacuation, and who as an "evacuated" holds a special experiential relationship with those who relocated me, the "evacuators."

### A Biographical Sketch

Among many of you as consociates or contemporaries, I lived for 13 years in Lethbridge, for 22 years in Southern Alberta, for 33 years in Alberta. Hence, when I speak of my lived experiences in Alberta, I speak not from the standpoint of a "visitor" looking on, but from the standpoint of an "insider" who lived his life with fellow Albertans for a third of a century.

I have chosen to speak of only a slice of my lived experiences — that of being and becoming a teacher in Alberta, dating back to 1945, the closing year of World War II, including my experiences as a teacher trainee at the Calgary Normal School, as a teacher for one year at a Hutterite School east of Calgary, as a teacher for two years at Foremost, south of Lethbridge, as a teacher for three years at Taber, and for thirteen years as a teacher and Lethbridge Collegiate Institute vice-principal in

Lethbridge, prior to becoming a teacher educator at the University of Alberta.

## A Typical "Becoming a Teacher"

What does it mean to become a teacher? I learned, from becoming one, that to become a teacher one undergoes a ritual that allows entry into a culturally shaped and culturally legitimated world in which are prescriptions of years of training, certification, compulsory membership, apprenticeship, scrutiny and evaluation by legitimated seniors, and so on. Once allowed into this culturally shaped world, one is governed by rules of conduct and socially expected behaviour, which are presumed to be "becoming" of people called teachers, and by codified ethical prescriptions of personal and interpersonal action. It is a domain of conduct governed socially by a codified School Act, provincially legislated, which sets out the bounds within which typical teachers are expected to act out their typical roles in typical ways. Those who learn the roles well are typified by being labelled "teachers."

However, looking at typicalities ignores the unique flavour of the experiences of becoming a teacher in my time and in my historical situation. My experiences are centred around me within my own experiential horizon and undergirded by my own biography of past experiences and my own aspirations and hopes.

## A Dialogue With Chief Maurice Wolfe

In the Fall of 1971, I chanced to meet Maurice Wolfe, Chief of the Ermineskin Band, the largest of the four bands of the Hobbema Reserves south of Edmonton. A friend of mine, Dr. Ralph Sabey, and I were at that time jointly seeking an opportunity to work with the people of Hobbema on a Native Indian curriculum project, firmly believing that a new curriculum development conception based on Native Indian involvement was sorely needed to develop meaningful school programs by Indians for Indian children attending Indian schools. Only by so doing could we begin to include in the curriculum the insiders perspective on what it means to be schooled.

On the appointed day I met Chief Wolfe, and we talked freely of many things, mainly about matters other than mounting a curriculum project — so I thought, naively, at that time. Although many of the details of our conversation have faded from my memory, I still remember vividly three items about which we chatted:

Item 1: We talked of Judo — in passing, we learned that our sons were in judo training at that time. Our discussion about judo led us to the notion of the dialectic between "defence" and "offence," between "the active" and "the passive," between "the gentle" and "the strong," between "the positive" and "the negative." We felt good about this dialectic talk, a momentary enjoyment of a non-positivistic world.

Item 2: Chief Wolfe led me to a discussion of a book on his shelf, Dr. Nitobe's *Bushido*. We dwelt to some extent on the meaning of being and becoming a warrior in the truest sense. We felt and experienced deep thoughts about being a human being and about human becoming and for a moment I thought he would be expounding to me the meaning of Zen. I wish he had.

Item 3: Then, he talked to me of what he knew about the experiences of the Japanese Canadian evacuees — the expropriation of their properties on the coast and their forced evacuation. He drew a parallel between the Japanese Canadian experience and his own forebears' experience — the expropriation of their lands and their appropriation to reserve lands — and of his own people then working as seasonal labour on the sugar beet farms in Southern Alberta. Then, he asked me of my experience and my fellow Japanese Canadians' experience as sugar beet workers in Southern Alberta, but particularly, he asked me how the Japanese Canadians transcended *the state of being economic objects* (that is how he viewed sugar beet workers), and how they transformed themselves "to become beings with increased control of their own destinies." I thought he was in search of a way — possibly resembling the way of a warrior — to help his people transform themselves.

Shortly thereafter, as I reflected upon our conversation, I could not help but envisage Chief Wolfe viewing human beings in a dialectical relationship between their subjective being and their objective world, in contrast to a popular view of humans as strictly economic beings, i.e., an objectified and "thingified" view of humans, shorn of much of their humanness and human dignity. I reinterpreted Chief Wolfe's earlier question to me as follows: How did the Japanese Canadian evacuees liberate themselves from the objectified condition, having been partially stripped of their history, of their familiar surroundings, of their circle of friendships and acquaintances? How did they move to a position where, in his eyes, they, the Japanese Canadians, could conduct themselves with promise, with dignity, as subjects of their thoughts and actions? Chief Wolfe wanted to know of the Japanese Canadian experience in this regard.

This leads me to a consideration, though brief, of the concept of "experience," which according to the conference planners seems to be a central concern if not "the" central concern. I define "experience", as Chief Wolfe defined it, as the meaning a person imparts to their action as the "subjective I" interacts with their "world." Experience thus viewed is seen as a dynamic dialectic between the subject and the object of which Chief Wolfe spoke, comparable to the dialectic between the "we" and "they" that Gordon Hirabayashi this morning spoke of in his sociological examination of the sense of community, and the "we" and "they" David Iwaasa commented on when he discussed the relationship between the evacuees and the non-evacuees in Southern Alberta.

## JOB OFFERS IN THE SPRING OF 1945

I told Chief Wolfe of my personal experiences in the only way I knew.

The invocation of the Emergency War Measures Act in 1941 undoubtedly brought about an abrupt change in the life of most Japanese Canadians. But it was another emergency measure, a little known one, that provided the setting for what turned out to be for me my personal transformation from a sugar beet worker to a teacher.

The emergency measure I am referring to is the Alberta Government's School Emergency Measure. During the War, the province faced a critical shortage in the teaching force and there was an urgent need to devise a way to throw warm bodies (labelled teachers) into many teacher-less classrooms. The normal school entrance requirement was lowered to allow entry of Grade 11 graduates, who with a three-month crash program (including nine days of practicum in teaching) enabled the graduates to receive a temporary licence which, followed by two summer schools at the University of Alberta, opened the way for a "bona fide" teaching certificate.

During the winter of 1944, a group of Japanese Canadians — Niseis most of us — were at Burmis in the Crows Nest Pass area felling timber as a winter passtime. It was there I saw a newspaper advertisement calling upon Grade 11 students to become teachers. I wrote the principal of the Calgary Normal School indicating my qualifications (a B.Comm. degree from U.B.C.) to which he responded, "fully qualified." So I dropped my bucking saw and double bit axe and off I went to Calgary. Here, I faced an unanticipated problem — a becoming-a-teacher problem for a Japanese Canadian aspirant — *that of where to live* since Calgary's bylaws forbade residence of any Japanese Canadian within the confines of Calgary city proper.

A kind Japanese couple working at Hay's Dairy just outside the city limits allowed me to stay with them. So for a brief while as a daily ritual I commuted to Calgary on the 7:00 a.m. milk wagon and I Greyhound-bussed home at night.

In the meantime I applied to the City Council for temporary permission to reside within Calgary. A report of the City Council deliberations hit the *Calgary Albertan* and the *Calgary Herald* on February 7, 1945, an event that catapulted me into a "cause celebre" at normal school. I felt good that the Council took time to discuss my application; I did not feel good about some of the comments that flew about in the City Council chambers:

> Alderman Starr referred to Japanese Canadians as "well-educated cultural devils" and shouted "If I had my way I'd take them all out to the middle of the Pacific Ocean and pull the cork."

> Alderman Brown stated: "They are treacherous. They are our enemies. And I don't like them — yellow bellies! And if there are no black marks against them, they will make good spies."

A six-to-five vote of the Council referred my case to the city commissioners and charged them that "if in conference with the RCMP and city police, there be no objection to the individual's character, he is to be permitted to attend Calgary Normal School for a period of two-and-a-half months."

From this experience I gained one important piece of knowledge, which I promptly offered freely to my Japanese Canadian friends. I told them: Find a city or town where Japanese Canadians are forbidden to live and apply for permission to reside there. One predictable outcome will be receipt of official information about their own character — gratis, at that!

By April of that year, I had a temporary ticket as a teacher. I learned quickly that when they said shortage of teachers, they had typical teachers in mind. There was no shortage of Japanese Canadian teachers. In fact, there was one too many.

I knew, however, that the normal school principal tried hard to locate a job for me. He did, eventually, at a Hutterite colony 60 miles east of Calgary — a one room school, Grades 1 to 8.

Interestingly enough — and remember this is in the spring of 1945 — out of the blue I received two other job offers:

1.  A job as a radio broadcaster at BBC, London, to do propaganda broadcasting in Japanese to Japan;
2.  A job in Vancouver as an instructor of the Japanese language, giving instruction to the Canadian Intelligence Service. (Previously I had done a two-year stint of COTC duties at U.B.C. but had received from C.O. Colonel Shrum an honourable discharge, essentially, I believe, for being of Japanese extraction.)

What job did I choose? I had no problem really. I found that no real alternatives faced me. I accepted the job at the Hutterite school (as caretaker, teacher, principal, all wrapped up in one package) and launched a pedagogic career — a move that, by the way, I have never regretted taking.

However, I found that teaching on a Hutterite colony was a stranger's existence in that the residents permitted me to enter only that sector of their world associated with the English school (the other school being the German school). Further, it was a life with little contact with fellow teachers or the mainstream of the community's social world, although, for me, the latter was not an unaccustomed kind of experience — for living apart from the mainstream has been the lot of most Japanese Canadians.

## FOREMOST

In the spring of '46, I scouted for a job. I had come to know T.C. Byrne, then Superintendent of Schools in Foremost (later Deputy Minister of Education and still later President of Athabasca University). I asked him for a job. I got an answer. Let me read a portion of that letter to you to give you the flavour of my lived world at that time. The letter is dated April 13, 1946.

> Dear Mr. Aoki:
>
> I have your letter of April 8th enquiring about vacancies in the Foremost Division for the next school year.
>
> My personal opinion is that men should be judged on their individual merits irrespective of race or creed. However, the problem of community reaction must be taken into account in teacher appointments.
>
> I will take up the matter of your appointment at the next Board meeting and I will advise you immediately as to their stand. Probably the only position available in any event will be in a rural school.
>
> Yours sincerely.

I received an appointment in the town school.

## Teachers' Convention, Lethbridge 1947

Marquis Hotel in downtown Lethbridge holds a special meaning for me. It revolves around a special episode 29 years ago, in the fall of 1947.

I was teaching in Foremost — just a year and a half out of normal school — and had come into the city of Lethbridge for the Annual Teachers' Convention. A group of us cronies from normal school settled in a circle around a little round table in the Marquis Hotel to seek strength, courage, and sustenance to continue the tough life as green teachers. The round-table conference had an aborted life. The beerhop, spotting me as a Japanese, served notice that "It is the policy of the management of the Marquis not to serve Japs."

I don't remember anything of the happenings at the Teachers' Convention, but I do have a strong indelible memory of that ten-second episode at the Marquis.

## Super Session 1947, University of Alberta

During the winter of 1946 I was already considering going to the 1947 Summer Session Studies at the University of Alberta. Despite the fact that earlier that year Deputy Minister Fred McNally had informed me, "I have telephoned the city authorities who assure me that there are no longer any restrictions on students of Japanese ancestry so far as residence in Edmonton is concerned," I received word from the Registrar of the University of Alberta that registration was impossible unless the city granted me permission to reside within the city. I despatched a letter, to which I received a reply from Mayor Harry Ainlay of Edmonton:

> Replying to your letter of the 27th instant, the City of Edmonton has granted your application for permission to reside in Edmonton temporarily, for the purpose of attending the 1947 Summer Session of the University of Alberta.

To my children, Harry Ainlay means a large composite high school in Edmonton (dedicated to Ainlay) — and it has for them mixed memories as students. For me the name Harry Ainlay represents "he who granted me the privilege of temporary residence" in Edmonton to attend Summer School in 1947.

I feel sure that Niseis of my vintage will be able to recall episodes somewhat akin to the ones I have cited. They add "charm" to the generalized reports and studies about Japanese Canadian experiences that are making their way into public view. These experiences that I narrated and the experiences of my fellow Japanese Canadians attest to the psychic walls and constraints that kept us caged in or caged out, depending on one's perspective — unwanted strangers in our own homeland.

These experiences we experienced; silently but bone deep we experienced them.

## Departure/Entry — Lethbridge

For 13 years I taught in Lethbridge. They were good years. But I left in 1964 when I was a budding Assistant Principal of the Lethbridge Collegiate Institute — in charge of locker keys, student attendance, and student assemblies, and really not enjoying being Assistant Principal.

During those 13 years, mostly happy years, the world of Lethbridge became very familiar and comfortable for me. I even dug into Lethbridge's past, for as a Master's study I had done a history of Lethbridge School District #51. I was even becoming familiar with many of my predecessors in Lethbridge. I was becoming one of many; I did the many things that many did; I had come to own many things that many owned; I had come to value the many things that the many valued. I was becoming very comfortable in the city, yet discomforted by the very comfort that seemed to surround me. So I struck anew — I became a stranger again, in a new surrounding — in a university setting as Assistant Professor at the University of Alberta. This time I became a stranger of my own volition.

Thinking about my departure from Lethbridge reminds me of the time I came to Lethbridge as a stranger 13 years earlier. The year was 1951. Although I was a stranger as a teacher, I was no stranger as a "consumer" in the business end of town: Fifth Street, Third Avenue, etc. But as a teacher, I was almost a total stranger in Lethbridge's world of teachers and teaching.

I applied for a teaching job — I was in Taber then — in answer to a want ad that appeared in the *Lethbridge Herald* calling for a junior high school social studies and physical education teacher. I was appointed to the staff of Hamilton Jr. High School.

They tell me I was the first teacher of oriental origin to be hired in Lethbridge — this I knew. What I did not know was the fact that I was hired as a test case, to see how the people of Lethbridge — parents and children — would react to the presence in their midst of a Japanese Canadian teacher. This I learned several years later from Superintendent L.H. Bussard. This was confirmed for me just two months ago by Nora Sinclair, one-time teacher in Lethbridge, now Assistant to the Dean, Faculty of Education, U.B.C.

But remember, 1951 was two years after 1949. What about 1949? A Japanese Canadian high school student said the following at a JCCA Annual Oratorical Contest in the early 50s held at the Capital Theatre in Lethbridge:

> March 31, 1949. To most Canadians this is a significant historical date, for on this day, Newfoundland became the tenth province of Canada. However, to 22,000 Canadians of Japanese ancestry, this day meant something more, for the hard, long struggle for enfranchisement was finally won. On that day, the Japanese Canadians became Canadians in the truest political sense.

This rings somewhat of the romantic but beautiful idealism of a young high school student in 1949. The real struggle for franchisement was undoubtedly still going on in Lethbridge in 1951 if the fact of my test case is true. But my presence in Lethbridge as a test case in itself reflects a new mood, a questioning of the walls erected, a re-examination of the Japanese Canadians in Southern Alberta society.

We in our turn tested out the attitude of the bigger world. Here is an illustrative case that occurred in 1952.

This same high school girl who spoke of the meaning of 1949 and her fellow Nisei students brought to my attention a high school social studies text in use at that time, Dr. L. A. Bagnall's *Contemporary Problems* published by the Western Canada Institute Ltd., Calgary. Their complaint was the reference to Japanese as "Jap" and "Japs." (Interestingly, the 1939 edition is clean; it is the 1946 that is contaminated.)

As a result I submitted a brief to the Lethbridge local of the Alberta Teachers' Association in the matter of the use of the terms "Jap" and "Japs" in a recommended reference book in social studies in Alberta. The resolution read in part

> Be It Resolved that the Alberta Teachers' Association strongly urge the Department of Education and offices concerned to take steps to withdraw from the list of recommended reference books in Social Studies the book entitled *Contemporary Problems* (Revised Edition) by Bagnall and Norton, until such time that terms "Jap" and "Japs" are revised to read "Japanese,"
>
> And Further Be It Resolved that the Alberta Teachers' Association notify of their action and attitude to the authors and publisher of the aforementioned book.

If the fire and heat of the activists of the 60s were lacking, the spirit and the soul were there. The book ceased to be used as a social studies reference book.

The young Niseis weren't vocal (in today's terms perhaps) but if one listened carefully, there were voices — naive, maybe, but nevertheless coming from deep within.

At an oratorical contest in Lethbridge in 1954 a Nisei high school student[2] spoke of the Niseis' role in *Building a Canadian Mosaic*. She asked, "Who is a Canadian?" and said, by the way,

> I have heard that one eminent Canadian artist toured from the Pacific to the Atlantic looking for a subject to whom he might refer to as "the typical Canadian." He searched in vain. He found no "typical Canadian." Who is a Canadian? I have a friend, a friend who is attending the Lethbridge Collegiate Institute. Her parents came from England. She is a Canadian. I met a girl, recently emigrated from Holland. Now, she's making her home in Lethbridge. She is a

Canadian. I met a student attending McGill University. Her
parents came from Japan 30 years ago. She is a Canadian.
Who is a Canadian?

From her own perspective she was indeed calling upon other
Japanese Canadians to join with her in search for their own identity
within the framework of multiculturalism — and this back in *1954*.

Viewing from my perspective in the context of my being and becoming
a Japanese Canadian teacher in the 40s and 50s, I have attempted a
gross characterization of what I experienced, reflecting the relationship
between myself and the dominant society.

Upon reflection I see the 1940s as a decade characterized by a feeling
of powerlessness and of helplessness. It was a decade of oppressive
economic and political servitude — denied even the right to domicile in
towns and cities or the right to service in a beer parlor. This was the
decade when we were objectified as the "enemy" — "the yellow devils"
— years when many of us felt alienated, shorn of some of our humanness.

But the 50s? How would you capture the Japanese Canadians and
the 50s?

I find the 50s, beginning with the enfranchisement in 1949, a decade
of enlarging possibilities for the Japanese Canadians. The popular climate
had changed: there seemed to be a feeling on the part of the dominant
society that "the enemy" may deserve humanitarian treatment; "that
some of the Japanese Canadians are like us, not enemies"; that the
Japanese Canadians could be bestowed a more human treatment. I call
the 1950s the decade of paternalistic humanitarianism.

Such an attitude toward the Japanese Canadians opened up
opportunities for them. The pent-up energies of the Japanese Canadians
had a chance to flow more freely. And as long as Japanese Canadians
did not deviate from the values system of the dominant society too much,
their opportunities seemed extensive.

For me, being and becoming a teacher in Alberta has been an
experience made richer by the fact of my ethnicity. I regard it as my
personal world of my own lived experiences, a world in which I
participated with others in its construction.

In my being and becoming, the tensions that were there created a
dynamic world within which I acted, which, after all is said and done,

has turned out to be my life as I have experienced it. I reflect upon it as a unique life in many ways, at times distorted but nevertheless providing me with meaning as a being doing my damnedest in my own personal becoming.

## Endnotes

1   *RIKKA*, Vol. 4, No. 2, 1977. Adapted from a paper given at *The Japanese Experience in North America Conference*, University of Lethbridge, Alberta, Canada, commemorating a century of Japanese Canadian experience in Canada.
2   Mary Aoki, high school student at the Lethbridge Collegiate Institute, Lethbridge, Alberta.

## Chapter 7

# "I Don't Want to Read This": Students' Responses to Illustrations of Black Characters in Children's Picture Books

## Andrew M.A. Allen

In recent years, there has been an increase in the number of multicultural children's picture books available that depict characters of various racial and ethnic backgrounds. Some of these books eventually become very popular and find their way into most libraries and classrooms. As an elementary school teacher, I was very excited about introducing my students to the rich variety of multicultural literature that was available. I was eager to establish a literature-based reading program in my class that presented the images and experiences that I believed were reflective of all my students and their backgrounds.

Hence, I purchased several multicultural picture books that I believed featured images of people that looked like the various groups of children in the class. I selected several other multicultural picture books from both our local and school libraries as additional reading material for the classroom to introduce the images and experiences of other cultures not represented in my class. I displayed them all around the classroom and in our classroom library or book corner. At that time, I was convinced that this would enhance my reading program by helping to stimulate students' interest and attract them to books, affirm individual self-worth, develop and promote respect and understanding between groups of students from different backgrounds, and enrich the overall classroom learning environment.

My Grade 2 class consisted primarily of students of immigrant and/ or working-class backgrounds, whose parents originated from the Caribbean, East Africa, and South and East Asia. I noticed that they seemed uninterested in reading most of the multicultural picture books I had brought to the class. Most of the multicultural literature, and even the more "popular" and award-winning picture books, went almost untouched the whole year. I also noticed that my Black students, in particular, became quiet and withdrawn during story time when I read particular picture books depicting Black characters. At times, they even became disruptive and had some difficulty sitting still through some stories.

I became even more interested when I observed that only the Black students continued to resist interacting with the literature with Black characters even after I tried to encourage them to select these books to read. When given a choice, they selected books with traditional European characters and avoided the books with Black characters. They did not seem to share my interest or excitement in the multicultural books. Why was this so? What were their perceptions of the images in the literature? How did this affect their literacy development and my attempts at teaching them to read?

As a way of further exploring my initial observations of the students in my classroom, I arranged to have a number of informal reading lessons with several groups of first- and second- grade Black students from other classes at my school. I wanted to investigate how these Black students from an urban working-class community respond to picture books depicting Blacks as the main characters. My investigation sought to answer the following questions:

1.  How do Black children select or choose picture books to read in their classrooms?
2.  How do they perceive Black characters or illustrations portraying the Black experience in books for children?
3.  What are the effects of using multicultural literacy materials in literacy programs for Black students?
4.  What are the implications of my findings for the education of Black children of working-class backgrounds?

## The Argument

The success or failure of Black working-class students in high school is likely to be related to some of their early experiences in school, as well as to the cumulative effect of the entire schooling process. The kinds of attitudes toward books and reading skills they develop in the primary grades might be dependent on a number of factors inherent in the school curriculum, and these factors have impact on their educational outcomes. Children's literature, including multicultural picture books, may be the children's first contact with literature, reading, and literacy learning (Kiefer, 1983). Thus they are an important starting point for examining the experiences of the students; understanding students' reactions to multicultural picture books would help me, I assumed, to learn more about their literacy development and develop proactive measures to help address the needs of my students.

This chapter attempts to examine Black children's particular reactions and responses to images in children's picture books and interprets those, making assumptions with respect to their experiences as Black children of working-class backgrounds. The students in my school live in a culturally, ethnically, and racially diverse urban community with high population density and significant economic disparities. The community has a high immigration and migration rate as well as a high unemployment and underemployment rate and a large amount of government subsidized housing. I will begin by examining the research that outlines the experiences, needs, and problems of Black students in the public school system in Ontario.

## The Black Experience in Ontario Schools

A review of the academic achievement and retention rates of Black students in the Ontario public school system reveals that these students do not receive the same quality of education as other groups of students, and that they face many barriers to academic success. A number of recent reports — including the *Report of the Royal Commission on Learning* (1994), the Toronto Board of Education *Every Student Survey* (1993), the Stephen Lewis Report (1992), and the Report of the Four Level Government and

African Canadian Community Working Group (1992) — all concluded that Black high school students typically had low academic achievement and retention rates, and high truancy and failure rates, and were most frequently streamed into low academic tracks. The studies concluded that the policies and actual practices of schools, as well as the curriculum and learning materials, were limiting the opportunities for academic advancement and achievement of Black students. The schools failed to respond effectively to the educational needs of Black students (Dei, 1993; Solomon, 1992; Curtis, Livingstone, and Smaller, 1992; James, 1990).

Black students of working-class families in particular were most likely to be affected by the "barriers" imposed by academic and social structures, and by ideologies, policies, and practices that serve to maintain hegemonic domination of the educational system and the larger social order. For working-class Black students, race and class both affect their school experiences and impact on their educational success. Schools help to reproduce class distinctions, because most working-class children, as a result of their educational and social experiences, tend to remain in their class of origin (Curtis et al., 1992).

Some of the problems of Black students can be attributed to their early schooling experiences, particularly with early classroom reading instruction and materials. Examining multicultural literature portraying Black characters and contexts and the ways Black children interpret them lead to an understanding of some of these experiences. The following sections examine the importance of illustrations and stories in children's literature; particularly the apparently implicit, yet powerful, information and social messages contained in the authors' or illustrators' words and images and their effects on the readers.

## THE IMPORTANCE OF ILLUSTRATIONS

Children's picture books are a major part of literacy programs. They are designed to be attractive and colourful to motivate children to want to read. Ralston (1990) describes children's literature as an essential teaching tool, a main focus and a springboard to creative activity in whole-language classrooms. Picture books enhance cognitive development; they help readers to form mental images of the information, decode words, and comprehend sentences better; they are designed to increase vocabulary levels, and offer opportunities to acquire and practice reading skills, spark imagination, and lead to the creation of writing or art; and they also highlight social and moral concerns (Harris, 1990; Elster and Simons, 1985; Schallert, 1980).

## Blacks in Children's Picture Books

Traditional representations of Blacks in children's literature and educational media have been characterized by omission or exaggeration. This pattern of selective tradition of domination and subordination of Blacks in children's literature favours the perspectives and world views of the dominant social group, and tends to focus on the exotic, sensational, or negative representations, based on the persistent and pervasive use of overgeneralizations, distortions, misconceptions, misrepresentations, stereotypes, and demeaning views of Blacks. Most books are written primarily by and for a middle-class audience and they are increasingly alienated from and irrelevant to the realities, concerns, and problems of the urban working-class Black children (Taxel, 1993; Harris, 1993; Sims, 1993; Walker and Rasamimanana, 1993; Pierterse, 1992; Harris, 1990; MacCann and Woodard, 1985; Broderick, 1973).

In a recent study examining the historical development of literature written for African American children, Harris (1990) described the depiction of Blacks in children's literature as "essentially stereotyped, pejorative, and unauthentic." She argues that illustrations in children's literature typically show Black people as grotesque caricatures of their race's physical features, simian-like or with protruding eyes and large red lips and extremely dark skin. She says Black children are portrayed as "pickaninnies": dark skinned, plain, mischievous, comical, and poor. She believes the literature reflects the values, knowledge, and interpretations of whites, particularly Anglo-Saxons. Harris (1990) also argues that children's literature is potentially a valuable and valued cultural commodity. It mediates between children, cultural knowledge, and socialization by adults and it shapes children's perceptions of the world and their roles in it.

The illustrations also reflect the ideologies, experience, and background of the illustrators. Images tell more about the feelings and ideas of the artist or illustrator than about the lives or perspectives of the subject they represent. A racist, sexist, and elitist society tends to reproduce race, class, and gender biases, and the literature it produces tends to mirror the societal attitudes toward particular racial and ethnic groups (Delpit, 1988; Taxel, 1993; Sims, 1993).

The values, principles, and assumptions affirmed in children's books are internalized by their readers to such an extent that they become a part of the way they learn to construct the social conventions of their social reality (Taxel, 1993; Sims, 1983). Children also learn not to question the established social order which supports poverty, social class, and the different values placed on various groups in society. When poverty and social class are apparent in the images and text, but the literature fails to define it and explain the reason for the disparity, the literature serves to socialize the children to maintain the "status quo" of passivity and conformity. The lack of discussion and explanation further perpetuates the "myth of a classless society" (Ramsay, 1993; Langston, 1988).

## THE EFFECTS ON THE LEARNER

James (1994) points out that when learning materials do not reflect the interests, needs, and life experiences of Black and other racial minority students, the information presented to them can serve to marginalize and disengage them from learning and participating in the classroom. When children perceive images as negative, and in conflict with their reality, or as denigrating their self-image and the world they experience, then the effect of the images is oppressive and damaging. James argues that low self-esteem may develop when a child's racial group is constantly portrayed through stereotypes as low achievers, primitive, or slum dwellers, particularly if there are no discussions which address the issues of bias around these images. He says that without discussion, the Black children may feel their voices are not valued or accepted, and as a result they may be silenced and rendered powerless and invisible in the classroom.

When Black students do not see positive reflections of themselves or positive affirmation of their heritage, they sometimes respond or react in negative ways; it is quite likely that they will not read or value schooling as much, and many of these students may respond by choosing not to learn (James, 1994; Delpit, 1995; Asante, 1991; Harris, 1990). The ways the behaviours of working-class Black students are perceived by the school system affect their educational success in school. Positive responses, attentiveness, or conformity and compliance are usually interpreted as reading readiness or academic ability and they maximize students' literacy success and academic achievement. Negative responses, social resistance, or lack of interest are interpreted as deficiency or deviance and impede their success in school (Gilmore, 1992; Solomon, 1992).

The students' disproportionately lower reading scores and reading levels may well be the result of their reactions to the curriculum and to instructional strategies. They may also reflect the way school personnel understand these students and respond to their behaviours. Since children's literature is such a powerful part of the schools' socialization and educational processes, it is necessary to interrogate the images we present in relation to the experiences of the readers. How are working-class Black children experiencing the books we use to teach them to read? How are their perceptions of the images in the literature informed by the experiences of their daily lives? Does the representation of Blacks in multicultural picture books reflect the reality of working-class Black children? The following section gives an account of my observations of the responses and reactions of a focus group of first- and second-grade Black students of working-class backgrounds to a collection of multicultural picture books with Blacks as the main characters.

## Black Students' Responses and Reactions Looking at Illustrations

I presented a collection of multicultural picture books depicting mostly Black characters, attractively displayed on a table in my classroom as part of a reading lesson. The selection consisted mostly of Black or "multicultural" literature from the students' classrooms. The children were invited to freely examine the books. I asked them to pick the stories they wanted to read or wanted me to read to them. I asked the students why they chose particular books or types of books to read. I also asked why they did not choose other books. I probed their responses to find out more about their reactions to the books, particularly their decisions to read or not to read particular books. I wanted to find out what it was about certain books that would make them avoid or refuse to read them.

Some of the children were eager to examine the books. Others, reluctant at first, began looking at the pictures after prompting from their more excited peers. All searched first for books they were familiar with. They looked at the covers, focusing for a longer time on some, and then leafed randomly through the pages, skipping several pages at a time. They continued to pay more attention to the pictures than to the text. They were eager to discuss what they remembered from the illustrations and passed some books on to one another; they scanned the covers of others.

The students were first attracted to, and looked for books or illustrations in books that were familiar to them. These were books they had seen or read before or ones the teacher had read. For example, the book *Daniel's Dog* (Bogart, 1990) was a favourite with many of the children.

> **Mike**: I know this book. Our teacher read this to us. I'm reading this. It is the best. I read it at school before, because he has a friend, he laughs, and he has a dog.
>
> **Kimberly**: It is such exciting. It is about a dog and it is about a baby sister. I like the pictures and I like the story. Because it is such lots of fun and you can learn new words in them. Some pages are very fun. It is a clean book.

The main character of the book *Daniel's Dog* is a Black boy who has an imaginary dog. The realistic images portray a range of expressions of the characters, from excitement to sadness. The pictures were brightly coloured and the background was filled with objects that reflected an environment familiar to those living in an urban setting.

Familiar or recognizable objects in the pictures, and the background or setting of the pictures, including the context or environment as perceived by the students, were other factors that prompted children to read certain books. These books included familiar situations or points of reference for children and related to their reality. For instance, the book

*Jonathan and his Mommy* (Smalls, 1992), elicited these responses from the students:

> **Trini**: Oh! I like this book. Because I just read it. They are walking down the street and stuff. And these kids are colouring with a chalk. She likes walking and talking with her mom and she likes skipping and all those stuff and she likes walking with her son.
> **Kimberly**: This one. Because it is interesting. I like this book. Because it has a lot of words to read and her little boy learns how to do good stuff. The pictures look very interesting. I enjoyed this one.

There were two main Black characters on the cover of the book *Jonathan and His Mommy:* a mother and her son strolling and playing in an outdoor urban environment. The features on the characters were realistically drawn to near photographic likeness. These images were familiar and recognizable to these children and reflected their own urban environment.

The students were attracted to images of characters that were recognizable or tended to closely resemble someone they knew. For instance, Billy was convinced that the character on the cover of the book *Jonathan and His Mommy* was that of their gym teacher.

> **Billy**: Mrs. Huxstable! That looks like Mrs. Huxstable. Mrs. Huxstable our teacher.

## Some Strategies

Both reading materials and teaching techniques used need to address the problem working-class Black emergent readers face when they select books to read. The following is a summary of the instructional strategies I would recommend for using multicultural literature in the primary grades:

- Involve students in selecting, reviewing, and critiquing books.
- Teach students to detect bias in materials they read.

- Help students develop critical thinking skills so that they learn to evaluate how genre, era, plot, setting, and images of characters might better represent various groups in the literature.
- Examine your own position or frames of reference with respect to your power, social class, access, privilege, and perpetuation of the status quo.
- Become aware of students' location or frames of reference and how it is implicated in reading materials.
- Be more careful when you introduce new materials and be particularly aware of how books are introduced and taken up in class.
- Select books featuring possible familiar frames of reference for your students, using books that connect with the community in which the school is located. Books that have familiar scenes and familiar names to the students and involve familiar children's objects and situations (including imaginative play) are especially important.
- Slowly introduce and expose students to new or unfamiliar situations in books, discussing any issues that arise in the class.
- Try to select even more multicultural picture books designed primarily to entertain. These may include poetry, rhymes, songs, and rhythmic play.
- Name and locate social class, poverty, and racial and other institutional forms of oppression displayed in the literature.

The following is a summary of the recommended strategies for evaluating multicultural literature in the primary grades:

- Take into account the perspectives and interpretations of the author and illustrator.
- Examine the type of images and illustrations to detect race, class and gender biases, and stereotyping.
- Examine the story context, backgrounds, situations, characters' clothing, and points of reference to detect bias and stereotyping.
- Examine the amount of text used in the book and plan a strategy for introducing books with a larger amount of text.
- Examine the quality of the text as it relates to the story plot and its relations to children's experiences and interests.

- Examine the social messages in the books being used in the classroom to ensure a balance between books that promote social or cultural information and books designed to entertain.
- Be attentive to the students' reactions and seek out their opinions and perspectives.

## CHILDREN'S BOOKS CITED

Bogart, J. (1990). *Daniel's Dog*. Toronto: Scholastic Inc.
Smalls, I. (1992). *Jonathan and His Mommy*. Toronto: Little, Brown and Company (Canada) Limited.

## REFERENCES

Asante, M. (1991). The Afrocentric idea in education. *Journal of Negro Education*, 60(2).
Broderick, D.M. (1973). *Images of the Black in Children's fiction*. New York: R.R. Bowker Company.
Curtis, B., D. Livingstone, and H. Smaller (1992). *Stacking the deck: The streaming of working-class kids in Ontario schools*. Montreal Our Schools/Our Selves Education Foundation.
Dei, G.J.S. (1993, April). (Re)Conceptualizing "dropouts" from narratives of Black high school students in Ontario. Presentation paper, Atlanta, GA: American Educational Research Association.
——— (1993). *The examination of high school dropouts among Black students in Ontario public schools. Preliminary Report*. Toronto: Ministry of Education and Training.
Delpit, L. D. (1988). The silenced dialogue: Power and pedagogy in educating other people's children. *Harvard Educational Review*, 58(3), pp. 380–398.
——— (1995). *Other people's children: Cultural conflict in the classroom*. New York: The New Press.
Elster, C., and H.D. Simons (1985). How important are illustrations in children's readers? *The Reading Teacher*, pp. 148–152.
Four-Level Government/African-Canadian Community Working Group (1992). *Towards a new beginning: Report on Metropolitan Toronto Black Canadian community concerns*. Toronto.
Gilmore, P. (1992). "Gimme room": School resistance, attitude, and access to literacy. In P. Shannon *Becoming political: Readings and writings in the politics*

*of literacy education* (pp. 113–127), Portsmouth, NH: Hienemann Educational Books Inc.

Harris, V.J. (1990). African American children's literature: The first one hundred years." *The Journal of Negro Education*, pp. 540–555.

———— (1993). Contemporary griots: African-American writers of children's literature. In V. Harris *Teaching multicultural literature in grades K–8*, Norwood, MA: Christopher-Gordon Publishers, Inc.

James, C.E. (1990). I don't want to talk about it. *Orbit*, 25(2), pp. 26–29.

———— (1990). *Making it: Black youth, racism and career aspirations in a big city*, Oakville, ON: Mosaic Press.

———— (1994). Access students: Experiences of racial minorities in a Canadian university. Paper presented at the society for Research into Higher Education Annual Conference, The University of York, England, Dec. 21.

———— (1994). I don't want to talk about it: Silencing students in today's classrooms. *Orbit*, 25(2).

———— (1994). Panel discussion on how Black students experience the schools. African Studies Association Conference. Toronto.

Kiefer, B. (1983). The responses of children in a combination first/second grade classroom to picture books in a variety of artistic styles. *Journal of Research and Development in Education*, 16(3), pp. 14–20.

Langston, D. (1988). Tired of playing monopoly? In J. Whitehouse Cochran, D. Langston, and C. Woodward (eds.) *Changing our power: An introduction to women's studies*, Dubuque, IA: Kendall-Hunt.

Lewis, S. (1992). *Report on race relations*. Toronto: Government of Ontario.

MacCann, D., and G. Woodard. (1985). *The Black American in books for children: Reading in racism* (2nd ed.), Metuchen, NJ: The Scarecrow Press Inc.

Pieterse, J.N. (1992). *White on black: Images of Africa and Blacks in western popular culture*, London, England: Yale University Press.

Ralston, M. (1990). Using literature in a whole-language program. In V. Froese *Whole-language practice and theory*, pp. 47–85, Scarborough, ON: Prentice-Hall Canada Inc.

Ramsay, J.G. (1993, November). Resignation and pretest: How children's picture books depict poverty. Paper presented at the American Educational Studies Association Annual Meetings, Chicago, IL.

Royal Commission on Learning (1994). *For the love of learning: Make it happen*. Volume IV. Toronto: Publications Ontario.

Royal Commission on Learning (1994). *For the love of learning: Report of the royal commission on learning*, Toronto: Ministry of Education

Schallert, D.L. (1980). The role of illustrations in reading comprehension. In R. Spiro, B. Bruce, and W. Brewer *Theoretical issues in reading comprehension*, pp. 503–524. Hillsdale NJ: Lawrence Erlbaum.

Sims, R. (1983). Strong black girls: a ten year old responds to fiction about Afro-Americans, *Journal of Research and Development in Education*, 16(3), pp. 21–28.

—— (1993). Multicultural literature for children: making informed choices. In V. Harris *Teaching multicultural literature in grades K–8*, Norwood, MA: Christopher-Gordon Publishers, Inc.

Solomon, R.P. (1992). *Black resistance in high school: A separatist culture*. Albany: State University of New York Press.

Taxel, J. (1993). The politics of children's literature: Reflections on multiculturalism and Christopher Columbus. In V. Harris *Teaching multicultural literature in grades K–8*, Norwood, MA: Christopher-Gordon Publishers, Inc.

Toronto Board of Education (1991). *Every student student survey*, Parts 1, 2, 3. Research Services.

Walker, S.S., and J. Rasamimanana (1993). Tarzan in the classroom: How "educational" films mythologize Africa and miseducate Americans. *Journal of Negro Education*, 62(1).

# Part 3

# Rethinking Inclusion: Representation and Stereotypes I

**Kivel**
"I'm Not White"; "I'm Not Racist"

**Hall**
"Heroes or Villains?";
"Stereotyping as a Signifying Practice"

**Tatum**
"Talking About Race, Learning About Racism:
The Application of Racial Identity
Development Theory in the Classroom"

**Short**
"Antiracist Education and Moral Behaviour:
Lessons from the Holocaust"

# Chapter 8

# "I'm Not White";
# "I'm Not Racist"

## Paul Kivel

### "I'm Not White"

Recently I was doing a workshop on racism and we wanted to divide the group into a caucus of people of color and a caucus of white people, so that each group could have more in-depth discussion. Immediately some of the white people said, "But I'm not white."

I was somewhat taken aback because although these people looked white they were clearly distressed about being labeled white. A white, Christian woman stood up and said, "I'm not really white because I'm not part of the white male power structure that perpetuates racism." Next a white gay man stood up and said, "You have to be straight to have the privileges of being white." A white, straight, working-class man from a poor family then said, "I've got it just as hard as any person of color." Finally, a straight, white middle-class man said, "I'm not white, I'm Italian."

My African American co-worker turned to me and asked, "Where are all the white people who were here just a minute ago?" Of course I replied, "Don't ask me, I'm not white, I'm Jewish!"

Most of the time we don't notice or question our whiteness. However, when the subject is racism many of us don't want to be white, because it opens us to charges of being racist and brings up feelings of guilt, shame, embarrassment, and hopelessness. There are others who proudly claim whiteness under any circumstances and simply deny or ignore the violence that white people have done to people of color.

Those of us who are middle class are more likely to assume we are white without having to emphasize the point, and to feel guilty when it is noticed or brought up. Those of us who are poor or working class are more likely to have had to assert our whiteness against the effects of economic discrimination and the presence of other racial groups. Although we share the benefits of being white, we don't share the economic privileges of being middle class and so we are more likely to feel angry and less likely to feel guilty than middle-class counterparts.

Whatever our economic status, most of us become paralyzed with some measure of fear, guilt, anger, defensiveness, or confusion if we are named as white when racism is being addressed.

In this country it has always been dangerous even to talk about racism. "Nigger lover," "Indian lover," and "race traitor" are labels which have carried severe consequences. You probably know the names of white civil rights workers who were killed for their actions against racism, such as Goodman, Schwerner, and Luizzo. Many of us have been isolated from friends or family because of disagreements over racism. A lot of us have been called "racist."

Saying "I am white" may make us feel either guilty of being racist or traitorous toward other whites. We don't want to be labeled or stereotyped. Talking about racism has often occurred in the context of angry words, hostility, accusations, and divisiveness. We also may have fears about people of color separating from us if we are clearly identified as white.

In any case, some of us are quick to disavow our whiteness, or to claim some other identity that will give us legitimate victim status. We certainly don't want to be seen as somehow responsible for or complicit with racism.

We must begin here — with this denial of our whiteness — because racism keeps people of color in the limelight and makes whiteness invisible. To change this we must take whiteness itself and hold it up to the light and see that it is a color too. Whiteness is a concept, an ideology that holds tremendous power over our lives and, in turn, over the lives of people of color.

Our challenge in this discussion will be to keep whiteness center stage. Every time our attention begins to wander off toward people of color or other issues, we will have to notice and refocus. We must notice when we try to slip into another identity and escape being white. We each have many other factors that influence our lives, such as our ethnicity, gender, sexual orientation, class, personality, and mental and physical abilities. Even when we're talking about these elements of our lives we must keep whiteness on stage with us because it influences each of the other factors.

What parts of your identity does it feel like you lose when you say aloud the phrase "I'm white"?

Part of our discomfort may come from the complex relationship our own family's ethnic and class background had to whiteness. Was your ethnic or cultural group ever considered not white? When they arrived in the United States, what did members of your family have to do to be accepted as white? What did they have to give up?

How has pride in being white (or becoming American) sustained you or your family? Has that identification or pride ever allowed you or your family to tolerate poverty, economic exploitation, or poor living conditions because "at least we're not colored"?

If, when you move down the streets of major U.S. cities, other people assume, based on skin color, dress, physical appearance, or total impression, that you are white, then in American society that counts for being white. This is where we are going to start talking about what it means to say, "I am white." I realize that there are differences between the streets of New York and Minneapolis, and between different neighborhoods within each city. But in American society there is a broad and pervasive division between white people and people of color, and most of us know from a very early age which side we are on. If we are white, we are told or learn in early childhood who to stay away from, who not to play with, who not to associate with, who isn't one of our kind.[1] This is true even if our parents are liberal or progressive. The training is too pervasive within our society for anyone to escape.

Whiteness is about more than skin color, although that is a major factor in this country. People of color and Jewish people are also marked as different by dress, food, the smells of cooking, religious ceremonies, celebratory rituals, and mannerisms. These features are all labeled racial differences, even though they may be related to culture, religion, class, or country of origin. I'm sure you know whether you are treated as "white" or as a person of color by most of the people you meet.

Say "I am white" to yourself a couple of times. What are the "but's" that immediately come to mind? Do you quickly add on another identity, perhaps one where you might claim a victim status such as female, poor, lesbian or gay, Jewish or Italian? Do you defend yourself with statements such as, "I have friends who are people of color," or "My family didn't own slaves"? Do you try to separate yourself from other white people? ("I don't feel white." "I'm not like other white people.") Do you try to minimize the importance of whiteness? ("We're all part of the human race.")

We are understandably uncomfortable with the label "white." We feel boxed in and want to escape, just as people of color want to escape from the confines of their racial categories. Being white is an arbitrary category that overrides our individual personalities, devalues us, deprives us of the richness of our other identities, stereotypes us, and yet has no scientific basis. However, in our society being white is also just as real, and governs our day-to-day lives just as much as being a person of color. To acknowledge this reality is not to create it nor to perpetuate it. In fact, it is the first step to uprooting racism.

Whiteness is problematic. All the fear, anger, frustration, helplessness, and confusion we experience about admitting that we are white is the result of racism. Many of these feelings are what keep us from recognizing and talking about the effects of racism in our own lives and the devastation that racism wreaks in our society.

We may claim that we aren't white because we simply don't (or refuse to) notice race. I sometimes like to think that I don't. But when I'm in an all-white setting and a person of color walks in, I notice. I am slightly surprised to see a person of color and I look again to confirm who they are and wonder to myself why they're there. I try to do this as naturally and smoothly as possible because I wouldn't want anyone to think that I wasn't tolerant. Actually what I'm surprised at is not that they are there, but that they are there as an equal. All of my opening explanations for their presence will assume they are not equal. "They must be a server or delivery person," I tell myself. It is usually not until another white person introduces me, or gives me an explanation, that my uneasiness is laid to rest. (And even then I may inwardly qualify my acceptance). We notice skin color all the time but we don't "notice" race unless our sense of the proper racial hierarchy is upset.

When I first meet someone, and I think this is true for most of us, I identify their gender (and get anxious when I can't), I identify as much about their class as I can figure out, and I identify what their racial identity is. I have two categories, white and other. I'm interested in the other. In fact, because of my assumptions about the commonness of whiteness, I often assume a person of color will be more interesting than another white person. But whether we value it positively or negatively, the difference counts and we notice it.

Since I've been taught to relate differently to people who are African American, or Latino/a, or Asian American, I may need more information than appearance gives me about what "kind" of person of color I am with. I have some standard questions to fish for more information, such as: "That's an interesting name. I've never heard it before. Where's it from?" "Your accent sounds familiar but I can't place it." "You don't look American, where are you from?"

Sometimes we ask these questions of white Americans who have unusual names or unfamiliar accents. Most often we use them to clarify who is white and who isn't, and secondarily, what kind of person of color we are dealing with.

Many of us were taught that it is not polite to notice racial difference. We may have learned that racial difference is an artificial basis used to discriminate against and exploit people of color, and therefore we may overcompensate by pretending to ignore it. White people often say, "I don't care whether a person is black, brown, orange, or green." Human beings don't come in orange or green. Those whose skin color is darker are treated differently in general and we, in particular, respond differently to them. As part of growing up white and learning racial stereotypes, we have been trained to stiffen up, be more cautious, fearful, and hesitant around people of color. These are physiological and psychological responses that we can notice in ourselves and see in other white people. These responses belie our verbal assurances that we don't notice racial differences.

There's absolutely nothing wrong with being white or with noticing the difference that color makes. We were born without choice into our families. We did not choose our skin color, native language, or culture. We are not responsible for being white or for being raised in a white-dominated, racist society in which we have been trained to have particular responses to people of color. We are responsible for how we respond to racism (which is what this book is about) and we can only do that consciously and effectively if we start by realizing that it makes a crucial difference that we are white.

## "I'M NOT RACIST"

Whether it is easy or difficult to say that we're white, the phrase we often want to say next is "…but I'm not racist." There are lots of ways that we have learned to phrase this denial.

> I'm not racist.
> I don't belong to the Klan.
> I have friends who are people of color.
> I don't see color, I'm color blind.
> I do anti-racism work.
> I went to an unlearning racism workshop.

This chapter is not about whether you are racist or not, or whether all white people are racist or not. We are not conducting a moral inventory of ourselves, nor creating a moral standard to divide other white people from us.

To avoid being called racist we may claim that we don't notice color and don't treat people differently based on color. However, we all notice color in just about every situation we're in. It's not useful or honest for any of us to claim that we don't. It is too pervasive a construct of our society to avoid. When we say things like, "I don't see color," we are trying to maintain a self-image of impartiality and fairness (and whiteness). Some of the motivation behind the claim that we are color neutral is to establish that we don't mistreat people or discriminate against them because of their race. Ultimately, this disclaimer prevents us from taking responsibility for challenging racism because we believe that people who see color are the problem.

The only way to treat people with dignity and justice is to recognize that racism has a profound negative effect upon our lives, and therefore noticing color helps to counteract that effect. Instead of being color neutral we need to notice much more acutely and insightfully exactly the difference that color makes in the way people are treated.

Just as it's not useful to label ourselves racist or not, it is not useful to label each other. White people, individually and collectively, have done and continue to do some very brutal things in the name of whiteness. We may want to separate ourselves from the white people who commit these acts by claiming that they are racist and we are not. But because racism operates institutionally, to the benefit of all white people, we are connected to the acts of other white people.

Of course we're not members of the Klan or other extremist groups. Of course we watch what we say and don't make rude racial comments. But dissociating from white people who do is not the answer. We need to dissociate from their actions and challenge their beliefs. We can't challenge them, or even speak to them, if we have separated ourselves from them, creating some magical line with the racists on that side and ourselves over here. This division leads to an ineffective strategy of trying to pull as many people as possible over to our (non-racist and therefore superior) side. Other white people will listen to us better and be more influenced by our actions when we identify with them. Then we can explore how to work from the inside out together.

Perhaps most importantly, the people who are more visibly saying or doing things that are racist are usually more scared, more confused, and less powerful than we are. (Or they are trying to increase their own power by manipulating racial fears.) It is often amazing how, when we get scared, confused, or powerless, we do and say the very same things. Since racism leads to scapegoating people of color for social and personal problems, we are all susceptible to resorting to racial scapegoating in times of trouble. Visible acts of racism are, at least in part, an indication of the lack of power that a white person or group of people have to camouflage their actions. More powerful and well-off people can simply move to segregated neighborhoods, or make corporate decisions that are harder to see and analyze as contributing to racism. Since the racism of the wealthy is less visible to us, those of us who are middle class can inadvertently scapegoat poor and working-class white people for being more overtly racist.

We do need to confront words and actions that are racist when we encounter them because they create an atmosphere of violence in which all of us are unsafe. We also need to understand that most white people are doing the best they can to survive. Overtly racist people are scared, and lack the information and skills to be more tolerant. We need to challenge their behavior, not their moral integrity. We also need to be careful that we don't end up carrying out an upper-class agenda by blaming poor and working people for being racist when people with wealth control the media, the textbooks, the housing and job markets, and the police. We need to stay focused on the institutions themselves.

## ENDNOTE

1.    Several studies have shown that young children between the ages of two and four notice differences of skin color, eye color, hair, dress, and speech and the significance that adults give to those differences. See McGinnis, Oehlberg, and Derman-Sparks.

## EXERCISES

1.    If race is not reducible to biological terms, then what is racial identity?
2.    How does racism go beyond explicit, conscious acts of discrimination or prejudice?
3.    Explore roles that blacks/whites/others are assigned in your life and the way we are compelled to be in these roles.
4.    What are some of the complexities of negotiating multiracial family and community within a racially hierarchical society?

# Chapter 9

# Heroes or Villains?; and Stereotyping as a Signifying Practice

## Stuart Hall

### HEROES OR VILLAINS?

Look, first, at the magazine cover on the next page. It is a picture of the men's 100 metres final at the 1988 Olympics, which appeared on the cover of the Olympics Special of the *Sunday Times* colour magazine. It shows the black Canadian sprinter Ben Johnson winning in record time from Carl Lewis and Linford Christie: five superb athletes in action, at the peak of their physical prowess. All of them men and — perhaps, now, you will notice consciously for the first time — all of them black!

ACTIVITY 1
How do you "read" the picture — what is it saying? In Barthes' terms, what is its "myth" its underlying message? One possible message relates to their racial identity. These athletes are all from a racially defined group — one often discriminated against precisely on the grounds of their "race" and colour, whom we are more accustomed to see depicted in the news as the victims or "losers" in terms of achievement. Yet here they are, winning!

In terms of difference, then, a positive message: a triumphant moment, a cause for celebration. Why, then,

"Heroes and Villains", cover of
*The Sunday Times Magazine*, October 9, 1988.

does the caption say, "Heroes and villains"? Who do you
think is the hero, who the villain?

Even if you don't follow athletics, the answer isn't difficult to discover.
Ostensibly about the Olympics, the photo is in fact a trailer for the
magazine's lead story about the growing menace of drug-taking in
international athletics — what inside is called "The Chemical Olympics."
Ben Johnson, you may recall, was found to have taken drugs to enhance
his performance. He was disqualified, the gold medal being awarded to
Carl Lewis, and Johnson was expelled from world athletics in disgrace.
The story suggests that all athletes — black or white — are potentially
"heroes" and "villains." But in this image, Ben Johnson personifies this
split in a particular way. He is *both* "hero" and "villain." He encapsulates
the extreme alternatives of heroism and villainy in world athletics in one
black body.

There are several points to make about the way the representation of
"race" and "otherness" is working in this photo. First, think about
Barthes' idea of "myth." This photo functions at the level of "myth."
There is a literal, denotative level of meaning: This is a picture of the 100
metres final and the figure in front is Ben Johnson. Then there is the more
connotative or thematic meaning: the drug story. And within that, there
is the sub-theme of "race" and "difference." Already, this tells us
something important about how "myth" works. The image is a very
powerful one, as visual images often are. But its meaning is highly
ambiguous. It can carry more than one meaning. If you didn't know the
context, you might be tempted to read this as a moment of unqualified
triumph. And you wouldn't be wrong since this, too, is a perfectly
acceptable meaning to take from the image. But, as the caption suggests,
it is not produced here as an image of unqualified triumph. So, the same
photo can carry several, quite different, sometimes diametrically opposite
meanings. It can be a picture of disgrace or of triumph, or both. Many
meanings, we might say, are potential within the photo. But there is no
one, true meaning. Meaning "floats." It cannot be finally fixed. However,
attempting to fix it is the work of a representational practice, which
intervenes in the many potential meanings of an image in an attempt to
privilege one.

So, rather than a right or wrong meaning, what we need to ask is,
"Which of the many meanings in this image does the magazine mean to

privilege?" Which is the *preferred meaning*? Ben Johnson is the key element here because he is both an amazing athlete, winner and record-breaker, *and* the athlete who was publicly disgraced because of drug-taking. So, as it turns out, the preferred meaning is *both* heroism and villainy. It wants to say something paradoxical like, "In the moment of the hero's triumph, there is also villainy and moral defeat." In part, we know this is the preferred meaning that the magazine wants the photo to convey because this is the meaning that is singled out in the caption, HEROES AND VILLAINS. Roland Barthes (1977) argues that, frequently, it is the caption that selects one out of the many possible meanings from the image, and *anchors* it with words. The "meaning" of the photograph, then, does not lie exclusively in the image, but in the conjunction of image *and* text. Two discourses — the discourse of written language and the discourse of photography — are required to produce and "fix" the meaning (see Hall, 1972).

As we have suggested, this photo can also be read, connotatively, in terms of what it has to say about race. Here, the message could be, black people shown being good at something, winning *at last!* But in the light of the "preferred meaning," hasn't the meaning with respect to race and otherness changed as well? Isn't it more something like, even when black people are shown at the summit of their achievement, they often fail to carry it off? This having-it-both-ways is important because, as I hope to show you, people who are in any way significantly different from the majority "them" rather than "us" — are frequently exposed to this binary form of representation. They seem to be represented through sharply opposed, polarized, binary extremes: good/bad, civilized/primitive, ugly/excessively attractive, repelling-because-different/compelling-because-strange-and-exotic. And they are often required to be *both things at the same time!* We will return to these split figures or tropes of representation in a moment.

But first, let us look at another, similar news photo, this time from another record-breaking 100 metres final. It shows Linford Christie, subsequently captain of the British Olympics squad, at the peak of his career, having just won the race of a lifetime. The picture captures his elation at the moment of his lap of honour. He is holding the Union Jack. In the light of the earlier discussion, how do you "read" this photograph? What is it saying about race and cultural identity?

**Linford Christie, holding a Union Jack, having won the men's 100 metres Olympic gold medal, Barcelona 1992.**

ACTIVITY 2

Which of the following statements, in your view, comes closest to expressing the message of the image?

a  This is the greatest moment of my life! A triumph for me, Linford Christie.

b  This is a moment of triumph for me and a celebration for black people everywhere!

c  This is a moment of triumph and celebration for the British Olympic team and the British people!

d  This is a moment of triumph and celebration for black people *and* the British Olympic team. It shows that you can be "black" *and* "British"!

There is, of courses no right or wrong answer to the question. The image carries many meanings, all equally plausible. What is important is the fact that this image both shows an event (denotation) and carries a message or meaning (connotation). Barthes would call it a "metamessage" or *myth* about race, colour, and otherness. We can't help reading images of this kind as saying something, not just about the people or the occasion, but about their otherness, their difference. *"Difference" has been marked.* How it is then interpreted is a constant and recurring preoccupation in the representation of people who are racially and ethnically different from the majority population. Difference signifies. It "speaks."

In a later interview, discussing his forthcoming retirement from international sport, Christie commented on the question of his cultural identity — where he feels he "belongs" (*The Sunday Independent*, November 11, 1995). He has very fond memories of Jamaica, he said, where he was born and lived until the age of seven. But "I've lived here [in the U.K.] for 28 [years]. I can't be anything other than British" (p. 18). Of course, it isn't as simple as that. Christie is perfectly well aware that most definitions of Britishness assume that the person who belongs is white. It is much harder for black people, wherever they were born, to be accepted as British. In 1995, the cricket magazine *Wisden* had to pay libel damages to black athletes for saying that they couldn't be expected to display the same loyalty and commitment to winning for England because they are black. So Christie knows that every image is also being read in terms of this broader question of cultural belongingness and difference.

Indeed, he made his remarks in the context of the negative publicity to which he has been exposed in some sections of the British tabloid press, a good deal of which hinges on a vulgar, unstated but widely recognized "joke" at his expense: namely, that the tight-fitting Lycra shorts that he wears are said to reveal the size and shape of his genitals. This was the detail on which *The Sun* focused on the morning after he won an Olympic gold medal. Christie has been subject to continuous teasing in the tabloid press about the prominence and size of his "lunchbox" — a euphemism that some have taken so literally that, he revealed, he has been approached by a firm wanting to market its lunchboxes around his image! Linford Christie has observed the following about these innuendoes: "I felt humiliated … My first instinct was that it was racist. There we are, stereotyping a black man. I can take a good joke. But it happened the day after I won the greatest accolade an athlete can win … I don't want to go through life being known for what I've got in my shorts. I'm a serious person …" (p. 15).

ACTIVITY 3

What is going on here? Is this just a joke in bad taste, or does it have a deeper meaning? What do sexuality and gender have to do with images of black men and women? Why did the black French writer from Martinique, Frantz Fanon, say that white people seem to be obsessed with the sexuality of black people?

## Stereotyping as a Signifying Practice

Before we pursue this argument, however, we need to reflect further on how this racialized regime of representation actually works. Essentially, this involves examining more deeply the set of representational practices known as *stereotyping*. So far, we have considered the essentializing, reductionist, and naturalizing effects of stereotyping. Stereotyping reduces people to a few simple, essential characteristics that are represented as fixed by nature. Here, we examine four further aspects: (a) the construction of otherness and exclusion; (b) stereotyping and power; (c) the role of fantasy; and (d) fetishism.

Stereotyping as a signifying practice is central to the representation of racial difference. But what is a stereotype? How does it actually work? In his essay on stereotyping, Richard Dyer (1977) makes an important distinction between *typing* and *stereotyping*. He argues that, without the use of *types*, it would be difficult, if not impossible, to make sense of the world. We understand the world by referring individual objects, people, or events in our heads to the general classificatory schemes into which — according to our culture — they fit. Thus we decode a flat object on legs on which we place things as a "table." We may never have seen that kind of table before, but we have a general concept or category of table in our heads, into which we fit the particular objects we perceive or encounter. In other words, we understand the particular in terms of its type. We deploy what Alfred Schutz called *typifications*. In this sense, typing is essential to the production of meaning.

Richard Dyer argues that we are always making sense of things in terms of some wider categories. Thus, for example, we come to "know" something about a person by thinking of the *roles* that he or she performs:

Is he/she a parent, a child, a worker, a lover, a boss, or an old age pensioner? We assign him/her to the *membership* of different groups, according to class, gender, age group, nationality, race, linguistic group, sexual preference, and so on. We order him/her in terms of *personality type* — is he/she a happy, serious, depressed, scatterbrained, overactive kind of person? Our picture of whom the person "is" is built up out of the information we accumulate from positioning him/her within these different orders of typification. In broad terms, then, "a *type* is any simple, vivid, memorable, easily grasped and widely recognized characterization in which a few traits are foregrounded and change or 'development' is kept to a minimum" (Dyer, 1977, p. 28).

What, then, is the difference between a type and a stereotype? *Stereotypes* get hold of the few "simple, vivid, memorable, easily grasped and widely recognized" characteristics about a person, *reduce* everything about the person to those traits, *exaggerate* and *simplify* them, and *fix* them without change or development to eternity. This is the process we described earlier. So the first point is that *stereotyping reduces, essentializes, naturalizes, and fixes difference.*

Secondly, *stereotyping deploys a strategy of "splitting."* It divides the normal and the acceptable from the abnormal and the unacceptable. It then excludes or expels everything that does not fit, that is different. Dyer argues that "a system of social- and stereo-types refers to what is, as it were, within and beyond the pale of normalcy [i.e., behaviour that is accepted as 'normal' in any culture]. Types are instances which indicate those who live by the rules of society (social types) and those who the rules are designed to exclude (stereotypes). For this reason, stereotypes are also more rigid than social types . ... [B]oundaries ... must be clearly delineated and so stereotypes, one of the mechanisms of boundary maintenance, are characteristically fixed, clear-cut, unalterable" (p. 29). So, another feature of stereotyping is its practice of closure and exclusion. *It symbolically fixes boundaries, and excludes everything that does not belong.*

Stereotyping, in other words, is part of the maintenance of social and symbolic order. It sets up a symbolic frontier between the normal and the deviant, the normal and the pathological, the acceptable and the unacceptable, what belongs and what does not or is other, between insiders and outsiders, Us and Them. It facilitates the binding or bonding together of all of Us who are "normal" into one imagined community;

and it sends into symbolic exile all of Them — the others — who are in some way different, — beyond the pale. Mary Douglas (1966), for example, argued that whatever is "out of place" is considered polluted, dangerous, taboo. Negative feelings cluster around it. It must be symbolically excluded if the purity of the culture is to be restored. The feminist theorist, Julia Kristeva (1982), calls such expelled or excluded groups "abjected" (from the Latin meaning, literally, "thrown out").

The third point is that *stereotyping tends to occur where there are gross inequalities of power*. Power is usually directed against the subordinate or excluded group. One aspect of this power, according to Dyer, is *ethnocentrism* — "the application of the norms of one's own culture to that of others" (Brown, 1965, p. 183). Again, remember Derrida's argument that, between binary oppositions like Us/Them, "we are not dealing with … peaceful coexistence … but rather with a violent hierarchy. One of the two terms governs … the other or has the upper hand" (1972, p. 41).

In short, stereotyping is what Foucault called a "power/knowledge" sort of game. It classifies people according to a norm and constructs the excluded as other. Interestingly, it is also what Gramsci would have called an aspect of the struggle for hegemony. As Dyer observes, "The establishment of normalcy (i.e., what is accepted as 'normal') through social- and stereo-types is one aspect of the habit of ruling groups … to attempt to fashion the whole of society according to their own world view, value system, sensibility and ideology. So right is this world view for the ruling groups that they make it appear (as it does appear to them) as 'natural' and 'inevitable' — and for everyone — and, in so far as they succeed, they establish their hegemony" (Dyer, 1977, p. 30). Hegemony is a form of power based on leadership by a group in many fields of activity at once, so its ascendancy commands widespread consent and appears natural and inevitable.

## REPRESENTATION, DIFFERENCE, AND POWER

Within stereotyping, then, we have established a connection between representation, difference, and power. However, we need to probe the nature of this *power* more fully. We often think of power in terms of direct physical coercion or constraint. However, we have also spoken, for example, of power *in representation*; power to mark, assign, and classify; of *symbolic* power; of *ritualized* expulsion. Power, it seems, has to be understood here, not only in terms of economic exploitation and physical coercion, but also in broader cultural or symbolic terms, including the power to represent someone or something in a certain way — within a certain regime of representation. It includes the exercise of *symbolic power* through representational practices. Stereotyping is a key element in this exercise of symbolic violence.

In his study of how Europe constructed a stereotypical image of the Orient, Edward Said argues that, far from simply reflecting what the countries of the Near East were actually like, Orientalism was the *discourse* "by which European culture was able to manage — and even produce — the Orient politically, sociologically, militarily, ideologically, scientifically and imaginatively during the post-Enlightenment period." Within the framework of Western hegemony over the Orient, he says, there emerged a new object of knowledge, "a complex Orient suitable for study in the academy, for display in the museum, for reconstruction in the colonial office, for theoretical illustration in anthropological, biological, linguistic, racial and historical theses about mankind and the universe, for instances of economic and sociological theories of development, revolution, cultural personalities, national or religious character" (pp. 7–8). This form of power is closely connected with knowledge, or with the practices of what Foucault called "power/ knowledge."

ACTIVITY 10

For an example of Orientalism in visual representation, look at the reproduction of a very popular painting, *The Babylonian Marriage Market* by Edwin Long. Not only does the image produce a certain way of knowing the Orient — as the mysterious, exotic, and eroticized Orient; but also, the women who are being sold into marriage are arranged, right to left, in ascending order of whiteness. The final figure approximates most closely to the Western ideal, the norm; her clear complexion accentuated by the light reflected on her face from a mirror.

**Edwin Long, *The Babylonian Marriage Market*, 1882.**

Said's discussion of Orientalism closely parallels Foucault's power/ knowledge argument: a *discourse* produces, through different practices of *representation* (scholarship, exhibition, literature, painting, etc.), a form of *racialized knowledge of the Other* (Orientalism) deeply implicated in the operations of *power* (imperialism).

Interestingly, however, Said goes on to define power in ways that emphasize the similarities between Foucault and Gramsci's idea of *hegemony*:

> In any society not totalitarian, then, certain cultural forms predominate over others; the form of this cultural leadership is what Gramsci has identified as *hegemony*, an indispensable concept for any understanding of cultural life in the industrial West. It is hegemony, or rather the result of cultural hegemony at work, that gives Orientalism its durability and its strength ... Orientalism is never far from ... the idea of Europe, a collective notion identifying 'us' Europeans as against all 'those' non-Europeans, and indeed it can be argued that the major component in European culture is precisely what made that culture hegemonic both in and outside

> Europe: the idea of European identity as a superior one in
> comparison with all the non-European peoples and cultures.
> There is in addition the hegemony of European ideas about
> the Orient, themselves reiterating European superiority over
> Oriental backwardness, usually overriding the possibility
> that a more independent thinker ... may have had different
> views on the matter.
>
> (Said, 1978, p. 7)

[Also,] *power* [is introduced] into questions of representation. Power ... always operates in conditions of unequal relations. Gramsci, of course, would have stressed "between classes," whereas Foucault always refused to identify *any* specific subject or subject-group as the source of power, which, he said, operates at a local, tactical level. These are important differences between these two theorists of power.

However, there are also some important similarities. For Gramsci, as for Foucault, power also involves knowledge, representation, ideas, cultural leadership and authority, as well as economic constraint and physical coercion. Both would have agreed that power cannot be captured by thinking exclusively in terms of force or coercion: Power also seduces, solicits, induces, wins consent. It cannot be thought of in terms of one group having a monopoly of power, simply radiating power *downwards* on a subordinate group by an exercise of simple domination from above. It includes the dominant *and* the dominated within its circuits. As Homi Bhabha has remarked, apropos Said, "it is difficult to conceive ... subjectification as a placing *within* Orientalist or colonial discourse for the dominated subject without the dominant being strategically placed within it too" (Bhabha, 1986a, p. 158). Power not only constrains and prevents: it is also productive. It produces new discourses, new kinds of knowledge (e.g., Orientalism), new objects of knowledge (the Orient), it shapes new practices (colonization) and institutions (colonial government). It operates at a micro-level — Foucault's micro-physics of power — as well as in terms of wider strategies. And, for both theorists, power is to be found everywhere. As Foucault insists, power circulates.

The circularity of power is especially important in the context of representation. The argument is that everyone — the powerful and the powerless — is caught up, *though not on equal terms*, in power's circulation. No one — neither its apparent victims nor its agents — can stand wholly outside its field of operation.

## REFERENCES

Barthes, R. (1977). Rhetoric of the image. In *Image-music-text*, Glasgow: Fontana.
Bhabha, H. (1986a). The Other question. In *Literature, politics and theory*, London: Methuen.
Brown, R. (1965). *Social psychology*, London/New York: Macmillan.
Derrida, J. (1972). *Positions*, Chicago: University of Chicago Press.
Douglas, M. (1966). *Purity and danger*, London: Routledge & Kegan Paul.
Dyer, R. (ed.) (1977). *Gays and film*, London: British Film Institute.
Hall, S. (1972). Determinations of news photographs. In *Working papers in cultural studies no. 3*, Birmingham: University of Birmingham.
Kristeva, I. (1982). *Powers of horror*, New York: Columbia University Press.
Said, E. (1978). *Orientalism*, Harmondsworth: Penguin.

## EXERCISES

1. Examine the idea of myth including denotative and connotative meanings as well as sub-themes of race and difference.
2. Discuss the production of preferred meanings.
3. Discuss binary forms of representations. Can you think of other binaries that might apply to our "others"?
4. Compare the idea of a type and a stereotype.
5. Examine stereotypes as reductions, the notion of splitting, and normalcy, as well as the issue of power in this practice.
6. What is symbolic violence?
7. What is Orientalism in reference to Said?
8. Discuss power as it pertains to the production of stereotypes, new discourses, new kinds of knowledge, new objects of knowledge, and as it shapes new practices and institutions.

# Chapter 10

# Talking About Race, Learning About Racism: The Application of Racial Identity Development

## Berverly Daniel Tatum

As many educational institutions struggle to become more multicultural in terms of their students, faculty, and staff, they also begin to examine issues of cultural representation within their curriculum. This examination has evoked a growing number of courses that give specific consideration to the effect of variables such as race, class, and gender on human experience — an important trend that is reflected and supported by the increasing availability of resource manuals for the modification of course content (Bronstein and Quina, 1988; Hull, Scott, and Smith, 1982; Schuster and Van Dyne, 1985).

Unfortunately, less attention has been given to the issues of process that inevitably emerge in the classroom when attention is focused on race, class, and/or gender. It is very difficult to talk about these concepts in a meaningful way without also talking and learning about racism, classism, and sexism.[1] The introduction of these issues of oppression often generates powerful emotional responses in students that range from guilt and shame to anger and despair. If not addressed, these emotional responses can result in student resistance to oppression-related content areas. Such resistance can ultimately interfere with the cognitive understanding and mastery of the material. This resistance and potential interference is particularly common when specifically addressing issues of race and racism. Yet, when students are given the opportunity to explore race-related material in a classroom where both their affective and intellectual responses are acknowledged and addressed, their level of understanding is greatly enhanced.

This article seeks to provide a framework for understanding students' psychological responses to race-related content and the student resistance that can result, as well as some strategies for overcoming this resistance. It is informed by more than a decade of experience as an African-American woman engaged in teaching an undergraduate course on the psychology of racism, by thematic analyses of student journals and essays written for the racism class, and by an understanding and application of racial identity development theory (Helms, 1990).

## Setting the Context

As a clinical psychologist with a research interest in racial identity development among African-American youth raised in predominantly White communities, I began teaching about racism quite fortuitously. In 1980, while I was a part-time lecturer in the Black Studies department of a large public university, I was invited to teach a course called Group Exploration of Racism (Black Studies 2). A requirement for Black Studies majors, the course had to be offered, yet the instructor who regularly taught the course was no longer affiliated with the institution. Armed with a folder full of handouts, old syllabi that the previous instructor left behind, a copy of *White Awareness: Handbook for Anti-racism Training* (Katz, 1978), and my own clinical skills as a group facilitator, I constructed a course that seemed to meet the goals already outlined in the course catalogue. Designed "to provide students with an understanding of the psychological causes and emotional reality of racism as it appears in everyday life," the course incorporated the use of lectures, readings, simulation exercises, group research projects, and extensive class discussion to help students explore the psychological impact of racism on both the oppressor and the oppressed.

Though my first efforts were tentative, the results were powerful. The students in my class, most of whom were White, repeatedly described the course in their evaluations as one of the most valuable educational experiences of their college careers. I was convinced that helping students understand the ways in which racism operates in their own lives, and what they could do about it, was a social responsibility that I should accept. The freedom to institute the course in the curriculum of the psychology departments in which I would eventually teach became a personal condition of employment. I have successfully introduced the course in each new educational setting I have been in since leaving that university.

Since 1980, I have taught the course (now called the Psychology of Racism) 18 times, at three different institutions. Although each of these schools is very different — a large public university, a small state college, and a private, elite women's college — the challenges of teaching about racism in each setting have been more similar than different.

In all of the settings, class size has been limited to 30 students (averaging 24). Though typically predominantly White and female (even in coeducational settings), the class make-up has always been mixed in terms of both race and gender. The students of color who have taken the course include Asians and Latinos/as, but most frequently the students of color have been Black. Though most students have described themselves as middle class, all socioeconomic backgrounds (ranging from very poor to very wealthy) have been represented over the years.

The course has necessarily evolved in response to my own deepening awareness of the psychological legacy of racism and my expanding awareness of other forms of oppression, although the basic format has remained the same. Our weekly three-hour class meeting is held in a room with movable chairs, arranged in a circle. The physical structure communicates an important premise of the course that I expect the students to speak with each other as well as with me.

My other expectations (timely completion of assignments, regular class attendance) are clearly communicated in our first class meeting, along with the assumptions and guidelines for discussion that I rely upon to guide our work together. Because the assumptions and guidelines are so central to the process of talking and learning about racism, it may be useful to outline them here.

## Working Assumptions

1. Racism, defined as a "system of advantage based on race" (see Wellman, 1977), is a pervasive aspect of U.S. socialization. It is

virtually impossible to live in U.S. contemporary society and not be exposed to some aspect of the personal, cultural, and/or institutional manifestations of racism in our society. It is also assumed that, as a result, all of us have received some misinformation about those groups disadvantaged by racism.

2. Prejudice, defined as a "preconceived judgment or opinion, often based on limited information," is clearly distinguished from racism (see Katz, 1978). I assume that all of us may have prejudices as a result of the various cultural stereotypes to which we have been exposed. Even when these preconceived ideas have positive associations (such as "Asian students are good in math"), they have negative effects because they deny a person's individuality. These attitudes may influence the individual behaviors of people of color as well as of Whites, and may affect intergroup as well as intragroup interaction. However, a distinction must be made between the negative racial attitudes held by individuals of color and White individuals, because it is only the attitudes of Whites that routinely carry with them the social power inherent in the systematic cultural reinforcement and institutionalization of those racial prejudices. To distinguish the prejudices of students of color from the racism of White students is *not* to say that the former is acceptable and the latter is not; both are clearly problematic. The distinction is important, however, to identify the power differential between members of dominant and subordinate groups.

3. In the context of U.S. society, the system of advantage clearly operates to benefit Whites as a group. However, it is assumed that racism, like other forms of oppression, hurts members of the privileged group as well as those targeted by racism. While the impact of racism on Whites is clearly different from its impact on people of color, racism has negative ramifications for everyone. For example, some White students might remember the pain of having lost important relationships because Black friends were not allowed to visit their homes. Others may express sadness at having been denied access to a broad range of experiences because of social segregation. These individuals often attribute the discomfort or fear they now experience in racially mixed settings to the cultural limitations of their youth.

4. Because of the prejudice and racism inherent in our environments when we were children, I assume that we cannot be blamed for learning what we were taught (intentionally or unintentionally). Yet as adults, we have a responsibility to try to identify and interrupt the cycle of oppression. When we recognize that we have been misinformed, we have a responsibility to seek out more accurate information and to adjust our behavior accordingly.

5. It is assumed that change, both individual and institutional, is possible. Understanding and unlearning prejudice and racism is a lifelong process that may have begun prior to enrolling in this class, and which will surely continue after the course is over. Each of us may be at a different point in that process, and I assume that we will have mutual respect for each other, regardless of where we perceive one another to be.

To facilitate further our work together, I ask students to honor the following guidelines for our discussion. Specifically, I ask students to demonstrate their respect for one another by honoring the confidentiality of the group. So that students may feel free to ask potentially awkward or embarrassing questions, or share race-related experiences, I ask that students refrain from making personal attributions when discussing the course content with their friends. I also discourage the use of "zaps," overt or covert put-downs often used as comic relief when someone is feeling anxious about the content of the discussion. Finally, students are asked to speak from their own experience, to say, for example, "I think ..." or "In my experience, I have found ..." rather than generalizing their experience to others, as in "People say ...."

Many students are reassured by the climate of safety that is created by these guidelines and find comfort in the nonblaming assumptions I outline for the class. Nevertheless, my experience has been that most students, regardless of their class and ethnic background, still find racism a difficult topic to discuss as is revealed by these journal comments written after the first class meeting (all names are pseudonyms):

> The class is called Psychology of Racism, the atmosphere is
> friendly and open, yet I feel very closed in. I feel guilt and
> doubt well up inside of me. (Tiffany, a White woman)

Class has started on a good note thus far. The class seems rather large and disturbs me. In a class of this nature, I expect there will be many painful and emotional moments. (Linda, an Asian woman)

I am a little nervous that as one of the few students of color in the class people are going to be looking at me for answers, or whatever other reasons. The thought of this inhibits me a great deal. (Louise, an African-American woman)

I had never thought about my social position as being totally dominant. There wasn't one area in which I wasn't in the dominant group .... I first felt embarrassed .... Through association alone I felt in many ways responsible for the unequal condition existing in the world. This made me feel like shrinking in a hole in a class where I was surrounded by 27 women and 2 men, one of whom was Black and the other was Jewish. I felt that all these people would be justified in venting their anger upon me. After a short period, I realized that no one in the room was attacking or even blaming me for the conditions that exist. (Carl, a White man)

Even though most of my students voluntarily enroll in the course as an elective, their anxiety and subsequent resistance to learning about racism quickly emerge.

## SOURCES OF RESISTANCE

In predominantly White college classrooms, I have experienced at least three major sources of student resistance to talking and learning about race and racism. They can be readily identified as the following:

1. Race is considered a taboo topic for discussion, especially in racially mixed settings.
2. Many students, regardless of racial-group membership, have been socialized to think of the United States as a just society.

3. Many students, particularly White students, initially deny any personal prejudice, recognizing the impact of racism on other people's lives, but failing to acknowledge its impact on their own.

## Race as a Taboo Topic

The first source of resistance, race as a taboo topic, is an essential obstacle to overcome if class discussion is to begin at all. Although many students are interested in the topic, they are often most interested in hearing other people talk about it, afraid to break the taboo themselves.

One source of this self-consciousness can be seen in the early childhood experiences of many students. It is known that children as young as three notice racial differences (see Phinney and Rotheram, 1987). Certainly preschoolers talk about what they see. Unfortunately, they often do so in ways that make adults uncomfortable. Imagine the following scenario: A White child in a public place points to a dark-skinned African-American child and says loudly, "Why is that boy Black?" The embarrassed parent quickly responds, "Sh! Don't say that." The child is only attempting to make sense of a new observation (Derman-Sparks, Higa, and Sparks, 1980), yet the parent's attempt to silence the perplexed child sends a message that this observation is not okay to talk about. White children quickly become aware that their questions about race raise adult anxiety, and as a result, they learn not to ask the questions.

When asked to reflect on their earliest race-related memories and the feelings associated with them, both White students and students of color often report feelings of confusion, anxiety, and/or fear. Students of color often have early memories of name-calling or other negative interactions with other children, and sometimes with adults. They also report having had questions that went both unasked and unanswered. In addition, many students have had uncomfortable interchanges around race-related topics as adults. When asked at the beginning of the semester, "How many of you have had difficult, perhaps heated conversations with someone on a race-related topic?", routinely almost everyone in the class raises his or her hand. It should come as no surprise then that students often approach the topic of race and/or racism with both curiosity and trepidation.

## The Myth of the Meritocracy

The second source of student resistance to be discussed here is rooted in students' belief that the United States is a just society, a meritocracy where individual efforts are fairly rewarded. While some students (particularly students of color) may already have become disillusioned with that notion of the United States, the majority of my students who have experienced at least the personal success of college acceptance still have faith in this notion. To the extent that these students acknowledge that racism exists, they tend to view it as an individual phenomenon, rooted in the attitudes of the "Archie Bunkers" of the world or located only in particular parts of the country.

After several class meetings, Karen, a White woman, acknowledged this attitude in her journal:

> At one point in my life — the beginning of this class — I actually perceived America to be a relatively racist free society. I thought that the people who were racist or subjected to racist stereotypes were found only in small pockets of the U.S., such as the South. As I've come to realize, racism (or at least racially orientated stereotypes) is rampant.

An understanding of racism as a system of advantage presents a serious challenge to the notion of the United States as a just society where rewards are based solely on one's merit. Such a challenge often creates discomfort in students. The old adage "ignorance is bliss" seems to hold true in this case; students are not necessarily eager to recognize the painful reality of racism.

One common response to the discomfort is to engage in denial of what they are learning. White students in particular may question the accuracy or currency of statistical information regarding the prevalence of discrimination (housing, employment, access to health care, and so on). More qualitative data, such as autobiographical accounts of experiences with racism, may be challenged on the basis of their subjectivity.

It should be pointed out that the basic assumption that the United States is a just society for all is only one of many basic assumptions that might be challenged in the learning process. Another example can be seen in an interchange between two White students following a discussion about cultural racism, in which the omission or distortion of historical information about people of color was offered as an example of the cultural transmission of racism.

"Yeah, I just found out that Cleopatra was actually a Black woman."
"What?"

The first student went on to explain her newly learned information. Finally, the second student exclaimed in disbelief, "That can't be true. Cleopatra was beautiful!" This new information and her own deeply ingrained assumptions about who is beautiful and who is not were too incongruous to allow her to assimilate the information at that moment.

If outright denial of information is not possible, then withdrawal may be. Physical withdrawal in the form of absenteeism is one possible result; it is for precisely this reason that class attendance is mandatory. The reduction in the completion of reading and/or written assignments is another form of withdrawal. I have found this response to be so common that I now alert students to this possibility at the beginning of the semester. Knowing that this response is a common one seems to help students stay engaged, even when they experience the desire to withdraw.

Following an absence in the fifth week of the semester, one White student wrote, "I think I've hit the point you talked about, the point where you don't want to hear any more about racism. I sometimes begin to get the feeling we are all hypersensitive." (Two weeks later she wrote, "Class is getting better. I think I am beginning to get over my hump.")

Perhaps not surprisingly, this response can be found in both White students and students of color. Students of color often enter a discussion of racism with some awareness of the issue, based on personal experiences. However, even these students find that they did not have a full understanding of the widespread impact of racism in our society. For students who are targeted by racism, an increased awareness of the impact in and on their lives is painful, and often generates anger.

Four weeks into the semester, Louise, an African-American woman wrote in her journal about her own heightened sensitivity:

> Many times in class I feel uncomfortable when White students
> use the term Black because even if they aren't aware of it
> they say it with all or at least a lot of the negative connotations

they've been taught goes along with Black. Sometimes it just causes a stinging feeling inside of me. Sometimes I get real tired of hearing White people talk about the conditions of Black people. I think it's an important thing for them to talk about, but still I don't always like being around when they do it. I also get tired of hearing them talk about how hard it is for them, though I understand it, and most times I am very willing to listen and be open, but sometimes I can't. Right now I can't.

For White students, advantaged by racism, a heightened awareness of it often generates painful feelings of guilt. The following responses are typical:

After reading the article about privilege, I felt very guilty. (Rachel, a White woman)

Questions of racism are so full of anger and pain. When I think of all the pain White people have caused people of color, I get a feeling of guilt. How could someone like myself care so much about the color of someone's skin that they would do them harm? (Terri, a White woman)

White students also sometimes express a sense of betrayal when they realize the gaps in their own education about racism. After seeing the first episode of the documentary series *Eyes on the Prize*, Chris, a White man, wrote:

I never knew it was really that bad just 35 years ago. Why didn't I learn this in elementary or high school? Could it be that the White people of America want to forget this injustice? ... I will never forget that movie for as long as I live. It was like a big slap in the face.

Barbara, a White woman, also felt anger and embarrassment in response to her own previous lack of information about the internment of Japanese Americans during World War II. She wrote:

> I feel so stupid because I never even knew that these existed.
> I never knew that the Japanese were treated so poorly. I am
> becoming angry and upset about all of the things that I do
> not know. I have been so sheltered. My parents never
> wanted to let me know about the bad things that have
> happened in the world. After I saw the movie *(Mitsuye and
> Nellie)*, I even called them up to ask them why they never
> told me this …. I am angry at them too for not teaching me
> and exposing me to the complete picture of my country.

Avoiding the subject matter is one way to avoid these uncomfortable feelings.

## "I'm Not Racist, But …"

A third source of student resistance (particularly among White students) is the initial denial of any personal connection to racism. When asked why they have decided to enroll in a course on racism, White students typically explain their interest in the topic with such disclaimers as, "I'm not racist myself, but I know people who are, and I want to understand them better."

Because of their position as the targets of racism, students of color do not typically focus on their own prejudices or lack of them. Instead they usually express a desire to understand why racism exists, and how they have been affected by it.

However, as all students gain a better grasp of what racism is and its many manifestations in U.S. society, they inevitably start to recognize its legacy within themselves. Beliefs, attitudes, and actions based on racial stereotypes begin to be remembered and are newly observed by White students. Students of color as well often recognize negative attitudes they may have internalized about their own racial group or that they have believed about others. Those who previously thought themselves immune to the effects of growing up in a racist society often find themselves reliving uncomfortable feelings of guilt or anger.

After taping her own responses to a questionnaire on racial attitudes, Barbara, a White woman previously quoted, wrote:

> I always want to think of myself as open to all races. Yet
> when I did the interview to myself, I found that I did respond

differently to the same questions about different races. No one could ever have told me that I would have. I would have denied it. But I found that I did respond differently even though I didn't want to. This really upset me. I was angry with myself because I thought I was not prejudiced and yet the stereotypes that I had created had an impact on the answers that I gave even though I didn't want it to happen.

The new self-awareness, represented here by Barbara's journal entry, changes the classroom dynamic. One common result is that some White students, once perhaps active participants in class discussion, now hesitate to continue their participation for fear that their newly recognized racism will be revealed to others.

Today I did feel guilty, and like I had to watch what I was saying (make it good enough), I guess to prove I'm really *not* prejudiced. From the conversations the first day, I guess this is a normal enough reaction, but I certainly never expected it in me. (Joanne, a White woman)

This withdrawal on the part of White students is often paralleled by an increase in participation by students of color who are seeking an outlet for what are often feelings of anger. The withdrawal of some previously vocal White students from the classroom exchange, however, is sometimes interpreted by students of color as indifference. This perceived indifference often serves to fuel the anger and frustration that many students of color experience, as awareness of their own oppression is heightened. For example, Robert, an African-American man, wrote:

I really wish the White students would talk more. When I read these articles, it makes me so mad and I really want to know what the White kids think. Don't they care?

Sonia, a Latina, described the classroom tension from another perspective:

I would like to comment that at many points in the discussions I have felt uncomfortable and sometimes even angry with people. I guess I am at the stage where I am tired of listening to Whites feel guilty and watch their eyes fill up with tears. I do understand that everyone is at their own stage of development and I even tell myself every Tuesday that these people have come to this class by choice. Some days I am just more tolerant than others .... It takes courage to say things in that room with so many women of color present. It also takes courage for the women of color to say things about Whites.

What seems to be happening in the classroom at such moments is a collision of developmental processes that can be inherently useful for the racial identity development of the individuals involved. Nevertheless, the interaction may be perceived as problematic to instructors and students who are unfamiliar with the process. Although space does not allow for an exhaustive discussion of racial identity development theory, a brief explication of it here will provide additional clarity regarding the classroom dynamics when issues of race are discussed. It will also provide a theoretical framework for the strategies for dealing with student resistance that will be discussed at the conclusion of this article.

## STAGES OF RACIAL IDENTITY DEVELOPMENT

Racial identity and racial identity development theory are defined by Janet Helms (1990) as

a sense of group or collective identity based on one's *perception* that he or she shares a common racial heritage with a particular racial group... racial identity development theory concerns the psychological implications of racial-group membership, that is belief systems that evolve in reaction to perceived differential racial-group membership. (p. 3)

It is assumed that in a society where racial-group membership is emphasized, the development of a racial identity will occur in some form in everyone. Given the dominant/subordinate relationship of Whites and people of color in this society, however, it is not surprising that this developmental process will unfold in different ways. For purposes of this discussion, William Cross's (1971, 1978) model of Black identity development will be described along with Helms's (1990) model of White racial identity development theory. While the identity development of other students (Asian, Latino/a, Native American) is not included in this particular theoretical formulation, there is evidence to suggest that the process for these oppressed groups is similar to that described for African Americans (Highlen et al., 1988; Phinney, 1990).[2] In each case, it is assumed that a positive sense of one's self as a member of one's group (which is not based on any assumed superiority) is important for psychological health.

## Black Racial Identity Development

According to Cross's (1971, 1978, 1991) model of Black racial identity development, there are five stages in the process, identified as Preencounter, Encounter, Immersion/Emersion, Internalization, and Internalization-Commitment. In the first stage of Preencounter, the African American has absorbed many of the beliefs and values of the dominant White culture, including the notion that "White is right" and "Black is wrong." Though the internalization of negative Black stereotypes may be outside of his or her conscious awareness, the individual seeks to assimilate and be accepted by Whites, and actively or passively distances him/herself from other Blacks.[3]

Louise, an African-American woman previously quoted, captured the essence of this stage in the following description of herself at an earlier time:

> For a long time it seemed as if I didn't remember my background, and I guess in some ways I didn't. I was never taught to be proud of my African heritage. Like we talked about in class, I went through a very long stage of identifying with my oppressors. Wanting to be like, live like, and be accepted by them. Even to the point of hating my own race

and myself for being a part of it. Now I am ashamed that I ever was ashamed. I lost so much of myself in my denial of and refusal to accept my people.

In order to maintain psychological comfort at this stage of development, Helms writes:

> The person must maintain the fiction that race and racial indoctrination have nothing to do with how he or she lives life. It is probably the case that the Preencounter person is bombarded on a regular basis with information that he or she cannot really be a member of the "in" racial group, but relies on denial to selectively screen such information from awareness. (1990, p. 23)

This de-emphasis on one's racial-group membership may allow the individual to think that race has not been or will not be a relevant factor in one's own achievement, and may contribute to the belief in a U.S. meritocracy that is often a part of a Preencounter worldview.

Movement into the Encounter phase is typically precipitated by an event or series of events that forces the individual to acknowledge the impact of racism in one's life. For example, instances of social rejection by White friends or colleagues (or reading new personally relevant information about racism) may lead the individual to the conclusion that many Whites will not view him or her as an equal. Faced with the reality that he or she cannot truly be White, the individual is forced to focus on his or her identity as a member of a group targeted by racism.

Brenda, a Korean-American student, described her own experience of this process as a result of her participation in the racism course:

> I feel that because of this class, I have become much more aware of racism that exists around. Because of my awareness of racism, I am now bothered by acts and behaviors that might not have bothered me in the past. Before when racial comments were said around me I would somehow ignore it and pretend that nothing was said. By ignoring comments such as these, I was protecting myself. It became sort of a

> defense mechanism. I never realized I did this, until I was confronted with stories that were found in our reading, by other people of color, who also ignored comments that bothered them. In realizing that there is racism out in the world and that there are comments concerning race that are directed towards me, I feel as if I have reached the first step. I also think I have reached the second step, because I am now bothered and irritated by such comments. I no longer ignore them, but now confront them.

The Immersion/Emersion stage is characterized by the simultaneous desire to surround oneself with visible symbols of one's racial identity and an active avoidance of symbols of Whiteness. As Thomas Parham describes, "At this stage, everything of value in life must be Black or relevant to Blackness. This stage is also characterized by a tendency to denigrate White people, simultaneously glorifying Black people ...." (1989, p. 190). The previously described anger that emerges in class among African-American students and other students of color in the process of learning about racism may be seen as part of the transition through these stages.

As individuals enter the Immersion stage, they actively seek out opportunities to explore aspects of their own history and culture with the support of peers from their own racial background. Typically, White-focused anger dissipates during this phase because so much of the person's energy is directed toward his or her own group- and self-exploration. The result of this exploration is an emerging security in a newly defined and affirmed sense of self.

Sharon, another African-American woman, described herself at the beginning of the semester as angry, seemingly in the Encounter stage of development. She wrote after our class meeting:

> Another point that I must put down is that before I entered class today I was angry about the way Black people have been treated in this country. I don't think I will easily overcome that and I basically feel justified in my feelings.

At the end of the semester, Sharon had joined with two other Black students in the class to work on their final class project. She observed that the three of them had planned their project to focus on Black people specifically, suggesting movement into the Immersion stage of racial identity development. She wrote:

> We are concerned about the well-being of our own people. They cannot be well if they have this pinned-up hatred for their own people. This internalized racism is something that we all felt, at various times, needed to be talked about. This semester it has really been important to me, and I believe Gordon [a Black classmate], too.

The emergence from this stage marks the beginning of Internalization. Secure in one's own sense of racial identity, there is less need to assert the "Blacker than thou" attitude often characteristic of the Immersion stage (Parham, 1989). In general, "pro-Black attitudes become more expansive, open, and less defensive" (Cross, 1971, p. 24). While still maintaining his or her connections with Black peers, the internalized individual is willing to establish meaningful relationships with Whites who acknowledge and are respectful of his or her self-definition. The individual is also ready to build coalitions with members of other oppressed groups. At the end of the semester, Brenda, a Korean American, concluded that she had in fact internalized a positive sense of racial identity. The process she described parallels the stages described by Cross:

> I have been aware for a long time that I am Korean. But through this class I am beginning to really become aware of my race. I am beginning to find out that White people can be accepting of me and at the same time accept me as a Korean.
> I grew up wanting to be accepted and ended up almost denying my race and culture. I don't think I did this consciously, but the denial did occur. As I grew older, I realized that I was different. I became, for the first time, friends with other Koreans. I realized I had much in common with them. This was when I went through my "Korean friend" stage. I began to enjoy being friends with Koreans more than I did with Caucasians.

> Well, ultimately, through many years of growing up, I
> am pretty much in focus about who I am and who my friends
> are. I knew before I took this class that there were people
> not of color that were understanding of my differences. In
> our class, I feel that everyone is trying to sincerely find the
> answer of abolishing racism. I knew people like this existed,
> but it's nice to meet with them weekly.

Cross suggests that there are few psychological differences between the fourth stage, Internalization, and the fifth stage, Internalization-Commitment. However, those at the fifth stage have found ways to translate their "personal sense of Blackness into a plan of action or a general sense of commitment" to the concerns of Blacks as a group, which is sustained over time (Cross, 1991, p. 220). Whether at the fourth or Fifth stage, the process of Internalization allows the individual, anchored in a positive sense of racial identity, both to proactively perceive and transcend race. Blackness becomes "the point of departure for discovering the universe of ideas, cultures and experiences beyond blackness in place of mistaking blackness as the universe itself" (Cross, Parham, and Helms, 1991, p. 330).

Though the process of racial identity development has been presented here in linear form, in fact it is probably more accurate to think of it in a spiral form. Often a person may move from one stage to the next, only to revisit an earlier stage as the result of new encounter experiences (Parham, 1989), though the later experience of the stage may be different from the original experience. The image that students often find helpful in understanding this concept of recycling through the stages is that of a spiral staircase. As a person ascends a spiral staircase, she may stop and look down at a spot below. When she reaches the next level, she may look down and see the same spot, but the vantage point has changed.[4]

## WHITE RACIAL IDENTITY DEVELOPMENT

The transformations experienced by those targeted by racism are often paralleled by those of White students. Helms (1990) describes the evolution of a positive White racial identity as involving both the abandonment of racism and the development of a non-racist White identity. In order to do the latter, he or she must accept his or her own Whiteness, the cultural implications of being White, and define a view of Self as a racial being that does not depend on the perceived superiority of one racial group over another (p. 49).

She identifies six stages in her model of White racial identity development: Contact, Disintegration, Reintegration, Pseudo-Independent, Immersion/Emersion, and Autonomy.

The Contact stage is characterized by a lack of awareness of cultural and institutional racism, and of one's own White privilege. Peggy McIntosh (1989) writes eloquently about her own experience of this state of being:

> As a white person, I realized I had been taught about racism as something which puts others at a disadvantage, but had been taught not to see one of its corollary aspects, white privilege, which puts me at an advantage .... I was taught to see racism only in individual acts of meanness, not in invisible systems conferring dominance on my group. (p. 10)

In addition, the Contact stage often includes naive curiosity about or fear of people of color, based on stereotypes learned from friends, family, or the media. These stereotypes represent the framework in use when a person at this stage of development makes a comment such as, "You don't act like a Black person" (Helms, 1990, p. 57).

Those Whites whose lives are structured so as to limit their interaction with people of color, as well as their awareness of racial issues, may remain at this stage indefinitely. However, certain kinds of experiences (increased interaction with people of color or exposure to new information about racism) may lead to a new understanding that cultural and institutional racism exist. This new understanding marks the beginning of the Disintegration stage.

At this stage, the bliss of ignorance or lack of awareness is replaced by the discomfort of guilt, shame, and sometimes anger at the recognition of one's own advantage because of being White and the acknowledgement of the role of Whites in the maintenance of a racist system. Attempts to reduce discomfort may include denial (convincing oneself that racism doesn't really exist, or if it does, it is the fault of its victims).

For example, Tom, a White male student, responded with some frustration in his journal to a classmate's observation that the fact that she had never read any books by Black authors in any of her high school or college English classes was an example of cultural racism. He wrote, "It's not my fault that Blacks don't write books."

After viewing a film in which a psychologist used examples of Black children's drawings to illustrate the potentially damaging effect of negative cultural messages on a Black child's developing self-esteem, David, another White male student, wrote:

> I found it interesting the way Black children drew themselves without arms. The psychologist said this is saying that the child feels unable to control his environment. It can't be because the child has notions and beliefs already about being Black. It must be built in or hereditary due to the past history of the Blacks. I don't believe it's cognitive but more biological due to a long past history of repression and being put down.

Though Tom's and David's explanations seem quite problematic, they can be understood in the context of racial identity development theory as a way of reducing their cognitive dissonance upon learning this new race-related information. As was discussed earlier, withdrawal (accomplished by avoiding contact with people of color and the topic of racism) is another strategy for dealing with the discomfort experienced at this stage. Many of the previously described responses of White students to race-related content are characteristic of the transition from the Contact to the Disintegration stage of development.

Helms (1990) describes another response to the discomfort of Disintegration, which involves attempts to change significant others' attitudes toward African Americans and other people of color. However, as she points out,

> due to the racial naivete with which this approach may be undertaken and the person's ambivalent racial identification, this dissonance-reducing strategy is likely to be met with rejection by Whites as well as Blacks. (p. 59)

In fact, this response is also frequently observed among White students who have an opportunity to talk with friends and family during holiday visits. Suddenly they are noticing the racist content of jokes or comments of their friends and relatives and will try to confront them, often only to find that their efforts are, at best, ignored or dismissed as a "phase," or, at worst, greeted with open hostility.

Carl, a White male previously quoted, wrote at length about this dilemma:

> I realized that it was possible to simply go through life totally oblivious to the entire situation or, even if one realizes it, one can totally repress it. It is easy to fade into the woodwork, run with the rest of society, and never have to deal with these problems. So many people I know from home are like this. They have simply accepted what society has taught them with little, if any, question. My father is a prime example of this .... It has caused much friction in our relationship, and he often tells me as a father he has failed in raising me correctly. Most of my high school friends will never deal with these issues and propagate them on to their own children. It's easy to see how the cycle continues. I don't think I could ever justify within myself simply turning my back on the problem. I finally realized that my position in all of these dominant groups gives me power to make change occur .... It is an unfortunate result often though that I feel alienated from friends and family. It's often played off as a mere stage that I'm going through. I obviously can't tell if it's merely a stage, but I know that they say this to take the attention off of the truth of what I'm saying. By belittling me, they take the power out of my argument. It's very depressing that being compassionate and considerate are seen as only phases that people go through. I don't want it to be a phase for me, but as obvious as this may sound, I look at my environment and often wonder how it will not be.

The societal pressure to accept the status quo may lead the individual from Disintegration to Reintegration. At this point the desire to be accepted by one's own racial group, in which the overt or covert belief in White superiority is so prevalent, may lead to a reshaping of the person's belief system to be more congruent with an acceptance of racism. The guilt and anxiety associated with Disintegration may be redirected in the form of fear and anger directed toward people of color (particularly Blacks), who are now blamed as the source of discomfort.

Connie, a White woman of Italian ancestry, in many ways exemplified the progression from the Contact stage to Reintegration, a process she herself described seven weeks into the semester. After reading about the stages of White identity development, she wrote:

> I think mostly I can find myself in the disintegration stage of development …. There was a time when I never considered myself a color. I never described myself as a "White, Italian female" until I got to college and noticed that people of color always described themselves by their color/race. While taking this class, I have begun to understand that being White makes a difference. I never thought about it before but there are many privileges to being White. In my personal life, I cannot say that I have ever felt that I have had the advantage over a Black person, but I am aware that my race has the advantage.
>
> I am feeling really guilty lately about that. I find myself thinking: "I didn't mean to be White, I really didn't mean it." I am starting to feel angry towards my race for ever using this advantage towards personal gains. But at the same time I resent the minority groups. I mean, it's not our fault that society has deemed us "superior." I don't feel any better than a Black person. But it really doesn't matter because I am a member of the dominant race …. I can't help it … and I sometimes get angry and feel like I'm being attacked.
>
> I guess my anger toward a minority group would enter me into the next stage of Reintegration, where I am once again starting to blame the victim. This is all very trying for me and it has been on my mind a lot. I really would like to be able to reach the last stage, autonomy, where I can accept being White without hostility and anger. That is really hard to do.

Helms (1990) suggests that it is relatively easy for Whites to become stuck at the Reintegration stage of development, particularly if avoidance of people of color is possible. However, if there is a catalyst for continued self-examination, the person "begins to question her or his previous definition of Whiteness and the justifiability of racism in any of its forms …." (p. 61). In my experience, continued participation in a course on racism provides the catalyst for this deeper self-examination.

This process was again exemplified by Connie. At the end of the semester, she listened to her own taped interview of her racial attitudes that she had recorded at the beginning of the semester. She wrote:

> Oh wow! I could not believe some of the things that I said. I was obviously in different stages of the White identity development. As I listened and got more and more disgusted with myself when I was at the Reintegration stage, I tried to remind myself that these are stages that all (most) White people go through when dealing with notions of racism. I can remember clearly the resentment I had for people of color. I feel the one thing I enjoyed from listening to my interview was noticing how much I have changed. I think I am finally out of the Reintegration stage. I am beginning to make a conscious effort to seek out information about people of color and accept their criticism …. I still feel guilty about the feeling I had about people of color and I always feel bad about being privileged as a result of racism. But I am glad that I have reached what I feel is the Pseudo-Independent stage of White identity development.

The information-seeking that Connie describes often marks the onset of the Pseudo-Independent stage. At this stage, the individual is abandoning beliefs in White superiority, but may still behave in ways that unintentionally perpetuate the system. Looking to those targeted by racism to help him or her understand racism, the White person often tries to disavow his or her own Whiteness through active affiliation with Blacks, for example. The individual experiences a sense of alienation from other Whites who have not yet begun to examine their own racism, yet may also experience rejection from Blacks or other people of color who are suspicious of his or her motives. Students of color moving from the Encounter to the Immersion phase of their own racial identity development may be particularly unreceptive to the White person's attempts to connect with them.

Uncomfortable with his or her own Whiteness, yet unable to be truly anything else, the individual may begin searching for a new, more comfortable way to be White. This search is characteristic of the Immersion/Emersion stage of development. Just as the Black student seeks to redefine positively what it means to be of African ancestry in the United States through immersion in accurate information about one's culture and history, the White individual seeks to replace racially related myths and stereotypes with accurate information about what it means and has meant to be White in U.S. society (Helms, 1990). Learning about Whites who have been anti-racist allies to people of color is a very important part of this process.

After reading articles written by anti-racist activists describing their own process of unlearning racism, White students often comment on how helpful it is to know that others have experienced similar feelings and have found ways to resist the racism in their environments.[5] For example, Joanne, a White woman who initially experienced a lot of guilt, wrote:

> This article helped me out in many ways. I've been feeling helpless and frustrated. I know there are all these terrible things going on and I want to be able to do something .... Anyway this article helped me realize, again, that others feel this way, and gave me some positive ideas to resolve my dominant class guilt and shame.

Finally, reading the biographies and autobiographies of White individuals who have embarked on a similar process of identity development (such as Barnard, 1987) provides White students with important models for change.

Learning about White anti-racists can also provide students of color with a sense of hope that they can have White allies. After hearing a White anti-racist activist address the class, Sonia, a Latina who had written about her impatience with expressions of White guilt, wrote:

> I don't know when I have been more impressed by anyone.
> She filled me with hope for the future. She made me believe
> that there are good people in the world and that Whites
> suffer too and want to change things.

For White students, the internalization of a newly defined sense of oneself as White is the primary task of the Autonomy stage. The positive feelings associated with this redefinition energize the person's efforts to confront racism and oppression in his or her daily life. Alliances with people of color can be more easily forged at this stage of development than previously because the person's anti-racist behaviors and attitudes will be more consistently expressed. While Autonomy might be described as "racial self-actualization, ... it is best to think of it as an ongoing process ... wherein the person is continually open to new information and new ways of thinking about racial and cultural variables" (Helms, 1990, p. 66).

Annette, a White woman, described herself in the Autonomy stage, but talked at length about the circular process she felt she had been engaged in during the semester:

> If people as racist as C.P. Ellis (a former Klansman) can
> change, I think anyone can change. If that makes me idealistic,
> fine. I do not think my expecting society to change is naive
> anymore because I now *know* exactly what I want. To be
> naive means a lack of knowledge that allows me to accept
> myself both as a White person and as an idealist. This class
> showed me that these two are not mutually exclusive but
> are an integral part of me that I cannot deny. I realize now
> that through most of this class I was trying to deny both of
> them.
>
> While I was not accepting society's racism, I was accepting
> society's telling me as a White person, there was nothing I
> could do to change racism. So, I told myself I was being
> naive and tried to suppress my desire to change society.
> This is what made me so frustrated — while I saw society's
> racism through examples in the readings and the media, I
> kept telling myself there was nothing I could do. Listening

to my tape, I think I was already in the Autonomy stage when I started this class. I then seemed to decide that being White, I also had to be racist which is when I became frustrated and went back to the Disintegration stage. I was frustrated because I was not only telling myself there was nothing I could do but I also was assuming society's racism was my own which made me feet like I did not want to be White. Actually, it was not being White that I was disavowing but being racist. I think I have now returned to the Autonomy stage and am much more secure in my position there. I accept my Whiteness now as just a part of me as is my idealism. I will no longer disavow these characteristics as I have realized I can be proud of both of them. In turn, I can now truly accept other people for their unique characteristics and not by the labels society has given them as I can accept myself that way.

While I thought the main ideas that I learned in this class were that White people need to be educated to end racism and everyone should be treated as human beings, I really had already incorporated these ideas into my thoughts. What I learned from this class is being White does not mean being racist and being idealistic does not mean being naive. I really did not have to form new ideas about people of color; I had to form them about myself — and I did.

## IMPLICATIONS FOR CLASSROOM TEACHING

Although movement through all the stages of racial identity development will not necessarily occur for each student within the course of a semester (or even four years of college), it is certainly common to witness beginning transformations in classes with race-related content. An awareness of the existence of this process has helped me to implement strategies to facilitate positive student development, as well as to improve interracial dialogue within the classroom.

Four strategies for reducing student resistance and promoting student development that I have found useful are the following:

1. The creation of a safe classroom atmosphere by establishing clear guidelines for discussion;
2. The creation of opportunities for self-generated knowledge;
3. The provision of an appropriate developmental model that students can use as a framework for understanding their own process;
4. The exploration of strategies to empower students as change agents.

## Creating a Safe Climate

As was discussed earlier, making the classroom a safe space for discussion is essential for overcoming students' fears about breaking the race taboo, and will also reduce later anxieties about exposing one's own internalized racism. Establishing the guidelines of confidentiality, mutual respect, "no zaps," and speaking from one's own experience on the first day of class is a necessary step in the process.

Students respond very positively to these ground rules, and do try to honor them. While the rules do not totally eliminate anxiety, they clearly communicate to students that there is a safety net for the discussion. Students are also encouraged to direct their comments and questions to each other rather than always focusing their attention on me as the instructor, and to learn each other's names rather than referring to each other as "he," "she," or "the person in the red sweater" when responding to each other.[6]

## The Power of Self-Generated Knowledge

The creation of opportunities for self-generated knowledge on the part of students is a powerful tool for reducing the initial stage of denial that many students experience. While it may seem easy for some students to challenge the validity of what they read or what the instructor says, it is harder to deny what they have seen with their own eyes. Students can be given hands-on assignments outside of class to facilitate this process.

For example, after reading *Portraits of White Racism* (Wellman, 1977), some students expressed the belief that the attitudes expressed by the White interviewees in the book were no longer commonly held attitudes. Students were then asked to use the same interview protocol used in the book (with some revision) to interview a White adult of their choice.

When students reported on these interviews in class, their own observation of the similarity between those they had interviewed and those they had read about was more convincing than anything I might have said.

After doing her interview, Patty, a usually quiet White student, wrote:

> I think I learned a lot from it and that I'm finally getting a
> better grip on the idea of racism. I think that was why I
> participated so much in class. I really felt like I knew what I
> was talking about.

Other examples of creating opportunities for self-generated knowledge include assigning students the task of visiting grocery stores in neighborhoods of differing racial composition to compare the cost and quality of goods and services available at the two locations, and to observe the interactions between the shoppers and the store personnel. For White students, one of the most powerful assignments of this type has been to go apartment hunting with an African-American student and to experience housing discrimination firsthand. While one concern with such an assignment is the effect it will have on the students of color involved, I have found that those Black students who choose this assignment rather than another are typically eager to have their White classmates experience the reality of racism, and thus participate quite willingly in the process.

## Naming the Problem

The emotional responses that students have to talking and learning about racism are quite predictable and related to their own racial identity development. Unfortunately, students typically do not know this; thus they consider their own guilt, shame, embarrassment, or anger an uncomfortable experience that they alone are having. Informing students at the beginning of the semester that these feelings may be part of the learning process is ethically necessary (in the sense of informed consent), and helps to normalize the students' experience. Knowing in advance that a desire to withdraw from classroom discussion or not to complete assignments is a common response helps students to remain engaged when they reach that point. As Alice, a White woman, wrote at the end of the semester:

You were so right in saying in the beginning how we would
grow tired of racism (I did in October) but then it would get
so good! I have *loved* the class once I passed that point.

In addition, sharing the model of racial identity development with
students gives them a useful framework for understanding each other's
processes as well as their own. This cognitive framework does not
necessarily prevent the collision of developmental processes previously
described, but it does allow students to be less frightened by it when it
occurs. If, for example, White students understand the stages of racial
identity development for students of color, they are less likely to
personalize or feel threatened by an African-American student's anger.

Connie, a White student who initially expressed a lot of resentment
at the way students of color tended to congregate in the college cafeteria,
was much more understanding of this behavior after she learned about
racial identity development theory. She wrote:

I learned a lot from reading the article about the stages of
development in the model of oppressed people. As a White
person going through my stages of identity development, I
do not take time to think about the struggle people of color
go through to reach a stage of complete understanding. I
am glad that I know about the stages because now I can
understand people of color's behavior in certain situations.
For example, when people of color stay to themselves and
appear to be in a clique, it is not because they are being rude
as I originally thought. Rather they are engaged perhaps in
the Immersion stage.

Mary, another White student, wrote:

I found the entire Cross model of racial identity development
very enlightening. I knew that there were stages of racial
identity development before I entered this class. I did not
know what they were, or what they really entailed. After
reading through this article I found myself saying, "Oh. That
explains why she reacted this way to this incident instead of

> how she would have a year ago." Clearly this person has
> entered a different stage and is working through different
> problems from a new viewpoint. Thankfully, the model
> provides a degree of hope that people will not always be
> angry, and will not always be separatists, etc. Although I'm
> not really sure about that.

Conversely, when students of color understand the stages of White racial identity development, they can be more tolerant or appreciative of a White student's struggle with guilt, for example. After reading about the stages of White identity development, Sonia, a Latina previously quoted, wrote:

> This article was the one that made me feel that my own
> prejudices were showing. I never knew that Whites went
> through an identity development of their own.

She later told me outside of class that she found it much easier to listen to some of the things White students said because she could understand their potentially offensive comments as part of a developmental stage.

Sharon, an African-American woman, also found that an understanding of the respective stages of racial identity development helped her to understand some of the interactions she had had with White students since coming to college. She wrote:

> There is a lot of clash that occurs between Black and White
> people at college which is best explained by their respective
> stages of development. Unfortunately schools have not
> helped to alleviate these problems earlier in life.

In a course on the psychology of racism, it is easy to build in the provision of this information as part of the course content. For instructors teaching courses with race-related content in other fields, it may seem less natural to do so. However, the inclusion of articles on racial identity development and/or class discussion of these issues in conjunction with the other strategies that have been suggested can improve student receptivity to the course content in important ways, making it a very useful investment of class time. Because the stages describe kinds of behavior that many people have commonly observed in themselves, as well as in their own intraracial and interracial interactions, my experience has been that most students grasp the basic conceptual framework fairly easily, even if they do not have a background in psychology.

## Empowering Students as Change Agents

Heightening students' awareness of racism without also developing an awareness of the possibility of change is a prescription for despair. I consider it unethical to do one without the other. Exploring strategies to empower students as change agents is thus a necessary part of the process of talking about race and learning about racism. As was previously mentioned, students find it very helpful to read about and hear from individuals who have been effective change agents. Newspaper and magazine articles, as well as biographical or autobiographical essays or book excerpts, are often important sources for this information.

I also ask students to work in small groups to develop an action plan of their own for interrupting racism. While I do not consider it appropriate to require students to engage in anti-racist activity (since I believe this should be a personal choice the student makes for him/herself), students are required to think about the possibility. Guidelines are provided (see Katz, 1978), and the plans that they develop over several weeks are presented at the end of the semester. Students are generally impressed with each other's good ideas, and, in fact, they often do go on to implement their projects.

Joanne, a White student who initially struggled with feelings of guilt, wrote:

> I thought that hearing others' ideas for action plans was interesting and informative. It really helps me realize (reminds me) the many choices and avenues there are once I decided to be an ally. Not only did I develop my own concrete way to be an ally, I have found many other ways that I, as a college student, can be an active anti-racist. It was really empowering.

Another way all students can be empowered is by offering them the opportunity to consciously observe their own development. The taped exercise to which some of the previously quoted students have referred is an example of one way to provide this opportunity. At the beginning of the semester, students are given an interview guide with many open-ended questions concerning racial attitudes and opinions. They are asked to interview themselves on tape as a way of recording their own ideas for future reference. Though the tapes are collected, students are assured that no one (including me) will listen to them. The tapes are returned near the end of the semester, and students are asked to listen to their own tapes and use their understanding of racial identity development to discuss it in essay form.

The resulting essays are often remarkable and underscore the psychological importance of giving students the chance to examine racial issues in the classroom. The following was written by Elaine, a White woman:

> Another common theme that was apparent in the tape was that, for the most part, I was aware of my own ignorance and was embarrassed because of it. I wanted to know more about the oppression of people in the country so that I could do something about it. Since I have been here, I have begun to be actively resistant to racism. I have been able to confront my grandparents and some old friends from high school when they make racist comments. Taking this psychology of racism class is another step toward active resistance to racism. I am trying to educate myself so that I have a knowledge base to work from.
>
> When the tape was made, I was just beginning to be active and just beginning to be educated. I think I am now starting to move into the redefinition stage. I am starting to feel ok about being White. Some of my guilt is dissipating, and I do not feel as ignorant as I used to be. I think I have an understanding of racism; how it effects (sic) myself, and how it effects this country. Because of this I think I can be more active in doing something about it.

In the words of Louise, a Black female student:

> One of the greatest things I learned from this semester in general is that the world is not only Black and White, nor is the United States. I learned a lot about my own erasure of many American ethnic groups .... I am in the (immersion) stage of my identity development. I think I am also dangling a little in the (encounter) stage. I say this because a lot of my energies are still directed toward White people. I began writing a poem two days ago and it was directed to White racism. However, I have also become more Black-identified. I am reaching to the strength in Afro-American heritage. I am learning more about the heritage and history of Afro-American culture. Knowledge = strength and strength = power.

While some students are clearly more self-reflective and articulate about their own process than others, most students experience the opportunity to talk and learn about these issues as a transforming process. In my experience, even those students who are frustrated by aspects of the course find themselves changed by it. One such student wrote in her final journal entry:

> What I felt to be a major hindrance to me was the amount of people. Despite the philosophy, I really never felt at ease enough to speak openly about the feelings I have and kind of watched the class pull farther and farther apart as the semester went on.... I think that it was your attitude that kept me intrigued by the topics we were studying despite my frustrations with the class time. I really feel as though I made some significant moves in my understanding of other people's positions in our world as well as of my feelings of racism, and I feel very good about them. I feel like this class has moved me in the right direction. I'm on a roll I think, because I've been introduced to so much.

Facilitating student development in this way is a challenging and complex task, but the results are clearly worth the effort.

## IMPLICATIONS FOR THE INSTITUTION

What are the institutional implications for an understanding of racial identity development theory beyond the classroom? How can this framework be used to address the pressing issues of increasing diversity and decreasing racial tensions on college campuses? How can providing opportunities in the curriculum to talk about race and learn about racism affect the recruitment and retention of students of color specifically, especially when the majority of the students enrolled are White?

The fact is, educating White students about race and racism changes attitudes in ways that go beyond the classroom boundaries. As White students move through their own stages of identity development, they take their friends with them by engaging them in dialogue. They share the articles they have read with roommates, and involve them in their projects. An example of this involvement can be seen in the following journal entry, written by Larry, a White man:

> Here it is our fifth week of class and more and more I am becoming aware of the racism around me. Our second project made things clearer, because while watching T.V. I picked up many kinds of discrimination and stereotyping. Since the project was over, I still find myself watching these shows and picking up bits and pieces every show I watch. Even my friends will be watching a show and they will say, "Hey, Larry, put that in your paper." Since they know I am taking this class, they are looking out for these things. They are also watching what they say around me for fear that I will use them as an example. For example, one of my friends has this fascination with making fun of Jewish people. Before I would listen to his comments and take them in stride, but now I confront him about his comments.

The heightened awareness of the White students enrolled in the class has a ripple effect in their peer group, which helps to create a climate in which students of color and other targeted groups (Jewish students, for example) might feel more comfortable. It is likely that White students who have had the opportunity to learn about racism in a supportive atmosphere will be better able to be allies to students of color in extracurricular settings, like student government meetings and other organizational settings, where students of color often feel isolated and unheard.

At the same time, students of color who have had the opportunity to examine the ways in which racism may have affected their own lives are able to give voice to their own experience, and to validate it rather than be demoralized by it. An understanding of internalized oppression can help students of color recognize the ways in which they may have unknowingly participated in their own victimization, or the victimization of others. They may be able to move beyond victimization to empowerment, and share their learning with others, as Sharon, a previously quoted Black woman, planned to do.

Campus communities with an understanding of racial identity development could become more supportive of special-interest groups, such as the Black Student Union or the Asian Student Alliance, because they would recognize them not as "separatist" but as important outlets for students of color who may be at the Encounter or Immersion stage of racial identity development. Not only could speakers of color be sought out to add diversity to campus programming, but Whites who had made a commitment to unlearning their own racism could be offered as models to those White students looking for new ways to understand their own Whiteness, and to students of color looking for allies.

It has become painfully clear on many college campuses across the United States that we cannot have successfully multiracial campuses without talking about race and learning about racism. Providing a forum where this discussion can take place safely over a semester, a time period that allows personal and group development to unfold in ways that day-long or weekend programs do not, may be among the most proactive learning opportunities an institution can provide.

## ENDNOTES

1   A similar point could be made about other issues of oppression, such as anti-Semitism, homophobia and heterosexism, ageism, and so on.

2   While similar models of racial identity development exist, Cross and Helms are referenced here because they are among the most frequently cited

writers on Black racial identity development and on White racial identity development, respectively. For a discussion of the commonalities between these and other identity development models, see Phinney (1989, 1990) and Helms (1990).

3    Both Parham (1989) and Phinney (1989) suggest that a preference for the dominant group is not always a characteristic of this stage. For example, children raised in households and communities with explicitly positive Afrocentric attitudes may absorb a pro-Black perspective, which then serves as the starting point for their own exploration of racial identity.

4    After being introduced to this model and Helms's model of White identity development, students are encouraged to think about how the models might apply to their own experience or the experiences of people they know. As is reflected in the cited journal entries, some students resonate to the theories quite readily, easily seeing their own process of growth reflected in them. Other students are sometimes puzzled because they feel as though their own process varies from these models, and may ask if it is possible to "skip" a particular stage, for example. Such questions provide a useful departure point for discussing the limitations of stage theories in general, and the potential variations in experience that make questions of racial identity development so complex.

5    Examples of useful articles include essays by McIntosh *(1983)*, Lester *(1987)*, and Braden *(1987)*. Each of these combines autobiographical material, as well as a conceptual framework for understanding some aspect of racism that students find very helpful. Bowser and Hunt's *(1981)* edited book, *Impacts of Racism on Whites*, though less autobiographical in nature, is also a valuable resource.

6    Class size has a direct bearing on my ability to create safety in the classroom. Dividing the class into pairs or small groups of five or six students to discuss initial reactions to a particular article or film helps to increase participation, both in the small groups and later to the large group discussions.

## References

Barnard, H.F. (ed.) (1987). *Outside the magic circle: The autobiography of Virginia Foster Durr*, New York: Simon & Schuster. (Originally published in 1985 by University of Alabama Press)

Bowser, B.P., and R.G. Hunt (1981). *Impacts of racism on whites*. Beverly Hills: Sage.

Braden, A. (1987, April–May). Undoing racism: Lessons for the peace movement. *The Nonviolent Activist*, 3–6.

Bronstein, P.A., and K. Quina (eds.) (1988). *Teaching a psychology of people: Resources for gender and sociocultural awareness*, Washington, DC: American Psychological Association.

Cross, W.E., Jr. (1971). The Negro to black conversion experience: Toward a psychology of black liberation. *Black World*, 20(9), 13–27.

Cross, W.E., Jr. (1978). The Cross and Thomas models of psychological nigrescence. *Journal of Black Psychology*, 5(1), 13–19.

Cross, W.E., Jr. (1991). *Shades of black: Diversity in African-American identity*, Philadelphia: Temple University Press.

Cross, W.E., Jr., T.A. Parham, and J.E. Helms (1991). The stages of black identity development: Nigrescence models. In R. Jones (ed.), *Black psychology* (3rd ed.), pp. 319–338, San Francisco: Cobb and Henry.

Derman-Sparks, L., C.T. Higa, and B. Sparks (1980). Children, race and racism: How race awareness develops. *Interracial Books for Children Bulletin*, 11(3/4), 3–15.

Helms, J.E. (ed.) (1990). *Black and white racial identity: Theory, research and practice*, Westport, CT: Greenwood Press.

Highlen, P.S., A.L. Reynolds, E.M. Adams, T.C. Hanley, L.J. Myers, C. Cox, and S. Speight (1988, August 13). *Self-identity development model of oppressed people: Inclusive model for all?* Paper presented at the American Psychological Association Convention, Atlanta, GA.

Hull, G.T., P.B. Scott, and B. Smith (eds.) (1982). *All the women are white, all the blacks are men, but some of us are brave: Black women's studies*, Old Westbury, NY: Feminist Press.

Katz, J.H. (1978). *White awareness: Handbook for anti-racism training*, Norman: University of Oklahoma Press.

Lester, J. (1987). *What happens to the mythmakers when the myths are found to be untrue?* Unpublished paper, Equity Institute, Emeryville, CA.

McIntosh, P. (1988). *White privilege and male privilege: A personal account of coming to see correspondences through work in women's studies*. Working paper, Wellesley College Center for Research on Women, Wellesley, MA.

McIntosh, P. (1989, July/August). White privilege: Unpacking the invisible knapsack. *Peace and Freedom*, 10–12.

Parham, T.A. (1989). Cycles of psychological nigrescence. *The Counseling Psychologist*, 17(2), 187–226.

Phinney, J. (1989). Stages of ethnic identity in minority group adolescents. *Journal of Early Adolescence*, 9, 34–39.

Phinney, J. (1990). Ethnic identity in adolescents and adults: Review of research. *Psychological Bulletin*, 108(3), 499–514.

Phinney, J.S., and M.J. Rotheram (eds.) (1987). *Children's ethnic socialization: Pluralism and development*, Newbury Park, CA: Sage.

Schuster, M.R., and S.R. Van Dyne (eds.) (1985). *Women's place in the academy: Transforming the liberal arts curriculum*, Totowa, NJ: Rowman & Allanheld.

Wellman, D. (1977). *Portraits of white racism*, New York: Cambridge University Press.

## Exercises

1. What are some of the advantages and disadvantages of using multiple ways of learning and sharing about racism and racial identity.
2. Racism hurts us all. What are your thoughts on this?
3. Racial identity development theory illustrates five stages of the process of learning about oneself and openly dealing with racism and racial identity. What are some of the important points of this theory? What are some of its limitations? Please explain in each case.
4. How would you factor in other forms of oppression without subsuming race (or any other) in teaching about racial identity and racism?

# Chapter 11

# Anti-Racist Education and Moral Behaviour: Lessons from the Holocaust

## Geoffrey Short

Yad Vashem, the Holocaust memorial and documentation centre in Israel, honours not only the millions of Jews murdered by the Nazis but also the "Righteous Gentiles" throughout Europe (and elsewhere) who attempted to protect them. The exceptional courage of around 11,000 rescuers has so far been recorded and more names are likely to be added in the future. But whatever the final tally, the number will remain infinitesimal compared with those who preferred to look the other way — the bystanders, whose passivity facilitated the destruction of the bulk of European Jewry. In the words of the historian Ian Kershaw (1983), "the road to Auschwitz was built by hate but paved with indifference." It was the indifference of ordinary people, the international community, and the Protestant and Catholic churches that calls to mind Edmund Burke's warning that "the one condition necessary for the triumph of evil is that good men do nothing."

In Germany, the bystanders were not, for the most part, rabid antisemites. On the contrary, the Nazis never secured much more than one-third of the popular vote and according to Ronnie Landau (1992, p. 223), while "antisemitic propaganda may have played a fundamental role in unifying the Nazi party ... it certainly did not perform the same function with the public at large." Landau goes on to quote from a Gestapo report of September 1934.

> Undoubtedly the Jewish question is not the main problem
> of the German public …. Utterances on the Jewish peril are
> dismissed as of no account and those engaged in enlightening
> the population are to a certain extent depicted as fools. (cited
> in Landau, p. 223)

Large sections of German society, for a variety of reasons, disapproved of Nazi violence towards Jews and many were genuinely appalled by the brutality of the *Kristallnacht* pogrom of November 1938. None the less, the fact remains that throughout the Nazi reign of terror, the overwhelming majority of Germans offered no succour to their Jewish compatriots.

It is not only historians who have shown an interest in the role of the bystander. Social psychologists have been intrigued by the phenomenon ever since a woman was murdered in New York in 1964 in the presence of around 40 neighbours, none of whom came to her assistance (Latiné and Darley, 1970). A considerable literature on bystanders, both historical and psychological, has built up over the years, but its self-evident implications for anti-racist education appear to have gone unheeded. An analogous situation has arisen in respect of another well-known phenomenon in social psychology, namely, the power of the peer group to impose conformity on its members. Anti-racists have failed to recognise the relevance of experimental work in this area to their own practice despite the fact that "racist actions are generally performed by *groups* and very rarely by lone individuals" (Hewitt et al., 1996, p. 24, original emphasis). Holocaust historians have confirmed the part played by peer group pressure in racist atrocities, with Christopher Browning (1992) providing a particularly powerful illustration in his book *Ordinary Men: Reserve Police Battalion 101 and the Final Solution in Poland*. He describes how 500 men in their thirties and forties, from working- and lower-middle-class backgrounds, were sent to Poland in 1942 to murder Jews inhabiting the country's smaller cities. Many of them were drawn from a social milieu that was relatively unreceptive to Nazi ideology, yet in the space of 11 months they killed nearly 40,000 Jews and dispatched a further 45,000 to their deaths at Treblinka. The most significant detail in Browning's account is that the men were not compelled to participate in the killing of their defenceless victims. There was no punishment for opting out, as the battalion commander made quite clear. None the less, no more than 10–20% of the men took up the offer to withdraw. In attempting to explain the behaviour of the others, Browning concluded that it could best be understood in terms of an urge to conform.

Anti-racists cannot afford to ignore the lessons of history. In the light of what is known of the consequences of bystander behaviour and conformity to the peer group, anti-racist education must be directed towards nurturing in students a willingness to *act* against racism. In his seminal work, *The Nature of Prejudice*, the American psychologist. Gordon Allport (1954) referred to the need for action against racism as the promotion of "militant tolerance." Those who display it, he wrote, "are fighters. They will not put up with any infringement of the rights of others. They are intolerant of intolerance." He acknowledged that some of these militants were "bigots in reverse," hating, for example, "Southern whites as irrationally as some whites hate Negroes." Nevertheless, he went on to observe that:

> Other militants ... seem capable of a finer analysis of the issue. They see that a particular act at a particular time, perhaps the passage of a particular legislative bill, will advance the interests of minority groups, and thereupon throw themselves into the battle. They do so on the basis of a realistic appraisal of their own values, and without stereotyping the opponent. Or they may deliberately choose to flaunt social custom and risk ostracism in order to demonstrate friendship for the outcast, again for the realisation of personal values. (Allport, 1954, p. 430)

A necessary condition of militant tolerance is that students care about ethnic groups other than their own. For white students to care about ethnic minorities they ought, in the first instance, to acquire knowledge about racism and this, historically, has been the principal achievement of anti-racist education. There are, however, other constraints on militant tolerance that anti-racists have neglected and continue to neglect despite vigorous debate on other matters. In this article I am concerned to show that the latter is a distraction as far as anti-racist activity is concerned. After drawing attention to research pertinent to encouraging such activity, I consider ways in which anti-racist education might be re-shaped in order to obviate its current limitations. Although I make my case with reference to Britain, the issues raised are relevant to all countries which aim to combat racism through formal education. They are, perhaps, particularly relevant in countries such as Canada where anti-racist education, in some provinces, has been heavily influenced by the British model (Bonnett and Carrington, 1996).

## Anti-racism Past and Present

Since the late 1970s, Britain's educational system has sought increasingly to advance racial justice by committing itself to anti-racist education — "a range of organizational, curricular, and pedagogical strategies which aim to promote racial equality and to eliminate attendant forms of discrimination and oppression, both individual and institutional" (Troyna and Carrington, 1990). Troyna had previously argued that of all the policy initiatives implemented in the name of anti-racism,

> the formal curriculum has received most attention. As numerous books and pamphlets have indicated, a politicised curriculum would discuss the origins and manifestations of racism and would be directed as much to white as (to) black students. (Troyna and Williams, 1986, p. 47)

From the outset, anti-racists appear to have given little thought to the means by which their aspirations were to be realised. There seems rather to have been a tacit assumption that by a process akin to osmosis students would acquire a disposition to act against racism simply by learning (in pedagogically appropriate contexts) about its "origins and manifestations." In the literature on anti-racist education, psychological discussion about how best to deal with the problem of racism has been all but drowned out by the welter of philosophical and sociological discussion about the nature of racism. As long ago as 1986, Ann Dummett wrote that "debate on race, culture, religion and moral education is often bogged down in abstract definition and theoretical arguments ..." (1986,

p. 10) and it would appear from relatively recent contributions to the literature (from among those most committed to anti-racism) that her criticism remains valid. For example, Tariq Modood (1989) objects to the municipal anti-racism of the 1980s (associated with Labour-controlled local authorities and especially the Greater London Council) on the grounds that it treats race and racism only in terms of colour. Concerned in particular about the situation facing British Muslims, he demurs at the emphasis within conventional anti-racist education given to "colour racism" and the concomitant rejection of cultural issues. In his view, municipal racism's obsession with colour has meant that it inevitably failed to connect with the most pressing concerns of the ethnic minority population.

Ali Rattansi (1992) is another critic who argues forcefully for the centrality of culture. He regards it as fundamental to anti-racist education but insists, along with Paul Gilroy (1990), that it be treated critically. In other words, he wishes to underline its dynamic and fluid quality. Rattansi also alleges that anti-racist education has "produced only patchy evidence of success" (1992, p. 33). He attributes this undistinguished track record to the rationalist pedagogy with which it is associated.

A further assault on anti-racist education emanating from the Left was mounted by the Burnage enquiry (MacDonald et al., 1989). The latter had been set up in the wake of the murder of an Asian teenager at a secondary school in Manchester and was especially hostile towards what it called "symbolic" or "moral" anti-racism. This approach was condemned for treating all blacks as victims of racism and all whites as perpetrators.

In the light of these strictures (not to mention those from less supportive quarters (e.g., Phillips, 1996) it would seem that anti-racism, at least in Britain, is currently under siege. David Gillborn (1995) sums up its parlous condition as follows:

> Given our current state of knowledge, it is difficult to arrive
> at any secure judgement about the overall success or failure
> of anti-racism in education: we simply know too little about
> what constitutes good anti-racist practice. (Gillborn, 1995,
> pp. 79-80)

I have already intimated that one of the things that does not constitute good anti-racist practice is to assume that knowledge of racism, however competently it may be imparted, is sufficient to guarantee anti-racist behaviour. In any given situation, knowledge may be a necessary condition of acting in one way rather than another or of not acting at all, but it is only one such condition and not necessarily the most important. Anti-racist education has been at fault in failing to recognise this basic truth. While a major aim of such education is to develop in the young a propensity to act against racism, this aim will not be achieved unless anti-racists engage with constraints on moral behaviour and particularly with the tendency towards bystander behaviour and conformity to the peer group. If anti-racists were to concern themselves with these inhibitory influences they would, perforce, acknowledge a number of issues (other than knowledge of racism) that need to be addressed if students are to take action against manifestations of racism.

## BYSTANDER BEHAVIOUR AND CONFORMITY

Over the past two to three years, the United Kingdom has experienced a certain moral panic following the murder of a London headmaster and the massacre of young children at Dunblane. According to an editorial in *The Times* (January 16, 1996) these outrages prompted "an anguished examination of the national conscience." Calls for a moral renewal came from many quarters, but most of the press coverage was devoted to publicising the views of the nation's religious leaders and the government's chief adviser on the curriculum, Dr. Nick Tate. The Archbishop of Canterbury exhorted parents, schools, and churches to bring about a return to the Ten Commandments and Tate actually proposed his own version. His list of "commandments" contained no surprises, making reference to such time-honoured virtues as honesty, patience, and politeness. Equally unsurprising was the outcome of the National Forum for Values in Education and the Community set up in 1996 to consider "whether there is any agreement on the values, attitudes and behaviours that schools should promote on society's behalf." There was agreement on a number of values, including truth, human rights, and justice but, predictably perhaps, in view of its remit, the Forum made no mention of the need for schools to foster in students *appropriate* nonconformity and the courage to act on their convictions. The absence of these qualities from the curriculum is highly significant precisely because they constitute potential constraints on bystander behaviour and conformity to the peer group. Their absence is doubly regrettable because teachers are, in fact, able to draw on a considerable body of research literature that has accumulated in both areas. I discuss below some of the more salient findings from this literature before elaborating, in a subsequent section, on their educational implications.

Psychologists studying bystander behaviour (and the related phenomena of altruism and prosociality) have observed that people possess a stronger tendency to help those they see as similar to themselves and with whom they have a special bond or commitment. They are, for example, more likely to respond sympathetically towards compatriots than towards foreigners (Feldman, 1968), a tendency well illustrated by the history of the Holocaust in France. The Vichy government protected Jews who were French citizens but willingly handed over to the Nazis those who had entered the country seeking refuge. In view of the importance of perceived similarity as a determinant of altruistic behaviour (Wrightsman and Deaux, 1981), it may be no coincidence that in occupied Europe during World War II,

> the readiness to protect Jews, regardless of risk, was most pronounced in societies where they were a small minority, *integrated into the fabric of the nation.* [They were least vulnerable in] countries whose identity was unchallenged, where Jews posed no threat, cultural, political or economic. (Silver, 1992, p. 161, emphasis added)

In the light of this comment, my recent work with Bruce Carrington on the development of children's understanding of their national identity would appear to have major implications for bystander behaviour (e.g., Carrington and Short, 1995; et seq.). We found that a small but significant minority of 8 to 12-year-olds in England, Scotland, and the United States construed their national identity in culturally monolithic terms. In other words, their conception of national belonging entailed an adherence to a given set of cultural practices and values. The danger in this way of thinking is not simply that it treats the cultural distinctiveness of ethnic minorities as evidence of their detachment from the nation, but that students who operate with such a mindset are unlikely to feel any kind of bond or commitment towards minorities, let alone a special one. The ability to display empathy — the vicarious experience of another person's perceptions and emotions — is also related to altruism (Hoffman, 1976) but here, too, research suggests that people generally display more empathy towards those they regard as similar to themselves.

The study of altruistic behaviour that is of most interest in relation to racism was undertaken just over a decade ago by Sam Oliner and Pearl Oliner (1988). They focused on the rescue of Jews during World War II and claimed, on the basis of interviews with hundreds of rescuers, bystanders, and survivors that:

> What distinguished rescuers was not their lack of concern with self, external approval or achievement, but rather their capacity for extensive relationships — their stronger sense of attachment to others and their feeling of responsibility for the welfare of others, including those outside their immediate familial or communal circles. (Oliner and Oliner, 1988, p. 249)

They noted that "no one developmental course inevitably produces an extensive person." However, certain characteristics were common among rescuers. For example, they more often came from families in which parents modelled caring behaviour (towards other family members and neighbours) and communicated caring values. Parental discipline was relatively lax but included discussing with children the consequences of their behaviour for others. At the same time, parents set high standards that they expected their children to attain in respect of caring. The themes of identification with a moral parent and the use of nonphysical punishment echoed the findings of earlier studies, e.g., London, 1970; Hoffman, 1975.

Research in the area of conformity has largely been laboratory-based. The best known investigations were conducted in the 1950s by Solomon Asch, who found that many of his subjects would proffer what they knew to be an incorrect response to a question having witnessed others (who were, in fact, paid stooges) commit the same "error." He went on to record that his subjects were far less willing to go along with the majority view if they believed they were in the presence of at least one other nonconformer (Asch, 1958).

Efforts have been made to define the conformist personality but no clear-cut picture has emerged; different people tend to conform under different circumstances. None the less, there is a strong suggestion in the literature that conformers are prone to low self-esteem (e.g., Stang, 1972). This is consistent with Browning's analysis of the ordinary men of Reserve Police Battalion 101 who participated in the killing. They were found to conform partly because they could not tolerate the threat of isolation, rejection, and ostracism, especially as there was no one other than their comrades to turn to for support and social contact. They also feared that refusal to conform would be interpreted by their fellow men as a form of moral reproach; in other words, they were keen not to appear morally superior.

## Educational Implications

### Bystander Behaviour
It has been pointed out that we are more willing to demonstrate altruistic behaviour towards those we see as similar to ourselves in significant respects. This suggests, in the first instance, that anti-racists need to pay attention not only to the perception that young people have of different ethnic groups, but specifically to their misconceptions of those groups. Indeed, anti-racists should have as one of their priorities the need to challenge any misconception that depicts ethnic minorities as culturally divorced from the mainstream. More generally, they should work towards developing a common sense of belonging, a task that clearly resonates with the current debate in the United Kingdom over the role of education in forging a national identity. The debate essentially revolves around the extent to which cultural pluralism should inform the curriculum. While some commentators, such as Nick Tate (*The Times*, October 31, 1996) and Melanie Phillips (1996), argue that the interests of minorities are best served by strengthening what they describe as "the dominant culture," others maintain that inclusivist notions of British identity are

more likely to result from a curriculum that draws heavily on a range of cultural traditions (Carrington and Short, 1995; Short and Carrington, 1996). Certainly, the present situation in France, where a school system that generally abjures multiculturalism exists alongside a thriving racist political party, does not inspire confidence in the line taken by Phillips and Tate. However, if teachers are to be effective in promoting the idea of Britain as a society to which all ethnic groups feel a sense of belonging, they must take steps to counter the "new racism" (Barker, 1981), a hallmark of the still influential cultural restorationist wing of the Conservative party. The central tenet of this form of racism is that cultural pluralism threatens national cohesion, a belief that implicitly identifies ethnic minorities as "the enemy within." In the words of the Conservative journalist T.E. Utley, "No Tory can accept the view that the existence in one small and homogeneous island of a huge variety of divergent cultures and religions is in itself a source of strength" (cited in Rich, 1986, p. 64). The same point was made at the 1997 annual conference of the Conservative party by Lord Tebbitt, the party's former chairman. He said:

> You can't have a whole load of different cultures in one society. You have one culture for one society and if you get different societies mixed up, living close, cheek by jowl, you will splinter our society in the way that devolution is splintering the UK.

What we have to do is, with the more recent arrivals, imbue in them and their children a sense that the Battle of Britain is part of their history. Otherwise we're not going to have a single society. We're going to have a splintered, fractured society which will be at odds with itself. (cited in the Guardian, October 7, 1997)

In order to promote an inclusivist view of national identity it is important for teachers to make their pupils aware that Britishness is not, and never has been, culturally monolithic. They should know that the social fabric of the United Kingdom has long been able to withstand the tensions stemming from different religious affiliations as well as those arising from social class, ethnic, and regional divisions.

The message that ethnic minorities do not pose any sort of threat to British society is likely to have a greater impact on white students if it is reinforced by the students' own experiences. It is for this reason that, wherever possible, schools should encourage inter-ethnic contact. It needs to be borne in mind, however, that contact between different ethnic groups will only have beneficial consequences if it meets certain conditions. From the standpoint of challenging negative stereotypes (and thereby helping to encourage an inclusivist view of national identity) it has been found that "the attributes of the disliked group members with whom the contact occurs [must be] such as to disconfirm the prevailing beliefs about them" (Cook, 1978).

The benefits of mixing with members of other ethnic groups are not restricted to the cognitive for, in addition to undermining stereotypes, contact may lead to friendship. The value of friendship in relation to bystander behaviour is self-evident. Indeed, as Latané and Darley (1970) have shown, even the briefest acquaintance with someone else diminishes the likelihood of standing aside should that person subsequently require assistance. The head of the SS, Heinrich Himmler, implicitly recognised this psychological truth in a speech delivered before some of his henchmen in October 1943:

> "The Jewish people is to be exterminated" says every party member. "That's clear, it's part of our programme, elimination of the Jews, extermination, right we'll do it". And then they all come along, the eighty million good Germans, and each one has his decent Jew. Of course, the others are swine, but this one is a first-class Jew (cited in Bauman, 1991, p. 187).

Turning to the link between empathy and altruism (Hoffman, 1976), research suggests that, other things being equal, the greater a student's capacity for empathy, the less chance there is of that student becoming a bystander. Schools should therefore do what they can to develop their pupils' ability to see things as others see them, and the teaching of English and drama have traditionally been recognised as useful in this respect. There is, however, no automatic connection between high levels of empathy and altruistic behaviour. The critical issue is whether the victim is thought to be deserving. As Derek Wright (1971) argues:

> One of the striking features of racially prejudiced people is
> their failure to respond empathically to the sufferings of the
> members of the groups they have rejected. This failure ... is
> probably related to their prejudiced belief that the others
> are not quite human, or that their suffering is merited.
> (Wright, 1971, p. 136)

Thus, in the context of race relations, teaching to promote empathy is likely to have the desired result only if it is undertaken as part of a programme which aims to subvert the view of ethnic minorities as less deserving of the good life than the ethnic majority.

One further aspect of the literature on bystanders with clear-cut implications for education concerns the value of teaching about the literature itself. Research indicates that students who have acquired knowledge of the bystander phenomenon are less likely to fall prey to it (Beaman et al., 1978). Ideally, such teaching would constitute an aspect of citizenship education.

## Conformity to Peer Group Pressure

A priori, one would expect higher levels of nonconformity in societies where (appropriate) nonconformity is widely recognised as a virtue. One means of creating a society of this kind might be through the teaching of history. Specifically, we should consider the merit of reconceptualising, or at least of broadening, our notion of a hero so that students are encouraged to laud acts of nonconformity (on condition that such acts are compatible with natural justice). In studying the life of Sir Winston Churchill, for instance, less attention might be given to his role as a wartime leader and rather more to "the wilderness years," when, at considerable personal cost, he championed the unpopular cause of re-armament. The Holocaust, of course, offers considerable scope for teaching about heroism in the context of nonconformity, but recent research (in the south of England) into the way the subject is taught indicates that full advantage is not being taken of this opportunity (Short, 1995). It was found that some teachers did not raise the issue of rescuers with their pupils and those who did tended to discuss only the exploits of Oskar Schindler. The vast majority of textbooks also made no mention of rescuers. In a follow-up study, a group of 14- and 15-year-olds was asked, among other things, if there were any heroes in the Holocaust (Short, 1999). Predictably, some mentioned Schindler, but most said either that there were none or claimed that the Jews themselves were heroes simply for having survived. Individual acts of rescue such as those highlighted by Eric Silver (1992) in his *Book of the Just* should form an integral part of any course on the Holocaust. Indeed, it could be argued that from the standpoint of promoting moral behaviour and appropriate nonconformity in particular, we devote too much time to victims and not enough to rescuers. Perhaps we need to redress the balance, giving less attention to Anne Frank and rather more to the likes of Mip Giess (who risked her life looking after the Frank family when they were in hiding). Social learning theory (e.g., Bandura, 1977) leaves little doubt about the importance of role models in shaping behaviour. The fact that the overwhelming majority of rescuers were ordinary members of the public makes them particularly potent as role models because of the relative ease with which students can identify with them.

It is not only the history curriculum that lends itself to teaching about nonconformity, for religious education is also important in this respect. Teaching about different faith communities should concentrate on more than just their beliefs and values and their festivals, rituals, and places of worship, as demanded by traditional multiculturalism; it should also stress what each teaches about nonconformity. In Christianity, for example, students should learn about and discuss the risks that Jesus took in violating the religious conventions of his time. A similar approach could be followed in relation to the prophet Mohammed and, as far as Judaism is concerned, students could usefully focus on the Old Testament prophets as exemplars of nonconformity.

Anti-racists should not only be concerned with the curriculum in their efforts to create a climate more receptive to nonconformity. Evidence of low self-esteem among those with a tendency to conform demands that they also take an interest in the multiplicity of ways in which schools and individual teachers can influence this crucial dimension of their pupils' personality. As intelligence is known to be correlated positively with ability to resist peer-group pressure (Gahagan, 1975), schools should be especially concerned to celebrate the achievements (and thereby enhance the self-esteem) of their academically less talented pupils.

One of the drawbacks in helping students to withstand peer group pressure is that they may come to see nonconformity per se as a virtue, particularly if it derives from the exercise of moral autonomy. The distinguished historian Lucy Dawidowicz (1992), when examining a number of Holocaust curricula in the United States, warned of the consequences:

> Some curricula teach that following one's "conscience" is morally superior to obeying one's parent or the just laws of society. None recommend that students read Plato's *Crito*, where they might come upon Socrates' refusal to accept his friends' plan to organise his escape from prison: "Do you imagine that a city can continue to exist and not be turned upside down if the legal judgements that are pronounced in it have no force, but are nullified and destroyed by private persons?" Nor does any curriculum question the reliability of conscience as a guide to distinguishing between good and bad, right and wrong. (Dawidowicz, 1992, pp. 79–80)

Oliner and Oliner (1988) adopt a similar line. They are strongly opposed to the view, expressed most famously by Adorno et al. (1950) in *The Authoritarian Personality*, that links moral courage to autonomy and independence. The corollary is that "those who behave (ethically) but do so in compliance with social norms or standards set by individuals or groups close to them or because of empathic arousal are presumed to be in some way morally deficient" (Oliner and Oliner, p. 257). In rejecting this view, the Oliners maintain that:

> Empathy and concern with social norms simply represent alternative but equally profound ways of apprehending moral claims, as Blum, Gilligan and Noddings have so eloquently argued. According to our study, they are the most common ways. Like principles, they too can inspire heroic moral courage. (Oliner and Oliner, 1988, p. 258)

It has certainly not been my intention to play down the importance of either empathy or social norms as sources of moral behaviour. On the contrary, I advocate anti-racist education precisely because I wish its core values to become the norm governing relations between different ethnic groups. Realising this goal, however, will require anti-racists to re-think their role.

## Re-Shaping the Anti-racist Agenda

If anti-racist education is to succeed in combating the tendency to bystander behaviour and in helping students to resist peer group pressure, its remit will have to change. This is not, of course, to deny that reducing racial inequality and opposing all forms of racial oppression must remain central to its raison d'être. It is imperative that anti-racist educators continue to identify discriminatory practices, undermine stereotypes, and deconstruct ethnocentric myths. It must, however, go further and do what it can to ensure that students, at all times, act in accordance with anti-racist values. To this end, I have argued that anti-racists ought to embrace a range of concerns that they appear hitherto and mistakenly to have regarded as irrelevant to the achievement of their aims. In relation to promoting appropriate nonconformity I have suggested that they take an interest in the many and diverse ways in which schools can influence their pupils' self-esteem and in how history and religious education can be taught with a different emphasis.

To obviate bystander behaviour I have stressed the value of an inclusive sense of national identity and urged anti-racists to recognise the importance of cultural pluralism in establishing such an identity. In the United States, Pearl Oliner (1986) has similarly stressed the benefits of inclusiveness, albeit in the form of community development. She argues that:

> It is out of a sense of community that people are more likely to engage in those acts of kindness, civility and helpfulness which enhance the quality of life. It is in the context of community consciousness that individuals begin to feel expansive responsibilities towards each other. (Oliner, 1986, p. 397)

She maintains that prosocial behaviours are vital in creating a sense of community. They "demonstrate caring and concern and they increase feelings of benevolence, bonding and rootedness." Specifically, she argues for schools to be transformed into more caring communities where:

> students, teachers, bus drivers, principals, and all others receive positive affirmation for kindness empathy, and concern . ... What is required is nothing less than institutionalised structures that promote supportive relationships with the same seriousness as is currently devoted to academic achievement. (Oliner and Oliner, 1988, pp. 258–259)

She recognises that in order to facilitate such a transformation it will be necessary, among other things, to re-structure the nature of citizenship education. The approach she derides is one which concentrates on the institution of government dealing with matters such as political parties, elections, and the Constitution and essential political concepts such as democracy. Oliner believes that this emphasis on government is excessive and decries the absence in social studies programmes of any reference to prosocial citizenship behaviours. In the light of her criticism, the situation in England and Wales, shortly after the inauguration of the National Curriculum in 1988, appeared more sanguine. "Education for Citizenship," introduced in 1990 as one of the five cross-curricular themes in the curriculum, aimed to go beyond "the machinery and processes of government" and actually referred to "shared values, such as concern for others" (National Curriculum Council, 1990, p. 4). However, the history of citizenship within the National Curriculum has been one of large-scale neglect (Whitty et al., 1992; Roberts, 1996). While the reason is due partly to its status as a cross-curricular theme, making it a matter of guidance rather than of law, it has also been sidelined as a result of the national obsession with raising standards in numeracy and literacy (Alexander, 1997). Anti-racists need to campaign not only for compulsory citizenship education, but for a content heavily marked by prosociality. The latter, according to Oliner (1983), "should acquaint students with the conventions of expressing care and concern for others regardless of social role, age, sex, ethnic identification or occupation" (p. 76). Students also "need to become aware of the prosocial activities of ordinary people much like themselves, so that they perceive opportunities for directing their own prosocial impulses in potentially effective ways" (p. 76).

The recent interim report of the advisory group on citizenship (Qualifications and Curriculum Authority, 1998) makes no direct reference to the teaching of prosocial skills. It does, however, define effective education for citizenship partly in terms of promoting "socially and morally responsible behaviour both in and beyond the classroom" (p. 13). This definition is entirely compatible with the changes to citizenship education that Oliner advocates. (It is, incidentally, equally compatible with my own recommendation that schools teach about the psychology of bystander behaviour.)

While acknowledging the value of prosociality, anti-racist educators, paradoxically, have displayed almost no interest in teaching the Holocaust, the subject which demonstrates *par excellence* the consequences of a failure of prosociality (Short, 1997). In my survey of 14- and 15-year-olds, referred to earlier, I asked them to consider what they had learnt about citizenship and about life generally as a result of studying the Holocaust. A handful spoke of the importance of dissenting from the popular view when necessary and a girl alluded to the immorality of doing nothing in the face of evil. She said: "(The Holocaust) shows how cruel humans can be to one another and that people just turn a blind eye to it." The dearth of responses to bystander behaviour and conformity illustrates the extent to which Holocaust education is failing to realise its anti-racist potential. It also illustrates the extent to which anti-racist educators, in continuing to neglect the Holocaust, are failing to fulfil their responsibilities.

## REFERENCES

Adorno, T.W., E. Frenkel-Brunswick, D. Levinson, and N. Sanford (1950). *The authoritarian personality*, New York: Harper.

Alexander, R. (1997). Beyond basics. *Times Educational Supplement*, 2, June 13.

Allport, G.W. (1954). *The nature of prejudice*, Cambridge, MA: Addison-Wesley.

Asch, S.E. (1958). Effects of group pressure upon modification and distortion of judgments. In E.E. Maccoby, T.M. Newcombe and E.L. Hartley (eds.) *Readings in social psychology*, 3rd ed., New York: Holt, Rinehart & Winston.

Bandura, A. (1977). *Social-learning theory*, Englewood Cliffs, NJ: Prentice Hall.

Barker, M. (1981). *The new racism*, London: Junction Books.

Bauman, Z. (1991). *Modernity and the Holocaust*, Oxford: Polity Press.

Beaman, A.L., P.J. Barnes, B. Klentz, and B. McQuirk (1978). Increasing helping rates through information dissemination: Teaching pays. *Personality and Social Psychology Bulletin*, 4, 406–411.

Bonnett, A., and B. Carrington (1996). Constructions of anti-racist education in Britain and Canada. *Comparative Education*, 32, 271–288.

Browning, C. (1992). *Ordinary men: Reserve police battalion 101 and the final solution in Poland*, New York: Harper Perennial.

Carrington, B., and G. Short (1995). What makes a person British? Children's conceptions of their national culture and identity. *Educational Studies*, 21, 217–238.

Cook, S.W. (1978). Interpersonal and attitudinal outcomes in cooperating interracial groups. *Journal of Research and Development in Education*, 12, 97–113.

Dawidowicz, L. (1992). *What is the use of Jewish history*, New York: Schocken Books.

Dummett, A. (1986). Race, culture and moral education. *Journal of Moral Education*, 15, 10–15.

Feldman, R.E. (1968). Response to compatriot and foreigner who seek assistance. *Journal of Personality and Social Psychology*, 36, 156–179.

Gahagan, J. (1975). *Interpersonal and group behaviour*, London: Methuen.

Gillborn, D. (1995). *Racism and anti-racism in real schools*, (Buckingham: Open University Press).

Gilroy, P. (1990). The end of anti-racism. *New Community*, 17, 71–83.

*The Guardian* (1997). Tebbit's "Battle of Britain test" revives row (News Report), October 7, 1997.

Hewitt, R., London Borough of Greenwich Central Race Equality Unit and Greenwich Youth Service (1996). *Routes of Racism; the social basis of racist action*, Stoke-on-Trent: Trentham Books.

Hoffman, M.L. (1975). Altruistic behaviour and the parent-child relationship. *Journal of Personality and Social Psychology*, 31, 937–943.

Hoffman, M.L. (1976). Empathy, role taking, guilt and development of altruistic motives. In T. Lickona (ed.) *Moral development and behaviour: theory, research and social issues*, New York: Holt, Rinehart & Winston.

Kershaw, I. (1983). *Popular opinion and political dissent in the Third Reich*, Oxford: Oxford University Press.

Landau, R. (1992). *The Nazi Holocaust*, London: I.B. Tauris.

Latané, B., and D. Darley (1970). *The unresponsive bystander: why doesn't he help?* New York: Appleton-Century-Crofts.

London, P. (1970). The rescuers: motivational hypotheses about Christians who saved Jews from the Nazis. In J. Macaulay and L. Berkowitz (eds.) *Altruism and helping behaviour: social psychological studies of some antecedents and consequences*, New York: Academic Press.

MacDonald, L, R. Bhavnani, L. Khan, and G. John (1989). *Murder in the playground: The report of the MacDonald Enquiry into Racism and Racial Violence in Manchester Schools*, London: Longsight.

Modood, T. (1989). Religious anger and minority rights, *Political Quarterly*, 60(3), 280–284.

National Curriculum Council (1990). *Education for citizenship*, York: National Curriculum Council.

Oliner, P. (1983). Putting "community" into citizenship education: The need for prosociality, *Theory and Research in Social Education*, 11, 65–81.

Oliner, P. (1986). Legitimating and implementing prosocial education. *Humboldt Journal of Social Relations*, 13, 389–408.

Oliner, S., and P. Oliner (1988). *The altruistic personality*, New York: Free Press.

Phillips, M. (1996). *All must have prizes*, London: Little, Brown & Co.

Qualifications and Curriculum Authority (1998). *Education for citizenship and the teaching of democracy in schools, part one: Advisory group initial report*, London: Qualifications and Curriculum Authority.

Rattansi, A. (1992). Changing the subject? Racism, culture and education. In J. Donald and A. Rattansi (eds.) *Race, culture and difference*, London: Sage.

Rich, P. (1986). Conservative ideology of race in modern British politics. In Z. Layton-Henry and P. Rich (eds.) *Race, government and politics in Britain*, London: Macmillan.

Roberts, M. (1996). A state of forgetfulness, *Times Educational Supplement*, June 7.

Short, G. (1995). The Holocaust in the national curriculum: a survey of teachers' attitudes and practices. *Journal of Holocaust Education*, 4, pp. 167–188.

Short, G. (1997) The role of the Holocaust in anti-racist education: A view from the United Kingdom, *New Community*, 23, pp. 75–88.

Short, G. (1999). Holocaust education and citizenship: A view from the United Kingdom. In M. Leicester, C. Modgil and S. Modgil (eds.) *Values, education and cultural diversity, vol. 6. Political and citizenship education*, London: Falmer Press.

Short, G., and B. Carrington. (1996). Anti-racist education, multiculturalism and the new racism. *Educational Review*, 48, 65–78.

Silver, E. (1992). *The book of the just*, London: Weidenfeld & Nicholson.

Stang (1972). Conformity, ability and self-esteem. *Representative Research in Social Psychology*, 3, 97–103.

Tate, N. (1996). Deliver us from these fallacies. *The Times*, October 31.

*The Times* (1996). Core of the curriculum: The commanding message of Tate and Lawrence (Editorial), January 16, 1996.

Troyna, B., and B. Carrington (1990). *Education, racism and reform*, London: Routledge.

Troyna, B., and J. Williams (1986). *Racism, education and the state*, Beckenham: Croom Helm.

Whitty, G., P. Aggleton, and G. Rows (1992). *Cross curricular work in secondary schools: Summary of results of a survey carried out in 1992: report to participating schools*, London: Institute of Education.

Wright, D. (1971). *The psychology of moral behaviour*, Harmondsworth: Penguin Books.

Wrightsman, L., and K. Deaux (1981). *Social psychology in the '80s*, 3rd ed., Monterey: California, Brooks/Cole Publishing Company.

## Exercises

1. What is the main argument in this article?
2. Why do you think it is important?
3. What is your understanding of the Holocaust?
4. Short states: Anti-racists cannot afford to ignore the lessons of history. Explain.
5. Discuss ways that you could incorporate anti-racist education in your teaching.

# Part 4

# Rethinking Inclusion: Representation and Stereotypes II

**Doxtator**
*Fluffs and Feathers:*
*An Exhibit on the Symbols of Indianness:*
*A Resource Guide*

**Slapin, Seale & Ganzales**
*How to Tell the Difference:*
*A Guide for Evaluating Children's*
*Books for Anti-Indian bias*

**TVOntario**
*Anti-Racist Education*
*(Selected Readings and Resources)*

# Chapter 12

# Fluffs and Feathers:
# An Exhibit on the
# Symbols of Indianness:
# A Resource Guide

## Deborah Doxtator

### THE IDEA OF INDIANNESS

Just a little more than a hundred years ago Canadian school texts were describing Indians as being "ferocious and quarrelsome," "great gluttons," "great drunkards." How have attitudes toward Indian people changed? Do people still carry in their minds the idea, even if it goes unsaid, that Indian culture is "primitive" and incapable of survival in a twentieth-century environment? Are some people still looking for the disappearing Indian? What does "Indian" really mean?

Teepees, headdresses, totem poles, birch bark canoes, face paint, fringes, buckskin, and tomahawks — when anyone sees images, drawings, or paintings of these things they immediately think of "Indians." They are symbols of "Indianness" that have become immediately recognizable to the public. To take it one step further, they are the symbols that the public uses in its definition of what an Indian is. To the average person, Indians, *real* Indians, in their purest form of Indianness, live in a world of long ago where there are no highrises, no snowmobiles, no colour television. They live in the woods or in mysterious unknown places called "Indian reserves." The Indians that people know best are the ones they have read about in adventure stories as a child, cut out and pasted in school projects, read about in the newspaper. They may have "played Indian" as a game, or dressed up as an Indian for Halloween. To many people Indians are not real, anymore than Bugs Bunny, Marilyn Monroe, or Anne of Green Gables are real to them. So it is not surprising that when they do meet Indian people they have some very strange ideas about how Indians behave, live, and speak.

In their excitement at meeting this celebrity, this Indian, people sometimes say foolish things, that if they thought about it, they would never say to anyone: "Is that your own hair?"; "What is the significance of that design, is it sacred?"; "Say something in *Indian*." Other Indian people have been asked whether or not their blood is red, or if feathers once grew out of their heads.

It is very difficult to discuss Indianness with any measure of neutrality. The emotions and experience of both parties in the relationship between Indians and Whites has been such that there is no easy way to discuss the facts. It is impossible to discuss the concept of Indianness without addressing racism and the injustices that have occurred. It is impossible to talk about Indianness without facing the uncomfortable reality of the dispossession of one people by another.

There is no one true perspective on Indianness. There are ranges of reactions and feelings and interpretations. What *Fluffs and Feathers* attempts to do is to present a small sample or range of images in historical and contemporary Canadian society. The viewpoint in this catalogue is my own and it is, of course, only one way of looking at how Indians have been perceived and defined by European and Canadian societies.

*Fluffs And Feathers* is about images associated with the word *Indian* — an English word that comes from a mistaken impression made by a man from Portugal in the fifteenth century. This is hardly a good reason for using it to refer to the peoples of North America's First Nations, yet that word, Indian, has certain associations and connotations that have been developing over the five centuries since contact. Indian has meant so many things, both good and bad: from an idealized all-spiritual environmentalist, to a "primitive" down-trodden welfare case. These popular images of Indians have very little to do with actual people. Instead they reflect the ideas that one culture has manufactured about another people. These images influence the concept of Indianness held by many people.

Definitions of Indianness have changed over the past four hundred years. But the change is often a development of, not a departure from, an earlier concept. In the seventeenth century, there were debates concerning whether or not Indians were animals or human beings. In the twentieth century, the debate about Indians shifted to whether or not Indians were competent human beings, capable of running their own affairs. As a result, for decades, Indian children grew up being told that their culture was inferior, their religion was wrong, and their language useless.

The concept of "The Indian" as primitive, undeveloped, and inferior has a long history that extends back into the sixteenth century (Dickason, 1984, p. 35). Ever since the two races first met, non-Indians have been trying to teach, convert, "improve," or otherwise change Indian peoples. Throughout the nineteenth century and into the twentieth, the idea persisted among government administrators that somehow Indians were really just undeveloped human beings in desperate need of training in the proper way to live.

Academic disciplines still have great difficulty accepting Indian art, history, literature, music, and technology as art, history, literature, and technology without first placing it in an anthropological context. Museums continue to foster the view of Indians as "pre-historic." It seems essential for museums to create special galleries that focus on presenting ethnographic, "pre-contact" "Native Culture" in ways that are perceived inappropriate for displaying Canadian history. Culture can be presented as anonymous, almost divorced completely from real human beings. History involves the actions of actual named individuals. Since Indians are perceived to have culture, not history, it is not particularly unusual for museums such as the National Museum of Civilization to display native skeletal remains in their archaeological exhibits as part of their interpretation of Native culture. It is seen as being comparable to scientific displays of the skeleton of Early Man. But it is not likely that the bones of Laura Secord will be installed in any museum exhibit in the near future to illustrate an episode in Canadian history. Indians, like the Iron-Age Man, are seen as being separated from modern technological society by the fact that their technology, or rather perceived lack of it, makes them "primitives" or "wildmen," ancient ancestors that just don't exist anymore and have no real connection to living human beings. They are "pre-history."

It has been difficult for industrial Canadian society to accept that non-industrial cultures are still viable. To Canadian society Indian cultures are based firmly in the past, and Western culture has a tradition of repudiating the past as out of date and irrelevant to the present. Since the sixteenth century, Indians have been seen as representing earlier, less-civilized versions of Europeans. They have, in the minds of some Europeans and Canadians come to symbolize human beings at an earlier, less complex stage of development. This idea has made it possible for some New Age spiritualists like Lynne Andrews to discover their own roots in Native cultures.

This has also meant that images of Indians created by Western society have emphasized two perceptions of Indian inferiority. Indians were seen as either morally inferior to white "civilized" society or as inferior to an ideal version of "the noble savage."

In the nineteenth and early twentieth centuries Indian culture is either denounced as immoral or seen as having degenerated from a higher form of culture. To those who were inclined to see the world as a struggle between good and bad, God and the Devil, Indians were pagans, devil worshippers. To those who accepted Darwin's theories of evolution, Indians were seen as half way between men and beasts, simple people who needed to be eventually raised to the level of Western civilization through education and training.

To those who saw the world in terms of a "golden past" against which everything in the present could never measure up, Indians were simply no longer what they used to be (Barbeau, 1923). Indians were judged against the sentiments of romanticized literature and found lacking. Although in the current decade these ideas are no longer expressed in terms of morality or level of civilization, there are nevertheless very similar ideas being expressed in a new idiom. For example, in land claims judgements such as the Gitksan-Wet'en case in British Columbia, Indian oral history was largely dismissed by the judge as "unscientific," as "faith made fact," their claims to land as merely romantic pretension. Indian people are often criticized for seeking special treatment and not adjusting to western society. And absurdly, they have often been charged by judges and academics such as William Fenton in the 1970s New York wampum controversy, with not being "really Indian."

Every culture creates images of how it sees itself and the rest of the world. Incidental to these images of self-definition are definitions of the "other." Canadian society through control over such tools as advertising, literature, history, and the entertainment media has the power to create images of other peoples, and these images often operate as a form of social control. For example, images in the media of women as incompetent, physically inferior, and scatterbrained have in the past been used to justify why women should not hold executive positions in Canadian business. Racial stereotypes in television situation comedies have in the past justified why it is all right to deny other racial groups access to power and financial rewards. Indians have been subject to this type of "control" but also to a unique form of psychological warfare. Minority groups often endure discrimination but they never experience situations in which the discriminating group usurps their identity. For example, no Canadians of East Indian descent have experienced other Canadians identifying with them and pretending to be them. The image of the "romantic Indian princess" was created for the benefit and imagination of the Euro-Canadian, not for the benefit of Indian people. It uses symbols derived from Indian cultures and changes them so that they better suit the needs of Canadian society. Through use of the romantic images of Indian princesses and Indian chiefs, non-Indian people can become "noble Indians" in their own minds.

It is not surprising that the dominant society should use the media to tell the stories about Indians that interest their own members the most. If the past five years are any indication of public interest in the idea of Indianness, there is a seemingly endless audience for the story of the victimized "Dances With Wolves" Indian who suffers at the hands of the sadly misguided, yet completely powerful dominant society. In this way, past injustice is revealed but only by underscoring the powerlessness of Indian people. To present Indians as victims is a much safer way of discussing the injustices of history than by suggesting to Indian people that they might have expected a different result.

At its heart, this exhibit and Resource Guide is about the creation and manipulation of symbols. It is also about the power of symbols to justify what is and to control what will be. Many of the mechanisms describe in this Resource Guide can be used to understand how stereotypes define and limit people in general. They are designed to not only influence how society views certain groups, but also attempt to control how people see themselves.

## Once Upon a Time: The Role of Indians in History

> In disposition the Savages were fierce, cruel and cunning. They seldom forgave an affront. They used to SCALP the enemies whom they had killed, and to torment those whom they had taken alive.... .However, as the Indians were so cruel and bloodthirsty, we cannot but lament and condemn the practice of using their services in warfare. Those who used them were often unable to manage them.
>
> Henry Miles, *The Child's History of Canada*

> Eighteen days after setting out Davis handed over his charges to the personnel at Fort Battleford — from outside the buildings. Realizing from personal experience the effect of such close contact with over a thousand Indians, the personnel there suggested that before presenting his dispatches it might be well for Davis to strip to the skin, burn his clothing and take a bath.
>
> "West by North," in *A Pocketful of Canada*

Interpretations of history can best be understood as a series of stories or myths. My generation grew up with the story of how North America was "discovered" by Christopher Columbus and of how civilization was "started" by the French. There were lots of statements in the textbooks about "virgin land," "uninhabited territories." Then suddenly into the picture came the Indians. Sometimes they were portrayed as tools, sometimes as threats, sometimes as allies. Indians were incidental because the story was not about them. They were just there — in the way.

I remember learning about Cartier, about Frontenac, about Brock, and feeling disappointed that the Indians always lost. When we studied the fur trade, the Indians were always doing foolish things, giving up all their valuable fur resources worth thousands of dollars for a few pots and pans, selling huge tracts of land for a handful of shiny beads. I didn't want to accept it, but there it was in print, in the textbook that never lied.

It wasn't until I went to university that I understood that what I had read, studied, and reiterated in my test answers was a type of story. It was somebody else's story about how Canada was settled, and it functioned as a justification and explanation for "the way things happened." This fall I discovered that the story still functions in this way. One of my tutorial students remarked to me that he felt it was unfair to blame the Canadian government for the reserve system and broken treaties because it was unintentional that the treaty promises were not kept, that no one had planned that the Cree in Saskatchewan would starve, that it "just happened."

The Canadian history textbook I was to use was sprinkled with references to the clash between "primitive and civilized societies." It stated that "despite their nomadic habits and their mixed blood the Métis were not savages," but "unsophisticated peoples." Métis people had "primitive nationalism," Crees didn't advance to the battle, they "prowled" around neighbourhoods frightening townspeople. Riel himself was said to be filled with "primitive aggressiveness and hostility" (Francis et al., 1986). In the bulk of the reading, Indians still were in the peripherary of the story, their part was still that of the obstacle and source of conflict.

Historically, these stories about Indians being primitive, violent, and generally incompetent at self-government justified two elements of Canadian Indian policy: non-Indian land settlement and non-Indian control over Indians. For example, it was easy for nineteenth- and often twentieth-century analysts to justify why Indians no longer should control the land. They simply didn't know how to use it properly. They built no roads, no fences, raised no cattle, they were not "improving" the land with European technology. Regulations were passed in the Canadian Parliament to control Indians: where they could live, how they were governed, how they should make their living. In the years following the second Riel Rebellion, the Canadian Parliament passed laws forbidding Indians in the West to leave their reserves without the written permission of their Indian agent. The Canadian government passed laws to decide who was an Indian and who was not, what form Indian government should take and what power those governments should have, all without the consent of Indian people being required. In 1884 an amendment to the Indian Act made certain religious ceremonies illegal (Titley, 1966, p. 63). Indians were prohibited from purchasing or consuming alcohol, and limits were placed on their economic activities in the Western grain and ranch markets. All resolutions passed by the band councils were subject to the approval or disallowance of the officials of the Indian Department in Ottawa. During the nineteenth century, no other group in Canada was as closely regulated and controlled.

Why were Indian people so closely watched and regulated? Why has this regulation seemed understandable to the public? Why does the phrase "wild Indians" make the public feel uneasy if not frightened? Conflict between Indians fighting for their land and settlers fighting to take the land happened in the relatively recent past, only a hundred years ago. Or it may be, as some have argued, that Indians have always been viewed by historians and other scholars as being a submerged, frighteningly violent part of the Euro–North American psyche (Fiedler, 1968).

Indians have always been viewed by Euro–North Americans in comparison with themselves. In the seventeenth century, Europeans believed that all of mankind was descended from Adam, the first man. Europeans also believed in a hierarchy of mankind. At the top of the hierarchy of societies, not surprisingly, were Europeans, and under them in development and "civilization" were all of the other peoples who were not Europeans.

From the beginning, Europeans had tried to set Indians into this order of peoples. The earliest perceptions of Indians were that they were more like the ancient Romans or Biblical Israelites than they were like Europeans. Lafitau, an early French "Indian" scholar went to great pains to demonstrate the similarity of North American customs and language to classical models. Early engravings of Indians often present them in poses and clothing that suggests a connection with ancient Greece or Rome.

Among the first illustrations of Indians in historical accounts was a woodcut from the title page to Guiliano Dati's account of the voyage of Christopher Columbus, printed in 1493. It shows the Indians in profile, naked, bearded with long flowing hair and laurel wreaths about the hips. Another woodcut by Hohann Froschauer, from the German printing of Vespucci's voyages in 1505, shows the Indians in dignified Roman poses. Later seventeenth-century engravings continue to depict Indians in a style that suggests a classical setting.

This tradition of presenting Indian individuals as classical figures has continued well into the twentieth century in the form of heraldry on coats of arms of Canadian cities, (City of Toronto, City of Brantford), provinces (Newfoundland, Nova Scotia) and historical cultural organizations (coat of arms of Ontario Historical Society).

In establishing the hierarchy of societies, the major criteria for classification was industrial technology and material wealth — two accomplishments of which Europeans were very proud. When this criteria were applied to Indians, most Europeans came to the conclusion that Indians were "savages." They lacked all the things that were necessary to be accepted as "civilized" and as Europeans. They had no printing presses, no books, no wine, no factories, no European-style government, no Christianity, no guns, and "no polite conversations" (Dickason, 1984, p. 52). The associations of Indians with the European tradition of the "primitive" half-animal "wild man" was so strong that Indians were often depicted with long flowing beards and body hair even though explorers repeatedly remarked upon the fact that, surprisingly, Indians were not very hairy and did not have beards.

To Cartier on the Gaspé coast in 1534, there was no doubt that the occupants of the new land were to be considered "wild" men:

> This people may well be called savage; for they are the sorriest folk there can be in the world and the whole lot of them had not anything above the value of five sous, their canoes and fishing nets excepted.... They have no other dwelling but their canoes which they turn upside down and sleep on the ground underneath. They eat their meat almost raw, only warming it a little on the coals and the same with their fish. (Hoffman, 1961, p. 135)

Described as being without houses, possessions, and comforts, the Indian nonetheless attracted some interest from those Europeans who were interested in changing materialistic European society. Like unfallen man, Adam, the Indians appeared to be very generous with their possessions and as some saw them, completely, "without evil and without guile" (Berkhofer, 1979, p. 11). This idyllic "Adam" side to the "savage," "uncivilized" man was used to great effect by those who were dissatisfied with society and sought to reform it. They presented "Indians" in ways that directly criticized European society.

Peter Martyr's sixteenth-century history of the conquest of the "New World" contrasted the "crafty deceitful" Europeans with the Indians who lived instead in a world of innocence, liberty, and ease uncorrupted by civilized ideas of property, greed, and luxury (Crane, 1952, p. 4). In Montaigne's "On Cannibals," Brazilian people were used to criticize French poverty and social inequality. He contrasted the Aboriginal practices of cannibalism with the common European practice of torture and concluded "better to eat your dead enemy as do the Amerindians than to eat a man alive in the manner of the Europeans" (Dickason, 1984, p. 56). Similarly the women of France were chastened for their lack of affection for their children, scarcely waiting "the birth of their children to put them out to nursemaids," unlike "savage women" who breasted-fed their own children with no ill physical effects (Jaenan, 1976, p. 33).

By the seventeenth century, Europeans had certain fixed ideas about what an Indian was supposed to look like. The "official costume" of Indians in European art was a feather skirt and upright headdress, occasionally with some feathers at the wrists and ankles (Chiapelli, 1976, p. 504). The physical remoteness of Indians to Europeans made it possible to create representations of abstract Indians that bore no resemblance to reality. In a sixteenth-century illustration depicting Amerigo Vespucci awakening "America" from the sleep in her hammock, America is represented as being a nude Indian woman. She is surrounded by European-looking animals in a forest scene; a spear is propped against a tree. These abstract depictions of Indians created a visual symbolic language that was immediately recognizable as Indianness: nudity, feathers, headdresses, bows, and arrows. It was upon this system of symbols that nineteenth- and twentieth-century symbolic language about Indianness was elaborated and developed.

Whenever Canadian and American society has found itself in competition with Indians over land and resources, the images generated about Indians by the non-Indian public are predictably negative. They are designed to create feelings of hate and anger. The newspaper engravings of the late nineteenth century provide ample examples of images of hate. "The Sentinel's Evening Visitors," depicting Indian women waiting to get a drink of the guard's whiskey possibly in exchange for certain services, and the sketch entitled "Indian Loafers," both from Canadian newspapers, illustrate the feeling of disgust that the public was expected to share with the artist. Depictions of leering crazed Indians threatening women and children, riding demented through their camps crying for scalps, making off with stock animals and anything else that was portable, were common in newspapers of the 1870s and 1880s such as *The Graphic* and *The Illustrated War News*. It is no coincidence that this was also the era of the dispossession of Indian Peoples in the West of their lands.

The pictorial story in these same newspapers of the Canadian and American participants in the wars with the Indians are strikingly heroic. Although an Indian may be depicted as scowling, demented, savage beyond all reason, the settler or the soldier is neat, calm, and in control. Although threatened, they appear as though they will never be defeated. This sense of superiority, of "British cheer and pluck" in the Battle of Batoche was reflected in the newspaper coverage of the victory for the Canadian forces:

> The charge started at high noon by routing them out of the advanced pits. At 3:30 p.m. the enemy were totally routed, many having been killed and wounded, many more were prisoners in our hands and others had fled and were hiding in the surrounding bushes. Col. Williams said simply: "Men will you follow me?" The answer was drowned in a roar of cheering such as I never heard before. Over the bluff we went, yelling like mad. The Indians fired one volley and ran. Neither the Indians nor halfbreeds stood their ground. (*Winnipeg Free Press*, 1910)

In the *Fluffs and Feathers* exhibit, by far the greatest number of negative images of Indians are found in the history section. This is because in telling the story of European and English Canadian survival in and conquest of North America there must be the protagonist; the force against which the victors struggle and overcome. In most versions of this story Indians have been placed in the peripheral roles of "savage threat," "faithful but brutal ally," and "vanquished disappearing race."

# References

Barbeau, Marius (1923). *Indian days in the Canadian Rockies*, Toronto: MacMillan.

Berkhofer, Robert (1979). *The white man's Indian*, New York: Vintage Books.

Chiapelli, Fredi (1976). *First images of America*, vol. 1, Berkeley: University of California.

Crane, Fred (1952). The noble savage in America, 1815–1860. Unpublished PhD Thesis, Yale University.

Dickason, Olive (1984). *Myth of the savage*, Calgary: University of Alberta Press.

Fielder, Leslie (1968). *The return of the vanishing American*, Toronto: Stern and Day.

Francis, Douglas, et al (eds.) (1986). *Readings in Canadian history: Post confederation*, Toronto: Holt Rinehard & Winston.

Hoffman, Bernard (1961). *Cabot to Cartier*, Toronto: University of Toronto Press.

Jaenan (1976). *Friend and foe*, New York: Columbia University Press.

Miles, Henry (1870). *The child's history of Canada: For the use of the elementary schools and of the young reader*, Montreal: Dawson Brothers.

Robins, John D. (ed.) (1948). West by north. In *A pocketful of Canada*, written for the Canadian Council of Education for Citizenship, Toronto: Collins.

Titley, E. Brian (1966). Senseless drumming and dancing. In *A narrow vision*, Vancouver: University of British Columbia Press.

*Winnipeg Free Press* (1910). Souvenir reprint, Glenbow Archives, May 13.

# Chapter 13

# How to Tell the Difference: A Guide for Evaluating Children's Books for Anti-Indian Bias

Beverley Slapin
Doris Seale
Rosemary Gonzales

## LOOK AT PICTURE BOOKS

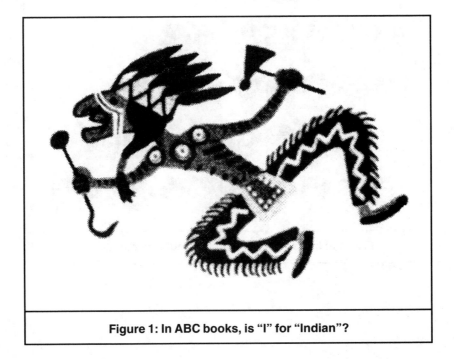

Figure 1: In ABC books, is "I" for "Indian"?

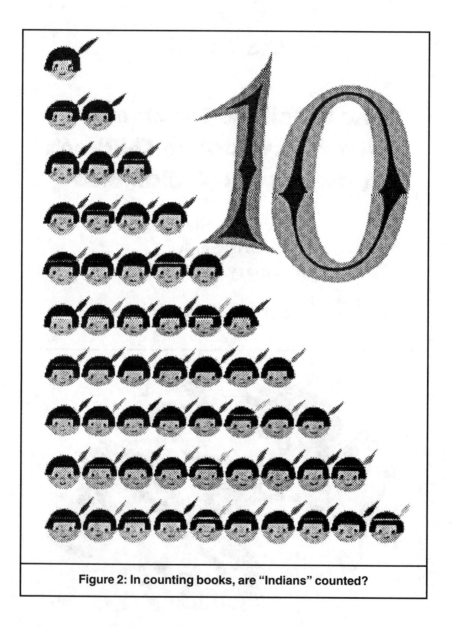

**Figure 2: In counting books, are "Indians" counted?**

## LOOK FOR STEREOTYPES

Are Native cultures oversimplified and generalized? Are Native people all one color, one style?

> *And what would America have been without the Indians themselves, with their magnificent feathered headdresses, their colorful blankets, their bows and arrows and wampum belts, their wigwarns and moccasins and birch-bark canoes that cut through the water like steel ploughs — their poetry and their history.*

Figure 3

or

Are Native cultures presented as separate from each other, with each culture, language, religion, dress, unique?

> *The People of the many Nations visited each other's lands. The People from the North brought elk meat. The People from the West gave them fish. The People from the South brought corn. The People from the East gave them hides. When there were arguments, their leaders would say, "Let us respect each other. We will bring you corn and baskets. You will bring us meat and flint knives. That way we will lead a peaceful life. We must respect each other, and the animals, the plants, the land, the universe. We have much to learn from all the Nations."*

Figure 4

## LOOK FOR LOADED WORDS

Are there insulting overtones to the language in the book? Are racist adjectives used to refer to Indian peoples?

> *A huge Indian came forward. He was over six feet tall, his half-naked body superbly muscled. His long black hair hung loosely to his waist.*

> *His brutal face gleamed with malice and under his low brows shone eyes like a wolf's.*

Figure 5

or

Is the language respectful?

> *My grandchildren, I am glad that you, the young Ojibway of today, are seeking to learn the beliefs, the customs, and the practices of our people, for these things have too long been alive only within the memories of the Old Ones. I am glad that you are asking, for it has always been the custom for us to tell what must be passed on so that our ways will be known to the Ojibiway children of the future.*

Figure 6

## Look for Distortion of History

Is there manipulation of words like "victory," "conquest," or "massacre" to justify Euro-American conquest of the Native homelands? Are Native Nations presented as being responsible for their own "disappearance?" Is the U.S. government only "trying to help?"

> *Vast, dark, unknown, the land lay for thousands of years, hardly used at all by men and women, for the few Indians never knew how to use it and never cared to learn. The wolf, the bear, the panther, and the bison flourished and increased faster than people. The land waited for a master who did not come for a long, long time.*

Figure 7

or

Is history put in the proper perspective: the Native struggle for self-determination and sovereignty against the Euro-American drive for conquest?

> *Soon, the People saw the destruction of their Nations. They soon found out it was the aim of the English, French, and Dutch to take their lands. The rich and the powerful of these men formed an American government. They wanted the land because it was fertile with forests and farmland and wealthy with precious minerals. And they wanted the People to serve them as slaves. When the People saw these men did not respect them and their land, they said, "We must fight to protect ourselves and the land."*

Figure 8

## LOOK AT THE LIFESTYLES

Are Native cultures presented in a condescending manner? Are there paternalistic distinctions between "them" and "us"?

> *In our half of the world, which we call the Western Hemisphere, there was no civilization five hundred years ago except in Mexico and Peru, where people built cities with houses of stone and knew how to carve statues and paint pictures.*

Figure 9

or

Is the focus on respect for Native peoples and understanding of the sophistication and complexity of their societies?

> *Long before the white man came, civilizations flourished in the American Southwest. Elegant stone masonry cities were built high in the walls of sheer cliffs, and adobe villages clustered along rivers and next to mesas and hills. The Pueblo people had learned how to farm the*

> *dry land of the region. They made beautiful pottery and baskets in which to serve and store the food they grew. They had mastered their environment and lived in harmony with it.*

Figure 10

Is there an ethnocentric Western focus on material objects, such as baskets, pottery, rugs?

> *The old and new Indian crafts are found to be well suited for modern home decoration. In the living room, the den, or a child's room, one or more Navajo rugs create warmth and color. A pair of kachina dolls hung on the wall or standing on the mantel, or a fine piece of pottery on a bookshelf, adds much charm to a room. A painting made by an Indian artist has an interesting subject, and its soft earth colors blend with almost any decor. Large baskets, serving as wastebaskets, are a unique touch, and since those from different tribes rarely clash, they may be mixed in the same room.*

Figure 11

or

Does the writer show any understanding of the relationship between material and non-material aspects of life?

> *Art is a fundamental activity in tribal cultures, an integral part of the daily life of ordinary people. It is an expression of the basic need of people in all times and environments to communicate with others, to record experience and impressions, to cope with a finite existence by passing on something of oneself and one's heritage to future generations .... The "art object" is valued not only for aesthetic reasons, as it is in Western society, but also for its utilitarian and religious functions. A Navajo basket is used in healing ceremonies. A Pueblo pot is treasured because the clay comes from Mother Earth and contains "the spirit of those who have gone before. "*

Figure 12

## Look for Standards of Success

In modern times, are Indian people portrayed as childlike and helpless? Does a white authority figure — pastor, social worker, teacher — know better than Native people themselves what is "good for them"? Are Indian children "better off" away from their families?

> *"You know what I wish?" Mary Beth tried not to cringe when Melody's fingers combed quickly through her hair. "I wish we could have another Indian mother. Why do you s'pose Indian people don't adopt all the Indian children like us who need homes?"*
>
> *"You know perfectly well why not," retorted Melody. "They're too poor, and they have no nice place to live, and not enough food." She listed all the reasons Miss Perry, the social worker, had mentioned when they asked.*

Figure 13

or

Are Native adults seen as mature individuals who work hard and make sacrifices, in order to take care of their families, and for the well-being of the people?

> *The next day Father called the people together. He told them that they must all agree either to move to the big Ojibway village or to stay in their forest place.*
>
> *The people were afraid of the sickness in the big village. Every time of cold the sickness was there. "We have been favored," they said, "because we did only what we have always done." They did not want to leave the old place. Father said, "If this is your wish, then we will stay."*
>
> *Grandfather said, "Each ricing time the man will come for the children. If they live in the longhouse of the school they will never know our ways. Our strength will be lost. If we move close to the big village, the children will stay home at night and we can still teach them the old ways. We must decide — shall we stay separate and not*

> *see the children from ricing to planting, or shall we speak to them each*
> *night about the good of our people?"*
>     *The people said, "We shall go to the big village."*

Figure 14

## LOOK AT THE ROLE OF WOMEN

Are women completely subservient to men? Do they do all the work while the men loll around, waiting for the next hunt?

> *Originally, the travois had been drawn by squaws or by dogs. The*
> *Spaniards introduced the Indians to the horse, and horsepower proved*
> *superior to dog or "squaw power."*

Figure 15

or

Are women portrayed as the integral and respected part of Native societies that they really are?

> *Among the Cherokee, there was a women's council, as there was among*
> *the Iroquois, which could override the authority of the chiefs. Other*
> *seaboard tribes probably had similar councils. The Cherokee council*
> *was made up of one woman from each clan, chosen by the clan members.*
> *The head of this assembly was called the Beloved Woman and she*
> *spoke for the women at all meetings of the chiefs. It was said that she*
> *represented and spoke for the Great Spirit.*

Figure 16

## LOOK AT THE ROLE OF ELDERS

Are Elders treated as a dispensable burden upon their People to be abandoned in times of trouble or famine; querulous, petulant, demanding, nagging, irritating, and boring?

> *"Try everything. Deer songs, rabbit songs, maybe the horse songs, too. That stuff I can handle …. But when she starts up about her soul wandering…and wants those old songs …that's a lot more complicated. Takes time. I can't just snap my fingers and dance around the fire like some witch doctor in a movie!"*

Figure 17

or

Are Elders treated as the loved and valued custodians of a people's history, culture, and lifeways? Are they cherished in the words of the writer as they were and are in the reality of the lives of the people?

> *Every evening, after a day of playing, exploring, and learning, Oona returned to the lodge of Grandfather and Grandmother. She sat before them, and they said, "Our daughter, what has been done today? Can you ask in truth and peace, 'Have I done enough today to earn the right to live tomorrow?'" Oona would count and think about the things she had done that day. Grandmother would touch her fingers to the back of Oona's hand, and Grandfather would place his hand on her head in blessing.*

Figure 18

## Look for the Effects on a Child's Self-Image

Is there anything in the story that would embarrass or hurt a Native child?

> *…she saw two naked, wild men coming,…. They were tall, thin, fierce-looking men. Their skin was brownish-red. Their heads seemed to go up to a peak, and the peak was a tuft of hair that stood straight up and ended in feathers. Their eyes were black and still and glittering, like snake's eyes …. The naked wild men stood by the fireplace … she smelled a horribly bad smell..*

Figure 19

or

Are there one or more positive role models with which a Native child can identify?

> *Emma Yazzie is a hero who is living right now in the Navajo Nation of New Mexico. She is a hero in our modern age — the time we all live in. Emma is brave and strong and courageous. And she is not alone. Many of her people work and struggle with her. They are brave, strong, and courageous heroes, too. They are the rural Navajo people. They call themselves "grassroots" people because, like the hardy grass on their reservation, they have to be tough to survive. Grassroots means that, like the grass, they have their roots in the land.*

Figure 20

## ENDNOTES

Figure 1. Eastman, P.D., *The cat in the hat beginner book dictionary* (Random House, 1964).

Figure 2. Seiden, Art, *Counting rhymes* (Crossett and Dunlap, 1959).

Figure 3. Commager, Henry Steele, *The first book of American history* (Franklin Watts, 1957).

Figure 4. Ortiz, Simon, *The people shall continue* (Children's Book Press, 1977).

Figure 5. Daugherty, James, *Trappers and traders of the far west* (Random House, 1952).

Figure 6. Broker, Ignatia, *Night flying woman, an Ojibway narrative* (Minnesota Historical Society Press, 1983).

Figure 7. Johnson, Gerald W., *America is born* (William Morrow & Company, 1959).

Figure 8. Ortiz, *The people shall continue.*

Figure 9. Johnson, *America is born.*

Figure 10. Yue, Charlotte and David, *The pueblo* (Houghton Mifflin Company, 1986).

Figure 11. Hofsinde, Robert, *Indian arts* (Morrow Junior Books, 1971).

Figure 12. Katz, Jane, *This song remembers: Self-portraits of Native Americans in the arts* (Houghton Mifflin Company, 1980).

Figure 13. Warren, Mary, *Walk in my moccasins* (Westminster, 1966).

Figure 14. Broker, *Night flying woman.*
Figure 15. Sutton, Felix, *The how and why wonder book of North American Indians* (Price/Stern/Sloan, 1985).
Figure 16. Gridley, Marion E., *American indian women* (Hawthorne, 1974).
Figure 17. Wallin, Luke, *Ceremony of the panther* (Bradbury Press, 1987).
Figure 18. Broker, *Night flying woman.*
Figure 19. Wilder, Laura Ingalls, *Little house on the prairie* (Harper & Row, 1971) (first published 1935).
Figure 20. New Mexico People and Energy Collective, *Red ribbons for Emma* (New Seed Press, 1981).

## Exercises

The following questions are provided to help the reader examine the contents of chapter 12 and chapter 13.

1.  Discuss the impact of stereotypes of "Indians" as produced in European and Canadian culture including
    a)  where the word Indian came from;
    b)  Indian myths and the impact of these myths in justifying mistreatment of Native peoples.
2.  Why were Native people so closely watched and regulated? Why was this understandable to the public? Why did the phrase "wild Indians" make the public feel uneasy if not frightened?
3.  Examine hierarchical thinking about "mankind" and the benchmark of industrial technology and material wealth when it is applied to "others" to place them in a hierarchy.
4.  Applying Hall (from last section) and considering Doxtator and Slapin, et. al.:
    a)  What is the "new" kind of knowledge produced?
    b)  What/who is the object of the knowledge?
    c)  What "new" practices were carried out?
    d)  What "new" institutions were created?
    e)  How do these continue today?
Next, consider the question:
5.  What are the implications of communications/media for your pedagogy, your classroom, for education in Canada?

# Chapter 14

# Anti-Racist Education (Selected Readings and Resources)

## TVOntario

### PRINCIPLES OF ANTI-RACIST EDUCATION

### BARB THOMAS

Several terms have gained currency in the recent attempts to recognize that Canada's population is both diverse and has been accorded unequal treatment and in the efforts to make the discussion of diversity and unequal treatment palatable to dominant-group Canadians: "cross-cultural education," "intercultural education," "multiculturalism," and "race relations training." While there are some differences in meaning between these four terms, they all share certain assumptions about the nature of the problem and the approaches necessary for the desired change.

The concept of "multiculturalism" was formulated by the state, and promoted as policy in Canada by the federal government from 1971.[1] While multiculturalism as an ideology has been and should continue to be critiqued, it is fair to say that its presence has legitimized a more open discussion of the place of different cultures in this country, and their unequal treatment in our history and our present.

The term "anti-racist education" has developed through the work of community organizations and activists, particularly those in Britain and the United States,[2] and over the past few years it has been making tentative, halting inroads into discussions of racism in Canada. Indeed, it can be seen to be enriching the thinking of major proponents of multiculturalism.[3] However, it departs from the tenets of multiculturalism in quite substantial ways. It is important to define, clearly, the oppositional nature of anti-racist education before the uncomfortable edges are smoothed, and we are left with yet another term for "dealing with diversity." This article, in the spirit of furthering debate and clarity on these issues, will attempt to summarize some of the main principles and assumptions behind anti-racist education; where appropriate, to remark on its divergence from multiculturalism; and to suggest a few of its implications for the school system.

## Defining the Problem

Multiculturalism views the cultural diversity of the Canadian population with some ambivalence. On the one hand, diversity is a potential problem because it may threaten — and, indeed, has been seen to threaten in the past — Anglo security. On the other hand, proponents of multiculturalism urge the celebration of that diversity. The problem for multiculturalists is that the differing cultures that make up Canada are not accorded the same value. Culture, here, is seen primarily in terms of one's ethnic heritage. Canada should be a place where everyone's culture can be preserved and lived out with respect and without penalty At present, it is not. Indeed, the very people who should be enjoying the preservation of their heritage have been and continue to be denied equal opportunity and equal access to programs, training, and jobs.

Anti-racist education posits that diversity per se is not the problem nor, necessarily, is preservation of one's ethnic heritage (more about this below). It is the significance that is attached to differences, and more importantly, the way that differences are used to justify unequal treatment, that is the problem. In short, racism is the problem. While it would be nice if all cultures were considered equally valuable, it is a fact that not all cultures are equally powerful in this country — whether one is talking about the aspects of culture that derive from one's gender, class, race, or ethnicity. Unequal power not only limits the dimensions of one's culture that can be legitimately expressed. More significantly, unequal power limits one's ability to earn a living, meet basic needs, make one's voice heard. Unequal power makes the struggle for self-respect, let alone the respect of one's neighbours, a formidable one. Racism is the message that one deserves unequal power if one is not part of the dominant cultural/racial group because one is "different," "lazy," "less well educated," "overeducated," "trying to take over all the professional positions," "incapable of being a professional," "privileged to be here," "clannish," "not able to assimilate," "expects too much," "exploits one's own community," "allows oneself to be exploited," "speaks dialect," "has a chip on one's shoulder," "takes away jobs," "won't get a job." This racism is deeply entrenched in our history and everyday understandings of ourselves, of others, and of the world around us. The very term "anti-racist" presumes the existence and extent of racism, and the need to confront and stamp it out.

The anti-racist educator knows that the problems of racism and unequal power are present in schools as they are in every institution of a society with a history of racism. In the school, racism says that more black, native, and Portuguese children will end up in dead-end streams; that European languages such as French and Spanish are more valuable than Punjabi, Cree, Greek, or Jamaican English; that children from Britain, United States, or European countries are more likely to "fit in" and bring with them knowledge that the school can credit than those who come from Third World countries; that heritage or third-language classes interfere with children's ability to learn English; that black students create trouble by hanging around together and playing loud music; that immigrant parents are either uninformed or expect too much from the school system; that Chinese students are better at and should be encouraged to excel in sciences and maths; that in schools where all the children are white Anglo-Saxon there is no problem of racism because there are no "visible minorities" — suggesting that it is the presence of minority children which creates racism.

However, I am reminded that the above litany may go nowhere at all in proving the existence of racism by the comment of a person being interviewed about her experience with racism. She said, "We have been told what racism is, and we think it is somebody calling us a "Paki," or a "Chink," or a "nigger." But in fact, most racism you can't prove. The main factor about racism is that you cannot prove it."[4]

For anti-racist educators, the prevalence and persistence of racism and unequal power need no further proof.

## Causes of the Problem

If multiculturalism views unfavourable reactions to differences and the resulting unequal access to goods and services as the problem, it sees ignorance and prejudiced attitudes as the causes of the problem. However, in the last few years, there is an increasing recognition among adherents of multiculturalism that institutional discrimination both feeds such prejudices and is nourished by them.

Anti-racist education also acknowledges the persistence of stereotypes and prejudices. And it is in accord with multiculturalism in its recognition that minority groups have been denied equal access and equal opportunity. But it asks what practices and history those stereotypes and prejudices support. It insists on examining and revealing where racist ideas come from, and how they become translated into the everyday "common sense" notions that see and justify the immigrant as "alien," and the native person as second class. Anti-racist education explores the history of racism in Canada and the ways it has been used to invite, maintain, and exploit cheap labour in the development of this country. It identifies those who have defined our history — those whose music, literature, art, technology, and struggles are present and whose are absent. It examines the ways in which the subjugation of Third World peoples is explained by such characterizations as "hungry," "dependent," "passive," "incompetent," "troubled," "poor," "ignorant," and "overpopulated." It asks why, when oppressed peoples fight back against the very injustices that harness them to dependency, their struggles are labelled "extremist," "militant," "leftist," "hardline," "radical," "anti-democratic," and "anti-American." Why is fighting against racism and unequal power in an organized and clear-eyed way viewed with such alarm by some of the same people who wish sincerely to change attitudes? Anti-racist education examines the ways in which racism convinces people that they have less rather than more in common. In short, anti-racist education probes the manner in which racism rationalizes and helps perpetuate injustices and continued unequal power.

## Approaches to Change

Multiculturalism seeks changes in the attitudes of Canadians toward each other. People (usually meaning members of the dominant culture) require more information about different cultures and some soul searching about their attitudes toward those cultures. Institutional practices which are unfair need to be identified and made fair. People who currently don't have equal access to programs, services, training, and jobs need to be provided with equal access. However, changes should be promoted in a "positive light" so that people (again, meaning primarily members of the dominant culture) will not be "turned off the whole thing."

Anti-racist education would also hope to accomplish these changes, but there are significant differences in the underlying understandings of how this might happen. First, in the experience of the anti-racist educator, providing information about other cultures does not always result in "increased tolerance." This is because stereotypes of other peoples have already been learned — have been "taught" through parents, peers, teachers, significant others, toys, games, books, comics, movies, textbooks, ads, television comedies, news coverage, limited equal contact, politicians, absence or presence of role models, and through the observed social status of particular groups in the society and globally. Unless these learnings are identified and examined critically, new information can simply be organized to reinforce existing understandings. For the teacher, this means several things: creating a climate in the classroom where stereotypes and racist ideas can be exposed and argued out; where sources of information can be examined; where children can be equipped to examine the accuracy of the information they receive; where alternative and missing information can be provided; and where the historical and current reasons for the continued unequal social status of different groupings can be explored.

Secondly, culture is viewed as a static body of information that can be transmitted easily. The aspects of culture that have currency with multiculturalism tend to be the more consumable dimensions of food, dress, "customs," and habits. The oppositional elements, which cause people to resist and challenge those things that hurt and oppress them, are usually marginalized in multiculturalism's portrayal of culture. Culture, then, in anti-racist education is not just the study of how people lived and what they did in their countries of origin. It should take into account the social class, gender, age, physical mobility, political affiliations, tie of immigration, work, experience of discrimination, rural or urban origins. It is the lived, everyday responses of people to the circumstances in which they find themselves, and the manner in which they attempt to act on and change those circumstances. People don't just identify their culture in terms of their ethnic group, but in terms of those others who are attempting to survive and act on their conditions in similar ways to themselves. For example, people of Chinese origin from Trinidad, Indonesia, Hong Kong, Uganda, China, Britain, or Canada may have little in common except for the way in which they are perceived and treated by the dominant culture.

For the teacher, such a notion of culture implies using the lived experiences of children and their parents as the starting point for understanding "culture"... their experiences at home, at work, in their communities, however they might define those communities. It means searching out a broad range of literature, poetry, music, art, oral history, and biographies; it means teaching children how people have tried to change things that are wrong and unjust and nurturing the courage and skills it takes to do this. It means respecting and reflecting in the classroom the languages that children speak; it means according all languages an equal status in their role of shaping and communicating people's experience. It means supporting the efforts of parents to teach and have the school teach those programs that it may not currently provide. It means engaging children in examining how people develop and adapt cultures to survive in particular circumstances.

Thirdly, while anti-racist education would also welcome "equal access" to programs, services, training, and jobs, it also recognizes that there are some hitches to this notion. For example, at the moment in Canada, the official estimate of unemployment is over 10 percent. If we include welfare and other forms of social assistance, 15 percent of the employable Canadian population is without work. This does not encompass the numbers of underemployed or part-time workers who need full-time employment. Equal access in this context means the continuing struggle not to be the one in seven without a job. Equal access can only mean hoping that the skills and qualifications you have will be the ones you will be able to use if you do get work. Equal access to limited jobs and training programs will still mean competing to beat someone else, who may also need equal access, out of the job or program. Anti-racist education recognizes that the resulting frustration and helplessness of such an insecure situation is fertile breeding for finger-pointing and racist scapegoating, whether the sorting process is based on class, race, ethnicity, gender, or "on merit." It also recognizes the important role of the school in socializing, sorting, and preparing children for the job market as it is. If the economy continues as it is, the schools cannot, in fact, provide children with equal access.

While teachers may not be able to change the economy (although some would argue they should try) they can continue to help children develop the necessary skills for living and acting on the conditions that may oppress them. Such skills are recognized by all good educators: communicating effectively, arguing a position, working with others, analyzing problems, locating relevant and full information. Teachers can strengthen and encourage self-respect, an ability to work cooperatively, a clear and critical understanding of the way in which our society works, a sense of what is fair, and a commitment and competence to work to change those things that are unjust. Teachers can recognize and develop the very real abilities in young children to think through issues, debate, argue, and organize. They can structure their classrooms in such a way as to maximize the abilities and knowledge of all students. This means legitimizing the lived experiences and knowledge of children, as well as "school knowledge." It means encouraging, wherever possible, "mixed ability" groupings. And it means resisting the separation of manual and mental skills and the undervaluing of the one and overvaluing of the other, which is reflected in the streaming system of our schools.

Fourthly, anti-racist education seeks to engage the energies of both those who experience racism and those who are members of the dominant culture, in the challenge to racism. However, it recognizes that there are some who will resist such engagement because of fear, or because they are doing just fine in their current situation. People who have power or who benefit from current power relations are not likely to be in the forefront of changing those power relations. Women seeking to uncover and challenge sexism have certainly learned this. While there are many men who have wrestled personally with their own beliefs about and practices toward women, and who have fought alongside women for equal rights, the fight has been led by women. Similarly, the fight against racism has been led by those who suffer most from their effects. It is difficult for those who are hurting from racism to put racism "in a positive light" so as not to offend or "turn off" those who do not want to see it.

For educators, this means learning more about how people have resisted and are resisting racism, both from the children and from the larger community and its organizations. It means putting community and world events squarely into the classroom. It implies a commitment to work with other staff, confront racist jokes from colleagues, support parents and children and colleagues when they attempt to rectify injustice. It means helping children identify the symptoms and causes of racism and supporting their efforts to challenge racism. Finally, it means recognizing that such efforts will be met with resistance and equipping children to deal with that resistance.

Fifthly, anti-racist education presumes that racism can only be challenged effectively through informed, collective action. Racism is not an individual problem — it is lodged squarely in the policies, structures, practices, and beliefs of everyday life. Teachers can and should be encouraged to reduce their own isolation as teachers, and to deepen adult working relationships with their colleagues. Breaking down the barriers of autonomous professionalism can provide opportunities to talk though tough issues frankly; to share materials and approaches in the classroom; to cooperate more meaningfully with heritage and third-language programs in the school; to plan for their own personal and professional development; to maximize the resources in the library and of special programs in the school; and to work more collaboratively and equally with parents. Collective action is crucial to the development of a school where racism can be discussed frankly, and where it can be resisted effectively.

In these ways, anti-racist education is also political education, for it examines critically those explanations and practices that misinform and oppress people. It challenges current power relations by attempting to create effective ways of working together, and by educating, equipping, and mobilizing people — both children and adults — to recognize injustice and change it.

The author acknowledges her debt to three sources in particular, whose thinking, talking, and writing have helped clarify her own:

Enid Lee, *Letters to Marcia: Anti-Racist Education in School*, forthcoming publication of Cross-Cultural Communication Centre.

Dionne Brand for her poetry and her interviews with over 100 people in
    Toronto.
All-London Teachers against Racism and Fascism, Challenging Racism,
    ALTARF, 1984.

## GUIDELINES FOR USING FILMS AND VIDEOS ON RACISM

### BARB THOMAS

### Why Talk about Racism?

Racism is a word that Canadians have generally preferred to associate
with other countries, places where relations between black people and
white people have been polarized, places like South Africa and the United
States. However, events of the last ten to fifteen years have pushed racism
onto the agendas of a variety of institutions. Debate about immigration
policy has raised questions about who is welcome in Canada and who
is not. The persistent struggle for redress by Japanese Canadians has
forced acknowledgment that Canada is capable of labelling and
imprisoning a whole group of people, based on racial identification. The
inquiry into the Donald Marshall case in New Brunswick has raised
awareness of systemic racism in the delivery of justice, particularly as
meted out to native people. And in cities like Halifax, Toronto, and
Montreal, blacks have protested racism at the hands of police, in
employment practices, and in the biased assessment and placement of
their children in schools. Racism is, at last, being recognized as a force
that continues to influence current social life.

Many people understand racism to be bigotry or prejudice acted out
between members of different racial groups. But people are not born
with racist ideas about others. They learn these attitudes from observing
the social status and unequal treatment of some groups of people, and
the greater privilege of others. Racism requires the social *power* to limit,
exclude, and marginalize a group of people, based on their physical
characteristics. Racism is also the message that one *deserves* unequal
treatment because one is "different," "lazy," "uneducated," "overeducated," "trying to take over all the professional positions," "incapable
of being a professional," "expects too much," "expects too little," "won't

learn English," "expects English classes at the expense of the taxpayer," "works for too little," "wants too much," "exploits one's community," "allows oneself to be exploited," "speaks dialect," "is only good at math," "is only good at sports," "has a chip on one's shoulder," "takes away jobs," "won't get a job." These are the everyday, "common sense" explanations that derive from, and provide permission for systemic racism. Systemic racism involves structures, practices, behaviours, and attitudes that result in the unequal treatment and oppression of people of colour. Racism exists in all of our institutions because it has a long history, and a continuing active presence in our society.

Canadians of all backgrounds are beginning to understand that, while racism has a particularly vicious impact on its targets, it also limits the humanity and the knowledge of people who do not experience it. This is why racism must be understood by all Canadians who want accurate information about themselves and others; and who seek just and equal relations with their neighbours.

## The Advantages of Film and Video in Examining Racism
Whatever the group, school class, union meeting, community organization, audiovisuals offer tremendous advantages in grounding the examination of racism. In particular, they can:

1. Show the *dynamics* of racism, the tone of voice, the physical gestures, the specific relations of power;
2. Show, visually, the *social context* in which racism occurs;
3. Provide insights on the *impact* of racism in the everyday lives of people;
4. Encourage *recognition* of familiar situations through specific images and voices;
5. Introduce *new situations* to which the viewer would otherwise have no access;
6. Ensure the *presence and voice* of those who experience racism;
7. Invite *identification* with those who are resisting and challenging racism.

Through the power of image and sound, films and videos can cut through abstract discussion of racism to focus on *what racism looks and sounds like*, and *what people can do about it*.

## Finding "Bias"

Some viewers, uncomfortable with the issue of racism, may claim that audiovisuals that challenge racism "are biased." This, of course, is true. Every audiovisual does have a perspective. For example, a film or video about the lives of a particular community of native people can catalogue a litany of social problems, confirming stereotypes of native people as alcoholics and dependents of the Canadian government. Or the film can pose the Canadian government as a major benefactor of native people, confirming the notion that white people have "saved" and "civilized" people who couldn't save themselves. Or the video can probe the forces that have produced dependency of native people, and show how native people themselves are challenging this condition. A film can confirm stereotypes, or implicitly condone racism, or actively challenge it. There is no such thing as a *neutral* audiovisual, even when it appears to show "both sides." Every film or video *selects* some images and discards others; includes some information and excludes other facts; emphasizes some points and marginalizes others. The business of selecting and discarding reflects a perspective.

Viewers are not just passive recipients of the messages of audiovisuals. They bring to an audiovisual their own experience and explanations of life. These explanations are shaped by what passes for common sense or truth in the society in which they live.

There is a dynamic relationship, then, between the viewer, the film or video, and the social context in which the viewer and film meet.

Audiovisual

Social Context                    Viewer

Hence, analyzing racism in or *through* a film can illuminate racism in the viewer's life and in the society.

Whatever the group, viewers should be encouraged to assess the perspective of an audiovisual critically. This enables people both to identify racism in the visual messages that bombard them daily, and to assess inadvertent racism in films claiming to be anti-racist.

## Ten Questions to Consider

1. Who speaks and who doesn't? Whose voice predominates? Is the voice speaking from personal experience or about the experience of others? How is language used? Whose accents are present? Are they the main voice, or peripheral voices?
2. What is the sequencing? What follows what? What is the effect?
3. What is in the foreground? What is in the background? What is the effect?
4. When is there music/any other sound/silence? What is the effect?
5. When is there light, and when darkness or dim lighting? What is the effect?
6. Are there "physical types" identifiable in the films? Whom do they remind you of?
7. What activities and experiences make people in the film happy, unhappy, anxious, or angry? Would you respond similarly to such experiences?
8. How is life accounted for in the film? What problems are identified? Whose problems are they? What causes are suggested?
9. Who makes decisions in the film? Do things happen as a consequence of people's actions, or do they just "happen"?
10. How might this film have been made differently if it had been produced by _____?

## Preparing to Use Film or Video

1. *Who* will be seeing the film/video? What are their ages, racial/ethnic backgrounds, gender? What experience might they have of racism? What resistance might they feel in talking about racism?
2. What impact might your own racial identity have on how viewers respond to the film? For example, a white person showing a film

about racism to an entirely native audience may elicit responses different from those evoked by a person of colour. Similarly, but for different reasons, a black educator conducting discussion with an all-white community group will face dynamics different from those faced by a white person.

3. What time do you have for showing the film, and for discussion? Is it adequate for probing the key questions and issues the film raises?

4. Why are you showing the film? Do you want to encourage viewers to develop indicators for recognizing racism? Do you want the group to draw connections between racism in another country and racism in their own community? Is the film to promote discussion of action against racism? Clarifying your goals ahead of time will help you steer discussion more usefully.

5. How will you use the film? What preparation do viewers require? What questions do you want the film to assist viewers to examine? What activities could strengthen the insights you hope viewers will gain?

## Using the Resource

The following are offered as guidelines to ensure that the film assists in frank and productive discussion of racism.

1. Establish some level of acceptance and trust. This presupposes that some discussion and work have occurred *before* the film is shown, and that people know something about each other.

2. Listen for points where people shuffle, whisper, laugh, cough, or move around, while the film is running. These may denote tension, disagreement, apprehension. You can then use these observations in questions such as, "I noticed that at such and such a point in the film several of you seemed agitated, or may have had something to say. What was going on for you at that point in the film?"

3. Begin discussion with questions that pinpoint and clarify what was going on in the film. Questions such as:
   "What did X mean when she said…?"
   "What does the film tell us about…?"

"How did Y feel when...?"

"What were the similarities and differences between the situations of ...?"

"What was the impact of ...?"

"What actions did people take in response to X?"

These initial discussions are often more effective in pairs or small groups for just a few minutes before a large-group examination of issues. Many people have difficulty in finding words for their responses to films, and large groups can inhibit them further.

4. Move from what happened in the film to how viewers feel about what happened. Use questions such as:

"X said .... Do you agree or disagree?"

"Who did you identify most with in the film? Why?"

"Did you agree with Y's analysis of ...?"

"How effective was X group's actions in response to ...?"

5. Encourage reflection on the parallels between the film and racism here and now. This is particularly important if the film is about a blatant situation of racism such as South Africa, or about racism at some point in the past. Viewers uncomfortable with racism may want to condemn this extreme racism, while reassuring themselves that, by comparison, they are not now racist.

6. Don't allow one, or a few people, to dominate the discussion. Encourage others in the group to respond to people's statements or questions.

7. Don't avoid the issues that arouse people's emotions in the film. Probe responses. Encourage clarification of viewpoints. People may have reasons other than the ones they are stating for their responses.

8. Don't engage in a long debate over whether the experience related in the film is true or exaggerated. People in the film are relating what they have experienced. What are the implications?

9. Don't be defensive about wanting to challenge racism. People who make racist comments, or who are offended by an anti-racist stance, should be pushed to defend their position.

10. Invite people to see possibilities for action suggested by the film. This is important whether viewers are white, people of colour, or a mixed group.

11. Enjoy yourself. Good discussion should be fun as well as hard. It is not racist to laugh at the idiocy of racism, or to laugh, with recognition, at practices in which one has engaged, or to which one has been subjected. Laughter is needed as people come together to try to make change.

## GUIDELINES FOR THE SELECTION OF ANTI-RACIST MATERIALS

### NORA ALLINGHAM

1. Wherever possible, select work written from within the culture or gender, rather than from an external observer's or commentator's point of view. Don't perpetuate the practice of white validation of everyone's experience.

2. Balance the selection; for example, a collection should neither exclude white writers nor focus exclusively on South Asian writers.

3. Ensure that materials selected provide a realistic, authentic, non-patronizing, and non-exotic account of their subjects.

4. Canadian material should include the history, culture, and experience of immigration and settlement of visible-minority communities. This material will include the experience of racism in Canada.

5. Questions, assignments, and topics should never imply that the experience of a minority person, whomever it is, can be validated by the majority experience or by a judgement made from an outsider (e.g., questions like "Do you think the author is making a legitimate comment on racism in Canada?" or "Is the author justified in her reaction to her experience with X?").

6. Ensure that you are familiar enough with the material to be reasonably certain that its use will not confirm existing biases against or stereotypes about minority groups. Always provide material that provides a counterbalance to negative portrayals.

The "interpreter" (often the instructor) must be capable of providing a context that will counteract negative portrayals.

7. First Nations people do not see themselves as part of the "multicultural" community. Ensure that the unique position of First Nations people is identified, and avoid using the voice of the outsider.

8. The theme or central focus of the material does not necessarily have to do overtly with racism or issues of inequity — the work that is done with it can be anti-racist. Choose material, as always, for age appropriateness and interest.

9. Ensure that racist, sexist, or classist views are identified as such eventually, even though they may be expressed by a person of colour or the "insider" of the culture (e.g., Naipaul, Bissoondath).

10. The value of the written material you select is reinforced or diminished by the environment in which it is studied. Ensure that posters, illustrations, symbols, logos, team and group names, announcements, seating arrangements, etc., reinforce the value you place on anti-racist work.

11. DO NOT provide this material as an add-on, or as supplementary to the core curriculum. It must be legitimized by its position at the centre of the curriculum, along with the conventionally used work.

## ENDNOTES

1   James Fleeting, "Multiculturalism: Who's it for?" A speech to the Fourth Canadian Conference on Multiculturalism: October 23, 1981.

2   See in particular the publications of the Council for Interracial Books for Children in New York and those of the All-London Teachers Against Racism and Fascism in Britain.

3   See for example *A handbook for enhancing the multicultural climate of the school*, John W. Kehoe, Western Education Development Group, University of British Columbia, 1984.

4   *Speaking of racism*, interviews by Dionne Brand and Krishantha Sri Bhaggiyadatta, forthcoming publication of the Cross-Cultural Communication Centre.

# Part 5

# Gender Equity

**Goldstein**
"Working Toward Equity"

**Toronto Board of Education**
*S.T.A.R.S. Equity Advisory Kit:*
*Challenging Sexism*

**Hanrahan**
"Producing the Female Reserve Labour Force:
Women and Schooling"

**Orenstein**
*Schoolgirls: Young Women,*
*Self-Esteem, and the Confidence Gap*

**Coulter**
*Gender Equity and Schooling:*
*Linking Research and Policy*

**Bravo and Miller**
"What Can Teachers Do About Sexual
Harassment?"

# Chapter 15

# Working Toward Equity

## Tara Goldstein

Of the many issues raised during the province-wide protest of Bill 160 last fall, discussion of what the bill might mean for the pursuit of equity initiatives in our schools was almost non-existent. In this article, I look at the ways different forms of discrimination still characterize the world in which we teach and learn and discuss how Bill 160 ignores equity issues in three important areas of schooling: curriculum and program development; student evaluation and assessment; and staff development.

## CHALLENGING DISCRIMINATION IN OUR SCHOOLS

A review of some of the research on how successful we have been in challenging discrimination in our schools reveals that sexism, racism, and homophobia are still enormous issues for high school students in Ontario. For example, in the early 1990s, researcher June Larkin (1994) asked 60 young women from four high schools in Toronto to describe their experiences of sexual harassment at school. This is what they said:

> I really hate going to this class because where I sit I'm surrounded by guys and they keep talking about hookers, strip bars, women's body parts, "making it" with girls, and

> so on. It really makes me angry. It makes me sick to my
> stomach.
>
> I was sitting in class and the guys behind me kept flipping
> my skirt. When I turned around to tell them to stop the
> teacher yelled at me. I tried to tell her what they were doing
> but she told me to be quiet and stop interrupting the class.

Around the same time, right after "The Yonge Street Riot" in which young people from all the over Toronto protested against racism in the aftermath of the Rodney King affair in Los Angeles, educator Doug Little (1992) asked Black students from three high schools in Toronto about their experiences of racism in school. Here is some of what they said:

> The most fundamental problem is the "Eurocentric
> curriculum." The changing face of Toronto is just not reflected
> in the curriculum. The only compulsory course in history is
> Canadian history and although Blacks made a contribution
> to Canada, we do not get a chance in a compulsory history
> course to tell the full story of African and Black history. Only
> a compulsory world history course can give the full history
> of Blacks and all others peoples.
>
> Some teachers right from elementary school give us subtle
> messages that being Black isn't so good. For instance, a few
> days ago a teacher was handing back work we had done.
> She had handed work to a Black friend of mine and said,
> "Don't worry, 60 percent is a good mark for you." She then
> handed work to a white girl and said, "I thought you would
> get 80 on this work, you could have." We all interpret that as
> a teacher giving higher expectations for the white student
> than the Black one. Too many Black students, even if they
> are having only a little trouble, are told that maybe they
> should go to General level or to an alternative school where
> they can work slower.

In a 1995 documentary that aired on the local television program *Cable 10*, several young gay men and lesbian women were asked to describe their experiences of homophobia at school. This is what they said:

> There was no atmosphere of support or understanding or anything. Or even any acknowledgment that there are gay people at our school. And there'd be people calling you names, whatever — "I'm going to beat those girls up if I ever catch one of them alone." They never did, it was, like, a threatening atmosphere and I had to leave. I dropped out a couple of times.
>
> Well, I'm from a small little town named Welland and my experience was terrible. It was like a nightmare. I would get to school and well, I came out more, more to my best friend. And my best friend kind of told some of his friends and it went around the school and I was bothered about being gay and called names and I got beat up twice by my best friend and my other friends ... I dropped out in Grade 10.

A number of recent research studies offer additional evidence of discrimination in our classrooms and schools. For example, in a survey entitled "Student to Student Harassment in Secondary Schools," the Ontario Secondary School Teachers' Federation (OSSTF) in partnership with the Ontario Women's Directorate and the Ministry of Education and Training (1995) revealed that 80 percent of female students surveyed reported that they had been sexually harassed in a school setting. Students' top three responses to the question, "What types of sexual harassment have you experienced?" were (1) sexual comments, jokes, gestures, or looks; (2) being touched, grabbed, or pinched in a sexual way; and (3) hearing negative comments made about their gender.

Around issues of racism, a 1991 high school survey done by one board of education in Toronto revealed that African Canadian youth were not achieving as well as other students in terms of credit accumulation. The survey reported that 36 percent of Black students were "at risk" of dropping out because of failure to accumulate sufficient credits to graduate within six years. This compared to 28 percent of the entire student body placed in those two streams (Brown et al., 1992; Cheng et al., 1993). In a three-year qualitative study on the "dropout" phenomenon among Black students (May 1992 to June 1995), educational researcher George Dei (1996) identified three primary concerns that pervade Black student narratives about their school experiences: (1)

differential treatment by race; (2) communicative and pedagogic practices that do not reflect the diversity of experiences, ideas, and events that have shaped the students' lives; and (3) the absence of Black and minority teachers in the school system.

Finally, around the issues of homophobia and gay-bashing, a study on American gay and lesbian youth by researchers Gilbert Herdt and Andrew Boxer (1996) revealed that two-thirds of the teenagers felt they had to hide their sexual orientation partially or totally in school. Unfortunately, the issue of homophobia has not been widely studied by educational researchers in Ontario. If we are not even asking questions about homophobic harassment in our schools, how can we begin to come up with any answers.

## Past Initiatives to Challenge Discrimination

In the early and mid-1990s, under the leadership of the New Democratic Party government, Ontario education policy makers made a bold attempt to challenge systemic racism and sexism in schools with the publication of two policy documents: the 1993 *Anti-racism and Ethnocultural Equity in School Boards Guidelines* and the curriculum support document *Engendering Equity: Transforming Curriculum.*

With ten areas of focus for policy development and implementation, the *Guidelines* reflect a commitment to addressing the racism issues raised earlier: the school system's Eurocentric curriculum, low expectations for students of colour, and overrepresentation of Black students in General and Basic level programs. As a support document, *Engendering Equity* was designed to help teachers address gender equity issues through the Common Curriculum.

With our election of the current Progressive Conservative government, implementation of these policies has come to a halt. While current education reform does not reflect our earlier commitment to equitable outcomes for all students, racism and discrimination have not disappeared from Ontario's school system. All over the province, there are parents, students, teachers, administrators, and community groups who continue to work hard to develop and implement anti-discriminatory policies and practices in their neighbourhood schools.

## Anti-Discriminatory Curriculum and Program Development

In order to develop or modify current curriculum so that it reflects our linguistically, culturally, and racially diverse society in an equitable way, teachers need new materials and new books. What kind of funding will be available to schools working on new, inclusive curriculum projects? What kind of funding will be available to school libraries working on diversifying their collections of books, periodicals, and newspapers?

Earlier, several gay and lesbian high school students talked about how physically and emotionally unsafe they felt in their high schools. Unable to bear the physical and verbal abuse they experienced at school, they dropped out of high school despite their personal desire and ability to succeed academically. Two years ago, the Toronto Board of Education began an alternative high school program for gay and lesbian students called the Pink Triangle Program. Shayne, one of the students enrolled in the 1995–96 program, had this to say about her experience in the Triangle Program.

> I'm learning a lot now. I probably wouldn't be going to school this year if it weren't for this program. And I probably wouldn't even be thinking of going to a regular high school next year. That's right. I would just drop out. Work for a year. And most likely after the year I wouldn't go back. (*Cable 10%*, 1995)

With the passing of Bill 160, what kind of funding will be available for innovative programming like the Triangle Program? What will happen to gay and lesbian students who are not safe at school and have nowhere else to finish their high school courses?

## Student Evaluation, Assessment, and Placement

The purpose of student evaluation and assessment is to obtain as accurate a picture as possible of students' capacities in order to ensure that they are provided with a program that enables them to fulfill their potential.

Educational reform accompanying Bill 160 will bring us province-wide testing so that parents and schools will be able to rank the results of their children's scores with the scores of other children in the province. Many tests measure knowledge and experiences that have been acquired within a given cultural and linguistic environment. What kind of validity will province-wide tests have for students whose culture and/or first language are different? How might results from such tests lead to misconceptions about students' capabilities and to their placement in appropriate academic programs?

## Staff Development for Anti-Discriminatory Education

Staff development for anti-discriminatory education is an integral part of changing both organizational culture and the behaviour and practices of individual teachers and students. Bill 160 means the loss of teaching jobs and further cuts to education. How many school board consultants and teachers will be available to assist their colleagues to deal confidently and effectively with issues of discrimination and incidents of harassment? How many will be available to help colleagues develop skills to identify and deal with bias in learning materials? How many will be available to run anti-racist leadership camps for students or to conduct student workshops that challenge homophobia and sexual harassment in classrooms and schools? There has been some progress since the early '90s around challenging discrimination in our schools. There is still much to be done before we can say that we have a high-quality school system for all students. How will Bill 160 help us meet that goal?

## References

Brown, R., M. Cheng, and S. Ziegler (1992). *The every secondary student survey: Initial findings*, Toronto: Toronto Board of Education.

*Cable 10%*. (1995, November). Education (Toronto).

Cheng, M., M. Yau, and S. Ziegler (1993). *The every secondary student survey: Parts 1, 2, 3*, Toronto: Research Services, Toronto Board of Education.

Dei, G. (1996). Listening to voices: Developing a pedagogy of change from the narratives of African-Canadian students and parents. In K. Braithwaite and C. James (eds.) *Educating African-Canadians*, Toronto: Our Schools/ Our Selves.

Herdt, G., and A. Boxer (1996). *Children of horizons: How gay and lesbian teens are leading a new way out of the closet*, Boston: Beacon Press.

Larkin, J. (1994). *Sexual harassment: High school girls speak out*, Toronto: Second Story Press.

Little, D. (1992). The meaning of Yonge Street: What do the kids say? *Our Schools/Our Selves*, 4(1), 16–23.

Ontario Ministry of Education and Training (1993). *Anti-racism and ethnocultural equity in school boards: Guidelines for policy development and implementation*, Toronto: Queen's Printer for Ontario.

Ontario Secondary School Teachers' Federation (OSSTF) (1995). *The joke's over — Student to student sexual harassment in secondary schools*, Toronto: OSSTF, Ontario Women's Directorate, and the Violence Prevention Secretariat. Ministry of Education and Training.

Ontario Women's Directorate (ND). Engendering equity: Transforming curriculum. Draft Document.

## EXERCISES

1.  How are schools failing to meet the needs of all students?
2.  How can schools, curriculum, and government policy begin to address the needs of all students?
3.  What is the impact of Bill 160 in regard to equity?

# Chapter 16

# S.T.A.R.S. Equity Advisory Kit — Challenging Sexism

## Toronto Board of Education

### Scenario 1

Mena is in Grade 7 and is one of Mr. Williams' math students. Almost no one likes Mr. Williams. Besides being boring and a hard marker, he bugs the girls more than the boys. One day, he tells Mena, "It's okay that you are not doing that well in math. Everyone knows that girls aren't smart enough to understand such a difficult subject."

Mena can't believe it. She knows most of her classmates are sick of Mr. Williams' comments but every time she talks to them about complaining to someone, they tell her to get a life. She doesn't feel right about not doing anything but doesn't know where to start.

### Questions
1. Is this sexual harassment, and why?
2. How do you think Mena feels? How does the rest of the class feel?
3. What should Mena do about it?
4. Is this something that needs to be talked about in a small group, with a teacher, or with the office? What should happen in the meeting?

## Scenario 2

Len has always been shy and never big on sports. He's gotten used to being the last one picked for different teams. Recently, a couple of guys have begun to bug him. They call him faggot and queer. At first he didn't even know what it meant. Then last week in the school yard somebody said, "Hey let's go queer-bashing," and a gang of guys began to push him around. He now feels scared to go into the yard at lunch.

### Questions
    1. Is this sexual harassment?
    2. What should Len do?

## Scenario 3

Frank is in Grade 8. Doreen, who is in his class, has developed a major crush on him. She hangs around his locker and she and her friends giggle whenever he walks by. On the one hand, Frank likes the attention. It makes him feel grown up. On the other hand, he doesn't really like Doreen and wishes she would just lay off because often he gets embarrassed. His friends kid him about her too. "Have you had Doreen yet? Man she's really hot on you." He doesn't know what to say.

### Questions
    1. Is this sexual harassment?
    2. What should Frank do?

## Scenario 4

Marilyn and Jimmy are twins and live with their mom. They are in Grade 7. Their mother isn't like a lot of the other kids' moms. She drives a truck. One day the kids in the class are all talking about the project they have to do for their teacher about their families. Tanya, one of the kids in the class, just got into a fight with her best friend and is angry. When Marilyn and Jimmy say that they are going to talk about their mom's job driving a truck, Tanya yells out, in front of everyone, that Marilyn and Jimmy's mom must be a lesbian because she drives a truck.

## Questions
1. Is Tanya sexually harassing Marilyn and Jimmy?
2. How do you think Marilyn and Jimmy feel?
3. If you were one of the kids in the class, what would you do about it?
4. Is this something that needs to be talked about in a small group, with the teacher, or with the office?

## What Are the Issues in Your School?

The Toronto Board of Education is committed to a school system free of sexual harassment. Together we must all work toward this goal. Once you understand what sexual harassment is and the damage it does, then the next step is to take a close look at what goes on in your own school.

1. Is there sexist graffiti in your school? Where is it? What happens if you complain about it?
2. Do students get sexually harassed at your school? In what ways do students get sexually harassed? How do incidents get dealt with?
3. What about homophobic harassment? Do you hear any homophobic name-calling at your school?
4. How do incidents get dealt with?
5. Are there places in the school where female students feel uncomfortable? Where and why? Is the school office aware of this?

## What Can You Do to Create a Harassment-Free School?

1. Once you understand about sexual harassment, then you can help your school create an environment free of it.

2. What can you do to tell other students about harassment?
3. What can you do for students who come to you feeling they are being harassed?
4. How can you create a school environment where all students feel comfortable and safe?
5. What else can you do?

## School/Classroom Survey for Examining Equity Practices

Always/Sometimes/Never

1. Do some teachers unconsciously segregate students according to sex; e.g., lining up, games, etc?
2. Are some students seated in the classroom according to their sex?
3. Have most teachers adopted non-sexist vocabulary? (e.g., firefighters for "firemen")
4. Do some teachers talk more with one sex during discussions or let one sex take over the discussion?
5. Are only male students asked to build something for a teacher in shop classes?
6. Do only boys get asked to pass out books, set up the film projector, carry boxes, etc.?
7. Do girls usually bring in the food for class parties?
8. Are sexist statements, — e.g., "Women can't be doctors" — discussed and challenged?
9. Do most teachers examine the images of women in the curriculum materials being used?
10. Do male students sometimes receive more reprimands and criticisms from teachers than female students?
11. Do female students generally receive more verbal praise than the boys?
12. Do most schools' bulletin boards show both boys and girls performing a variety of activities in close to equal numbers?
13. Do some teachers tend to expect girls to excel in verbal areas and boys to do better in math and science?
14. Are girls and boys equally involved in drama, art, dance, and music activities?

15. Does there tend to be equality in sports in your school? e.g., equipment, coaching, teams.
16. Are there equal numbers of girls' and boys' interschool teams?
17. Are physical education classes co-educational?
18. Are students encouraged to examine the broadened roles for family and work?

## EXERCISES

1. Discuss examples of events (in regard to each of the statements) that would be considered sexual harassment and examples that would not be.
2. Each group is to read one of scenarios 1–4 and discuss (a) their answers to the questions and (b) how this could be used with secondary students.
3. Answer all of the questions in the section entitled "What can you do...?"
4. Discuss your responses to the survey in regard to a school setting you are familiar with.

# Chapter 17

# Producing the Female Reserve Labour Force: Women and Schooling

## Maura Hanrahan

It does not seem to be the true end of education to make women of fashion, dancers, singers, players, painters, actresses, sculptors, gilders, varnishers, engravers and embroiderers …. The profession of ladies, to which the bent of their instruction should be turned, is that of daughters, wives, mothers and mistresses of families.

Hannah More, *Strictures on the Modern System of Female Education*, 1799

We must think positively about how the position of women in their own societies and in international affairs could not only be improved, but their large potential contribution be better utilized for the benefit of all.

Kurt Waldheim, Secretary General, United Nations, 1975

Like women the world over, most Canadian women are characterized by a socioeconomic status that is inferior to men's. Women hold low-paying, low-status jobs (if they work outside the home), many of which are vulnerable to labour-saving technology. In the capitalist system, the work women perform is dispensable; they constitute a reserve labour force. It is their experience in the education system that encourages and helps to guarantee this sort of female participation in the labour force.

Writing in 1799, Hannah More concluded that well-bred young ladies (at the time only upper-class women were being educated at all) might "lawfully" learn most of the fashionable arts (More, [1799]1974, 97). Yet the message of her well-received treatise is that women's education was not presently and ought not to be goal-oriented or vocational in any sense; only boys and men were to be trained to take up professions. More advocated a rigidly structured society in which choices available to men and to women were extremely limited. Social and economic roles were determined by sex rather than talents, abilities, or inclinations. In More's sex-segregated society women lived in the private sphere and men in the public sphere. The respective educations prepared them for these roles.

More's view was prevalent in a society making the transition to capitalism. Abigail Adams wrote to her husband, John, in 1817:

> I was never sent to any school .... Female education in the
> best families went no further than writing and arithmetic, in
> some few and rare instances, music and drawings. (cited in
> Goodsell, 1923, 12)

The nineteenth century saw the establishment of academies and female seminaries where girls were taught French, math, history, geography, and "a smattering of book science" (Goodsell, 1923, 17). These institutions were the successors of boarding and finishing schools but they provided the opportunity for a more thorough education than had the earlier schools. The academies and seminaries were open to only upper-class women. Female education was left to private educators who usually emphasized "showy accomplishments" in music, drama, and the arts (Goodsell, 1923, 18). Left to the private sector, competition was a feature of educational institutions for women. Willystine Goodsell criticized these in 1923 (p. 18), calling them "temporary institutions, formed by individuals, whose object is present emolument." Women's education was not seen as a right. The demand for public education for women began to grow in the first quarter of the nineteenth century and several large cities in the Western world established public high schools for girls. (One of these, in Boston, was closed because it quickly became overcrowded.) By the twentieth century, there were thousands of such public schools, in Britain, Canada, and other countries. Colleges for women began springing up, especially in the United States, mid-way through the nineteenth century. Some of these were just "ladies' schools," similar to the old finishing schools, but Vassar opened in 1865 and became a solid model for women's colleges. Universities started opening their doors to women in the late 1800s and early 1900s and beyond.

These changes occurred in the face of much opposition. Women's education was, after all, a threat to the existing social order. As Simone de Beauvoir noted, "Once she [woman] ceases to be a parasite, the system based on her dependence crumbles" (cited in Byrne, 1978, 64). Women's education would allow for the possibility of female participation in government and the economy; marriage would no longer be the only female vocation.

Even before women gained access to it, public education was characterized by overt class differentiation. In Britain in 1868, sons of gentlemen and men in the upper professions were provided with secondary education until the age of 18 or 19. Sons of the mercantile classes were given a more practical education until age 16. The sons of artisans were taught "very good" reading, writing, and arithmetic until they turned 13. Education has been one of the most decisive determinants of people's life-chances; the nineteenth-century public school system blocked individual and group advancement and securely reproduced class membership.

This brings us to the question of the purpose of contemporary education. Children are taught in school that the purpose of education is to facilitate the development of their intelligence, talents, and abilities. Education affords them the opportunity to prepare for a career or a job, to advance in life, to succeed, and to enjoy personal fulfillment. The view is widely held that public education provides children of all classes, races, religions, and both sexes, with an equal chance to accomplish all of these things. It is often assumed that if a child fails at obtaining a job or a position in a post-secondary institution, it is his or her fault. The socioeconomic differences among former classmates in later life are usually attributed to the individual talents and abilities. Some educators say the purpose of education is measurable by output, that is, students' educational achievements, the success rates in exams, percentages of literate students, numbers of students that do and do not continue on to postsecondary education, skilled and unskilled employment. Educators and others in positions of authority are accused of refusing to monitor the direct relationship of discriminatory practices of resource allocation to education and work-related achievement.

This failure or refusal is a major cause of continuing and even worsening inequality between the sexes and between social classes. It is not only a primary cause of such inequality but it is related to the primary aim of the educational system, to perpetuate the status quo which is marked by social and economic inequality. Such inequality is necessary for the continuation of the capitalist system; in order to sustain itself, capitalism needs a reserve labour force, as we shall see later. Before examining men's and women's participation in this social and economic system and how it is preserved by public education, we will look at the nature of the capitalist system itself.

In hunting and gathering societies, work is all pervasive and not divided from other activities. Unemployment does not exist. Status is derived from family membership, age, and other factors. When status is derived from work in more agrarian or maritime societies, it is not the nature of work that counts, as most or all members perform the same sort of work; rather, the status indicator is one's ability to hunt or to fish. These features survive, to a large extent, for example, in Newfoundland and Labrador where the main indicator of status is "how hard you work," not what work you do.[1] This is true, as well, of Inuit society and other cultures in Canada. Most Canadians, however, are urban and live and work in a capitalist world. In capitalist society, the Protestant ethic survives in secular form as cultural norms attribute status and dignity to the worker while denying it to the unemployed. In a cash economy where labour power is bought and sold, social identity is very dependent on the type of occupation one holds.[2] Although sub-cultural membership cannot be overlooked, traditional indicators as outlined above have been eroded as cities get larger (Parker 1972; Parkin 1971). In the capitalist system, work becomes synonymous with the nature of one's employment. It also structures time and is tied in with the need to achieve, which is a cultural feature of capitalism. In other societies work means survival and survival is its primary, if not only, purpose. In capitalism, work has other functions such as providing an opportunity for social interaction and a major source of identity. (Because of all these factors, unemployment results in psychological trauma for the individual, as well as financial hardship.)

In the capitalist system, the unemployed serve as a reserve labour force, which will be needed in times of economic booms. In Canada, the Atlantic provinces have served to supply reserve labour;[3] witness the migration to and employment of Atlantic people in oil-rich Alberta in the 1970s. Women also comprise a temporary labour supply; during World War II, women performed "male" jobs and alleviated a severe labour shortage. Since the beginning of the post-war period, women have served as a reserve labour force:[4] they have filled most of the clerical and secretarial jobs, many of which are now performed by computers.

Women have served as a stop gap as the world of work has become more bureaucratized. Rigid sex segregation by occupation is likely to decrease only in times of labour shortages, such as wartime, or where new types of occupations are opening up. Note that the latter scenario did not, and is not, happening in Alberta's oilfields, the Beaufort Sea, and Newfoundland's offshore oilfields where new types of oil-related jobs are springing up. This is due partly to women's other ascribed responsibility of child care, which is difficult to combine with offshore work; women's education is another factor. Even when women begin to enter such jobs, the status and prestige associated with the occupation may begin to decrease and men enter that occupation in declining numbers.[5] An example is secretarial work at the turn of the century; as these jobs were performed less and less by upper-class men, they lost prestige and financial rewards.

Many of the jobs women do are seasonal. Women (and increasingly, youth of both sexes) whose unemployment rate is high, whose labour force participation rate is low, and whose choices are limited, are recruited temporarily.[6]

Marginal groups, such as women, are used on a last-hired, first-fired basis (Armstrong and Armstrong 1981). There is sufficient competition in the labour market to keep wages low and unions away. The mere existence of a reserve labour force can be used to threaten men who are unsatisfied with their wages and working conditions; they know others are willing and able to take their jobs. Employer control over women occurs both in the labour market and in the workplace, although it is often not recognized as control.

These facts are not cited by employers and may not be recognized by them; they may simply be carrying on previous business practices without even bothering to question why. If the question is addressed at all, employers point to a high turnover rate and high absenteeism among women. Most studies indicate, however, that a small number of employers account for most of the absenteeism that occurs. The two most important variables are age and job level; young people and less skilled workers have higher rates of absenteeism and women are overrepresented in both these groups, particularly the latter. Studies show that older women and professional women miss work less often than their male counterparts (Statistics Canada 1984). Myths abound and many reasons are given for the failure to hire women for certain types of jobs. Stereotyped differences ("women are too emotional") are pointed to as are differences in physical strength. Old concepts of propriety and beliefs about women's inability to get along are still not uncommon. Some potential employers fear female superiors will not be taken seriously even by their female subordinates. Some of these fears are based on realism as most women have been, and still are, raised to fill supportive, dependent roles, and hence, to be part of a secondary labour force.

How are boys and girls raised? What part does education play in preparing them for their respective roles in the world of work? The most obvious feature of education is the differences between boys' curricula and girls' curricula. There are also differences here between urban and rural, and between religions (especially in Newfoundland and Labrador where a denominational school system, with five religions each having their own school boards and schools, exists).[7] Even in the other nine provinces and two territories where education is almost exclusively the responsibility of the state, state education has failed to bring about equality of educational opportunity. In far too many schools woodworking and mechanics classes are open only to boys. If they are not closed, teachers all too often perpetuate that status quo by not encouraging female students to take such courses. Girls' motor skills are not afforded the chance to develop. In their primary years, girls are often discouraged from mathematical work; by junior high they either hate it or think they can't do it, or both. When students lack physics and math they lose the opportunity for further science education, industrial training, and the high wages and job satisfaction associated with such skilled labour. There are few female candidates for high-ranking positions in the science and technical industries; women have no input and these sectors remain very male-dominated. With their choices severely curtailed, most girls are headed for unskilled jobs usually in the service sector.

There exists a major problem with role models; because of the sort of education girls receive there are few female automechanics teachers. Role models play a significant part in a child's career or work orientation; many girls may not see mechanical work as a possible choice for them. Women teach home economics, men do not.

Teachers treat female children differently from male children. Almost inevitably if a boy asks the teacher for help, the teacher will show him how to perform the task; if a girl asks for assistance, the teacher will often complete the job for her, cultivating dependence rather than initiative. The message is emphasized that it is more important for a boy to achieve academically; girls must do well socially. An education professor of mine told his class a true story of how an extremely intelligent girl hid her Grade 5 reading level because she was afraid she wouldn't be popular; she was in kindergarten at the time. Experts say the case of this child was not an unusual one.

It has been argued by many that a different or inferior education (for girls, native children, Catholics, rural children) is legitimate. Proponents of this argument claim the educational opportunities are there (and on the surface, they may be) but these groups don't take advantage of them and underachieve because they don't work hard enough or don't need the chance for development. Note that even today the vast majority of people who make up the "government of education" are male. Support for "equal but different" education is alive and well even today.

Discrimination is an act, and is usually not subtle. Inequality, however, is less obvious, taken for granted and unrecognized; therefore, it is more difficult to attack. As Eileen Byrne (1978) says in *Women and Education*, "inequality in education has its roots in social history, which records the stereotyping of expected adult roles (social, economic, etc.) for men and women and the translation of them into different curricula." Certainly women on the whole are not as skilled or educated as men and they are not adequately prepared to do the jobs with high financial and social rewards. It is necessary to look at the causal relationship between the educational experience of girls and the inferior socioeconomic status of the women they become.

Women participate in a relatively small number of occupations, most of which have little or no promotional opportunities, low pay, and a vulnerability to replacement through technological advancement. The Dodge Task Force Report, *Labour Market Development in the 1980's* (Dodge 1 981), reveals that almost 80 percent of clerical workers are women while 99 percent of workers in the highly-unionized, high-paying construction industry are men. Female participation in "highly qualified" occupations is increasing slowly; from 39 percent in 1973 to 45 percent in 1982. However, as we entered the 1980s, over 62 percent of all Canadian women who worked outside the home worked in the occupational categories of clerical, sales, and services. If teaching, medicine, and health were added, the percentage would be 78. Only 11 percent of women were in jobs traditionally considered "male jobs."

According to this report, Canada pays women a far smaller proportion of wages than any other industrialized country; for every dollar paid to a man, a woman earns $0.58. Wage differentials range from $2,000 annually to $10,000 annually *within* occupations. There are also huge differences *between* occupations, such as construction worker and secretary. Dodge pointed out that the gap shows little sign of closing as teenage women continue to enter traditional female fields in large numbers. Official poverty data show poverty is increasingly associated with women, especially single mothers and elderly women who are widowed or single; this is referred to as "the feminization of poverty." In 1981, 30 percent of all poor families were headed by women, and 62 of every one hundred elderly women were poor (Canadian Advisory Council on the Status of Women 1984; Canadian Council on Social Development 1984; Proulx 1978). Hand in hand with poverty are hunger, cold, lack of sanitation, as well as feelings of inadequacy, illegitimacy, and failure. Single mothers and elderly women are in very vulnerable, powerless positions and have little hope of improving their lives; members of these groups are likely to become the long-term poor. Their children will most likely be subject to the same sort of lifestyle; poverty means a day-to-day existence and an inability to plan for the long term.

Education and training will not necessarily lead to equal status for men and women but without education, especially improved education, and training, women's inferior socioeconomic status is guaranteed.[8]

Today boys are socialized to develop competitiveness and aggressiveness; they are socialized to be comfortable in hierarchies and impersonal relationships. Men are trained to make work the focal point in their lives. This serves to enhance production in the workplace but it does not allow for full personal growth and well-being. Women, on the other hand, are not provided with the chance to develop and utilize their intelligence and abilities in a public and influential manner. Both boys and girls should be trained for full participation in government, the economy, personal relationships, parenthood, and community development. The men who dominate the governments of today were educated in a system in which individual value over the community and achievement, at large cost, was emphasized. Male-dominated governments are increasingly prioritizing preparation for war and ignoring growing poverty, bad housing, mental illness, disease, crime, and unemployment. As these problems become more and more widespread and institutionalized, children of both sexes need to be educated to deal with them.

How might inequalities in the schooling system be corrected? The obvious answer is through a new education that results in awareness, first of all for teachers to raise their consciousness about how boys and girls are treated and fare differently in school.

If teachers are educated about stereotyping in their teacher-training courses, the cycle will be broken, at least partly, and more avenues will be open to girls and women. Experts agree that most children are sexist by age 5 so parents need to be educated, and the media, including children's media, must be surveyed very closely. Women themselves must take up the challenge by encouraging each other in their career pursuits, by asserting themselves as individuals and groups to legislators and others in positions of power and influence, and by trying to develop a balance of achievement-orientation and nurturance. As many women carry out the dual roles of worker and parent and serve as role models for their own sons and daughters, the foundations are already laid.

# ENDNOTES

1    For a more complete examination of work and status in Newfoundland society, see Wadel (1973) and Hill (1983).

2    For a more complete examination of this, see Hayes and Nutman (1981). This book provides much information on the other issues surrounding work in the capitalist context.

3    For a deeper understanding of the role of the regions in Canada in relation to the Canadian economy, see Matthews (1981).

4    This topic and related ones were discussed at an international conference entitled "Women and Oil" sponsored by the Institute of Social and Economic Research, Memorial University, St. John's, Newfoundland and Labrador, September, 1985.

5    The facts and myths surrounding women in the labour force and absenteeism are discussed more fully in *Sex and Caste in America* by Carol Andreas (1971).

6    This contrasts with non-industrial societies in which production centres wholly on the home and women's economic value is enormous, not just as the producer of children, but also as the producer of food, clothing, and shelter. Even in these societies, however, women's work lacks status and the division of labour is legitimized by religion. With industrialization, the family becomes separate from the economy, the division of labour strengthened, and women became more ghettoized into low-paying, low-status occupations.

7    For more information on the denominational school system in Newfoundland and Labrador, consult *Education and Culture in Newfoundland* by Frederick W. Rowe (1976). The denominational school system was guaranteed in the Terms of Union with Canada in 1949 and the Canadian Constitution.

8    It should he stressed that the arena of sexual politics is much wider than just the labour market; women's participation is restricted in religion, electoral government, and elsewhere. A new form of education could help alleviate these discrepancies as well.

# REFERENCES

Andreas, Carol (1971). *Sex and caste in America*, Englewood Cliffs: Prentice Hall, Inc.

Armstrong, Pat, and Hugh Armstrong (1981). *Women and jobs: The Canadian case*, Ottawa: Canadian Centre for Policy Alternatives.

Byrne, Eileen (1978). *Women and education*, London: Tavistock Publications.

Canadian Advisory Council on the Status of Women. (1984). *Annual report: 1983–84*. Ottawa: The Canadian Advisory Council on the Status of Women.

Canadian Council on Social Development. (1984). *Not enough: The meaning and measurement of poverty in Canada*, Ottawa: Report of the Canadian Council on Social Development National Task Force on the Definition and Measurement of Poverty in Canada.

Dodge, David (1981). *Labour market development in the 1980s*, Ottawa: Employment and Immigration Canada.

Goodsell, Willystine (1923). *The education of women: Its social background and its problems*, New York: The Macmillan Company.

Hayes, John, and Peter Nutman (1981). *Understanding the unemployed: The psychological effects of unemployment*, London: Tavistock Publications.

Hill, Robert H. (1983). The meaning of work and the reality of unemployment in the Newfoundland context. Research Report, Community Services Council, Newfoundland and Labrador.

Matthews, Ralph (1981). *The creation of regional dependency*, Toronto: University of Toronto Press.

More, Hannah (1974). *Strictures on the modern system of female education with a view to the principles and conduct prevalent among women of rank and fortune, vol 1*, New York: Garland Publishing Inc. (First published by T. Cadell Junior and W. Davies of London, 1799).

Parker, Richard (1972). *The myth of the middle class*, New York: Harper and Row.

Parkin, Frank (1971). *Class inequality and political order: Social stratification in capitalist and communist societies*, London: MacGibbon and Kee, Ltd.

Proulx, Monique (1978). *Five million women: A study of the Canadian housewife*, Ottawa: Canadian Advisory Council on the Status of Women.

Rowe, Frederick W. (1976). *Education and culture in Newfoundland*, Toronto: McGraw-Hill Ryerson.

Statistics Canada (1984). *Women in the work world*, Ottawa: Minister of Supply and Services.

Wadel, Cato (1973). *Now whose fault is that? The struggle for self-esteem in the face of chronic unemployment*, Newfoundland Social and Economic Studies No. 11, St. John's: Institute of Social and Economic Research, Memorial University of Newfoundland.

## Exercises

1. In history how have schools functioned to reproduce gender and class discrimination?
2. Discuss woman as a "reserve labour force." Who are the "others" that also fill this need? How does this create control of women and marginalized persons?
3. How are boys and girls treated differently in schools?
4. How are stereotypes and prejudices part of these practices?

# Chapter 18

# Schoolgirls: Young Women, Self-Esteem, and the Confidence Gap

## Peggy Orenstein

### Unbalanced Equations: Girls, Math, and the Confidence Gap

Although the skewed equations of voice and silence are not the exclusive province of math or science, they are arguably the most damaging in those classes, where the tradition of male dominance is most entrenched. *Shortchanging Girls, Shortchanging America* showed that girls and boys who like math and science have higher levels of self-esteem than other children (and, for that matter, that children with high self-esteem tend to like math and science). For girls in particular, those subjects are also tied to ambition: Girls who like math and science — who are, perhaps, more resistant to traditional gender roles — are more likely to aspire to careers as professionals. As adults, women who have taken more than two math courses in college are the only ones who subsequently achieve pay equity and even earn more than their male counterparts.[1]

Unfortunately, girls are far less likely than boys to retain their affection for math and science. As they move through school, their confidence in their mathematical abilities falters and their competence soon follows suit.[2] It's important to note that the confidence drop often *precedes* the competence drop: Even in early adolescence, girls who perform as well as boys often evaluate their skills as lesser. By their senior year, convinced of their ineptitude, they become less persistent in solving problems than their male peers and less likely than boys with poorer grades in the same class to believe they can pursue a math-related career.[3]

Amy is one of those girls who have little faith in her math skills, although her performance is well above average. "School is important to me," she says during lunch one day, when I catch her struggling with a homework assignment. "I want to do good in school and be proud of myself. I don't want to be a lazy bum. And I'll need math when I'm older. There's math in everything, no matter what, so it's important to learn. So I know I should have a better attitude, but I just want to give up. It's not that I don't try, it's just that I don't believe in myself and I don't get it. I'm just so slow." She glares down at her paper.

Amy goes on to say that a person has to be smarter to do well at math than at English. She also believes that girls — herself included — have a natural bent toward English and boys toward math, which, by her logic, would make girls less intelligent than boys. When I point this out, she begins to backtrack, but then stops, leans forward, and drops her voice, continuing in a solemn, confidential tone. "Boys do better in math, believe me, they do. Girls, we have other things on our minds, I guess."

Yet in spite of this purported genetic disadvantage, Amy receives an A in math, which clinches her spot on the school honor roll. The news doesn't change her assumptions one whit.

"It's not hard to get an A in here," she says. "Basically you just have to show up. And I still think I've done it wrong every day. I'll probably be in, like, special ed. math next year."

From her vantage point in the front of the class, Mrs. Richter says she can see the girls' waning interest in her subject, and it frustrates her. She is especially disturbed by a trend she's recently noticed: The boys in her class tend to improve over the course of the school year — some even jump from D's to B's or A's — while girls stay exactly where they were in September, the good students remaining good students, the poor students remaining poor. She worries that, for the girls, the holding pattern is simply temporary. Next year, perhaps the year after, even the good students may begin to slide; they simply don't trust their ability.

"The boys see math as something that shows they're brainy and they like being able to show off that way," Mrs. Richter explains. "And they're more risk-taking than the girls, so they'll do better on tests every time, even if the girls turn in all their work and the boys don't. It's like the girls set themselves up to fail. They do the work. I see them practice one kind of problem over and over because I've told them it'll be on a test. But then the test comes and they miss it anyway. I've heard them say, 'Oh no, I got that kind of problem wrong last time.' So even though they practiced it, they go and get it wrong again. Amy does that. She'll look at a problem and say, 'There's no way I can do this,' and give up, even though I know she has the skills. But the boys are different: They can get all the homework wrong, but they don't care as long as they tried. And then they figure out why it's wrong instead of being embarrassed about it. That makes them more confident."

Mrs. Richter considers parents, more than teachers, to be responsible for girls' confidence gap. Every year, she says, her female students tell her, "My mother said she couldn't do math either," as if math skills are genetic, which, the teacher hastens to add, they are not.[4] Still, she admits, the classroom culture can further undercut the girls. "I try to teach them the same; I try to call on them the same. But I know I don't always hold them accountable the same way. I let the girls off the hook because they get so embarrassed when they're wrong. And the boys want control of the class, so sometimes they get it …." She trails off, shaking her head. "I don't know," she says. "We try, but somehow we're still not getting to the girls, and we're going to lose them."

## You Can Say "I Think" in There

Teachers at Weston varied tremendously in their reactions to boys' dominance in their classroom. Some, like Mr. Sinclair, simply didn't see it. Others fought the boys for control: One eighth-grade history teacher — who proudly told me that his wife had founded the local NOW chapter — would break into class discussions to say, "We haven't heard from any of the girls in the room. What do you think?" The girls seemed to be uncomfortable with such attention at first, but, as the year progressed, they became increasingly vocal. During a lesson on England's debtor's prisons one girl even yelled out, "What about the women? What happened to them?"

Another teacher, Liz Muney, who runs the district's gifted program and teaches sixth grade at Weston, told me that when *Shortchanging*

*Girls, Shortchanging America* was first released, she discussed its findings with her class. She explained that, from now on, she was going to call equally on girls and boys, and, just to make sure that she did, she held her attendance roster during class.

"After two days the boys blew up," she told me one afternoon during a break between classes. "They started complaining and saying that I was calling on the girls more than them. I showed them it wasn't true and they had to back down. I kept on doing it, but for the boys, equality was hard to get used to; they perceived it as a big loss."

Like the teachers, the girls I interviewed were not always aware that they were being ignored in class (in some classes, such as math, they even preferred it), but their favorite teachers just happened to be the ones who actively wrestled with the hidden curriculum. For Amy, Evie, and Becca that teacher is Ms. Nellas, with whom they study American history.

"She teaches good," Becca assures me one day during lunch.

"Yeah," Evie says. "She makes you want to strive to be better. She'll do 'the power clap' and say how good you're doing …."

"Even if your work sucks," interrupts Amy, whose work rarely "sucks." "So you try really hard. And you can say what you want in there and no one ever says you're wrong; it's like, you're not afraid to say 'I think.'"

Becca returns to her original assessment: "She teaches good," she says, nodding her head.

Amy's demeanor in Ms. Nellas' class is utterly different than it is in math, science, or even English: She uncrosses her legs and plants both feet on the floor. She sits up straight, leans forward, and thrusts her hand in the air. Once, she even gives an impatient (and uncharacteristic) little wave for attention.

This is election year, and when I first visit Ms. Nellas' class in late October, she is discussing the electoral college. She stands at the front of the room, a craggy-faced woman with an easy smile, and offers a blunt explanation of that esoteric organization: "The reason there's an electoral college is that people who wrote the constitution — who were all men — *didn't* really want everyone to participate in electing officials," she says. "They only trusted people like themselves, so they said, 'We don't want the common people to vote. They can't read or write and we can't trust them to elect leaders.' And they certainly didn't trust *women*, so they weren't about to let *them* vote."

During the lesson, boys raise their hands roughly twice as often as girls, but Ms. Nellas has a trick for making sure that girls who do volunteer are recognized: After she asks a question she looks around the room to see whose hands are up, then says, "Okay, first Randy, then Jeffrey, then Amy." If she inadvertently continues without exhausting the list, the slighted students are quick to protest. She also promotes a more tolerant culture through her classroom decor: Among the encouraging messages she has posted on the classroom walls are "You Have a *Duty* to *Assist* Anyone Who Asks for Help" and the somewhat convoluted "Everybody Is Good at *Some* of the Abilities." Under the clock, in the most strategic spot in the room, there is a yellowed poster depicting a teacher in Renaissance garb saying to his student, "Columbus, will yer [sic] sit down and stop asking all those dumb questions?" Beneath it a caption reads: "'Dumb' questions lead to learning. Don't be afraid to ask."

Amy's class meets just before Ms. Nellas' free period, so, one afternoon after the bell rings, I linger behind to chat. Ms. Nellas invites me to sit at one of the students' recently vacated desks and settles in opposite me. As a veteran teacher — she's been in the profession for over 20 years — Ms. Nellas is comfortable discussing both her strengths and her weaknesses. She looks pleased when I tell her that girls seem to feel the most comfortable in her class, but adamantly denies that she's solved the gender dilemma.

"I definitely play to the boys," she says, shaking her head. "I know I do. The squeaky wheel gets the grease and they're louder."

She mentions Andrew, a curly haired, slightly pudgy boy in Amy's class who shoots his hand up — sometimes snapping his fingers for attention — whenever she asks a question. When called on, he tends not only to answer but to offer up an additional mini-lecture of his own.

"Andrew's into history," Ms. Nellas says. "He knows a lot and he teaches the class things with what he has to say, so he's a good resource and I like that. But on the other hand he's loud, and, like a lot of boys, he pulls my attention. I know that means they walk out of here with greater self-esteem, they feel more valued. For the girls, it seems more important that they feel a personal bond, that makes them feel valued. I have that with Amy, Evie, and Becca, but I don't have that with all of them. I try to make it up some by encouraging girls to talk, by stressing that a question is a question and every question is worthwhile" — Ms. Nellas gestures to her Columbus poster — "but I know some girls end up feeling bad, they feel reduced by the experience of my class."

Like many teachers at Weston, Ms. Nellas is an advocate of cooperative learning: students collaborating on projects in groups, each with an assigned role. Cooperative learning — in which success is not contingent on quick response time or a loud voice — is said to be especially beneficial for girls and has become somewhat voguish in progressive schools. But, as with lab groups, the interactions, if not effectively monitored, can merely reinforce the students' stereotypes. "I've noticed that when they do group work, the boys want to be the leader," Ms. Nellas says, "and the girls always take the recorder role and that's a problem. I suppose I let it happen, too, but I don't want to assign them the roles in groups because I'm afraid of my own prejudices. I think I'd pick the quick students to lead the group, and so I might end up with the boys too, although I think I'd pick more girls than they do.

"The dynamics are already in place when they get here," she continues, "and they don't improve as they get older: When I teach high school, boys put their arm around me, pat my head like I'm a pet or something because I'm a woman. It can be funny, but it's still a power play. It's all about control, about who's in charge. When they really act out, though, I'll just stop the class and wait, even if it takes 30 seconds and it's driving me crazy. That sounds like a long time, but it's less of a waste, in the end, than sending them to the principal or yelling at the student. That way, they don't get the power, they don't get the attention, and they don't get the control. And *maybe* you can make it a little more equal."

## Too Cute to Be Competent

The lessons of the hidden curriculum teach girls to value silence and compliance, to view those qualities as a virtue. In fact, students tend to believe that, although they pay more attention to boys, teachers actually like girls better: As one Weston girl once told me, ticking the list off on her fingers, "teachers like us because we're nicer, quieter, and better behaved."[5] And the girls are right: Teachers *are* more likely to describe girls as "ideal" pupils.[6] Yet since, in practice, educators reward assertiveness and aggression over docility, the very behavior that is prized in girls becomes an obstacle to their success. Furthermore, the praise girls earn for their exemplary passivity discourages them from experimenting with the more active, risk-taking learning styles that would serve them better in the long run.[7] As the author of one study put it, by adolescence, girls have learned to get along, while boys have learned to get ahead.[8]

Girls like Lindsay and Suzy are the biggest losers: Gifted girls, who best combine tractability with superior performance, receive less attention from their teachers, and often their talents are overlooked entirely. When Liz Muney, who directs the gifted program in the Weston school district, reviewed her files in the late 1980s, she discovered that boys were referred to her twice as often as girls for special testing, precisely because giftedness is seen as aberrant, and girls strive to conform. Since she alerted teachers to her findings, she says, the ratio in the district has improved.

Although they're ignored in the classroom, smart girls are singled out by their peers for stigmatization.[9] Asked directly, most of the girls at Weston will say that it is acceptable for a girl to excel, to get good grades. Yet behind their backs, girls like Lindsay and Suzy are referred to as "schoolgirls," an insult so great that, once tipped off, I never revealed the title of this book. The social pressure, Liz Muney says, has prompted innumerable Weston girls to repudiate their intelligence (as well as their self-esteem) and drop out of the district's gifted program.

As they proceed through school — and, in the case of Lindsay and Suzy, as they consider career options — gifted girls who remain academically engaged must negotiate between the independence necessary to fulfill their potential and the compliance which, although expected of them, is in direct conflict with standing out and shining bright. The task is daunting: How can they, after all, be both selfless and selfish, silent and outspoken, cooperative and competitive?

In their extensive work on girls' psychological development conducted in two private all-girls schools, psychologists Lyn Mikel Brown and Carol Gilligan found that, confounded by this irresolvable dilemma, their subjects invented a superior self who could solve it — "the perfect girl": "the girl who has no bad thoughts or feelings, the kind of person everyone wants to be with ... [it is] the girl who speaks quietly, calmly, who is always nice and kind, never mean or bossy."[10] The "perfect girl" acts as an imaginary companion and a constant reproach. She reminds young women to silence themselves rather than speak their true feelings, which they come to consider "stupid," "selfish," "rude," or just plain irrelevant. To achieve the ideal that this exemplary creature represents, Brown and Gilligan's girls believed they must suppress the unruly self, with all of its nasty opinions and rebellious feelings; as Carolyn Heilbrun has written, they believed they must sacrifice "truth on the altar of niceness."[11]

In her relentless selflessness, the "perfect girl" is painfully reminiscent of the Victorian "angel in the house," the woman who, through saintlike virtue, conquers personal desire and lives only to enhance the lives of others. In that era, if women unleashed anger or rebelliousness they were deemed monsters; they were shut away, depicted, like Bertha in Charlotte Brontë's *Jane Eyre*, as the "madwoman in the attic."[12] Such renunciation of self inevitably caused ill health: The nineteenth century saw an upswing of emotional "hysteria" in upper-class women, as well as an epidemic of "fasting girls," who willfully refused food, sometimes unto death.[13]

But today's "perfect girl" doesn't just bludgeon young women into a bland silence: she wreaks havoc on their academic self-image as well. Girls like Lindsay and Suzy believe that, in addition to being perfectly nice, they must be perfectly smart. In his study of the effects of gender, race, and class on self-esteem, psychologist Charles L. Richman found that high-achieving white girls in particular are subject to unrealistic standards of success. When they fell short, they overgeneralized failures with an intense self-punitiveness; by late adolescence, their self-esteem had spiraled downward."

## ENDNOTES

1    Clifford Adelman, "Women at Thirtysomething: Paradoxes of Attainment," Washington, DC: Office of Educational Research and Improvement, 1991. Adelman tracked over 12,000 high school graduates from their high school graduation in 1972 until they were 32. Although the women received higher grades, were awarded more scholarships, and completed their

BAs faster, they subsequently received lower pay than their male counterparts, were awarded fewer promotions, and were more frequently unemployed. Women who had taken two or more math courses in college were the sole exception to this pattern.

2    Confidence is the variable most strongly correlated with achievement in math, particularly for girls. Yet even when they perform as well as boys, girls' confidence drops significantly during their middle school years, with girls who view the subject as "male" showing consistently poorer performance than girls who do not hold that view. The AAUW Educational Foundation, *The AAUW Report, p.* 28; Margaret R. Meyer and Mary Schatz Koehler, "Internal Influences on Gender Differences in Mathematics," in *Mathematics and Gender*, Elizabeth Fennema and Gilah C. Leder, eds., New York: Teachers College Press, 1990, pp. 91–92; Peter Kloosterman, "Attributions, Performance Following Failure, and Motivation in Mathematics," *Mathematics and Gender*, p. 119; Elizabeth Fennema and Julia Sherman, "Sex-Related Differences in Mathematics Achievement, Spatial Visualization and Affective Factors," *American Educational Research Journal*, 14, 1 (1977), pp. 51–71. American Association of University Women, *Shortchanging Girls, Shortchanging America: Executive Summary*, Washington, DC: American Association of University Women, 1991, p. 13, Graph G.

3    Heather Featherstone, "Girls' Math Achievement: What We Do and Don't Know," *The Harvard Education Letter*, January 1986, p. 3. Girls are also more likely than boys to lose heart after a failure in math and, subsequently, to achieve at a lower level. This may largely be due to a difference in what psychologists call "effort attribution." When girls do well, they assume it is because they've worked hard or are lucky, while boys attribute success to ability. Meanwhile, girls blame failure on incompetence, while boys ascribe it to laziness or bad luck. Girls' relatively poorer performance on standardized tests may derive from this difference: since girls attribute success to hard work, they approach a test that purports to measure raw ability with less confidence than do boys. Unfortunately, standardized tests determine students' futures. In 1993, three out of five semifinalists for the National Merit Scholarship, which is based on Preliminary Scholastic Aptitude Test (PSAT) scores, were boys. That same year, a new federally funded college scholarship program intended to encourage students to enter math- and science-related fields, used students' performance on the American College Testing Program Assessment (ACT) as its sole criterion, and conferred 75 percent of its awards on boys. Malcolm Gladwell, "Pythagorean Sexism," *Washington Post*, March 14, 1993, p. C3; "Boys

Predominate in a Contest, Fueling Complaint of Test Bias," *New York Times*, May 26, 1993, p. B7; Michael Winerip, "Study Finds Boys Receive 75% of New Science Scholarships," *New York Times*, November 17, 1993, p. B7.

4   The "math gene" is a persistent, mythical explanation for girls' disinclination toward math. Yet Patricia B. Campbell points out that in studies conducted after 1974 (not, incidentally, coincident with the rise of the feminist movement in this country), gender differences in achievement have declined by 50 percent. Even the oft-cited gender difference in spatial ability declines dramatically when girls are exposed more frequently to spatial tasks. If math skills were biologically determined they would be impervious to changing political ideology. Nor can the "math gene" explain why girls' math achievement relative to boys' varies across ethnic lines: In a study of students in Hawaii, for instance, non-Caucasian girls both outperformed and outnumbered males in top math classes. Further, the studies that are most often used to support gender differences in math — conducted by Camilla Benbow and Julian Stanley of Johns Hopkins University — are flawed. Not only did they rely on the Scholastic Aptitude Test (SAT), which is considered by many to be biased against both girls and minority boys, but they assumed that, because the students were in the same classes, they had identical learning experiences. Finally, according to biologist Robert Sapolsky, the studies turned up enormous overlap between boys' and girls' scores, making it impossible to predict who would perform better in any randomly selected pair. Given these factors, a biologically driven achievement gap does not explain girls' reluctance to pursue math: a confidence gap, however, does. Patricia B. Campbell, "Math, Science and Too Few Girls: Enough Is Known for Action," documentation developed under the auspices of the Women's Educational Equity Act by Campbell-Kibler Associates, Groton, MA, 1991; Marcia C. Linn and Janet S. Hyde, "Gender, Mathematics, and Science," *Educational Researcher*, 18, 8, pp. 17–27; P.R. Brandon, B.J. Newton, and O. Hamond, "Children's Mathematics Achievement in Hawaii: Sex Differences Favoring Girls," *American Educational Research journal*, 24, 3 (1987), pp. 437–61; Robert Sapolsky, "The Case of the Falling Nightwatchmen," *Discover*, July 1987, p. 44.

5   *Shortchanging Girls, Shortchanging America* confirmed that children believe teachers like girls more, but boys receive more overall attention. American Association of University Women, *Shortchanging Girls, Shortchanging America: Full Data Report*, Washington, DC: American Association of University Women, 1990, p. 65.

6    American Association of University Women, "Equitable Treatment of Girls and Boys in the Classroom," *AAUW Equity Brief*, June 1991, p. 3.

7    AAUW, "Equitable Treatment," p. 3.

8    Bruce Bower, "Gender Paths Wind Toward Self-Esteem," *Science News*, 143, 20, (1993), p. 308.

9    Richard L. Luftig and Marci L. Nichols, "Assessing the Social Status of Gifted Students by Their Age Peers," *Gifted Child Quarterly*, 34, 3 (1990), p. 111. Luftig and Nichols found that gifted girls were the least popular among their peers of all ability/gender groups.

10   Lyn Mikel Brown and Carol Gilligan, "The Psychology of Women and the Development of Girls," paper presented at the Laurel-Harvard Conference on the Psychology of Women and the Education of Girls, Cleveland, OH, April 1990, p. 16. See also Brown and Gilligan, *Meeting at the Crossroads: Women's Psychology and Girls' Development*, Cambridge, MA: Harvard University Press, 1992; and Carol Gilligan, Nona P. Lyons, and Trudy J. Hanmer, eds., *Making Connections: The Relational Worlds of Adolescent Girls at Emma Willard School*, Cambridge, MA: Harvard University Press, 1990. Brown, Gilligan, and their colleagues' work was conducted largely among white middleclass girls at all-girl schools and so is, perhaps, most appropriately applied to girls such as Lindsay and Suzy, who are demographically similar.

11   Carolyn G. Heilbrun, review of *Meeting at the Crossroads*, by Lyn Mikel Brown and Carol Gilligan, in *The New York Times Book Review*, October 4, 1992, pp. 12–13.

12   Sandra M. Gilbert and Susan Gubar, *The Madwoman in the Attic: The Woman Writer and the Nineteenth Century Literary Imagination*, New Haven, CT: Yale University Press, 1979, pp. 22, 336–71. See also Tillie Olsen, *Silences*, New York: Delacorte Press, 1965; reprint, New York: Delta/Seymour Lawrence, 1989, pp. 213–16. Olsen cites Virginia Woolf's "Professions for Women," in which Woolf wrote that the angel in the house "bothered me and wasted my time and so tormented me that at last I killed her," (p. 213).

13   Joan Jacobs Brumberg, *Fasting Girls: The Emergence of Anorexia Nervosa as a Modern Disease*, Cambridge, MA: Harvard University Press, 1988, pp. 61–62.

## References

Adelman, Clifford. (1991). Women at thirtysomething: Paradoxes of attainment. Washington, DC: Office of Educational Research and Improvement.

American Association of University Women (1991). *Shortchanging girls, shortchanging America: Executive summary,* Washington, DC: American Association of University Women.

—— (1991). Equitable treatment of girls and boys in the classroom. *AAUW Equity Brief.*

—— (1990). *Shortchanging girls, shortchanging America: Full data report,* Washington, DC: American Association of University Women.

—— (1992). *The AAUW report: How schools shortchange girls,* Washington, DC: The AAUW Educational Foundation and National Educational Association.

Bower, Bruce (1993). Gender paths wind toward self-esteem. *Science News,* 143(20), 308.

Brandon, P.R., B. J. Newton, and O. Hammond (1987). Children's mathematics achievement in Hawaii: Sex differences favoring girls. *American Educational Research Journal,* 24(3), 437–61.

Brown, Lyn Mikel, and Carol Gilligan (1990). The psychology of women and the development of girls. Paper presented at the Harvard-Laurel Conference on the Psychology of Women, Cleveland, OH.

—— (1990). *Meeting at the crossroads: Women's psychology and girls' development,* Cambridge, MA: Harvard University Press.

Brumberg, Joan Jacobs (1988). *Fasting girls: The emergence of anorexia nervosa as a modern disease,* Cambridge, MA: Harvard University Press.

Campbell, Patricia B. (1991). Math, science and too few girls: Enough is known for action. Documentation developed under the auspices of the Women's Educational Equity Act by Campbell-Kibler Associates, Groton, MA.

Featherstone, Heather (1986). Girls' math achievement: What we do and don't know. *The Harvard Education Letter,* January, 1–5.

Fennema, Elizabeth, and Julia Sherman (1977). Sex-related differences in mathematics achievement, spatial visualization and affective factors. *American Educational Research journal,* 14(1), 51–71.

Fennema, Elizabeth, and Gilah C. Leder (eds.) (1990). *Mathematics and gender,* New York: Teachers College Press.

Gilbert, Sandra M., and Susan Gubar (1979). *The madwoman in the attic: The woman writer and the nineteenth century literary imagination,* New Haven: Yale University Press.

Gilligan, Carol, Nona P. Lyons, and Trudy J. Hanmer (eds.) (1990). *Making connections: The relational worlds of adolescent girls at Emma Willard School,* Cambridge, MA: Harvard University Press.

Gladwell, Malcolm (1993). Pythagorean sexism. *Washington Post,* March 14, C3.

Linn, Marcia C., and Janet S. Hyde (1989). Gender, mathematics, and science. *Educational Researcher,* 18(8), 17–27.

Luftig, Richard L., and Marci L. Nichols (1990). Assessing the social status of gifted students by their age peers. *Gifted Child Quarterly*, 34(3), 111-15.

Olsen, Tillie (1965). *Silences,* New York: Delacorte Press; reprint, New York: Delta/Seymour Lawrence, 1989.

Richman, Charles L., M. L. Clark, and Kathryn P. Brown (1985). General and specific self-esteem in late adolescent students: Race x gender x SES effects. *Adolescence*, 20(79), 555–66.

Sapolsky, Robert (1987). The case of the falling nightwatchmen. *Discover*, July, 42.

Winerip, Michael (1993). Study finds boys receive 75% of new science scholarships. *New York Times*, November 17, B7.

## Exercises

1. Discuss the relationship of confidence and competence in mathematics.
2. How can teachers "treating girls the same" actually contribute to the problem of girls and confidence?
3. How could alternative action on the teacher's part help address this problem?
4. "Equity" is perceived as a loss to some boys. Discuss this as an example of privilege in inequity in classrooms and as a disadvantage in current inequitable classrooms.
5. How can teachers alter gender dynamics in classrooms?

# Chapter 19

# Gender Equity and Schooling: Linking Research and Policy

## Rebecca Priegert Coulter

Feminist research has had a noticeable effect on education policy makers.[1] Although a significant portion of the most important and influential research has come from the field of women's studies, feminist scholars in faculties of education as well as teacher-researchers[2] have also made key contributions. Indeed, the nature and purpose of feminist research in education, whether it occurs inside or outside faculties of education, is such that no artificial polarity between research and policy is created; rather, there is a conscious linking of the two — research informs policy making, and policy successes and failures inform research. At the same time, some specific types and forms of feminist research have been more widely influential in the policy arena than have others. The recent history of research and policy making illustrates both how these two activities are linked, largely through the efforts of female educators in a variety of roles, and why some research approaches are more acceptable to and are used more often by policy makers than are others.

## Sex Roles, Stereotyping, and Schooling

For centuries, access to education has been seen as a central policy initiative in the struggle for women's equality. With the resurgence of the women's movement in Canada during the late 1960s, education was again identified as a key policy domain. The Royal Commission on the Status of Women in Canada (1970) listed education as one of nine public policy areas "particularly germane to the status of women" (p. ix). By using the contemporary research on sex-role socialization, the Commission and many women's groups argued that sex-role stereotyping, the lack of strong female role models for girls, and inadequate career counselling were key factors contributing to women's inequality in Canada. For the best part of the next two decades, this type of analysis, as part of a larger liberal feminist[3] agenda, shaped policy making around women's education, and resulted in remarkably similar initiatives across the country.

The earliest initiatives centred on sex-role stereotyping in textbooks. During the 1970s several research studies were conducted (Ad Hoc Committee Respecting the Status of Women in the North York System, 1975; Batcher, Brackstone, Winter, and Wright, 1975; Cullen, 1972; Women in Teaching, 1975). They relied heavily on a quantitative approach to stereotyping and reported how many times women and men appeared in stories and illustrations, and in what types of roles in the work force and family. All studies came to the same conclusion. Textbooks were biased. Batcher et al. (1975), for example, concluded from their review of all the reading series approved for use in Grades 4 to 6 in Ontario schools, that none could be termed "positive image" or "non-sexist" (p. i). A North York study found ample evidence of sexism in the readers used in Grades 1 to 3 as well as "shocking evidence of various other kinds of rigid stereotyping and of racism" (Ad Hoc Committee, 1975, p. 16). Policy was developed in response to this research. By 1987 every Canadian province had guidelines for textbook selection and an evaluation grid designed to eliminate sex bias in learning materials (Julien, 1987, p. 53).[4]

Closely tied to the concern for sex-role stereotyping in textbooks was an emerging assessment of women's absence from the curriculum in general (Pierson, 1995). Beginning in the 1970s, a range of lesson plans and units was developed to assist teachers. For example, the British Columbia Teachers' Federation (BCTF), through its Lesson Aids Service, published a variety of kits and curriculum packages with titles such as "Women in the Community," "Famous Canadian Women," "Early

Canadian Women," and "From Captivity to Choice: Native Women in Canadian Literature." The Ontario Ministry of Education (1977) published a resource guide for teachers called *Sex-Role Stereotyping and Women's Studies*, which included units of study, resource lists, and teaching suggestions for teachers at all grade levels. In 1977, the British Columbia Department of Education published *Women's Studies: A Resource Guide for Teachers*. At the same time, other government agencies, institutions, and commercial publishers began producing materials for classroom use. The Ontario Institute for Studies in Education, for example, compiled *The Women's Kit* (1974), a collection of print and audio-visual materials. So began the first stage of curriculum reform, a clear illustration of what has been called "the add women and stir" model, an approach still prevalent today. Information about women continues to be added to existing curricula in the form of individual lessons or a special unit.

Education policies also were shaped in response to women's failure to enroll in mathematics, sciences, and technology courses, and women's apparent lack of interest in nontraditional work in the trades. This area of concern has been pursued vigorously in the policy domain because it maps onto the discourse about education for global competitiveness and schooling for the new economic realities. Again, based on sex-role theory, it was argued that girls lacked effective role models and received inadequate career counselling, and hence were socialized to consider only a narrow range of occupations. The policy response to this "problem" has been massive. As Julien (1987) discovered,

> The breadth of guidance materials made available by the provinces to female students concerning career options is enormous. Preparing young women for the new technology, broadening their career goals to include options that may have seemed unavailable to them, and introducing non-traditional occupations as career alternatives, are subjects of a seemingly constant flow of literature. (p. 5)

Across Canada, teacher federations, school boards, ministries of education and labour/employment, women's directorates/secretariats, and women's groups such as Women Into Scholarship, Engineering,

Science and Technology, and the Women Inventors' Project developed posters, pamphlets, videotapes, films, and workshops for girls, urging them to be all that they could be. Role modelling and mentoring programs, speakers' bureaus, girls-only career days, and girl-friendly computer courses were developed. The extent of these types of responses is illustrated in a 1992 survey of Canadian mathematics and science programs for girls and women conducted by the Nova Scotia Women's Directorate. This survey yielded information about 92 separate programs as well as a conclusion that there were many more programs not reporting (Armour and Associates, 1992, p. 5).

Across Canada, the dominant approach to gender-equity policies in education, and even then implemented unevenly and inconsistently, remains the relatively shallow one of sex-role stereotyping first articulated in the 1970s. A recent report from the Maritime Provinces Education Foundation (1991), for example, concluded that in education there was

> a) the need to promote a better self-image among female students beginning in the earliest grades; b) the need to expose female students to a broader range of career options, especially in the field of mathematics, science and technology; and c) the need to recognize and build on the positive effect that role modelling has on female students. (pp. i-ii)

Ontario's recent Royal Commission on Learning (1994) identified sex-role stereotyping, the absence of women in physics, engineering, and technology, and the lack of women's awareness about the range of career opportunities available as key gender-equity issues (pp. 42–43). These conclusions are no different from those in the 1970 report of the Royal Commission on the Status of Women.

Why sex-role socialization theory remains dominant in education can in part be explained by the fact that it is a form of critique easily accommodated within existing state arrangements and liberal notions of equality of opportunity. It sits very comfortably with a view of the state as a relatively benign institution, and one that is inherently fair. Coupled with this explanation is the force of a common understanding of teaching, an understanding shaped overwhelmingly by educational psychology and its emphasis on the individual. In this context, each student must be helped to realize his/her full potential and becomes responsible for his/her individual successes or failures. Each student is seen only as an individual, outside the social relations of sex, class, ethnicity, race, or sexual orientation. The gender reform and non-sexist strategies arising from the sex-role framework emphasize changing *individuals* and hence present no fundamental challenge to either the state or the schools.

## CHALLENGING SEX-ROLE EXPLANATIONS

Although the forms of policy development and implementation outlined above are still dominant today, some significant shifts in analysis and action have begun to develop. By the mid-1980s, a cogent critique of earlier research, and hence of the policies based on that research, emerged. Feminist scholars began to point out that many policies and practices of non-sexist education were based on assumptions that girls were "lesser boys" and the goal was to make girls more like boys, to make women "less defective men." That is, by adopting a non-sexist approach, teachers were, in essence, inadvertently reinforcing the notion of women's inferiority because girls were being pushed to be like boys or men. As Gaskell, McLaren, and Novogrodsky (1989) point out, interventions based on sex-role theory, especially role-modelling programs, "leave unchallenged the gender bias in schools ... [and are based] on the assumption that girls must be changed. Men are the model of achievement, and compared to men, women don't measure up" (p. 16). It was also observed that role-modelling programs, self-esteem workshops, and the like are based on the notion that individual girls must be helped. These types of programs rarely take account of the very real material circumstances and barriers young women will face. Even when these programs acknowledge barriers, the solution is to "empower" each girl to overcome the obstacles rather than to challenge the obstacles themselves.

The sex-role stereotyping approach also was criticized from the radical or cultural feminist position for devaluing women's "special" contributions, namely nurturing, care, and concern. The work of Noddings (1984), Martin (1985), and, most influentially, Gilligan (1982) became important in policy debates as some women began to demand the revaluing of the feminine and women's ways of knowing, caring, and teaching. How this new position intersects with the development of education policy is best seen in the arguments brought forward to support more women in positions of leadership in education.

Although it had long been obvious that women were underrepresented numerically and proportionally in administrative posts, the argument that women brought special attributes to leadership, that women were better listeners and team players, more democratic principals, and often were more effective in managing change (Shakeshaft, 1989), seems to have been more effective than simple justice or fairness arguments based on numbers and the concept of equal rights. What is at work here is women's use of the "different but equal" strategy. During the 1980s and early 1990s, female educators lobbied for more women in educational administration based on the research that suggested women bring different (and by implication better) perspectives and strengths to leadership tasks (Joly, McIntyre, Staszenski, and Young, 1992; Tabin and Coleman, 1993). In Ontario during the 1990s, the Federation of Women Teachers' Associations of Ontario (FWTAO) and others lobbying for change tied the radical/cultural feminist arguments about women's special abilities to the liberal feminist arguments about the importance of students seeing women in leadership roles in schools. The eventual success of this lobby led to an amendment to The Education Act in 1988 which allowed the Minister of Education to require school boards to implement employment-equity programs with respect to the promotion of women to positions of added responsibility. The Minister of Education indicated that, as a goal, 50 percent of the occupational categories of vice-principal, principal, and supervisory officer should be held by women by the year 2000. However, since the election of a Progressive Conservative government in Ontario in 1995, all references to employment equity have been removed from the statutes, a step the teacher federations regard as a setback. Nonetheless, it appears that many school boards, having begun the process of examining their hiring practices and policies, will continue with some form of employment equity at the local level.

Although research studies (Baudoux, 1995; Gill, 1995; Ontario Ministry of Education, 1992; Rees, 1990) suggest there is a long way to go in every province before women are well represented in administration, there is no doubt that women's access to leadership positions in schools is a well-established issue, and women are likely to continue to enter into administrative positions with school boards. By 1990, eight provincial ministries of education and school boards in six provinces had some form of equal-opportunity, affirmative-action, or employment-equity policy (Rees, 1990, p. 85) designed to improve women's representation in administrative positions. The prevalence of these policies attests to the power of female teachers' political lobbying and the combined influence of liberal and radical/cultural feminist research that united the discourses of equal opportunity and women's "special attributes."

The concepts of "a different voice," "women's ways of knowing," and "women-centred learning" (Belenky, Clinchy, Goldberger, and Tarule, 1986) have had other effects. Responding specifically to the research of Gilligan (1982) and her colleagues (Brown and Gilligan, 1992; Gilligan, Lyons, and Hanmer, 1990), a feminist girls' school, The Linden School, was recently established in Toronto (Moore and Goudie, 1995). In Edmonton, the Nellie McClung Program provides an alternative junior high school for girls within the public system (Sanford-Smith, 1996). Single-sex mathematics and science classes are being seriously considered or are already in operation in a number of jurisdictions across Canada (Conrad, 1996). The practice of women-centred learning is particularly obvious in specific job training or re-entry programs such as Women Into Trades and Technology (Gedies, 1994; Pierson, 1995) and in some literacy programs (Lloyd, 1992).

The focus on women's experiences has led to a number of studies of sexual harassment and of other forms of violence against female students (Larkin, 1994; Staton and Larkin, 1992, 1993), and the development and implementation of several projects designed to curb that violence. The Canadian Teachers' Federation (CTF) (1990b), for example, published a curriculum document called *Thumbs Down: A Classroom Response to Violence Towards Women* and several provincial federations and school boards have also provided materials for the use of classroom teachers. In Ontario, the Ontario Secondary School Teachers' Federation (OSSTF), the Ontario Women's Directorate, and the Ontario Ministry of Education and Training (1995) cooperated in the production of a teaching resource called *The Joke's Over: Student to Student Sexual Harassment in Secondary*

*Schools*. Staton and Larkin (1996) have produced a resource for elementary school teachers called *Harassment Hurts: Sex-Role Stereotyping and Sexual Harassment Elementary School Resources*.

In a unique study, the CTF (1990a), in cooperation with its provincial affiliates, used teachers to conduct a national, school-based, action research study of girls, which resulted in the publication of *A Cappella: A Report on the Realities, Concerns, Expectations and Barriers Experienced by Adolescent Women in Canada*. As a result of this report, follow-up activities to educate teachers and youth workers about the problems of adolescent girls, especially concerning self-esteem, harassment, and violence, have been undertaken (Canadian Teachers' Federation, 1993a, 1993b). At the same time, and most unfortunately, much policy currently being developed by ministries of education and teacher federations around the safe schools issue ignores the gendered dimension of violence, whether that violence is directed toward teachers or students (Robertson, 1996). Sexual harassment policies are unevenly developed across Canada and are non-existent in many locations (Rees, 1990). Where policy exists, it is often inadequate. As H.-J. Robertson (1993) discovered in her analysis of the assumptions underpinning policy and contract language, there is only "a superficial recognition that sexual harassment is the abuse of power in a system in which power has been distributed by gender" (p. 47) and "a conflicted view of culpability and responsibility in the event of harassment" (p. 46).

Ironically, the revaluing of women's contributions and experiences has also led to some small initiatives involving boys' education. Canadian schools have long encouraged boys to take home economics or family studies classes and some provinces make this mandatory. In New Brunswick and Quebec, for example, industrial arts/introductory technology and home economics courses are compulsory for both girls and boys (Julien, 1987). Another intervention occurs in the form of a program for pre-adolescent boys ranging in age from about 10 to 13. Known as "Boys for Babies" and sponsored by the Toronto Board of Education, the program description suggests that:

> Through learning to bathe, feed, diaper, play with and comfort real babies, boys overcome their doubts, fears and preconceptions about gender roles. The program validates

and rewards caring and nurturing feelings and behaviour in
a boys-only context just at the age when boys are most
urgently concerned with learning how to "be a man." ...
The boys are allowed and encouraged by their peers, as well
as by the instructor, to demonstrate gentleness, care, and
sensitivity to the babies' needs, and they see that this in no
way contradicts or diminishes their masculinity. (Wells, 1991,
pp. 8–9)

Although mentoring programs and career days based on sex-role
analysis often encouraged girls to be more like boys, this program took
the opposite approach and encouraged boys to be more like girls.

However, as the example of "Boys for Babies" illustrates, although
the research and policy approach, which reclaims and revalues women's
lives, has some important benefits, it also has the effect of emphasizing
women's difference and "otherness" from men as well as essentializing
women's experiences (Fuss, 1989).

MacKinnon (1987) puts the case against the "different but equal"
strategy well. She argues that Gilligan's emphasis on

the affirmative rather than the negative valuation of that
which has accurately distinguished women from men ....
mak[es] it seem as though those attributes, with their
consequences, really are somehow ours, rather than what
male supremacy has attributed to us for its own use. For
women to affirm difference, when difference means
dominance, as it does with gender, means to affirm the
qualities and characteristics of powerlessness. (pp. 38–39)

## Anti-Sexist Approaches

Another body of research suggests that analyses of sexism in schooling
that emphasize sex-role stereotyping rely on an oversimplified
understanding of complex issues and hide the ways the gendered nature
of education is played out in the content and practice of schooling
(Gaskell, 1992; Mac an Ghaill, 1994; Ng, Staton, and Scane, 1995; Thorne,

1993; Walkerdine, 1990). Classrooms do not exist in isolation and individual teachers, however well equipped with curriculum packages and videotapes, cannot alone eliminate sexism. Individual efforts to provide a non-sexist education are doomed to failure, for as Briskin (1990) argues,

> The goal of "non-sexism" (non-racism or non-classism) reflects a belief embedded in liberalism that discrimination is somehow incidental to the system — a result of prejudice — and that good attitudes and intent can erase that discrimination and make sex, race and class irrelevant, especially in the classroom. Such a view conceals rather than reveals structural inequality and institutional limits. (p. 12)

A focus on the systemic nature of sexism and schooling and on developing anti-sexist, as opposed to non-sexist, pedagogics is growing.

An explicit example of this can be found in the reasoning behind the Toronto Board of Education's parallel four-day retreats on sexism for selected female and male high school students, which began in 1991. In separate conference centres, male students, teachers, and facilitators and female students, teachers, and facilitators meet for three days to discuss a range of topics including sexism in schools, sexuality, homophobia, violence against women, and family life. On the fourth day, male and female participants meet together to share their experiences and to plan for follow-up activities in their schools. The organizers of the retreat, although acknowledging the importance of equal opportunity and compensatory programs for girls and women, argued for the importance of going beyond efforts to create gender equity within existing social structures. They wanted to help students and teachers

> to begin to understand some difficult concepts: One is that sexism is a form of systemic discrimination which ensures the power of one group in society over another group. Sexism isn't just what individuals say or do, it relates to the entire way we've set up a male-dominated society. The second is the perplexing idea that patriarchy is a system not only of oppression of women, but one that has a

> contradictory impact on men as well: men's privileges and
> power are linked to the pain and alienation suffered by men
> themselves. (Novogrodsky, Kaufman, Holland, and Wells,
> 1992, pp. 69–70)

As well, the organizers worked hard to create experiences for participants that would not disempower young women by creating a victimization mind-set but rather would emphasize women's collective ability to work for change through women's movements. Similarly, efforts were made to ensure that young men were not bogged down with feelings of guilt but could see ways of doing anti-sexist work in support of women and in challenging the sexist nature of society. All of this work was done within a context that situated gender in relation to race, class, ethnicity, and sexual orientation (Novogrodsky et al., 1992).

The possibility of a policy shift toward a more fundamentally critical anti-sexist approach can also be seen in the validation draft of the gender-equity support document recently issued by Ontario's Ministry of Education and Training (1994). Called *Engendering Equity* and reflecting some of the more recent debates in post-structuralist feminist scholarship about education (see Kenway, Willis, Blackmore, and Rennie, 1994), this document calls for a transformed curriculum that is much more than "adding on" women. It notes that an inclusive curriculum "means rethinking the content, form, and context of curriculum" and requires that the "causes and patterns of sexism, racism, and all forms of discrimination and prejudice are explored and challenged" (p. 4). The document critiques the Ministry's own earlier approaches based on the sex-role stereotyping analytical framework and argues for anti-sexist strategies that name inequitable power relations between men and women and take into account the whole social context and the intersections of race, class, and sexual orientation with gender (pp. 11–12). Given the election of the Progressive Conservative government in Ontario in 1995, it is not clear that *Engendering Equity* will ever receive final approval and be distributed widely throughout the province's schools.

A recent Ontario debate over textbooks contrasts the dominant liberal individualist position with a more radical alternative. In 1987, the FWTAO published a study of school readers as a follow-up to the study it had commissioned in 1975. The study concluded that:

> The ideal Reader world would be one where young people
> would be welcomed as cherished members of the human
> race and are denied nothing because of the accident of their
> birth. (Batcher, Winter, and Wright, 1987, p. 43)

It was suggested that readers should show women and men "in equal, caring and joyful partnerships" and that "human existence is changeable if we want it to be" (p. 43). The implication is that if educators just want something to happen badly enough, it will happen. Repo (1988) takes issue with the perspective adopted by the FWTAO study. Noting that the report recommends that readers portray a world in which all problems have been eliminated, she goes on to argue that:

> The real world out there is still sexist, racist and class-biased.
> Surely the challenge for School Readers which are trying to
> combat these inequalities is to both to [sic] clarify actual
> experience and to show protagonists struggling to change
> this world. This means that inequalities have to, in the same
> sense, be named .... The resourceful girl protagonist has to
> be seen functioning — not in some egalitarian paradise —
> [sic] but in a world where men are more powerful (and
> some of them more powerful than others), where she may
> not easily find role models and where the prince of her
> choice may indeed need reeducation. (Repo, 1988, pp. 150–
> 151)

At stake here is a vision of education. Many teachers, including feminist teachers, have accepted uncritically that the purpose of schooling is to maximize individual development and to help students fit happily into the world. Too few teachers recognize the political agenda of compliance underpinning this position and consequently they engage in gender-equity initiatives that do little to aid in a fundamental transformation of schooling. Gaskell et al. (1989) suggest an alternative:

> Children should be helped to see the world as it is, while
> being encouraged to develop a critical consciousness, a sense
> of active and co-operative participation that equips them to
> engage in the struggle for social change. (p. 38)

This debate about textbooks and teaching also provides evidence of a rich and flourishing feminist scholarship. As understandings of systemic sexism, gender relations, and patriarchy are developed, these understandings are applied to schooling, and are re-worked and refined through research on classroom interactions and language use, teaching practices, evaluation methods, gender dynamics among students, among teachers, and between teachers and students, sexual harassment in schools, and other topics. The feminist research on women's absence from curriculum content and the new scholarship on women evident in the traditional disciplines has affected debates about what knowledge is of most worth and what should be included in core and elective subjects.

It is possible to be guardedly optimistic about positive linkages between research and policy making on gender and education for a number of reasons. One has to do with the very nature of feminist research. Sydie (1987) has observed that feminist social scientists are the true granddaughters of the founding fathers such as Weber and Marx, for it is the feminists who continue to observe the principle that the purpose of research is to understand and solve social problems. That is, feminist educational research is, for the most part, openly and consciously about eliminating sexism and contributing to the realization of gender equity. Because feminist research is often about making change, it is not surprising that research and policy linkages are forged.

Furthermore, feminist scholars tend to be education activists as well, and hence their research informs their practice and their practice informs their research. The women's movement, too, through its lobbying efforts, focuses the attention of policy makers on gender, and the "femocrats" (Eisenstein, 1991) are instrumental in transforming research findings into policy statements. Finally, it should not escape attention that the majority of teachers are women, albeit white and middle-class, with a specific stake in understanding and re-working gender relations. Many research-policy linkages come from the work of teachers.

# ENDNOTES

1    An earlier version of this paper was presented at the 1994 symposium organized by the Canadian Society for the Study of Education to discuss "the widening gap between educational policy and research across the country" (S. Cook, personal communication, January 22, 1994).

2    Bailey (1993) provides an excellent example of work done by teacher-researchers. See also Barton (1994), Hart (1996), and Ortwoin (1996) for examples of teachers' research completed as part of their graduate work. Nor should it be forgotten that most professors of education, myself included, have been classroom teachers, as have researchers such a Briskin (1990) and Larkin (1994).

3    Until recently feminists have commonly been categorized as liberal, radical, or socialist. Liberal feminists argue for equal opportunities, seek to identify and remove barriers to women's success, and theorize sex inequalities through the sex-role socialization framework. Radical feminists, often called cultural feminists, are concerned with structural issues and tend to focus on the role of the school in reproducing the power relations of patriarchy and on the sexual politics of schooling. Socialist feminists, influenced by neo-Marxist theories, tend to focus on the economy and the family; to the extent that they consider education at all, they are concerned with how the schools work to replicate the social relations of gender, race, and class. This brief summary does not, of course, do justice to the three approaches to education, which are discussed in more detail in Acker (1994), Kenway (1990), and Stromquist (1990). These three authors note the difficulties of cleanly and simply categorizing approaches to gender reform in education and also remark on the growing influence of a post-structuralist feminism. Adamson, Briskin, and McPhail (1988) and Wine and Ristock (1991) claim that Canadian feminists have in practice, worked across their differing political positions and agree more than they disagree. Nonetheless, the three categories provide an heuristic device for broadly differentiating theoretical understandings and approaches to equity issues in education.

4    How effective these policies are is a different question. Recent assessments of learning materials (Butcher et al., 1987; Light, Staton, and Bourne, 1989) suggest that anti-bias policies have not been adequately implemented and textbooks are far from non-sexist.

# References

Acker, S. (1994). *Gendered education: Sociological reflections on women, teaching, and feminism*, Toronto: OISE Press.

Adamson, N., L. Briskin, and M. McPhail (1988). *Feminist organizing for change: The contemporary women's movement in Canada*, Toronto: Oxford University Press.

Ad Hoc Committee Respecting the Status of Women in the North York System (1975). *The rape of children's mind*, North York: Ad Hoc Committee Respecting the Status of Women in the North York System.

Armour and Associates (1992). *Expanding choices: Math and science programs for girls and women*, Halifax: Nova Scotia Women's Directorate.

Bailey, K.R. (1993). *The girls are the ones with the pointy nails: An exploration of children's conceptions of gender*, London, ON: Althouse Press.

Barton, M. (1994). Get real! Developing curricula that respond to women's lives. *Women's Education des Femmes*, 11(1), 37–41.

Batcher, E., D. Brackstone, A. Winter, and V. Wright (1975). *... And then there were none*, Toronto: Federation of Women Teachers' Associations of Ontario.

Batcher, E., A. Winter, and V. Wright (1987). *The more things change ... the more they stay the same*, Toronto: Federation of Women Teachers' Associations of Ontario.

Baudoux, C. (1995). Women managers in education in Quebec. In C. Reynolds and B. Young (eds.) *Women and leadership in Canadian education*, Calgary: Detselig.

Belenky, M.P., B.M. Clinchy, N.R. Goldberger, and J.M. Tarule (1986). *Women's ways of knowing: The development of self, voice, and mind*, New York: Basic Books.

Briskin, L. (1990). *Feminist pedagogy: Teaching and learning liberation*, Ottawa: Canadian Research Institute for the Advancement of Women.

British Columbia Department of Education (1977). *Women's studies: A resource guide for teachers*, Victoria: British Columbia Department of Education.

Brown. L.M., and C. Gilligan (1992). *Meeting at the crossroads: Women's psychology and girls' development*, Cambridge: Harvard University Press.

Canadian Teachers' Federation (1990x). *A cappella: A report on the realities, concerns, expectations and barriers experienced by adolescent women in Canada*, Ottawa: Canadian Teachers' Federation.

Canadian Teachers' Federation (1990b). *Thumbs down: A classroom response to violence towards women*, Ottawa: Canadian Teachers' Federation.

Conrad, P. (1996). Separating the boys from the girls. *The ATA Magazine*, 76(4), 18–22.

Cullen, L. (1972). *A study into sex stereotyping in Alberta elementary textbooks*, Edmonton: Alberta Department of Education.

Eisenstein, H. (1991). *Gender shock: Practicing feminism on two continents*, Boston: Beacon Press.

Fuss, D. (1989). *Essentially speaking: Feminism, nature and difference*, New York: Routledge.

Gaskell, J. (1992). *Gender matters from school to work*, Toronto: OISE Press.

Gaskell. J., A. McLaren, and M. Novogrodsky (1989). *Claiming an education: Feminism and Canadian schools*, Toronto: Our Schools/Our Selves Education Foundation.

Gedies, T. (1994). *A study of male faculty response to women learners in non-traditional college programs*, Unpublished master's thesis, University of Western Ontario, London, Ontario.

Gill, B. (1995). Breaking the glass ceiling or sliding back the sunroof? Women in educational administration in New Brunswick. In C. Reynolds and B. Young (eds.) *Women and leadership in Canadian education*, Calgary: Detselig.

Gilligan, C. (1982). *In a different voice: Psychological theory and women's development*, Cambridge: Harvard University Press.

Gilligan, C., N.P. Lyons, and T.J. Hanmer (eds.) (1990). *Making connections: The relational worlds of adolescent girls at Emma Willard School*, Cambridge: Harvard University Press.

Hart, S. (1996). Listening to a different voice: Using women's stories in the social studies: In C.E. Harris and N.E. Depledge (eds.) *Advancing the agenda of inclusive education: Proceedings of the first Canadian Association for the Study of Women and Education summer institute*, Thunder Bay, ON: Lakehead University, Faculty of Education.

Joly, L., S. McIntyre, D. Staszenski, and B. Young (1992). Leading from the heart: Toward a feminist reconstruction of educational leadership. In E. Miklos and E. Ratsoy (eds.) *Educational leadership: Challenge and change*, Edmonton: University of Alberta, Faculty of Education.

Julien. L. (1987). *Women's issues in education in Canada: A survey of policies and practices at the elementary and secondary levels*, Toronto: Council of Ministers of Education, Canada.

Kenway, J. (1990). *Gender and education policy: A call for new directions*, Geelong, Australia: Deakin University Press

Kenway, J., S. Willis, J. Blackmore, and L. Rennie (1994). Making "hope practical" rather than "despair convincing": Feminist post-structuralism, gender reform and educational change. *British Journal of Sociology of Education*, 15, 187–210.

Larkin, J. (1994). *Sexual harassment: High school girls speak out*, Toronto: Second Story Press.

8

Light. B., P. Staton, and P. Bourne (1989). Sex equity content in history textbooks. *The History and Social Science Teacher*, 25(1), 18–20.

Lloyd. B.A. (1992). Learner-centred/woman-positive: Research with adult literacy programs. *Women's Education des Femmes*, 9(3) 29–32.

Mac an Ghaill, M. (1994). *The making of men: Masculinities, sexualities and schooling*, Buckingham, UK: Open University Press.

MacKinnon. C.A. (1987). *Feminism unmodified: Discourses on life and law*, Cambridge: Harvard University Press.

Maritime Provinces Education Foundation (1991). *Women's issues in education: A cooperative approach*, No place: Maritime Provinces Education Foundation.

Marin. J.R. (1985). *Reclaiming a conversation: The ideal of the educated woman*, New Haven, CT: Yale University Press.

Moore, E., and D. Goudie (1995). The Linden School: A woman-centred school. In H. MacKinnon (ed.) *Encouraging gender equity: Strategies for school change*, Ottawa: Human Rights Research and Education Centre.

Ng. R., P. Staton, and J. Scarce (eds.) (1995). *Anti-racism, feminism, and critical approaches to education*, Westport, CT: Bergin and Garvey.

Noddings, N. (1984). *Caring: A feminine approach to ethics and moral education*, Berkeley: University of California Press.

Novogrodsky, M., M. Kaufman, D. Holland, and M. Wells (1992). Retreat for the future: An anti-sexist workshop for high schoolers. *Our Schools/Our Selves*, 3(4), 67–87.

Ontario Institute for Studies in Education (1974). *The women's kit*, Toronto: Ontario Institute for Studies in Education.

Ontario Ministry of Education (1977). *Sex-role stereotyping and women's studies: A resource guide for teachers including suggestions, units of study and resource lists*, Toronto: Ontario Ministry of Education.

Ontario Ministry of Education (1992). *The status of women and employment equity in Ontario school boards*, Toronto: Ontario Ministry of Education.

Ontario Ministry of Education and Training (1994). *Engendering equity: Transforming curriculum* (validation draft), Toronto: Ontario Ministry of Education.

Ontario Secondary School Teachers' Federation, Ontario Women's Directorate, and Ontario Ministry of Education and Training (1995). *The joke's over: Student to student sexual harassment in secondary schools*, Toronto: Ontario Secondary School Teachers' Federation.

Ortwein, E. (1996). Red wheelbarrow vision, purposeful poetic pedagogy and the echoes in the halls of student minds: Women's literature and feminist teaching. In C.E. Harris and N.E. Depledge (eds.) *Advancing the agenda of inclusive education: Proceedings of the first Canadian Association for the Study of Women and Education summer institute,* Thunder Bay, ON: Lakehead University, Faculty of Education.

Pierson, R.R. (1995). Education and training. In R. R. Pierson and M. G. Cohen (eds.) *Canadian women's: Issues: Volume 2. Bold visions: Twenty-five years of women 's activism in English-Canada,* Toronto: Lorimer.

Rees, R. (1990). *Women and men in education: A national survey of gender distribution in school systems,* Toronto: Canadian Education Association.

Repo, S. (1988). School readers and moral visions. *Our Schools/Our Selves,* 1(1), 147–151.

Robertson, H.-J. (1993). *Progress revisited: The quality of (work) life of women teachers,* Ottawa: Canadian Teachers' Federation.

Robertson, L. (1996). Safe schools: Gender issues are important. *FWTAO/FAEO Newsletter,* 14(4), 2–9.

Royal Commission on Learning (1994). *For the love of learning: Report of the Royal Commission on Learning for Ontario* (short version), Toronto: Queen's Printer.

Royal Commission on the Status of Women in Canada (1970). *Report of the Royal Commission on the Status of Women in Canada,* Ottawa: Information Canada

Sanford-Smith, K. (1996). Feminist pedagogy: Curriculum at an all-girls' school. *The ATA Magazine,* 76(4), 31–33.

Shakestaft, C. (1989). *Women in educational administration* (re. Ed.), Newbury Park, CA: Corwin.

Staton, P., and J. Larkin (1992). *Sexual harassment in high schools: We can do something about it!* Toronto: Green Dragon Press.

Staton, P., and J. Larkin (1993). *Sexual harassment: The intimidation factor,* Toronto: Green Dragon Press.

Staton, P., and J. Larkin (1996). *Harassment hurts: Sex-role stereotyping and sexual harassment elementary school resources,* Toronto: Green Dragon Press and Women's Caucus Against Sexual Harassment at OISE.

Stromquist, N.P. (1990). Gender inequality in education: Accounting for women's subordination. *British Journal of Sociology of Education,* 11, 137–153.

Sydie, R.A. (1987). *Natural women, cultured men: A feminist perspective on sociological theory,* Toronto: Methuen.

Tabin, Y., and P. Coleman (1993). From the dollhouse to the schoolhouse: The changing experience of women principals in British Columbia, 1980–1990. *Canadian Journal of Education,* 18, 381–397.

Thorne, B. (1993). *Gender play: Girls and boys in school,* New Brunswick, NJ: Rutgers University Press.

Walkerdine, V. (1990). *Schoolgirl fictions,* London, UK: Verso.

Wells, M. (1991). *A review of elementary and secondary programs on gender equity,* Toronto: Ontario Teachers' Federation.

Wine, J.D., and J.L. Ristock (eds.) (1991). *Women and social change: Feminist activism in Canada,* Toronto: Lorimer.

Women in Teaching (1975). *Text book study,* Vancouver: British Columbia Teachers' Federation.

## Exercises

1.  What behaviours do teachers and students value in girls?
2.  How does this "set girls up" and lead to skilled girls being overlooked?
3.  How does the imaginary "perfect girl" work to control and censor girls' behaviour?
4.  How can teachers and parents help girls to change these perceptions?
5.  Discuss sexism and curriculum including "the add women and stir" approach.
6.  How are the province, school institutions, curriculum, and educational policies not benign in regard to gender issues in education?
7.  Discuss the implications of a "different but equal" strategy for reform of policy and practice. In particular, examine the revaluing of women but also the emphasis on women's difference/"otherness" in this approach.
8.  Discuss structural inequality and the systemic nature of sexism particularly in regard to issues of power.
9.  What is an inclusive curriculum? How does it work?

# Chapter 20

# What Can Teachers Do About Sexual Harassment?

## Ellen Bravo
## Larry Miller

Theresa was the only girl in the metalworking class. When a teacher asked her how things were going with the boys, Theresa replied, "Oh, it's much better. They don't grab my breasts and butt anymore. They just call me all those names."

Paula hated walking past Leon and his friends. They would grab themselves and say things like, "Come on, now, you know you want it." Some of her friends yelled comments back, but Paula never knew what to say.

Anton took the long way to class. He didn't want to pass a certain group of girls who always made fun of him for being a virgin.

The eighth-grade girls didn't like the way the teacher would fondle their hair and then let his hand skim across their bodies. But because this had been going on for a while, they were afraid to tell their parents. And they didn't know who to tell at school.

These are just a few of the types of sexual harassment problems in our schools. Despite the headlines and well-publicized court cases, most administrators have focused little attention on the problem. But teachers don't have to wait for a directive that may be years in coming; we can take action right now in our classrooms.

Sexual harassment isn't the only problem kids face in school and, for many, it's not the worst problem. But it's an area where a lot of confusion exists — confusion that's been cultivated by many people in authority who have trivialized the issue, criticized those who have raised it, and distorted proposed solutions.

For high school students, the situation is further complicated by adolescence. If being preoccupied with sex makes someone a harasser, most teenagers would have to plead guilty. Where's the line between appropriate and inappropriate behavior — and who's drawing it?

Last year, when Larry Miller did a seven-day unit on sexual harassment, students afterward remarked that it was one of the highlights of the school year. He found that developing a unit on sexual harassment has several advantages:

> **The students love it.** Students repeatedly said throughout the year "Why can't class always be as interesting?" Sexual harassment is also a subject on which students are eager to talk and have a great deal to say. What adolescent hasn't spent an inordinate amount of time contemplating the complexities of intimate relations?
>
> **The students need it.** Most students don't understand the issue of sexual harassment and have many misconceptions. They need guidance and support to help figure out what is and isn't appropriate behavior.
>
> **The students benefit from it.** The benefits occur on a number of different levels. First, a sexual harassment unit empowers those individual girls and boys who may have been harassed. (For boys, it's almost always for being gay or not "manly" enough.) Such students urgently need validation that harassment is wrong, that they're not crazy, and that they're not at fault. They need to hear that someone in authority cares about the problem and isn't blaming them or dismissing their pain.

Second, it makes clear that harassment is unacceptable behavior — thus helping to create a classroom culture in which students will have a stronger understanding that their rights will be respected and defended, regardless of whether they have ever been harassed. While it is essential to go beyond dealing with harassment on a classroom-by-classroom basis, individual discussions of the issue are often an essential first step.

Third, it helps clear up confusion among boys who think they'll be in trouble for flirting or consensual joking. Larry found that while many boys initially felt hostile and suspicious during the unit (they feared the unit would demonize all boys and portray all girls as innocent victims), such attitudes changed when they found the focus was on inappropriate behavior and not on boys in general.

Fourth, it helps raise broader relationship and gender issues that the students need to talk about. One incident underscored this point to Larry. After the unit, a 16-year-old male student came up to him one day and asked to talk privately. It turned out the student had a common but simple biological question about sex — but had no adult male he felt comfortable talking to.

## A Good Curriculum

A good curriculum makes clear that while most harassers are male, most males are not harassers. It also encourages students to intervene when harassment occurs, to speak out not as champions of the "poor victims" but as people offended by such behavior.

At its minimum, the curriculum should have three goals. First, it must help the majority of students to understand why harassment is wrong. Second, it must help the harassers to stop their behavior. Third, in what is a more complex issue, it must address larger issues of gender stereotypes and power. Students need to understand that sexual harassment is part of a continuum of sexual misconduct that has to do with domination rather than sex. This takes the issue out of the battle-of-the-sexes mode and helps students better understand patterns of sexual discrimination.

It is also essential to deal with the perspective that those who challenge sexual harassment are merely whining "victims" rather than people with a legitimate anger. Some critics argue that sexual harassment awareness training contributes to a nation of "victims." Like any unit dealing with situations of oppression, the curriculum's purpose is not to create a sense of hopelessness but of understanding and power — the knowledge that each of us is important and deserves to be treated with dignity. We don't prevent or stop harassment by ignoring it any more than we do by condoning it. In fact, ignoring sexual harassment sends a powerful message that no one cares. This "hidden curriculum" can leave girls with a sense of powerlessness and, in essence, teaches girls to accept sexual inequality.

## Teaching Techniques

Obviously, good teaching is central to the unit's success. Teachers can use a variety of techniques, from videos to role plays, small-group discussions, and student essays. It is useful to begin with a "safe" lesson idea that encourages students to share their feelings, such as an anonymous survey asking students both their definition of sexual harassment and whether they have ever been harassed.

It's a good idea to include at least one lesson plan that helps students distinguish between flirting and harassment. In helping students distinguish between the two, Larry found that two questions were essential: Was the behavior unwelcome? Did the behavior make the recipient feel uncomfortable? If the answer is "yes" to the questions, the line is usually crossed between flirting and harassment.

Role plays and scenarios are a particularly useful technique. In his unit, Larry took a male and a female student that he knew were mature enough to act out what was, from their own experiences, the difference between flirtation and harassment. For example, the young man would look the girl up and down, make comments such as, "Hey, you want some of this," or grab himself in his private parts. The girl would respond, "Go away, boy, I don't need that crap." It was clear from the class's response to the role plays that the students, whether or not they could articulate it, often knew the difference between flirting and harassment.

Scenarios, in which the teacher describes a situation and asks for students' responses, are a useful way to open up discussion. Larry developed the following activities.

In one scenario, boys "rate" girls as they walk past them in the hallway. ("She's a 10"; "She's so ugly she'd be pretty if she were a dog.") During a discussion of such "ratings," some boys argued that rating girls can be a compliment. "It's just ugly girls who are offended," one said.

Some girls had a different view. "I don't care what I'm rated; it makes me uncomfortable," Betty replied. "I don't like it." Other girls backed her up and made the point that such ratings are degrading and make a woman feel less than a human being. Larry found that such conversations were much needed. Whether or not every student took Betty's comments to heart, her point was made.

Another scenario focused on how boys "eye" girls. James, for instance, argued that he can look at anything he wants. "These are my eyes," he insisted. But another student responded, "If I feel disrespected, then you're out of order" — picking up on common student concern with "respect" as a key factor in determining what's right and wrong.

In doing such scenarios, it is important that at least one deal with the most evident form of harassment: the use of abusive words such as "bitch" and "whore." In the discussion following such a scenario in Larry's class, one female student reflected a common view that, "If a girl is not a 'whore' then she should be tough enough not to be offended by these words."

Her view sparked a lively debate. A number of both young men and women shot back with comments such as, "We shouldn't have to put up with that kind of nonsense."

The power of the unit was most clear in the summary essays written by Larry's students. Many of the students came to clearly understand not only the difference between flirting and harassment, but the issue's importance.

Reflecting on flirting and harassment, Jamela wrote in her summary essay: "Flirting and sexual harassment are two different things. Flirting is when two people are joking and kidding around and none of them mind. But sexual harassment is when two people might be joking around and kidding around and one goes too far. Another form may be when two people are talking or playing and one of them touches the other in a way they don't like, or grabs the other in a way they don't like."

Jason, meanwhile, focused on the many responses to sexual harassment. Articulating a range of responses that most students were unaware of before the unit, he wrote, "Sometimes you can handle sexual harassment by ignoring it or asking the person to stop it, especially when it is name calling, rumors, light touching, or gestures. If it continues you need to go to someone in authority, either a teacher, parent, boss, or head of the department. If it still continues you need to keep taking action and not let them get away with it. Don't be afraid to talk to other students or co-workers about it. Perhaps it is happening to them too and you could build a better case against that person. Sexual harassment should be an important issue in all communities. Looking the other way and doing nothing about it is saying that sexual harassment is okay."

# Part 6

# Gender and
# Regulation of Bodies

**Iseke-Barnes**
"Readings of Cultural Narratives
of Diet, Technology, and Schooling
in Multimedia Stories"

**Wolf**
*The Beauty Myth*

# Chapter 21

# Readings of Cultural Narratives of Diet, Technology, and Schooling in Multimedia Stories[1]

## Judy M. Iseke-Barnes

Why are stories considered irrelevant in many school curricula? Why are students' lives, as reflected in the stories they tell, not a fuller part of educational contexts? This paper presents a case study of a high school student's activities in generating what her teacher termed a "living essay." This story is read through cultural narratives of diet and weight loss, through discourses about technology, and in discursive practices in computing classrooms.

Wells (1987, p. 16) questions the view that (1) "school is for learning about the 'real' world," (2) stories are frivolous, and (3) students' personal anecdotes are considered by some teachers "as annoying and irrelevant interruptions of the official matter of the curriculum." Wells further suggests that imaginative and affective responses to experience are connected to and not competing with practical and analytic responses. Educators are challenged by Wells to engage their students in multiple readings of texts and in storying that engages them in moral and aesthetic pursuits particularly in dealing with science and technology.

How can teachers engage students in "storying" in classes where the focus is not literature? This study offers the potential of the secondary computing classroom and multimedia story development as a place where students can tell stories and explore perspectives. The case study provided here describes one student's (we will call her Susan) production of what her teacher termed a "living essay" and defined as an autonomous creation in computer program form. The case study demonstrates that Susan's experiences were not autonomous, as her teacher expected, but that her multimedia story was produced through multiple discourses. Just as Carson, another student in Susan's class during the project of completing a living essay, suggested that his story about a prince who saves a princess from a fiery dragon came from his experiences and from his own imagination (further outlined in Iseke-Barnes, 1997), Susan's story about a mouse who loved cheese is produced in relation to her experiences and discourses in which she plays a role.

One example of cultural narrative through which we define our lives is in discussions of gender. Davies (1997, p. 9) explains that

> gender is constructed, through language, as two binary categories hierarchically arranged in relation to each other. This construction operates in a variety of intersecting ways, most of which are neither conscious nor intended. They are more like an effect of what we might call "speaking-as-usual"; they are inherent in the structures of the language and the storylines through which our culture is constructed and maintained.

This study examines one female student's production of a multimedia story, which is read through the cultural narratives of diet and weight loss, through discourses about technology, and in discursive practices in computing classrooms. While multiple other readings of Susan's story are possible, this discussion offers only this reading due to space constraints.

## SUSAN — STORY TELLING IN COMPUTER CONTEXTS

Susan was a Grade 11 student at the time of the study, enrolled in a computer studies class learning about creating multimedia. Susan had used a tutorial to learn about multimedia and had created a number of small multimedia documents as assignments in the class before beginning the creation of her living essay.

From the onset Susan described "pages" in her "story." Her approach was to generate a short text sequence and then to create an image to illustrate the text. The project was not outlined by the teacher to be about story. The teacher suggested that students were to create a computer file that contained images and text as well as sequences incorporating animation, sound, and imported graphics. The file for the teacher was for students to demonstrate their technical skills in the multimedia computing context. But Susan's interpretation of the assignment was to create a story. She began her story with the following sequence.

> Once upon a time there was a little mouse named Cheeser.
> As you can imagine he adored cheese. As a result of his love
> of cheese he grew very fat.

Susan's opening sentence suggests a fairy tale genre but given that this story is concerned with "fatness" which is not a usual topic of fairy tales, suggests that this story may not be of this genre. A concern about fatness is not uncommon amongst adolescent females and is explored through Susan's story about Cheeser.

## Story Telling as Cultural Activity

Figure 22 provides an image of Cheeser with a distended mid-section. This is a common concern of bulimics and anorexics who focus on particular bulges of the body (Sacker and Zimmer, 1987). But it is also common in our culture.

> In a ... magazine show "20/20," several ten-year-old boys
> were shown some photos of fashion models. The models
> were pencil-thin. Yet the pose was such that a small bulge of
> hip was forced, through the action of the body, into
> protuberance — as is natural, unavoidable on any but the
> most skeletal or the most tautly developed bodies. We bend
> over, we sit down, and the flesh coalesces in spots. These
> young boys, pointing to the hips, disgustedly pronounced
> the models to be "fat." Watching the show, I was appalled at

**Figure 22: Susan's Cheeser the mouse as she began her multimedia production.**

the boys' reaction. Yet I could not deny that I had also been surprised at my own current perceptions while reviewing female bodies in movies from the 1970s; what once appeared slender and fit now seemed loose and flabby. *Weight* was not the key element in these changed perceptions — my standards had not come to favor *thinner* bodies — but rather I had come to expect a tighter, smoother, more "contained" body profile. (Bordo, 1990, p. 88).

In the case of Cheeser his body is not "contained" but rather is large and distended in the midsection. His fatness is apparent in the roundness of his body, which is contrasted with the thinness of his tail and the insignificant size of his paws.

Susan's story continued.

Cheeser got so incredibly fat that his doctor ORDERED him to quit eating [sic] so much cheese. (Please help Cheeser with his diet and feed him the apple.)

Susan then copied another image of her mouse into the story and drew a table with an apple on it. She used the text *Please help Cheeser with his diet and feed him the apple* in building an interactive sequence in which a user of her program would move the apple to Cheeser's paws. If the apple was not moved to Cheeser's paws a feedback sequence presented the text *Please put the apple in the mouse's paws.* Susan emphasized order in her text. The doctor here is an authority figure who can impose order on people to change their lifestyles. Fatness is framed as a problem for which there is a mandated solution — a personal change by reducing eating. Did the doctor investigate the causes of the fatness? Accept it? Pose alternatives? Fatness in this culture is a disease state needing a cure: a diet (Orbach, 1978; Bordo, 1993). Duden (1991, p. 4) outlines Foucault's (1973) repeated suggestion that clinical and medical discourses about the body

> repressed, censored, masked, abstracted, and alienated modes of perception; at the same time it had the power to create new realities, to constitute new objects, to introduce new, inescapable rituals into daily life, rituals whose participants became epistemologically dependent on the newly created objects.

One of the cultural objects created by clinicians is the obsessions with thinness (Chernin, 1985). Indeed the subspecialty of American medicine called bariatrics is a group devoted to the treatment of obesity, demonstrating the prevalence of the medical profession and its interventions in matters of appetite and weight control (Brumberg, 1989). An apple in Susan's story is an appropriate part of a weight-loss diet. Cheese is not. How did Susan construct these standards of what to eat (or at least what a mouse who wants to lose weight must eat)? Brumberg (1989) demonstrates how "standardizing" the body by insurance company statistics and the acceptance and then promotion of these standards by the medical profession for adults lead to a heightened interest in body weight. Pediatrics built its early work on feeding and nutrition at a time when infant mortality was high and proposed standardized weights for children, and prescriptive diets in charts and tables were made available in doctors' offices and nurseries. The home economics movement also developed a field of dietetics and nutrition which devoted itself to the science of feeding and standard diets, making terms like protein, carbohydrate, and fat as well as the scientific notion of calorie counting a common occurrence. The food guides issued today by Canadian and U.S. governments are a continuation of this trend toward control in diet.

Increasing concerns about fat children have been evident since the 1940s but more recent data suggests that young girls and adolescents are making dieting a way of life. Eighty percent of nine-year-olds in one study were dieting (Stacey, 1987). Health and Welfare Canada (1988) statistics indicated that 70 percent of adult Canadian women wanted to reduce weight. Thirty-six percent of "normal weight" women thought they were overweight (Millar, 1991) and it was estimated by Berg (1992) that 40 percent of women and 61 percent of adolescent and young adult females were dieting. Feldman, Feldman, and Goodman (1986) reported that girls as young as five were restricting food intake in fear of getting fat.

Susan, in writing her story about fatness as a problem, reflects the cultural norms that are prevalent in this society. Crawford (1985), Silverstein (1984), and Schwartz (1986) all suggest that capitalism and its excessive productions require the cultivation of the work ethic and delayed gratification while it also demands excessive consumerism and immediate satisfaction. Total satisfaction is never allowed "as we find ourselves continually besieged by temptation, while socially condemned for overindulgence. ... Food and diet are central arenas for the expression of these contradictions (Bordo, 1993, p. 199). Bulimia embodies the unstable double bind of consumer capitalism, while anorexia and obesity embody an attempted resolution of that double bind (Bordo, 1993, p. 201).

Susan's story continued with the text:

> Cheeser was doing very well on his diet and seemed to be losing weight. All his friends were very proud of him, so they gave him presents.

Doing well on a diet for Cheeser means losing weight, not getting more fit, feeling better, reducing cholesterol, etc. Losing weight is something about which to be proud, worthy of the receipt of gifts in recognition of the achievement. And the achievement is not just a personal achievement but is a public event in which friends share. Foucault (1977, p. 155) suggests that power can work to produce individual compliance to standards and self-correction rather than the necessity of coercion. This means that "there is no need for arms, physical violence, material constraints. Just a gaze. An inspecting gaze, a gaze which each individual under its weight will end by interiorising to the point that he is his own overseer, each individual thus exercising this surveillance over, and against himself."

As Susan continued her storying she opened the graphics package and drew three gift-wrapped packages next to the image of Cheeser with a less rounded midsection which suggested thinness. She also added a title page to her story which read " Cheeser the Fat Mouse." In creating the new thinner image of Cheeser, she changed the oval shape of Cheeser's body to a greatly narrowed oval which she placed under Cheeser's head and then exclaimed that his head looked "too big." The body no longer looked like it could support the head. Bordo (1993, p. 335) describes Dolly Parton after weight loss as "truly looking as though she might snap in two in a strong wind ... whose television presence is now recessive, beseeching, desiring only to serve;" in Parton's words as she opened her show "I'll bust my but to please you" (Surely she already has?). Parton and Vanna White (of the television show "Wheel of Fortune," and who also lost a lot of weight and is obsessive about thinness) are known for large breasts which "now adorn bodies that are vulnerably thin, with fragile, spindly arms and legs like those of young colts. Parton and White suggest the pleasures of nurturant female sexuality without any encounter with its powers and dangers." (Bordo, 1993, p. 335)

Susan added the following passage and added an image of Cheeser above the text.

> Cheeser finished opening his gifts. All his friends went home, so he decided to take a better look at his presents. He got a new book from his friend the rabbit, a new pair of mittens from his friend the elephant and a new cook book from his friend the robin.

## Losing Weight — Looking Good, Feeling Good, Being Good

At the beginning of the next class Susan added more text to her story.

> All of a sudden Cheeser heard a knock on the door. Quickly
> he hurried to the door and to his surprise it was his cousin,
> Gary goat.

Susan added the image of the mountain goat (imported from the file server) who appeared to be saying *Cheeser you have lost weight. Are you on a diet?* Susan added more text to her story and an image of the mountain goat exiting through a door on the next page.

> Cheeser and his cousin sat down and talked for a while.
> Gary had told Cheeser how good he looked now that he
> had lost weight. Cheeser started to feel really good about
> himself. Gary realized it was now getting late so he decided
> to leave.

Looking good is the result of losing weight. Feeling good is about looking good and about weight loss. Susan, in her story about Cheeser, explores this prevalent orientation in our culture. Brown (1993) suggests that anorexics are often frustrated in trying to develop a sense of self that is acceptable to themselves and others. Others suggest that anorexics are actually struggling to develop a self (Chernin, 1985; Friedman, 1985; Orbach, 1986).

> Initial success with weight loss often brings praise from others
> and encouragement to continue to lose weight. The control
> established over the basic human urge to eat, especially when
> starving, is compelling as it makes the anorexic woman feel
> stronger. The anorexic woman feels she should be able to
> control her urge to eat. She experiences a personal sense of
> failure if she succumbs and eats, a reaction that is also
> common among bulimic women and most dieters.
> Conversely, women often feel a sense of power and personal
> satisfaction when they can contain and curb their appetites,

even when they are emaciated and near death. The accomplishment of self-control, not weight or food intake in themselves, becomes the central issue. For anorexic and bulimic women as well as dieters, controlling the body becomes one viable way to feel more in control of one's self and one's life. (Brown, 1993, p. 61)

Susan added further text and an image of Cheeser in bed.

Cheeser was so tired that he cleaned the kitchen the[n] went straight to bed.

This text is suggestive of the work ethic, which requires a clean home before sleeping. Compliance to societal standards of weight loss are also associated with the work ethic (Bordo, 1990, 1993).

## Diets, Desires, Binges, Purging

Susan returned to the task of adding text to her story adding images compiled from those she had created earlier above each excerpt of text.

Cheeser [sic] woke up at three o'clock in the morning and decided he was very hungry [sic]. Cheeser got out of bed and hurried to the kitchen.

This is a common experience of dieting — waking in the night hungry and rushing to the kitchen to fulfill one's bodily needs.

All Cheeser could find to eat was a carrot and he was sick of eating carrots!! All he could think about was the block of cheese he hid in the clipboard before he started the diet.

Many dieters experience both a fixation on a particular food item and then a dislike of this item. Cheeser just wants the things he is "not supposed to have" on a diet.

> Cheeser could not help himself, so he sat down and ate the huge block of cheese. Cheeser was so full when he was done, that he went straight to bed.

The "binge" of the diet is a common phenomenon and a difficulty with the structure of diets. In this story Cheeser succumbs to his desires as many dieters do. Dieters are not supposed to listen to their bodies and feed them. They are supposed to show willpower and deny their bodily needs for nutrients, which drive them to eat.

Bordo (1990) describes the constant effort and self-correction that is required to conform to increasingly slim images of female bodies. The most common way of conforming to these societal demands is dieting. But dieting often ensures its own failure, as the experience of deprivation leads to compensatory bingeing, with its attendant feelings of defeat, worthlessness, and loss of hope. Between the media images of containment and self-mastery and the reality of constant, everyday stress and anxiety about one's appearance lies the chasm that produces bodies habituated to self-monitoring and self-normalization. Ultimately, the body (besides being evaluated for its success or failure at getting itself in order) is seen as demonstrating correct or incorrect attitudes toward the demands of normalization themselves. (Bordo, 1990, p. 99–100)

Susan next added a sound icon to her file and explored various sounds stored on the computer network file server. She selected the sound of vomiting from the sounds provided. She then added more text.

> Good thing Cheeser made it to the bathroom in time!!! From that day on Cheeser never cheated on his diet again.

Binge and purge (through vomiting) is all too common a story in this culture where bulimia is becoming a common occurrence. The desire expressed is to never cheat again — to be completely faithful to a diet regiment — to never again binge (and thereby eliminate the need to purge). The desire for complete control is evident in this story excerpt about lack of control. This desire is to find resolution to the double bind of endless temptations and condemnation for partaking.

## Diet, Identity and "Being Good"

Susan added the text:

> He also changed his name to Chuck because he would never
> eat cheese again!

Chuck, alias Cheeser, has a whole new identity given his weight loss and now has a new name to go with the new identity. The new identity is based on never eating cheese again — in other words, never bingeing on cheese and needing to purge. The new name symbolizes the overcoming of the binge and purge scenario and resolution of the conflict.

Susan then created an interaction beginning with the question *For a good mouse to lose weight successfully what food must he eat?* Notice here that losing weight means that the mouse is "good" so by implication not losing weight is bad. In this story to be successful one must lose weight. Also note that some foods MUST be eaten on a diet. Choices, likes, and dislikes cannot dictate what is eaten. One MUST eat some foods to be on a diet and to be "good."

On the same computer page Susan added an image and text for *an apple, some cheese,* and *some pizza.* Denial of favoured foods — in this case cheese and pizza — and the requirement for eating certain "diet" foods like apples is a prerequisite for dieting in this story. The approach to dieting suggested here is the limiting of food intake to a subset of food choices rather than the idea of balance as an approach to healthy eating.

Susan created the "feedback" for various responses to the question. When the user chooses the apple the text appears *Correct. You read carefully!!!! The mouse would eat an apple.* In this response Susan indicates that her question was one of recall of previously presented information rather than a question requiring analysis on the part of the user of the program. By implication, dieting is not something requiring analysis but rather the following of a regiment that merely must be remembered.

For the other two possible answers (cheese, pizza) she added two feedback responses.

> No, the mouse loves cheese, but the apple is better for him.
> Click on the apple.

No, pizza is not the best for the mouse when he is on a diet.
The correct answer is the apple.

Here Susan indicates that an apple is better for the mouse than is cheese, even though the mouse formerly loved cheese. One is to deny wants in favour of "prescribed" foods when on a diet. The best choice of food for the mouse is the apple for the diet. Pizza, like cheese, is not a preferred food when dieting. But this implies that dieting is a temporary state of affairs and that pizza might well appear on the dieters menu once the weight is lost. But while dieting, choosing pizza or cheese is incorrect. This entire scenario of denial and desire is played out within the constructs of prescriptive discourses around diet. Diet is not merely what one eats for Cheeser but it takes on entirely new meanings as prescriptive discourses are internalized.

Susan added the sound of a harp playing (from a wide selection of sounds from which she could choose) to be executed after the choice of the apple. Harp music is commonly associated with angelic qualities as well as religious zeal. Is eating an apple when on a diet an "angelic" thing to do? Augustine (1961, p. 165) wrote of the "two wills" in him, "one the servant of the flesh, the other of the spirit." In Augustine there is a struggle to triumph over the body with what Woods (in Bordo, 1993, p. 148) describes as "absolute purity, hyperintellectuality and transcendence of the flesh. My soul seemed to grow as my body waned; I felt like one of those early Christian saints who starved themselves in the desert sun. I felt invulnerable, clean and hard as the bones etched into my silhouette."

Brown (1993, p. 56) suggests "a continuum framework which recognizes that there are more similarities than differences among anorexic and bulimic women and those who diet and exercise to control their weight." She challenges the view of anorexic women as more disturbed than others and suggests that western society views weight preoccupation as healthy and normal.

Many women who become weight preoccupied find themselves at different places on the continuum over their lives. Some women exchange anorexia and emaciation for bulimic bingeing and purging. Bulimic women may, at some points, vomit to purge, and at others use laxatives, diuretics, or exercise. Bulimic women may stop purging but continue to binge and find themselves gaining weight. These shifts, in themselves, are not uncommon and suggest that the psychological underpinnings remain quite similar, regardless of what form the weight preoccupation takes. (Brown, 1993, p. 58)

## SAVING FILES, SAVING STORIES

Susan handed her disk containing her story file to her teacher. The teacher in this case is the final judge of the student's success or failure in achieving the goal of creating a "living essay." This role of the teacher is acknowledged by both students and the teacher. The teacher is in control, dictating the technological skills students must acquire and assessing students' successes (or lack thereof). Alternative models of teaching and assessment suggest that students can collaborate in determining the usefulness of the tasks they undertake and the meaningfulness of the stories they tell (Britzman, 1991; Lewis, 1990).

## DISCUSSION

### Story Telling

In writing stories or engaging in learning activities of many kinds we may be aware of the intertextual nature of the stories and the cultural narratives in which they are produced. Intertextuality is used here to indicate the interpreting of texts through/with/in understandings of other texts where texts are discourses "held" in language that cut across many works (books, etc., which we can hold in our hands) achieving an irreducible plurality of meanings (Barthes, 1979). It is important to realize though that we cannot determine the origins of a text and that intertextuality is not confused with origins because sources of a text are irrecoverable and "yet *already read:* They are quotations without quotation marks" (Barthes, 1979, p. 77).

We create new meanings in telling a story to others (Rosen, 1984). This idea is elaborated by Hanssen, Harste, and Short (1990, p. 263) in their statement that "[w]hen a story is shared, that text becomes a source of further dialogue and storying by both the writer and the reader." In reading Susan's story one can recognize the importance of the cultural narratives of diet and weight loss as well as issues of technology and schooling.

In Susan's story she explored the narratives of bodies being "too big" and the need to lose weight. Our culture obsesses on weight loss and small bodies and sees any other form (particularly female form) as unfit. Susan's story reflects this cultural construct. In writing her story, Susan explored this cultural phenomenon. Cheeser's character represents the struggle for weight loss and small body and is rewarded by his friends for his achievements in this domain. The loss of his primary and favourite food is small sacrifice in this culturally significant achievement.

It is perhaps only through reading students' stories as cultural artifacts that we can come to understand the importance of stories in schools and the ways that students' stories reflect the cultural contexts in which students are situated. Part of Susan's situation is the computing context in which she works, which forms another thread in her storying.

## The Technical Threads of Susan's Story

Susan had begun the process of telling stories — an action that could have led her to explore cultural narratives and potentially could have led her to engage in resistance writing if this situation had encouraged this kind of activity. Davies (1993) demonstrates that students can explore cultural narratives, question hegemonic discourses, and engage in resistance writing through the writing of stories. This study, in suggesting that computing classrooms are places of cultural production (in this case even when unintended by the teacher) poses the possibility of computing classrooms as sites of resistance to hegemonic discourses, although it leaves how to engage students not only in the production of texts but in critique of their texts as an untried possibility. Wing (1997, p. 503) provides a method of interacting with children around a text composed to provide resistance to hegemonic discourses about gender and suggests that "to question and perhaps to change one's way of thinking may need more stimulus than simply reading a book." Dialogue with children around texts seems to be important in encouraging rethinking (Dobbo, 1982). But even this is not enough. Golden (1996, p.325) suggests that engaging students in "abundant story (consciously shaped by the teacher)" produces possibilities for work with imagination, which she describes "not as an essentialist attribute of an individual but as an effect of discourse, an accumulation of moments of being positioned and taking up positions in the interplay of meaning." Classrooms with this work on imagination taking place would still have dominant discourses present but would take up deconstructive work in order to change children's understandings of their classrooms, those working in them, and themselves. "Narrative knowing seems to be one of the basic ways of understanding or making sense of the world. So a well-considered approach to the use of stories ... is a vital part of any long-term strategy ... to make available the 'cultural capital' of the dominant discourse, and to voice another storyline" (Golden, 1996, p. 330). In the case of Susan's story she might have been encouraged to play with her story and produce variable endings for the same story — a reasonable task in multimedia — in order to 'try on' different storylines and she might have also enjoyed constructing the story with different characters, playing with the gender of the characters and the kinds of events that played out in her story. As Luke (1993, p. 150) suggests "you can't play the game unless you know the rules. But to change the game, you need to know that the rules are neither static nor non-negotiable." Susan may well not have seen the rules of this game as negotiable but this might have been created with her.

Changing the rules of the game though poses challenges for students in that schools base teaching and learning on a set of taken-for-granted meanings in a discourse that constructs an independent, active, and critical child who engages with the texts of the classroom including the teacher's words. Jones (1993, p. 330) suggests that these assumptions may not fit all students — particularly those of nondominant cultural groups or those from non–middle-class backgrounds. In her study, working-class Pacific Island girls

> ... interpret schooling and authority quite differently, through discourses shaped within their history, and their cultural beliefs in the wisdom and authority of elders. The subject position they usually take up as students in these discourses is that of a respectful and accepting recipient of knowledge; for them, "school work" is a closely directed activity with the teacher as "authority" providing the

> necessary, true and correct information. A good student
> then, is not critical .... Taking this sort of analysis there is a
> sense in which such working class minority children have
> failed before they begin; they cannot be "good students"
> within the dominant discourses of secondary schooling.

Of course Razack (1995, p. 67) describes the "perils of talking about cultural differences [that] arise due to the context of twentieth century racism, a context in which cultural differences have largely replaced biological differences as the marker of racial inferiority . ... Peoples of colour, including Aboriginal peoples and African Americans, are defined in the ethnicity paradigm as not having made it owing to their cultural incompatibility with the dominant culture. Culture talk, where race becomes a cultural inadequacy, deflects attention away from the structural relations of domination and subordination."

This suggests that teachers, classrooms, and schools not only need to engage students in story telling but that they need to change the rules of the game with students, taking into account the cultural diversity and gender difference in these classrooms in order that the rules of the game can be made malleable enough that students can work to change them.

## ENDNOTE

1   Research reported in this paper was supported in part by the Social Sciences and Humanities Research Council of Canada.

## REFERENCES

St. Augustine (1961). *The confessions,* Trans. R.S. Pine-Coffin, Middlesex: Penguin.
Barthes, R. (1979). From work to text. In J.V. Harari (ed.) *Textual strategies: Perspectives in poststructural criticism,* Ithaca, NY: Cornell University Press.
Berg, F. (1992). Who is dieting in the United States? *Obesity and Health,* May/June, 48–49.
Bordo, S. (1990). Reading the slender body. In M. Jacobus, E. Fox Keller, and S. Shuttleworth, *Body/politics: Women and the discourses of science,* New York: Routledge.

Bordo, S. (1993). *Unbearable weight: Feminism, Western culture, and the body,* Berkeley: University of California Press.

Britzman, D. (1991). *Practice makes practice: A critical study of learning to teach,* New York: State University of New York Press.

Brown, C. (1993). The continuum: Anorexia, bulimia, and weight preoccupation. In C. Brown, and K. Jasper (ed.) *Consuming passions: Feminist approaches to weight preoccupation and eating disorders,* Toronto: Second Story Press.

Brumberg, J.J. (1989). *Fasting girls: The history of anorexia nervosa,* Markham, ON: Penguin.

Chernin, (1985). *The hungry self: Women, eating, and identity,* Toronto: Random House.

Crawford, R. (1985). A cultural account of health — Self-control, release, and the social body. In J. McKinley (ed.) *Issues in the political economy of health care,* New York: Methuen.

Davies, B. (1993). *Shards of glass: Children reading and writing beyond gendered identities,* Cresshill, NJ: Hampton Press.

Davies, B. (1997). Constructing and deconstructing masculinities through critical literacy. *Gender and Education,* 9(1), 9–30.

Dobbo, P. (1982). Using literature to change attitudes to the handicapped. *The Reading Teacher,* 36, 290–292.

Duden, B. (1991). *The woman beneath the skin: A doctor's patients in eighteenth-century Germany,* Cambridge, MA: Harvard University Press.

Feldman, W., E. Feldman, and J. Goodman (1986). Health concerns and health related behaviours of adolescents. *Canadian Medical Association Journal,* 134, 489–493.

Foucault, M. (1973). *The birth of the clinic: An archaeology of medical perception.* Trans. A.M. Sheridan Smith, New York.

Foucault, M. (1977). The eye of power. In M. Foucault (ed.) *Power/knowledge,* Trans. C. Gordo. New York: Pantheon.

Friedman, M. (1985). Bulimia. *Women and Therapy,* 4(2), 63–69.

Golden, J. (1996). Critical imagination: Serious play with narrative and gender. *Gender and Education,* 8(3), 323–335.

Hanssen, E., J. Harste, and K. Short (1990). In conversation: Theory and instruction. In D. Bogdan and S. Straw (eds.) *Beyond communication: Reading comprehension and criticism,* Portsmouth, NH: Boynton/Cook.

Health and Welfare Canada (1988). *Promoting healthy weights: A discussion paper.* Ottawa.

Iseke-Barnes, J. (1997). Poststructuralist analysis of reading and writing through/with technology. *Curriculum Studies: A Journal of Educational Discussion and Debate,* 5(2), 195–211.

Jones, A. (1993). Becoming a girl: Post-structuralist suggestions for educational research. *Gender and Education*, 5(2), 157–166.

Lewis, M. (1990). Interrupting patriarchy: Politics, resistance, and transformation in the feminist classroom. *Harvard Educational Review*, 60, 467–488.

Luke, A. (1993). Stories of social regulation: The micropolitics of classroom narrative. In B. Green (ed.) *The insistence of the letter: Literacy studies and curriculum theorizing*, London: Falmer Press.

Millar, W. (1991). A trend to a healthier lifestyle. *Health Reports*, 3(4), 363–370.

Orbach, S. (1978). *Fat is a feminist issue: A self-help guide for compulsive eaters*, New York: Paddington Books.

Orbach, S. (1986). *Hunger strikes: The anorectic struggle as a metaphor for our age*, New York: W.W. Norton.

Razack, S. (1995). The perils of talking about culture: Schooling research on south and east Asian students. *Race, Gender, and Class*, 2(3), 67–82.

Rosen, H. (1984). *Stories and meanings*, Sheffield, England: National Association for the Teaching of English.

Sacker, I., and M. Zimmer (1987). *Dying to be thin*, New York: Warner.

Schwartz, H. (1986). *Never satisfied*, New York: Free Press.

Silverstein, B. (1984). *Fed up!* Boston: South End Books.

Stacey, J. (1987). Sexism by a subtler name? Postindustrial conditions and postfeminist consciousness. *Socialist Review*, 17(6), 7–30.

Wells, G. (1987). Apprenticeship in literacy. *Interchange*, 18 (1,2), 109–123.

Wing, A. (1997). How can children be taught to read differently? Bill's new frock and the "hidden curriculum." *Gender and Education*, 9(4), 491–504.

## EXERCISES

1. What are the main ideas in this article?
2. What are your interpretations of the various images highlighted in this article?
3. How would you use them in terms of teaching in a diverse situation?

# Chapter 22

# The Beauty Myth

## Naomi Wolf

At last, after a long silence, women took to the streets. In the two decades of radical action that followed the rebirth of feminism in the early 1970s, Western women gained legal and reproductive rights, pursued higher education, entered the trades and the professions, and overturned ancient and revered beliefs about their social role. A generation on, do women feel free?

The affluent, educated, liberated women of the First World, who can enjoy freedoms unavailable to any women ever before, do not feel as free as they want to. And they can no longer restrict to the subconscious their sense that this lack of freedom has something to do with — with apparently frivolous issues, things that really should not matter. Many are ashamed to admit that such trivial concerns — to do with physical appearance, bodies, faces, hair, clothes — matter so much. But in spite of shame, guilt, and denial, more and more women are wondering if it isn't that they are entirely neurotic and alone but rather that something important is indeed at stake that has to do with the relationship between female liberation and female beauty.

The more legal and material hindrances women have broken through, the more strictly and heavily and cruelly images of female beauty have come to weigh upon us. Many women sense that women's collective progress has stalled; compared with the heady momentum of earlier days, there is a dispiriting climate of confusion, division, cynicism, and above all, exhaustion. After years of much struggle and little recognition, many older women feel burned out; after years of taking its light for granted, many younger women show little interest in touching new fire to the torch.

During the past decade, women breached the power structure; meanwhile, eating disorders rose exponentially and cosmetic surgery became the fastest-growing medical specialty. During the past five years, consumer spending doubled, pornography became the main media category, ahead of legitimate films and records combined, and thirty-three thousand American women told researchers that they would rather lose ten to fifteen pounds than achieve any other goal. More women have more money and power and scope and legal recognition than we have ever had before; but in terms of how we feel about ourselves physically, we may actually be worse off than our unliberated grandmothers. Recent research consistently shows that inside the majority of the West's controlled, attractive, successful working women, there is a secret "underlife" poisoning our freedom; infused with notions of beauty, it is a dark vein of self-hatred, physical obsessions, terror of aging, and dread of lost control.

It is no accident that so many potentially powerful women feel this way. We are in the midst of a violent backlash against feminism that uses images of female beauty as a political weapon against women's advancement: the beauty myth. It is the modem version of a social reflex that has been in force since the Industrial Revolution. As women released themselves from the feminine mystique of domesticity, the beauty myth took over its lost ground, expanding as it waned to carry on its work of social control.

The contemporary backlash is so violent because the ideology of beauty is the last one remaining of the old feminine ideologies that still has the power to control those women whom second wave feminism would have otherwise made relatively uncontrollable: It has grown stronger to take over the work of social coercion that myths about motherhood, domesticity, chastity, and passivity, no longer can manage. It is seeking right now to undo psychologically and covertly all the good things that feminism did for women materially and overtly.

This counterforce is operating to checkmate the inheritance of feminism on every level in the lives of Western women. Feminism gave us laws against job discrimination based on gender; immediately case law evolved in Britain and the United States that institutionalized job discrimination based on women's appearances. Patriarchal religion declined; new religious dogma, using some of the mind-altering techniques of older cults and sects, arose around age and weight to functionally supplant traditional ritual. Feminists, inspired by Friedan, broke the stranglehold on the women's popular press of advertisers for household products, who were promoting the feminine mystique; at once, the diet and skin care industries became the new cultural censors of women's intellectual space, and because of their pressure, the gaunt, youthful model supplanted the happy housewife as the arbiter of successful womanhood. The sexual revolution promoted the discovery of female sexuality; "beauty pornography" — which for the first time in women's history artificially links a commodified "beauty" directly and explicitly to sexuality — invaded the mainstream to undermine women's new and vulnerable sense of sexual self-worth. Reproductive rights gave Western women control over our own bodies; the weight of fashion models plummeted to 23 percent below that of ordinary women, eating disorders rose exponentially, and a mass neurosis was promoted that used food and weight to strip women of that sense of control. Women insisted on politicizing health; new technologies of invasive, potentially deadly "cosmetic" surgeries developed apace to re-exert old forms of medical control of women.

Every generation since about 1830 has had to fight its version of the beauty myth. "It is very little to me," said the suffragist Lucy Stone in 1855, "to have the right to vote, to own property, etcetera, if I may not keep my body, and its uses, in my absolute right." Eighty years later, after women had won the vote, and the first wave of the organized women's movement had subsided, Virginia Woolf wrote that it would still be decades before women could tell the truth about their bodies. In 1962, Betty Friedan quoted a young woman trapped in the Feminine Mystique: "Lately, I look in the mirror, and I'm so afraid I'm going to look like my mother." Eight years after that, heralding the cataclysmic second wave of feminism, Germaine Greer described "the Stereotype": "To her belongs all that is beautiful, even the very word beauty itself ... she is a doll ... I'm sick of the masquerade." In spite of the great revolution of the second wave, we are not exempt. Now we can look out over ruined barricades: A revolution has come upon us and changed everything in its path, enough time has passed since then for babies to have grown into women, but there still remains a final right not fully claimed.

The beauty myth tells a story: The quality called "beauty" objectively and universally exists. Women must want to embody it and men must want to possess women who embody it. This embodiment is an imperative for women and not for men, which situation is necessary and natural because it is biological, sexual, and evolutionary: Strong men battle for beautiful women, and beautiful women are more reproductively successful. Women's beauty must correlate to their fertility, and since this system is based on sexual selection, it is inevitable and changeless. None of this is true. "Beauty" is a currency system like the gold standard. Like any economy, it is determined by politics, and in the modern age in the West it is the last, best belief system that keeps male dominance intact. In assigning value to women in a vertical hierarchy according to a culturally imposed physical standard, it is an expression of power relations in which women must unnaturally compete for resources that men have appropriated for themselves.

"Beauty" is not universal or changeless, though the West pretends that all ideals of female beauty stem from one Platonic Ideal Woman; the Maori admire a fat vulva, and the Padung, droopy breasts. Nor is "beauty" a function of evolution: Its ideals change at a pace far more rapid than that of the evolution of species, and Charles Darwin was himself unconvinced by his own explanation that "beauty" resulted from a "sexual selection" that deviated from the rule of natural selection; for women to compete with women through "beauty" is a reversal of the way in which natural selection affects all other mammals. Anthropology has overturned the notion that females must be "beautiful" to be selected to mate: Evelyn Reed, Elaine Morgan, and others have dismissed sociobiological assertions of innate male polygamy and female monogamy. Female higher primates are the sexual initiators; not only do they seek out and enjoy sex with many partners, but "every nonpregnant female takes her turn at being the most desirable of all her troop. And that cycle keeps turning as long as she lives." The inflamed pink sexual organs of primates are often cited by male sociobiologists as analogous to human arrangements relating to female "beauty," when in fact that is a universal, nonhierarchical female primate characteristic.

Nor has the beauty myth always been this way. Though the pairing of the older rich men with young, "beautiful" women is taken to be somehow inevitable, in the matriarchal Goddess religions that dominated the Mediterranean from about 25,000 B.C.E. to about 700 B.C.E., the situation was reversed: "In every culture, the Goddess has many lovers …. The clear pattern is of an older woman with a beautiful but expendable youth — Ishtar and Tammuz, Venus and Adonis, Cybele and Attis, Isis and Osiris … their only function the service of the divine 'womb.'" Nor is it something only women do and only men watch: Among the Nigerian Wodaabes, the women hold economic power and the tribe is obsessed with male beauty; Wodaabe men spend hours together in elaborate makeup sessions, and compete — provocatively painted and dressed, with swaying hips and seductive expressions — in beauty contests judged by women. There is no legitimate historical or biological justification for the beauty myth; what it is doing to women today is a result of nothing more exalted than the need of today's power structure, economy, and culture to mount a counteroffensive against women.

If the beauty myth is not based on evolution, sex, gender, aesthetics, or God, on what is it based? It claims to be about intimacy and sex and life, a celebration of women. It is actually composed of emotional distance, politics, finance, and sexual repression. The beauty myth is not about women at all. It is about men's institutions and institutional power.

The qualities that a given period calls beautiful in women are merely symbols of the female behavior that that period considers desirable: The beauty myth is always actually prescribing behavior and not appearance. Competition between women has been made part of the myth so that women will be divided from one another. Youth and (until recently) virginity have been "beautiful" in women since they stand for experiential and sexual ignorance. Aging in women is "unbeautiful" since women grow more powerful with time, and since the links between generations of women must always be newly broken: Older women fear young ones, young women fear old, and the beauty myth truncates for all the female life span. Most urgently, women's identity must be premised upon our "beauty" so that we will remain vulnerable to outside approval, carrying the vital sensitive organ of self-esteem exposed to the air.

Though there has, of course, been a beauty myth in some form for as long as there has been patriarchy, the beauty myth in its modern form is a fairly recent invention. The myth flourishes when material constraints on women are dangerously loosened. Before the Industrial Revolution, the average woman could not have had the same feelings about "beauty" that modern women do who experience the myth as continual comparison to a mass-disseminated physical ideal. Before the development of technologies of mass production — daguerrotypes, photographs, etc. — an ordinary woman was exposed to few such images outside the Church. Since the family was a productive unit and women's work complemented men's, the value of women who were not aristocrats or prostitutes lay in their work skills, economic shrewdness, physical strength, and fertility. Physical attraction, obviously, played its part; but "beauty" as we understand it was not, for ordinary women, a serious issue in the marriage marketplace. The beauty myth in its modern form gained ground after the upheavals of industrialization, as the work unit of the family was destroyed, and urbanization and the emerging factory system demanded what social engineers of the time termed the "separate sphere" of domesticity, which supported the new labor category of the "breadwinner" who left home for the workplace during the day. The middle class expanded, the standards of living and of literacy rose, the size of families shrank; a new class of literate, idle women developed, on whose submission to enforced domesticity the evolving system of industrial capitalism depended. Most of our assumptions about the way women have always thought about "beauty" date from no earlier than the 1830s, when the cult of domesticity was first consolidated and the beauty index invented.

For the first time new technologies could reproduce — in fashion plates, daguerreotypes, tintypes, and rotogravures — images of how women should look. In the 1840s the first nude photographs of prostitutes were taken; advertisements using images of "beautiful" women first appeared in mid-century. Copies of classical artworks, postcards of society beauties and royal mistresses, Currier and Ives prints, and porcelain figurines flooded the separate sphere to which middle-class women were confined.

Since the Industrial Revolution, middle-class Western women have been controlled by ideals and stereotypes as much as by material constraints. This situation, unique to this group, means that analyses that trace "cultural conspiracies" are uniquely plausible in relation to them. The rise of the beauty myth was just one of several emerging social fictions that masqueraded as natural components of the feminine sphere, the better to enclose those women inside it. Other such fictions arose contemporaneously: a version of childhood that required continual maternal supervision; a concept of female biology that required middle-class women to act out the roles of hysterics and hypochondriacs; a conviction that respectable women were sexually anesthetic; and a definition of women's work that occupied them with repetitive, time-consuming, and painstaking tasks such as needlepoint and lacemaking. All such Victorian inventions as these served a double function — that is, though they were encouraged as a means to expend female energy and intelligence in harmless ways, women often used them to express genuine creativity and passion.

But in spite of middle-class women's creativity with fashion and embroidery and child rearing, and, a century later, with the role of the suburban housewife that devolved from these social fictions, the fictions' main purpose was served: During a century and a half of unprecedented feminist agitation, they effectively counteracted middle-class women's dangerous new leisure, literacy, and relative freedom from material constraints.

Though these time- and mind-consuming fictions about women's natural role adapted themselves to resurface in the post-war Feminine Mystique, when the second wave of the women's movement took apart what women's magazines had portrayed as the "romance," "science," and "adventure" of homemaking and suburban family life, they temporarily failed. The cloying domestic fiction of "togetherness" lost its meaning and middle-class women walked out of their front doors in masses.

So the fictions simply transformed themselves once more: Since the women's movement had successfully taken apart most other necessary fictions of femininity, all the work of social control once spread out over the whole network of these fictions had to be reassigned to the only strand left intact, which action consequently strengthened it a hundredfold. This reimposed onto liberated women's faces and bodies all the limitations, taboos, and punishments of the repressive laws, religious injunctions and reproductive enslavement that no longer carried sufficient force. Inexhaustible but ephemeral beauty work took over from inexhaustible but ephemeral housework. As the economy, law, religion, sexual mores, education, and culture were forcibly opened up to include women more fairly, a private reality colonized female consciousness. By using ideas about "beauty," it reconstructed an alternative female world with its own laws, economy, religion, sexuality, education, and culture, each element as repressive as any that had gone before.

Since middle-class Western women can best be weakened psychologically now that we are stronger materially, the beauty myth, as it has resurfaced in the last generation, has had to draw on more technological sophistication and reactionary fervor than ever before. The modern arsenal of the myth is a dissemination of millions of images of the current ideal; although this barrage is generally seen as a collective sexual fantasy, there is in fact little that is sexual about it. It is summoned out of political fear on the part of male-dominated institutions threatened by women's freedom, and it exploits female guilt and apprehension about our own liberation-latent fears that we might be going too far. This frantic aggregation of imagery is a collective reactionary hallucination willed into being by both men and women stunned and disoriented by the rapidity with which gender relations have been transformed: a bulwark of reassurance against the flood of change. The mass depiction of the modern woman as a "beauty" is a contradiction: Where modern women are growing, moving, and expressing their individuality, as the myth has it, "beauty" is by definition inert, timeless, and generic. That this hallucination is necessary and deliberate is evident in the way "beauty" so directly contradicts women's real situation.

And the unconscious hallucination grows ever more influential and pervasive because of what is now conscious market manipulation: powerful industries — the $33-billion-a-year diet industry, the $20-billion cosmetics industry, the $300-million cosmetic surgery industry, and the $7-billion pornography industry — have arisen from the capital made out of unconscious anxieties, and are in turn able, through their influence on mass culture, to use, stimulate, and reinforce the hallucination in a rising economic spiral.

This is not a conspiracy theory; it doesn't have to be. Societies tell themselves necessary fictions in the same way that individuals and families do. Henrik Ibsen called them "vital lies," and psychologist Daniel Goleman describes them working the same way on the social level that they do within families: "The collusion is maintained by directing attention away from the fearsome fact, or by repackaging its meaning in an acceptable format." The costs of these social blind spots, he writes, are destructive communal illusions. Possibilities for women have become so open-ended that they threaten to destabilize the institutions on which a male-dominated culture has depended, and a collective panic reaction on the part of both sexes has forced a demand for counterimages.

The resulting hallucination materializes, for women, as something all too real. No longer just an idea, it becomes three-dimensional, incorporating within itself how women live and how they do not live: It becomes the Iron Maiden. The original Iron Maiden was a medieval German instrument of torture, a body-shaped casket painted with the limbs and features of a lovely, smiling young woman. The unlucky victim was slowly enclosed inside her; the lid fell shut to immobilize the victim, who died either of starvation or, less cruelly, of the metal spikes embedded in her interior. The modern hallucination in which women are trapped or trap themselves is similarly rigid, cruel, and euphemistically painted. Contemporary culture directs attention to imagery of the Iron Maiden, while censoring real women's faces and bodies.

Why does the social order feel the need to defend itself by evading the fact of real women, our faces and voices and bodies, and reducing the meaning of women to these formulaic and endlessly reproduced "beautiful" images? Though unconscious personal anxieties can be a powerful force in the creation of a vital lie, economic necessity practically guarantees it. An economy that depends on slavery needs to promote images of slaves that "justify" the institution of slavery. Western economies are absolutely dependent now on the continued underpayment of women. An ideology that makes women feel "worth less" was urgently needed to counteract the way feminism had begun to make us feel worth more. This does not require a conspiracy; merely an atmosphere. The contemporary economy depends right now on the representation of women within the beauty myth. Economist John Kenneth Galbraith offers an economic explanation for "the persistence of the view of homemaking as a 'higher calling'": the concept of women as naturally trapped within the Feminine Mystique, he feels, "has been forced on us by popular sociology, by magazines, and by fiction to disguise the fact that woman in her role of consumer has been essential to the development of our industrial society .... Behavior that is essential for economic reasons is transformed into a social virtue." As soon as a woman's primary social value could no longer be defined as the attainment of virtuous domesticity, the beauty myth redefined it as the attainment of virtuous beauty. It did so to substitute both a new consumer imperative and a new justification for economic unfairness in the workplace where the old ones had lost their hold over newly liberated women.

Another hallucination arose to accompany that of the Iron Maiden: The caricature of the Ugly Feminist was resurrected to dog the steps of the women's movement. The caricature is unoriginal; it was coined to ridicule the feminists of the nineteenth century. Lucy Stone herself, whom supporters saw as "a prototype of womanly grace ... fresh and fair as the morning," was derided by detractors with "the usual report" about Victorian feminists: "a big masculine woman, wearing boots, smoking a cigar, swearing like a trooper." As Betty Friedan put it presciently in 1960, even before the savage revamping of that old caricature: "The unpleasant image of feminists today resembles less the feminists themselves than the image fostered by the interests who so bitterly opposed the vote for women in state after state." Thirty years on, her conclusion is more true than ever: That resurrected caricature, which sought to punish women for their public acts by going after their private sense of self, became the paradigm for new limits placed on aspiring women everywhere. After the success of the women's movement's second wave, the beauty myth was perfected to checkmate power at every level in individual women's lives. The modern neuroses of life in the female body spread to woman after woman at epidemic rates. The myth is undermining — slowly, imperceptibly, without our being aware of the real forces of erosion — the ground women have gained through long, hard, honorable struggle.

The beauty myth of the present is more insidious than any mystique of femininity yet: A century ago, Nora slammed the door of the doll's house; a generation ago, women turned their backs on the consumer heaven of the isolated multiapplianced home; but where women are trapped today, there is no door to slam. The contemporary ravages of the beauty backlash are destroying women physically and depleting us psychologically. If we are to free ourselves from the dead weight that has once again been made out of femaleness, it is not ballots or lobbyists or placards that women will need first; it is a new way to see.

## Exercises

1.  What are the main arguments in this article?
2.  Why do you think these arguments are important in relation to this topic?
3.  Could you explain your understanding of the following: Beauty is a currency; Beauty is a commodity; Women have no control of their beauty?
4.  How can teachers create awareness in their teaching about the exploitative nature of the cosmetic industry?
5.  Why do you think women seem to have lost control of their beauty?

# Part 7

# Issues of
# Sexuality in Schools

**Mac an Ghaíll**
"(In)visibility: 'Race,' Sexuality, and
Masculinity in the School Context"

**Toronto Board of Education**
"Safely Out: Activities for
Challenging Homophobia in Schools"

**Gordon**
"What do you say
when you hear 'Faggot?'"

# Chapter 23

# (In)visibility: 'Race,' Sexuality, and Masculinity in the School Context

## Máirtín Mac an Ghaíll

We are only beginning to understand the complex articulation between schooling, masculine cultural formations and sexual/racial identities. Feminist theory has enabled us to move beyond the ahistorical gender/ sexual essentialism and determinism of sex-role theory, acknowledging that young people are not such *'tablae rasae*, to be injected or even constructed with the ideology of the day' (Rowbotham, 1989, p.18). As Carrigan, Connell and Lee (1985, pp. 88–9) argue:

> The history of homosexuality obliges us to think of masculinity not as a single object with its own history but as being constantly constructed within the history of an evolving social structure of power relations. It obliges us to see the construction as a social struggle going on in a complex ideological and political field in which there is a continuing process of mobilization, marginalization, contestation, resistance and subordination.

Modern schooling systems are significant cultural sites that actively produce and reproduce a range of differentiated, hierarchically ordered masculinities and femininities that are made available for students to inhabit. It is within historically specific school gender regimes that we may locate the development of black and white lesbian and gay sexualities (Mac an Ghaíll, 1993).

A main argument here is that the major problem in the schooling of black gay students is not their sexuality but the phenomena of homophobia, heterosexism, and racism which pervasively circumscribe their social world. Furthermore, these phenomena are mediated and reproduced both through existing formal and hidden curriculum, pedagogical and evaluative systems that set out to regulate subordinated young people, and through gender/sexual specific mechanisms, such as the processes of gender/sexual representations, which in turn are 'race,' class, and age specific. An idealist analysis of the curriculum that reduces the heterosexist structuring of schooling to aberrant teacher prejudice is insufficient to explain the complex social interaction of white male and female teachers with black male students in racialized, male-dominated institutions. For example, the students' teachers claimed that they found it difficult to discuss lesbian and gay issues within the school context. However, at a deeper level specific age relations operate in English schools that serve to marginalize and alienate many young people. White teachers' difficulty in communicating with black gay students is not simply an issue about sexuality and racism. It is also premised on the low epistemological status ascribed to all students.

## THE CASE STUDY[1]

The Asian and Afro-Caribbean young gay men involved in this qualitative study were aged between 16 and 19 years. They were all attending local post-16 education institutions situated in the Midlands. I taught a number of them, who were following A-level courses. Within their schools and colleges they were not "out" as gay. My own students informed me that they were open to me about their sexuality because of my anti-homophobic stance. In the staffroom, classroom, and more informal school arenas I presented a pro-gay perspective. They introduced me to their friends, who in turn introduced me to their friends. We operated as an informal support group. [...]

Our being together provided the conditions for us to start a conversation about the politics of oppression with particular reference to contemporary state schooling. This produced an unexpected and unintended effect. By the early 1990s in post-primary schools there tends to be less evidence among minorities of the "black unity" of the mid-1980s, with its emphasis on the shared experience of anti-black racism. The black gay students here in exploring the politics of complex difference involving the articulation of homophobia, heterosexism, and racism, are a sector of the younger generation among whom "syncretic black identities are being formed ..." (Mama, 1992, p. 80), focusing on racial gender and sexual communalities as well as on the specificities of personal histories, memories, desires, and expectations.

## Methodology

Space does not allow for a detailed discussion of the study's methodology, particularly with reference to questions concerning the politics and ethics of researching oppressed groups (see Mac an Ghaill, 1989a). Much of the material reported here was collected from observation, informal discussions, and recorded semi-structured interviews with the students and their teachers at their schools and colleges. The material is taken from life and school histories that involved discussion of family/kinship network, peer groupings, work experience, political views/activities, and school/college experiences. This methodological approach helped to locate schooling within the larger sociopolitical processes (see Connell, 1989; Morgan, 1992). Sharing our life histories helped to challenge the power asymmetries between the students and myself. My main influences include feminist methodology and praxis-based pedagogy (see Freire, 1985; Bryan, Dadzie, and Scale, 1985, and hooks, 1991). In adopting a student-centred methodological approach that prioritizes their epistemological accounts of schooling, I have attempted to operate within a framework that served to empower the students who were actively involved in the construction of the research stance (Griffin, 1987, p. 21; Bhavnani, 1991).

## ADMINISTRATIVE SYSTEMS OF TEACHER RACIAL AND GENDER/SEXUAL TYPIFICATIONS

As Westwood (1990, pp. 56–57) points out within the context of the need to de-essentialize black masculinity:

> The essentialism of the constructions that surround the black
> man and black masculinity have given plenty of scope for
> racist accounts through stereotyping and the construction
> of black men as "the other".[..] The fixity of these stereotypes
> places "races," genders, motivations and behaviours in such
> a way that they become naturalized and a substitute for the
> complex realities that they seek to describe.

For the young men in this study these processes of naturalization
and objectification were most immediately experienced through the
highly contradictory dominant systems of teacher racial and gender/
sexual discourses, which are "embedded in social relationships of
structured domination and subordination" (Bhavnani, 1991, p. 181).
These administrative systems operate as processes of teacher
signification, that form the basis for the creation of ethnically structured
student hierarchies. In turn, they serve to establish regulatory criteria by
which to develop allocative and exclusionary processes within specific
institutional sites, in relation to the Afro-Caribbean and Asian groups
(Miles, 1989).

In earlier work (Mac an Ghaíll, 1989b) I set out to reconceptualize
black students' experience of schooling within a framework that moved
beyond monocausal explanations and examined the multifaceted
dimensions of racially structured English schooling. The Afro-Caribbean
and Asian young men in this study, all of whom are academically
successful, recall schooling biographies that have significant
convergences and differences. What emerges is how racialized social
and discursive configurations with their own local histories are grounded
in specific material cultures at classroom and playground levels. For the
students, the white teachers' racial and gender/sexual typifications did
not take a unitary form but rather were differentially structured and
experienced, mediated by the specificity of different school cultures and
individual and collective student responses. In particular, the racial
and gender composition of each school was a significant variable in the
construction of teacher typifications. So, for example, in working-class
schools where there was a majority Asian student population with a
mainly white minority, the dominant representations of Asian youths
tended to be negative, with caricatures of them as "sly" and "not real

men." However, in working-class schools which included significant numbers of Afro-Caribbeans, the students felt that the Asians were caricatured in a more positive way in relation to the Afro-Caribbeans, who were perceived as of "low ability," "aggressive" and "anti-authority." In contrast, in middle-class grammar schools with predominantly white student populations, such attributes as "hard working" and "ambitious" were assigned to Asian students (Rattansi, 1992).

A major limitation of much "race relations" theoretical and empirical work in education has been the failure to incorporate psychodynamic explanations (Henriques, 1984; Cohen, 1987; Nava, 1992). As students point out, their schooling cannot be reductively conceptualized in terms of a simple binary social system, composed of a juxtaposed white straight superiority and a black gay inferiority. The relations between white teachers and black students also involve a psychic structure, including such elements as desire, attraction, repression, transference, and projection in relation to a racialized "sexual other." (Pajaczknowska and Young, 1992) [...] In the following accounts the young men discuss the range of split responses from white males to themselves, that were manifested in terms of the interplay between racial and sexual fear and desire and the accompanying contradictory elements of repulsion, fascination, and misrecognition (Klein, 1960; Rutherford, 1990).

**Andrew:** It's like with the straights, all the bits they don't like about themselves or they're afraid of, they push on to us.

**Rajinder:** Thinking about it, it's very complex. Straight men don't really have a problem with gays, they have a problem with themselves. Straight men seem to fear and love women but fear and hate gay men. Then whites, especially white men, have that fear and hatred for Asians and Afro-Caribbeans. So, black gay men are a real threat to white straight men. Like James Baldwin says, they act out their fears on us, on our bodies .... But then there's other complications. Like at our school, you could see some of the white teachers, the men, they really admired the Caribbeans and not just in sport and music, where it was really homoerotic, though of course they could never admit it to themselves. I think for a lot of teachers there, who felt trapped in their jobs, the macho black kids represented freedom from the system. There were anti-school macho whites and Asians but the teachers with their stereotypes fantasized about the Caribbean kids, who they saw as anti-authority, more physical and athletic, everything they couldn't be but greatly admired.

**Stephen:** Like you say black kids know that most white teachers would never live in our areas even though they make their living here. English middle-class people have always lived off immigrants; the blacks and the Irish around here. The teachers' kids go to their white grammar and private schools on the backs of the mis-education that their parents impose on us every day .... But at night the teachers creep out of their white ghettoes to live it up among the "black folk." Emotionally they're really screwed up. And somehow although they don't want us as neighbours, they are obsessed with our food, music, dance, with our sex. You see they fantasize that these poor black folk they're not repressed like the whiteys and in a different way their kids are doing the same ... another generation of patronization from the white boys and girls!

## SUBORDINATED BLACK MASCULINITIES: SUBCULTURAL RESPONSES AND SELF-REPRESENTATIONS

There is a danger in examining black gay students' schooling experiences of unintentionally adopting a passive concept of subject positioning, with the student portrayed as unproblematically accepting an over-determined racial and gender/sexual role allocation (Walkerdine, 1990). In fact, as the students here make clear, they are active curriculum and masculine makers. Male ethnographic research on white and black working-class males has finely illustrated how subordinated youth, drawing on resources from their own communities and wider youth cultural forms, have actively constructed a range of masculinities. This has taken place within the interrelated nexus of teacher authoritarianism, their own survivalist peer-group cultures, the negotiation of their sexual coming-of-age and the anticipation of their future location in low-skilled local labour markets. In the 1990s for many black and white working-class young people, their post-school anticipation is for the status of a condition of dependency as surplus labour in late-industrial capitalism (Cohen, 1987).

Cockburn (1987, p. 44) has pointed out that "The social construction of gender is riddled with resistance and the resistance is complex. While some boys refuse the macho mode of masculinity and pay the price of being scorned a 'wimp' or a 'poofter,' others resist the class domination by means of masculine codes." For black male students this resistance is also developed in relation to racially administered schooling systems. Here, the students reflected on the specific dynamics and interplay between state schooling and the construction of black ethnic masculinities. They were aware of how class-based differentiated curricula helped to shape differentiated masculinities, with sectors of black and white working-class students developing compensatory hyper-masculine forms in response to their experience of academic failure. They were also aware of how black students defensively responded to racialized and gendered discourses that constructed juxtaposed images of "weak" Asian and "tough" Afro-Caribbean males. They acknowledged the colonial legacy and present-day validity of Mercer and Julien's argument that:

> Whereas prevailing definitions of masculinity imply power, control and authority, these attributes have been historically denied to black men since slavery. The centrally dominant role of the white male slavemaster in eighteenth and nineteenth-century plantation society debarred black males from the patriarchal privileges ascribed to the male masculine role . ... Shaped by this history, black masculinity is a highly contradictory formation as it is a subordinated masculinity. (Mercer and Julien, 1988, p. 112)

What emerges are the specific dynamics for young black men of their psychosexual development within state school systems and a wider culture that systematically devalues and marginalizes black masculinities, while elevating and celebrating dominant forms of white straight masculinity. In the following extracts the students make clear the contextual contingency in which racial and sexual representations and typifications operate within specific sites.

**Amerjit:** Teachers can't see the way that schools make kids act bad. For a lot of blacks, it's the low classes, the non-academic subjects and being pushed into sport that makes them act macho. It's the way that black and white boys having been failed on the school's terms, try to get some status, some self respect .... At school you only hear of all the great whites. Most teachers don't respect black men, so the kids think they have no choice but to act it out.

**Assim:** At our school when we started, the whites and the Caribbeans were seen as the toughest. But by the fifth year, the Asian gangs were the worst. They were like the Warrior gang in Young, Gifted, and Black. They formed gangs, smoked, wore the right gear, trainers and tracksuits, watched violent videos, and hung around with older kids with fast cars and the music. Things that a lot of white working-class pupils do, acting hard all the time. But for the Asians, there is also racism. Outside of school, outside our own area, we are always under suspicion and likely to be attacked from the NF and respectable whites. We know that we get attacked because whites see us as easy targets, as weak. They also knew that the teachers were afraid of the Caribbeans because they saw them as tough. Like at school the teachers would avoid walking through groups of black kids but not Asians.

**Stephen:** In the last place (secondary school) the blacks were seen as the hardest and most against the teachers. There were only a few of them involved in the main anti-school gang but they were the leaders of the posse, as they called themselves. I think a lot of the teachers stereotyped all blacks as aggressive. And I think some of the kids came to believe this about themselves or thought the teachers believed it, so they may as well act it out as they were going to be picked on anyway .

[ … ] The black gay students examined the links between the institutional and male peer-group surveillance, regulation and control of female and male gender and sexual reputations. They were surprised at the way in which male teachers and students conflated assumed gay behaviour with femininity in order to traduce the former. The assimilation of masculine non-macho behaviour to feminine behaviour was most evident in relation to the ubiquity of the term "poof," which in "denoting lack of guts, suggests femininity-weakness, softness and inferiority" (Lees, 1987, p. 180). (See Cockburn 1987, p. 41, on the development of the term "lezzie.") Furthermore, they linked this form of "gay-bashing" to that of the use of the term "Paki" as a form of "Paki-bashing." Both these labels, "poof" and "Paki" have several meanings: sometimes they are used with a specific sexual or racial connotation; while at other times they are used as general terms of abuse. The notoriety and frequency of these labels acted as major mechanisms of policing gender and sexual boundaries with specific implications for Afro-Caribbean and Asian straight and gay youth.

> **Rajinder:** Nearly all the tough kids, the really hard lads were in the bottom two bands especially the bottom one. They got their status by fighting the system that they saw abusing them. Some of the toughest ones were the white kids from the estate, always in trouble with the police and teachers. They were obsessed with proving they were real men, like those kids you talked about with their fighting, football, and fucking — that was really them … They hated "poofs" and "Pakis" and used to argue with the teachers when they tried to stop fights say things like, "Sir, he's only a 'Paki' or a 'poof.' They felt that the teachers agreed with them and in some ways they were right. A lot of the men teachers were really into violence but it was official, so that was okay to them. Anything seen as soft in their terms was despised. Like there was all this sexist talk by teachers. They thought that the best way to control a boy was to say to him, "Stop acting like a girl." And they always said it loud so all their friends could hear. You see then outside the class the lads could carry on the sexual bullying that the teachers had set up.

Westwood (1990, p. 59) points out: "Discourses as registers of masculinity are worked through a variety of spaces." For the working-class students, territorial imperatives underpinned their inner-city school playgrounds. They constituted a military-like arena in which dominant forms of straight masculinity, physically and symbolically occupied key spatial sites including the central location of constructed football pitches, smoking areas, and school entrances and exits. Within these "safe" sites, male straight students ascribed the highest status to the toughest gang, projecting a version of working-class masculinity that overemphasized such traits as physical toughness, independence, and aggression (Tolson, 1977). Fighting was a key signifier, related to a class-specific and gendered use of the body as against the mind (Walkerdine, 1990, p. 178). Joyce Canaan, in a paper that examines the construction of white working-class masculinity as highly contradictory and multifaceted, notes that:

> Working-class violence is not something that singularly expresses working-class identity or masculine identity; it is a particular combination of these two, and other factors. In addition, this analysis suggests that male violence is constructed as much through gender as class, it is central to masculinity in general and takes particular forms among distinct groups of working-class young men, which reveals much about their class and gender as well as their sexual orientation and age. (Canaan, 1991, p. 123)

For the students there was an ethos of physical and symbolic intimidation that pervaded playground life that they were coerced into "learning to live with." Most immediately the specific student social hierarchies within this arena were translated into covert and overt dominant forms of straight male violence and abuse (Macdonald et al., 1989).

**Stephen:** Playgrounds are really cruel places if you're seen as different or weak. In our school the macho gangs treated girls very bad. And they persecuted me and a few friends, calling us poofs and queer and all that because we weren't like them, didn't act hard like them. We survived because we were big and did not show that we were afraid of them.

**Vijay:**   The tough kids were the best at football, could threaten anyone, had the best reputation with a lot of girls, wore the best gear. They bullied younger kids and girls, and any boys who they thought were soft. White kids joined the gang and together the black and white kids abused Asian kids. They were always talking about "Pakis" and "batty men" (a derisory homophobic comment).

**Assim:**   Looking back there wasn't probably that many fights but the physical pressure was there all the time. It was all to do with the way you looked. The clothes, hair, and most important the way you stood, walked about, how you talked, just little things that signalled whether you were hard or not.

In contrast to the working-class forms of physical violence, former grammar school students recalled the centrality of verbal violence in serving to police gender and sexual boundaries. The highest peer-group esteem was assigned to those who combined a display of linguistic competence and "put down" humour. One of the students, Denton Purcell, confided in his best friend that he was confused about his sexuality.

**Denton:**   The next day when some of our mates were around, my friend said "Your mom must be proud of you, that means she has two washing powders, Persil (Purcell) and Omo (homosexual)." They all started laughing. They all got the message, as they already thought I was effeminate. It was one of the worst things that ever happened to me. I felt so violated. Thinking about it since we started talking, I can see it was my friend's way of distancing himself from me, not just for the crowd but also for himself. We were very close, not in a sexual way, more emotionally. Like most straight men, he just couldn't cope.

## VISIBILITY OF "RACE" — INVISIBILITY OF HOMOSEXUALITY OR THE NORMALIZATION OF WHITE HETEROSEXUALITY

One of the major issues that emerged in the research was the question of the visibility of "race" and the invisibility of "homosexuality" within the context of the school. In order to more fully understand the absence of lesbians and gays from the curriculum, we need to examine the more general question of the official response to the place of sexuality within schools. Beverley Skeggs (1991, p. 1) has critiqued the way in which "the discourse on sexuality is either ignored or subsumed within a more general discourse on gender." Similarly, Wolpe (1988, p. 100) argues that: "The ideology on sex and sex education and its relation to the moral order, structure the official way in which sex and sexuality are handled within a school. In spite of these discourses and the tendency for teachers to accept these seemingly unquestioningly, sexual issues are ever present but not necessarily recognized as such by teachers."

The visibility of the students' secondary schools' racial structuring included predominantly white staff with majority black student populations, racially stratified curriculum and testing systems, the overrepresentation of specific ethnic groups in low status subject areas and racial divisions in classrooms and among student peer-groups. More positively at their different schools multi-cultural/anti-racist policies were in operation. Although these official local state interventions, often unwittingly, tended to reproduce reified conceptions of black ethnic cultures, and the accompanying reinforcement of images of "them" and "us," they also provided space to contest dominant racial representations. The students pointed out that "skin colour" is often read as a key signifier of social exclusion. However, as for their parents, it also has positive, productive elements for young blacks positioned within specific racist discourses, thus enabling them collectively to develop positive social identities. [...]

The students recalled the invisibility of femininities and subordinated masculinities that the dominant examples of white teachers and student masculinities serves constantly to devalue, marginalize, and threaten. Homophobia, compulsory heterosexuality, racism, and misogyny circumscribed the boundaries of what constituted "normal" male and female behaviour. The invisibility of homosexuality at their secondary schools was structured by a "policy of omission" — it was as if lesbians and gays did not exist. Much important work on the racial and gender structuring of the curriculum has emphasized how discriminatory practices operate against subordinated groups. Here, the students point out that of equal significance is what is excluded in shaping differential curriculum experiences and outcomes.

> **Raj:** It's like you are black, right, and you can accept the white view of blacks or you can reject it and challenge it. But to say I am a black gay, what does it mean? At school they never suggested that there was a history of gay people or any books on gays. They never presented any evidence of black gay people. So, you could think I must be the only one. At school you are totally on your own. It's really bad, you know what I mean? ... The only times teachers talked about gays was when they talked about AIDS a few times.

As part of the research, I interviewed the students' former and present teachers. Here, I am focusing on white male teachers. Within the context of a broader concern with the question of how schools produce a range of masculinities and femininities, I asked the teachers how they would respond to gay students "coming out" to them (Mac an Ghaíll, 1992). The following interview with a teacher in a senior pastoral care post was illustrative of their responses to the question of black students' sexual identities. Holding on to notions of a unitary self, the teachers were highly defensive in being unable to rationalize the contradictions of their own positions (Henriques, 1984).

> **Teacher:** I don't think a teacher is going to think an Asian or black kid is a homosexual, they just wouldn't. They've got enough problems dealing with being black. Like you wouldn't think of a handicapped person as a homosexual, would you? No, you just wouldn't, would you?
>
> **MM:** You said earlier that you would advise a student, if he told you he was gay, that he was going through a phase.
>
> **Teacher:** Yes, definitely. It's part of growing up. Often, these kids would be loners, one-parent families without a father figure, you know?

MM:      Is this phase true for all boys?

Teacher: I know, you are going to ask, did I go through it? It depends on what you mean. But, no. I was close to friends, male friends as you are at that age. But I was brought up in a normal family and all that and I've always known where I stood with the ladies.

MM:      But what about most boys?

Teacher: Well, the experts reckon so, don't they?

MM:      But wouldn't that include Asian and black boys?

Teacher: You've tricked me. I must say I've never thought of the black kids here like that. Well like a lot of theories they overgeneralize. If you saw the big black kids here, you'd see what I mean. We have to pull them away from the girls. The black kids are obsessed with them but to be fair to the lads, the girls do lead them on, hanging around all the time. I could say with certainty, there's no way they've got any homosexual ideas.

The intersection of these homophobic and racist discourses produced contradictions and confusions. On the one hand, in interviews with me, in relation to issues of gay sexuality, the teachers appealed to black parents' religious beliefs as legitimate justification for not taking a positive pedagogical stance towards gay students. On the other hand, as the students stressed, white teachers tended to caricature Asian and Afro-Caribbean male students and their parents as intrinsically more sexist than whites. In class discussions the teachers were preoccupied with explaining the difficulty of implementing an anti-sexist curriculum which they claimed conflicted with traditional ethnic cultures. Rajinder informed a teacher that he was gay and was most surprised that the teacher responded primarily in racial terms, projecting his own difficulties with the issue of sexuality on to the Asian community.

Rajinder: At school there's no such thing as sexuality, so it seems. Then one day you come out and say you're gay and then you find out that it's the most important thing in the world. The teachers try everything to change you: It's a phase, you need psychiatric help, it's unnatural, it's against your religion, your parents won't accept you, your friends will reject you, you won't get a job. I've heard it all. I think that teachers feel more threatened by gays than any other group.

## CONCLUSION

[ ... ] At present, young people, collectively and individually, are constructing their identities, at a time of rapid socioeconomic and political change, that has led to a major disruption in the process of coming-of-age in the "enterprise culture." For example, Willis, (1985, p. 6) speaks of how the unemployed now find themselves in a "new social condition of suspended animation between school and work. Many of the old transitions into work, into the cultures and organizations of work, into being consumers, into independent accommodation have been frozen or broken ...." As the students above demonstrate, their preparation for these transitions are further structured by an articulation of complex forms of social differences. Within this new social condition the young gay students here can be seen as an example of the new generation of black intellectuals, of whom Mercer (1992, p. 110) writes:

In the hands of this new generation of black diaspora intellectuals rethinking sex ... [they] simultaneously critique the exclusions and absences which previously rendered black lesbian and gay identities invisible, and reconstruct new pluralistic forms of collective belonging and imagined community that broaden the public sphere of multicultural society.

## ENDNOTES

1.  In order to maintain the anonymity of those involved, all the names of the students and teachers are pseudonyms.

## References

Bhavnani, K.K. (1991). *Talking politics: A psychological framing for views from youth in Britain*, Cambridge: Cambridge University Press.

Bryan, B., S. Dadzie, and S. Scale (1985). The heart of the race: Black women's lives in Britain, London: Virago.

Canaan, J. (1991). Is 'doing nothing' just boys' play?: Integrating feminist and cultural studies perspectives on working-class young men's masculinity. In S. Franklin, C. Lury, and J. Stacey (eds.) *Off centre: Feminism and cultural studies*, London: HarperCollins.

Carrigan, T., R.W. Connell, and J. Lee (1985). Hard and heavy phenomena: the sociology of masculinity. *Theory*, 14, 551–604.

Cockburn C. (1987). *Two-track training: Sex inequality and the YTS*, London: Macmillan.

Cohen, P. (1987). Racism and popular culture: a cultural studies approach. Working paper No. 9, London, Institute of Education.

Connell, R.W. (1989). Cool guys, swots and wimps: The inter-play of masculinity and education. *Oxford Review of Education* 15(3), 291–303.

Freire, P. (1985). *The politics of education*, London: Macmillan.

Griffin, C. (1987). The eternal adolescent: Psychology and the creation of adolescence. Paper presented at the Symposium of the Ideological Impact of Social Psychology, British Psychological Association Conference, Oxford University.

Henriques J. (1984). Social psychology and the politics of racism. In J. Henriques, W. Hollway, C. Urwin, C. Venn, and V. Walkerdine (eds.) *Changing the subject: Psychology, social regulation and subjectivity*, London: Methuen.

hooks, b. (1991). *Yearning: Race, gender and cultural politics*, Massachusetts: Turnaround.

Klein, M. (1960). *Our adult world and its roots in infancy*, London: Tavistock.

Lees, S. (1987). The structure of sexual relations in school. In M. Arnot and G. Weiner (eds.) *Gender and politics of schooling*, Milton Keynes: Open University Press.

Mac an Ghaíll, M. (1989a). Beyond the white norm: the use of qualitative research in the study of black students' schooling in England. *Qualitative Studies in Education* 2(3), 175–89.

——— (1989b). Coming-of-age in 1980s England: Reconceptualizing black students' schooling experience. *British Journal of Sociology of Education*, 10(3), 273–86.

——— (1992). *Acting like men: Masculinities, sexualities and schooling*, Milton Keynes: Open University Press.

Macdonald I., R. Bhavnani, L. Khan, and G. John (1989). *Murder in the playground*, London: Longsight Press.

Mama, A. (1992). Black women and the British state: race, class and gender analysis for the 1990s. In P. Braham, A. Rattansi, and R. Skellington (eds.) *Racism and antisexism: Inequalities, opportunities and policies*, London: Sage/Open University Press.

Mercer, K. (1992). Just looking for trouble: Robert Mapplethorpe and fantasies. In L. Segal and M. McIntosh (eds.) *Sex exposed: Sexuality and the pornography debate*, London: Virago.

Mercer, K., and I. Julien (1988). Race, sexual politics and black masculinity: A dossier. In R. Chapman and J. Ruthford (eds.) *Male order: Unwrapping masculinities*, London: Lawrence & Wishart.

Miles, R. (1989). *Racism*, London: Routledge.

Nava, M. (1992). *Changing cultures: Feminism, youth and consumerism*, London: Sage.

Paiaczkowska C., and L. Young (1992). Racism, representation and psychoanalysis. In J. Donald and A. Rattansi (eds.) *"Race," culture and difference*, Milton Keynes: Open University Press/Sage.

Rattansi, A. (1992). Changing the subject? racism, culture and education. In J. Donald and A. Rattansi (eds.) *"Race," culture and difference*, Milton Keynes: Open University Press/Sage.

Rowbotham, S. (1989). *The past is before us: Feminism in action since the 1960s*. Harmondsworth: Penguin.

Rutherford, J. (1990). A place called home: identity and the cultural politics of difference. In J. Rutherford (ed.) *Identity: Community, culture and difference*. London: Lawrence and Wishart.

Skeggs, B. (1991). The cultural production of 'Learning to Labour'. In M. Barker and A. Breezer (eds.) *Readings in culture*, London: Routledge.

Tolson, A. (1977). *The limits of masculinity*, London: Tavistock.

Walkerdine, V. (1990). *Schoolgirl fictions*, London: Verso.

Westwood, S. (1990). Racism, black masculinity and the politics of space. In J. Hearn and D. Morgan (eds.) *Men, masculinities and social theory*, London: Hyman.

Willis, P. (1985). Youth unemployment and the new poverty: A summary of local authority review and framework for policy development on youth and youth unemployment. Wolverhampton: Wolverhampton Local Authority.

Wolpe, A.M. (1988). *Within school walls: The role of discipline, sexuality and the curriculum*, London: Routledge.

## Exercises

1. How are invisibility and subordination part of the experiences of gay and lesbian students?
2. Mac an Ghaíll suggests that "homophobia, compulsory heterosexuality, racism, and misogyny circumscribed the boundaries of what constitutes 'normal' male and female behavior" in schools. What is the "policy of omission" that produces the discourses of heteronormativity (or heterosexual assumption)?
3. How do race and sexuality marginalize and threaten as different oppressions and complex forms of social difference?

# Chapter 24

# Safely Out: Activities for Challenging Homophobia in Schools

## Toronto Board of Education

### DEFINITIONS OF TERMS RELATED TO SEXUAL ORIENTATION

Developed by Laurie Chesley, Donna MacAulay, and Janice Ristock.

| | |
|---|---|
| *Homophobia* | Fear and hatred of homosexuals, often exhibited by prejudice, discrimination, harassment, and acts of violence. |
| *Sexual orientation* | The physical and emotional attraction of someone to the persons of the opposite sex, same sex, or both. Three forms of sexual orientation are labelled heterosexual, homosexual, and bisexual. |
| *Heterosexual* | Someone who is physically and emotionally attracted to people of the opposite sex. |
| *Straight* | A term for heterosexual. |
| *Homosexual* | Someone who is physically and emotionally attracted to people of the same sex. Because the term is associated historically with a medical model of homosexuality, most homosexuals prefer the terms lesbian, gay, and bisexual. |
| *Gay* | A term for homosexual. This can refer to both males and females, but increasingly is used only to refer to men. |

| | |
|---|---|
| *Lesbian* | A female homosexual. |
| *Bisexual* | Someone who is attracted physically and emotionally to persons of the same and opposite sexes. |
| *Sexual identity* | Someone's sense of being male or female. |
| *Transsexual* | Someone whose sexual identity is different from her or his biological sex; .for example, a biological male who would describe himself as a woman trapped inside a man's body. |
| *Gender role* | Refers to characteristics attached to culturally defined notions of masculinity or femininity. |
| *Coming out* | "Coming out" carries two meanings: |

(1) The developmental process through which gay and lesbian people recognize their sexual preferences and integrate this knowledge into their personal and social lives.

(2) It may also be used to mean disclosure, as in "I just came out to my parents."

| | |
|---|---|
| *Heterosexual assumption* | The assumption that everyone is heterosexual unless otherwise indicated. |
| *Heterosexism* | The belief that heterosexuality is better than any other form of sexual orientation. |

## DEBUNKING MYTHS

Originally developed by Vanessa Russell, Equity Studies Centre for Horizon Document.

1. *All gay men are pedophiles.*
   In fact, statistics show that most child molesters are heterosexual men who abuse children within the nuclear family and are related to the children they abuse.

2. *Homosexuality is a disease.*
   Because of prejudice, homosexuality was once listed as a disease but it was removed from the lists of mental illnesses by the American Psychiatric Association in 1973.

3. *All gay men are like women. All lesbians are like men.*
   Some gay men are effeminate and some lesbians are masculine but most are not. Many gays and lesbians resist homophobia by trying to challenge the rules about how "real" men and "real" women should behave. Sometimes gays and lesbians purposely choose to engage in more traditional "opposite sex" behaviours.

4. *All lesbians are man-haters.*
   Most lesbians are not sexually attracted to men but maintain many male friendships. Being lesbian has little to do with the way they feel about men. It has much more to do with the way they feel about women. Lesbians are women who love women.

5. *People become homosexual because they are unattractive and have no success with the opposite sex.*
   You just have to look at a Calvin Klein ad to be reminded that many lesbians and gay men are considered attractive by our society's standards and would have no trouble attracting interest from the opposite sex.

6. *All gays and lesbians have been abused in childhood or had some kind of negative experience to "make them that way."*
   There is no evidence linking child abuse with a homosexual orientation in adult life. If everyone who ever had a negative experience or was a victim of child abuse became gay or lesbian, there would be a lot more homosexuals around.

7. *All gay men have AIDS and it is a curse from God.*
   While the gay community in North America has been hard hit by AIDS, the vast majority of gay men are not infected by the HIV virus. Around the world, most people with AIDS are heterosexual. In Canada, 20 percent of all new cases of HIV infection are women. If AIDS was a curse from God, lesbians must be the chosen people since they are in the lowest-risk group for AIDS.

8. *Homosexuals are predominantly white.*
   Gays and lesbians come from all races, ethnicities, religions, and countries of origin. However, how individuals define themselves is culturally shaped.

9. *All religious groups oppose homosexuality.*
   There is a variety of religious opinion on homosexuality, from groups that consider homosexuality a sin to others who consider it a gift from God.

10. *Homosexuality is only about sex.*
    Being gay or lesbian is about people's lives, not just about what they do in bed. It's about who they love, who they spend time with, who they choose to have a child with, who they wash the car with, what movies they like, books they read, etc.

11. *Lesbians are not real women.*
    This myth is the primary, underlying one about lesbians. Obviously lesbians are biologically female, so this myth must be a comment on the traditional sexual roles all women are expected to play. The truth is that real women can be and want a variety of things, both sexually and otherwise. This would include loving women, nurturing children, and having friendships with men.

12. *Lesbians wear male clothing.*
    What is male clothing? It is sturdy, warm, and comfortable. Female clothing, on the other hand, is usually expensive and flimsy. It is designed to decorate us rather than to protect us from the elements or allow us to move freely in it. In fact, a lot of women's clothing is physically restraining and even crippling — girdles, high heels, straight skirts, tight pants, and so on. The major reason to differentiate between male and female clothing is to make the difference between men and women readily apparent. If men and women looked the same how would men know who to treat as inferior? Hire as secretaries? Rape?

## Twenty Questions About Homosexuality

Originally from the Gay Activists Alliance.

1. Who is a homosexual?
2. How is a person's sexual orientation determined?
3. Can a person change his or her sexual orientation?
4. How many homosexuals are there?
5. Are homosexuals easy to identify? By appearance? behaviour? choice of profession?
6. Are there two types of homosexual, active and passive?
7. Is homosexuality "against nature"?
8. Does religion tell us that it's immoral?
9. Is homosexuality socially destructive? Has it always accompanied decadent societies?
10. Is homosexuality a mental illness?
11. Are homosexuals all neurotic?
12. Are homosexuals more "promiscuous" than heterosexuals?
13. Are homosexual relationships as stable as heterosexual ones?
14. Is homosexual love different from heterosexual love?
15. Does our society discriminate against homosexuals?
16. Is there reason to bar homosexuals from certain kinds of employment? Are homosexuals security risks?
17. Should homosexuals be allowed to work with children in schools and camps? Are homosexuals child molesters?
18. Must there be any laws relating to homosexuals? What about prostitution? public sex?
19. If there weren't any anti-homosexual laws, would homosexuals be encouraged to proselytize? Would there be more homosexuals as a result?
20. Is it better, in this society, to be heterosexual?

## HOMOPHOBIA IN ELEMENTARY SCHOOLS: 4 SCENARIOS

Developed by Vanessa Russell and Tim McCaskell.

What follows are four scenarios that are interconnected. They should be used together simultaneously. As with all scenarios, you should break the class into smaller discussion groups. Each group should receive one scenario. Instruct the groups to read the scenarios, answer the questions, and be prepared to report back to the large group.

### Scenario 1

Michelle is a Grade 8 student who loves hockey. Her school has a boys' hockey team but does not have a girls' team. Michelle's parents, together with some teachers at the school, have fought hard to create a co-ed hockey team.

Michelle has proven herself to be an amazing player. She is better than most of the boys. As you can imagine, some of the boys are really angry about it. A bunch of the boys on the team have begun to play rough with Michelle by checking her hard. They also have begun to threaten her.

Yesterday was the last straw. One of the boys yelled at Michelle during Ms. Russell's class, "Girls aren't supposed to play hockey. You must be a big dyke. Only lezzies would play a boys' game. You're ruining our team. You better think of quitting or you're gonna get it... and where we're gonna give it to you, you won't be able to sit down for a week." Ms. Russell overheard most of the conversation and told everyone to "sit down and cut it out."

Michelle is scared. She doesn't want to be centred out all the time like another kid in her class named Leonard. He gets called faggot almost every day. Michelle doesn't know what to do.

1. Does the fact that Michelle plays hockey make her a lesbian?
2. Why do the boys on the hockey team think Michelle is a lesbian?
3. List all the ways that the boys are treating Michelle badly.
4. What does the teacher, Ms. Russell, do to handle the situation?
5. Do you think Ms. Russell handled this situation in the best possible way?

6.  What else could be done?
7.  Who else could help Michelle?

## Scenario 2

Brian is in Grade 8. His best friend is David. They hang out together and play sports at recess and weekends.

Last week Brian and David were wrestling and Brian got sexually excited. David noticed and said "Hey are you queer or something?" Brian was very embarrassed.

David seems to have forgotten the incident but Brian has been worrying ever since. He is afraid he is going to be gay. What if David tells and people tease him? What does it mean to be gay anyway? Brian had never really thought much about sex until David and his friends started making "dirty" jokes late last year.

Leonard is a boy in Brian's class. He doesn't play sports too much and he likes to read. The other boys sometimes tease him and call him a sissy.

Brian and Leonard happen to be coming into the classroom at the same time and Leonard bumps into Brian by accident.

"Don't you touch me you faggot!" Brian angrily shouts at Leonard. "Touch me again and I'll kick your head in!"

Leonard doesn't know what to say and just stands there surprised.

"Why don't you go touch Michelle the dyke if you want to touch somebody," Brian continues.

"Brian! Settle down. Don't shout in class. Go to your seat," says Ms. Russell, the classroom teacher.

1.  Why is Brian worried that he might be gay?
2.  Does the fact that Brian got excited while wrestling make him gay?
3.  What is Brian afraid of?
4.  Normally Brian wouldn't even notice Leonard had bumped into him. Why does he get so upset today?
5.  What is Brian trying to prove?
6.  What should Leonard do?
7.  Do you think Ms. Russell did the right thing?
8.  What more could she have done?

## Scenario 3

Frank has just moved to the neighbourhood and this is his first year in the school. He is in Grade 8 in Ms. Russell's class.

Frank has a secret that he has never told any of his new friends. He has two moms and doesn't know his father.

At home everything seems fine and normal. He has always lived with his two moms, and his is a family like anybody else's. His moms have been living together from before he was born. They take turns driving him to hockey practice and make his lunch and do all the things that parents normally do.

Outside home, though, he knows that people sometimes don't understand and don't approve. In this new class, he has heard some of the boys teasing Michelle who is the only girl on the hockey team. They call her a dyke and a lezzie. They also push around another boy, Leonard, and call him a sissy because he doesn't like sports. Sometimes that teacher tells them to stop and sometimes she just ignores it.

Yesterday Ms. Russell told everybody that they are going to have to write a short essay on their family and read it aloud to the class.

Frank doesn't know what to do. He's afraid if he writes the truth, people may make fun of him and he might lose friends. On the other hand, his moms have always told him that the most important thing about a family is that people love each other. He doesn't want to hide the truth. He shouldn't need to feel ashamed.

Frank decides he should talk to Ms. Russell about the assignment.

1. Why is Frank afraid to write the essay on his family?
2. What does he think might happen if everyone finds out he has two moms?
3. Should he talk to Ms. Russell?
4. If so, what should he say to her?
5. What would you do if you were Frank?

## Scenario 4

Ms. Russell teaches a Grade 8 class at an east-end school. She is tired and angry a lot lately. Over the last month, her students have been acting up in class all the time. Two of her students, Leonard and Michelle, are being teased every day about being gay and lesbian. She tells the boys who call them names to stop it but they never listen to her. She can barely stand it anymore.

A couple of days ago, she asked students to write a short essay on their families that they would present in front of the whole class. At the end of the day, one of her students named Frank told her that his mothers were lesbians and he was scared to tell the truth in his essay.

Ms. Russell didn't know what to say to him. With all the homophobic name calling going on in class these days, it may not be so safe for Frank to be honest. She decided that what she wants to do is to bring in some gay and lesbian people into the class to talk to the students about homophobia. Maybe this would make the class a safer place for Frank to be honest. However, Ms. Russell is afraid what parents might say.

Ms. Russell told Frank to come back in a few days but she still doesn't know what to say or do.

1. What things are happening in Ms. Russell's class that are making her tired and angry?
2. What has Ms. Russell done to try to stop name calling in the class?
3. Why do you think the students don't listen to her?
4. Why is Frank afraid to tell the class he has two mothers who are lesbians?
5. What do you think Ms. Russell should tell Frank?
6. Why is Ms. Russell afraid to have gays and lesbians talk about homophobia in her class?
7. What does your board of education say about talking to students about homophobia?

# Chapter 25

# What Do We Say
# When We Hear "Faggot"?

## Lenore Gordon

Alice is eleven. She walks down the school halls with her arm around her best friend, Susan. During lunch, they sit on the floor holding hands or combing each other's hair. Lately, Alice has been called "dyke," and boys have been told not to be her friend.

Brian refuses to take part in a fight on his block. As he makes his way home, he hears cries of "faggot" and "sissy." Suddenly he begins to run, realizing that the other children may now attack him.

Carl is gifted musically; he would like to join the elementary school chorus. Although he hesitates for several weeks, the music teacher persuades him to join. One morning soon after, he enters the classroom tense and angry after chorus, muttering that several boys have called him "gay."

Some children play a "game" called "Smear the Queer," in which one child suddenly attacks another, knocking him to the ground. The attacker shouts "Fag!" and then runs away.

Homophobic name calling is pervasive. Even first graders are now using such terms as "faggot" to ridicule others, and such name calling is increasingly common in the older grades. Homophobic name calling is devastating to young people experiencing homosexual feelings. For youngsters who are not gay, such name calling creates or reinforces hostility toward the gay and lesbian population. And it forces all children to follow strict sex-role behaviors to avoid ridicule.

Because homosexuality is such a charged issue, teachers rarely confront children who use homophobic name calling to humiliate and infuriate other children. Many teachers do not realize that this sort of name calling can be dealt with in much the same way as other kinds of bigotry and stereotyping.

Teaching children to be critical of oppression is teaching true morality, and teachers have the right, indeed the obligation, to alert their students to all forms of oppression. Educating children not to be homophobic is one way to show the difference between oppressive and non-oppressive behavior.

Challenging homophobic name calling by teaching children nonjudgmental facts about homosexuality and by correcting myths is also intrinsically connected to anti-sexist educational values, since homophobia is used to reinforce rigid sex roles. Furthermore, if adults criticize other forms of name calling but ignore anti-gay remarks, children are quick to conclude that homophobia is acceptable.

Boys are far more likely to be the object of homophobic name calling than girls, perhaps because sex roles for boys remain, to some extent, more rigidly defined. A boy involved in a traditional "female only" activity such as sewing or cooking risks out-and-out contempt from his peers, as well as the possibility of being called "faggot" or "sissy." Girls are more able to participate in activities that have traditionally been for boys, such as sports or shop, without loss of peer approval.

At the late elementary and junior high school levels, physical affection between girls is far more acceptable than between boys, but a girl will be called a "dyke" if she does not express, by junior high, a real interest in pleasing boys or in participating with other girls in boy-centered discussions.

As an elementary school teacher, I have made an awareness of oppression and of the concept of "majority" and "minority" a focus of current events, history, and social studies. Throughout the year we discuss those who are not in the majority in this country: Native Americans, Puerto Ricans, Blacks, Chicanos, disabled people, older people, and many others. We also discuss women, a generally powerless majority.

If oppression is being discussed, it is impossible to ignore lesbians and gay men as a group that faces discrimination. Children in the middle grades have a strong sense of justice, and they can understand the basic injustice of people being abused because they are different from the majority. They can also identify with the powerlessness of oppressed groups because children themselves are often a verbally and sometimes a physically abused group.

## TYPES OF NAME CALLING

When initiating a discussion of name calling, teachers can explain that there are two kinds of name calling. One kind of name calling, unrelated to any particular group, is often scatological or sexual (i.e., the four-letter words). The other is group-biased; it uses the name of a group — "nigger," "chink," "polack," etc. — as the insult and implies that there is something wrong with being a member of that group.

Group-biased name calling can be handled in a variety of ways. Sometimes children do not truly understand why a word is offensive. If a teacher simply takes the time to tell the class that a particular word insults or demeans a group of people, children will often stop using the word. (Occasionally, children do not even know what a term means. One New York City ten-year-old who frequently called others "faggot" told me that the word meant "female dog." A twelve-year-old said that a lesbian is a "Spanish Jew.")

Discussions about the meaning of homophobic words can often be quite consciousness-raising. When I hear a child use the word faggot, I explain that a "faggot," literally, is a stick used for kindling. I also explain that gay people used to be burned in medieval times simply for being gay, and they had to wear a bundle of sticks on their shirts to indicate that they were about to be burned. (At times, gay men were used as the kindling to burn women accused of witchcraft.) After the discussion that ensues from this revelation, I make it clear to my students that the word is not to be used again in my classroom, and it rarely is.

When I talk about the words "lesbian" and "gay men," there is always a stir of discomfort, so I ask what those words mean. I am also usually told that a gay man is an "effeminate" man. We discuss the stereotyping inherent in that myth, as well as the fact that "effeminate" means "behaving like a woman," and the class begins to realize that "behaving like a woman" is viewed negatively.

When asked what it really means to be called a "faggot" and why it is insulting for a boy to be called "gay," students will often respond that saying that a boy is like a girl is the worst insult imaginable. At this point, girls are likely to sense that something unjust has been touched upon, and they will often take up their own defense, while simultaneously having their own consciousness raised.

Before we go on with the lesson plan, I usually attempt to reach a consensus on definitions. Here are some that have seemed acceptable: "Someone who loves someone of the same sex, but can be close to people of the opposite sex if they want to" and "Someone who romantically loves someone of the same sex." We added the word "romantically" in one class after a boy commented in a confused tone, "But I love my father ...." When discussing definitions, it is important to tell children that gays and lesbians are as different from one another as are heterosexual men and women. There is no such thing as a "typical" lesbian or gay man.

## IMAGINING NAMES

When we continue with the lesson plan and students are asked to imagine being called names as they walk with a close friend of the same sex, they describe feeling "different," "dumb," "weird," "afraid," and " embarrassed." (One very different response was, "I'd feel loved, because the main thing would be walking with someone I loved.") When asked how they would feel as one of the name callers, children usually admit that they "would feel like part of the group." Suggested responses to homophobic attacks have included, "It's my choice," "We like each other, and for your information, we're not homosexual," "I'm not ashamed," "I'm just as different as you are," "I don't care," and "So what!"

I have also used the music of Holly Near to teach about oppression. Songs are an effective tool in reaching children, who seem to retain information presented in this mode quite easily. Near sings about the oppression of many different groups and her songs help students make linkages between their struggles.

Another way to combat homophobia — particularly for older students — is to invite a speaker from a gay organization to talk to the class. Listening to a gay or lesbian who is also a living, breathing human being — someone who has parents, siblings, and looks a little nervous in front of a group — is often a decisive factor in breaking down homophobic stereotypes.

Homophobic attitudes can also be countered in discussions about sex roles. Students can be asked, "What does a boy have to do to 'act like a girl?'" (and vice versa). The stereotypic behaviors that are mentioned can usually be quickly discounted by asking children to consider their own home lives. Many children, particularly those with single or divorced parents, have seen their mothers working and their fathers cleaning the house.

Another classroom activity is to ask students to look in any standard dictionary or thesaurus for the definitions of "male" and "female," "masculine" and "feminine," "husband," "wife," etc. The definitions are often so blatantly offensive and stereotypic that they create a small sensation when read aloud, thus challenging children to rethink their own definitions.

Discussing homophobic concepts is one thing; enduring homophobic name calling is an entirely different matter. The pressure to conform is especially overwhelming within the school/peer structure, and it is vital that teachers try to instill the courage needed to function independently when one is the object of ridicule.

I attempt to teach my students to be willing to defend not only their own rights but the rights of others. Because name calling is so common among children, and because it embodies the bigotry learned from adults, it is a good place for educators to begin.

# Part 8

# Students at Risk: Class, Poverty, and Marginality

**Baxter**
*A Child Is Not a Toy*

**Mitchell**
"The Poor Fare Worst in Schools"

**Bigelow and Diamond**
"The Organic Goodie Simulation"

**Toronto Board of Education**
*Challenging Class Bias*

**Wane**
"Students at Risk"

# Chapter 26

# A Child
# Is Not a Toy

## Sheila Baxter

### Journal

It is May 1992. I have been avoiding writing this book, but it has never left my mind. There is always a small voice saying, "What about the children? Who is listening to them?" In my last two books, adult voices were heard speaking out against poverty and homelessness. Now it's the children's turn.

For the next nine months I will try to give children a voice. I will interview children who live below the poverty line, and perhaps a couple of children who are not poor, to see how they relate to children who are poor. (How I hate this word "poor"; the very sound of it is so demoralizing.)

I look back, remembering the 15-year-old girl I interviewed in my last book, living in a run-down hotel with her family. I wonder, did she survive?

———

I was at a local community centre, having a cheap lunch. Two young girls came in. They said they were hungry. One, a small person about 15, looked really nervous and scared. The other I had met before. She had been homeless then. We talked. The two girls had been living in an empty house. The young people squatting in the house had been busted by the police. The older girl was trying to talk the younger into going to Toronto. The younger girl turned to me nervously and said, "I have spots. I'm really itchy." I looked at the spots and said, "Honey, you've got scabies." She said, "The mattress I slept on was really dirty." I talked to her about where she could go for help, and the older girl said she would take her to the youth clinic. After they ate, they took off real fast. They obviously didn't want to be picked up and questioned by any authority. In B.C. you are not an adult until you are 19, and till then, you can be picked up and returned to your family or put in foster care. These two were scared of being taken back to wherever they had run from. They lived scrounging, panhandling. They were street kids, hungry street kids.

I called Betty McPhee at Crabtree Corners. They have a daycare for children and a drop-in for street people. I asked her how she felt about me writing this book. She said, "It's wonderful. It just gives me goose bumps." Then I talked to Jean Swanson and Linda Marcotte at End Legislated Poverty and asked them for ideas. Linda said, "Perhaps you should make some rules for interviewing children." We agreed that it was something that had to be handled with great care.

When I talk to parents about the possibility of interviewing their children, I become even more aware of how gently I must tread. This is the most sensitive issue I have ever dealt with. I asked different anti-poverty activists and people who work with children how I could address the issue of poverty. I obviously can't say to a child, "Are you poor? What does It feel like?" I know that the self-esteem of children is often very fragile. I ask at what age does a child know that he or she is poor. Most say it starts in the school.

Flashing back to my poverty as a child, I have memories of deep shame, intense hunger, of begging for money, daydreaming about being adopted and having nice clothes and shoes, about going to school and having the children like and accept me. That didn't happen, and if it had, I wouldn't be the anti-poverty activist I am today.

I have given a lot of thought to what rules I should give myself when interviewing children. I decided on the following.

- They don't have to talk to me if they don't want to.
- No one will know who they are unless they choose to identify themselves.
- They don't have to answer any questions that they choose not to.
- Their interviews will be played back to them.
- A parent can be with them if they wish.
- I will believe what they tell me.

———

Chris, the coordinator of the Downtown Eastside Women's Centre, came across very strong on one point. She told me that I shouldn't label women as single mothers. As soon as someone reads the phrase "single mothers," all kinds of judgments and prejudices spring up, and society dumps the problem on the fact that there is a "single mother" involved. She is right, so in this book I will say "family." That can mean one or two people of any sex, or even an extended family. One woman I spoke to talked about her street brother and sister, her street mother and father.

As I speak to families who live below the poverty line, I realize that having their children talk about their poverty is really difficult for parents. Many go out of their way to hide it from their children. One parent told of a ten-year-old daughter who badly needed a pair of shoes. The daughter said, "I need shoes. How am I going to get them?" She wasn't asking her parent for the shoes, she was taking the responsibility as if she were an adult. I asked if I could interview the girl. Her parent said, "I'll think about it and I'll ask her."

A friend called me. She knew a family whose children are very artistic. She had asked if one of the children could do a drawing about poverty. She couldn't understand why the parent she asked got mad and said no. I understand. Poverty creates a terrible guilt feeling when you are a parent and you can't get your children the things they need.

My eldest son, now married with a family, is middle class as far as income goes. He said, "You know, Mom, the first time I knew we were poor was when the Baptist Church brought us a charity basket at Christmas." My husband was a low-paid blue-collar worker at the time. I remember the incident. It was a snowy cold Quebec winter. We lived in a third-floor walk-up flat. Laundry was done in a wringer washer, and a clothesline was strung along the hall to dry the clothes, because they froze when hung outside in the winter, and of course I didn't have a dryer. As they came into the hall, those church people looked at the laundry and I'm sure they judged us by it. Anyway, John was about ten years of age. He became enraged. He said, "We don't need your charity, we are not poor. Give it to somebody else." I remember hushing him. How he hated that moment when he first became aware that we were poor. It still bothers him, I think.

————

I ran into a friend on the street. It was a really nice sunny day. Spring in Vancouver is so beautiful. The flowers were in bloom, masses of reds and yellows and all kinds of colours — a joy to look at. I asked my friend, "What's happening?" She told me they couldn't afford a babysitter and a new friend of the family had volunteered to look after the children. The friend started to buy the daughter all kinds of clothes that the family couldn't afford. Now, two years later, the 13-year-old girl is a runaway and sexually active because this so-called friendly babysitter had been sexually abusing her and keeping her quiet by buying her stuff. My friend said, "He set my daughter up for prostitution. If I hadn't been poor and working an under-the-table job, I would not have been so desperate for a sitter." The daughter was missing. The family had tried to get help, but the girl just kept running away. After we parted, the spring flowers seemed less bright, even invisible.

I can't just switch off and on I guess. This is so frustrating. Poverty is a catch-22: You need to work but you can't afford a sitter, so if someone offers to sit for free, you accept, even though the person may be a threat to your children, a predator. Poverty can set kids up for sexual abuse.

————

Way back in 1959 the United Nations drafted a declaration on the rights of the child. Paragraph 4 says:

> The child shall enjoy the benefits of social security. He shall
> be entitled to grow and develop in health; to this end, special

care and protection shall be provided to him and his mother, including adequate pre-natal and post-natal care. The child shall have the right to adequate nutrition, housing, recreation, and medical services.

Thirty-odd years ago this was declared and yet in our affluent country we still have children living far below the poverty level. We have homeless children. Recently, the federal government cut back on social housing, even though the waiting lists are endless.

In November 1989, the Canadian parliament passed a resolution with the goal of eliminating poverty among Canadian children by the year 2000. A *Globe and Mail* article from November 1991 says that progress is not evident. Apparently the government established a children's bureau in the Health and Welfare Department to coordinate the anti-poverty campaign. The children's bureau has a budget of almost $2 million, and is run by Brian Ward, a former aide to Prime Minister Brian Mulroney, but it is not able to deliver any programs. In fact, it can't really do much because policy is controlled by the finance minister's office, and that office is more concerned about the recession than about social policy. I guess a lot of people earned a lot of money doing all these studies and reports, but wouldn't it be great if part of their salary depended on results, like sales people working on commission?

It's been my experience in the last 20 years of anti-poverty work that millions and millions of dollars go for studies that are supposed to find solutions to poverty. *Yet children are still not guaranteed good housing, good food, and good schools.*

———

Today my editor and publisher, Audrey and Rolf, came to see me. They looked over the proposal for this book and obviously supported it. I agreed to have it done by the end of the year. Then maybe it will be a spring book. They came bearing gifts: Audrey loaned me a typewriter that was decent and Rolf brought paper, files, and a notebook. I don't apply for Canada Council grants for my books, so the gifts really help. The benefit of working with a small publishing company is empowerment — it's like working with good, honest friends. None of us are rich, there's no classism. Instead, there's a gentle discussion of ideas and there's a feeling, for me, of trust that goes both ways. Having a publisher and editor who believe in my work is a must!

I had some disturbing news today, as well. A parent that I interviewed in my last book called me. The family had spent a lot of time in shelters because, at the time, it was very difficult to find affordable rentals on a welfare budget. One of the children is now a street kid; another is in foster care. How can children survive the trauma of being in a shelter? of being homeless?

———

As I talk to parents and workers, I am told that some children not only are poor but have been sexually abused too. That doesn't mean that because parents are poor they will sexually abuse their children. Rich and middle-class children are sexually abused too, but I think poor children are more at risk from outside sources because of non-safe housing, poor recreation resources, unscreened helpers who turn out to be pedophiles. Pedophiles buy children toys and clothes that families can't supply them with, and then sexually abuse them. Street kids are picked up and given drugs and money by johns who want to have sex with children. I realize that even though this is a book about children and poverty, sexual abuse will probably show up in some of the sketches and interviews.

———

As a society, do we love our children? The evidence is to the contrary. It's not so long ago that our children worked in the mines and industry from dusk to dawn. At one time, children were deliberately maimed so they could legally beg. According to Statistics Canada, in 1991 there were 1.2 million children living in poverty in Canada. This number is rapidly increasing.

Many single people, seniors, and couples without children (not all of them!) complain about other peoples' children. I have heard them say, "We didn't give birth to them; it's up to their parents to support them. They shouldn't have children if they can't support them." Many resent paying school taxes, or seeing their tax money go to child benefit payments or to fund daycare.

When I visited the Okanagan recently, I saw blocks and blocks of complexes surrounded by strong walls. Adult Only Complexes, the signs said, Adult, Adult, Adult, and more and more were being built. It was like the olden days, when forts were built and castles had moats. The family I was with had three children. They said, "You kinda get the feeling that kids are not welcome." Or even liked.

In the year 2021 there will be more than six million people in Canada over the age of 65 — one in every four Canadians will be a senior, and it is the children growing up now who will have the job of looking after us. They will be the doctors, nurses, homemakers, cooks, dentists, caregivers. So isn't it in society's best interest to take care of and nurture our children? If we set an example by being unloving and uncaring about their poverty, how do we expect them to treat us when we need them? They will have to pay the taxes to support medicare, and to keep social housing and long-term care faculties open. If we don't nourish and educate them, there will be huge numbers of unemployed and no money for medicare and pensions.

———

I have found some really neat people as I gather my research, and many of them give me helpful ideas. Rosemary, at the National Anti-Poverty Organization in Ottawa, suggested I look into child labour. She also sent me up-to-date, relevant material. The Ombudsman's office in Victoria sent me some reports that had been published, and some statistics for B.C. It's so important that I have up-to-date stats and information that pertain to child poverty and abuse, and I depend on a network of "good people" who are involved in the anti-poverty movement.

The people at End Legislated Poverty in Vancouver, as usual, opened their doors and their hearts, and gave me press clippings and articles. It was good to talk over my ideas for this book. I like community input; it keeps me on track.

Through my journal, I'm attempting to show you, my reader, the process I'm going through as I write about child poverty.

After doing all this preliminary research, I did my first interview with a child today. It was really spontaneous. I was spending time at the

Carnegie Community Centre, having a coffee, and I saw Paul. I have known Paul for many many years. He's 16 and he and his family have always lived below the poverty line.

---

I have had two major surgeries in the last seven months. Part of my therapy is to go three times a week to the local pool and do a water exercise class. Yesterday I was talking to a woman in my class about my book. S said, "I live below the poverty line, that's me .... My daughter likes to draw. She's four years old. I'll ask her to do a sketch for you." S told me that when she was a child she was very poor and had to work six days a week delivering newspapers. She said, "You know, I never got to keep the money. My parents used it. The money was kept in a big jar. It was hard work."

---

Yesterday I interviewed three children. They were sisters, three, five, and six years old. We were at an anti-poverty group's annual meeting and there was a lot of food around. The children kept saying, "Can we eat now? Can we eat? I want to eat now." So the interviews were kind of short, very different from the one I did with Paul. I know that each child will take his or her interview in a different direction. I won't be able to ask each the same questions.

---

I was feeling so miserable, totally wiped out. There is something so special, so vulnerable about children; it's impossible not to be extremely concerned about the ones I talk to, and I get involved emotionally from the innermost parts of my body and mind. I have just finished interviewing Patty, a sweet, bright 11-year-old who lives partly on the street, partly at home, and partly in a group home. She said children are not toys like video games and tapes. You can't just pick them up and play with them, then leave them. I interviewed her at a community centre. While I was talking to her, a staff person came up and said, "You are a truant. You are not supposed to be here. You are supposed to be in school. You can only come in this building after 3:30." She replied, "I'm here with my mother. She's downstairs." He: "I don't care. You should be in school." Patty said she wished there was a place that was safe to go, off the street, where she wouldn't get busted.

The interview bothered me. What was I supposed to do? Use her for my book and then forget her? I can't do that. But I also can't break my promise of anonymity. She told me she would go to school tomorrow. I said perhaps I could meet her after school at the community centre. She said she would bring me some drawings she had done.

I did meet Patty the next day. I was so happy that she had gone back to school. The plan is for her to return to her family soon.

She brought me some of her sketches and writings. She is really talented. I told her she could be a really good writer if she wanted. She replied, "I like writing poetry." I gave her a hug and my phone number, and told her to keep in touch. She only stayed a few minutes. How she reminded me of me, when I was a runaway.

———————

When I was researching *Under the Viaduct,* I interviewed staff from the City of Vancouver's Social Planning Department and talked to the city's child advocate. I was told that there were plans to create a safe place for street kids to go, a place where they wouldn't be busted but would have a few days to think about "which way they were going." There's a new child advocate at City Hall now. I called and asked what had happened with the safe house. She said, "It didn't happen. They never got the funding." I have to check this out. Two years ago everyone was supporting this idea, all the agencies and government departments were on-side, and the funding seemed to be in place. Why did it fall through?

There's a real need for a place for young people to go. I talked with a staff person at the community centre where I had interviewed Patty, and asked about the policy of not allowing children in during school hours. He replied, "It's a real problem. We can't encourage children to hang out here during school hours, but when we make them leave, they go out onto the street and are vulnerable to the drug and sex trade out there. There's nowhere for us to send them to." I asked, "Couldn't we meet with Social Planning and see what happened to the safe house project?" He replied, "If you can get them here, sure, I'd come."

It seems that, as I write, it's impossible not to look at solutions. It's impossible not to want to do something about it. I'm aware that there are many people working to eliminate child poverty. People have presented briefs, studies, ideas … great, but where the hell is the safe house??

Jeff Brooks of the city's Social Planning Department called me about it. He said it had taken four years to get a detox residential program for youth, and that it was well used. He was really disappointed that in spite of all the community and social services, and street children's planning for a safe home, the provincial government had turned down the funding request. He didn't know why. He said it is really needed. There's one in Victoria, and others in Alberta and Ontario, but they are too big. He felt that the solution isn't to "warehouse children" in a big institution. He says there are many people out there who are pushing for this safe house to happen.

I also spoke to Libby Davies, one of Vancouver's city counsellors, about the safe house. Even though it was a provincial decision, she still took the time to explain to me what was happening. Because the provincial government had turned funding requests down, there was no point in City Hall looking for a house that there was no funding for — it was to be a joint project. She agreed with me that there should be such a house, and she was glad that I did care enough to check it out. The request is being resubmitted. Perhaps it will still happen. I'll keep checking.

———

In October 1991 I was lying on a bed at St. Paul's Hospital. There were staples making train tracks all the way down my right leg. My grandson had suggested I have a train tattooed on the future scar. I had had a knee replacement and it was bloody sore. Rolf, the publisher of New Star Books, had dropped by to give me a hug, even though he was busy as usual. We sat and talked. I expressed a desire to write about children who were poor, and said that I'd like to give them a voice … but I didn't think I had a right to do it because so many people were presently working so hard with child poverty groups. I thought that perhaps they would want to do a book. Rolf said, "Sheila, that would be a great sequel to your other books, and you know there's room for more than one book." I lay on the bed thinking, I would really like to do it. I was also feeling a little strange because of the painkillers and the morphine machine that was attached to my arm. Now it is little more than a year later, and the children's book is nearly finished because I was given so much encouragement from friends, family, fellow anti-poverty workers, and New Star Books. I can't believe it has happened so fast.

I'm told that my work is "folk art." I like that. Grandma Moses was great, and she was a late bloomer, too.

When I give this manuscript to my editor, I will part company with you, the reader. Thank you for reading my journal. It's not meant to be a scholarly piece of work, just a story of the book as it progressed. I didn't know what way it would take me, what paths it would lead me to. I never expected the school to play so large a role in how children see themselves in their poverty. The sexual abuse is there, and so few resources to deal with it when a child is poor.

As Patty said, a child is not a toy. I say, a book is not a solution. It's what you do with the book. Hear the children that cry out for help in this book. Hear them, help them. Help society change its attitude. Talk to governments and to corporations about paying decent wages. Make sure that poverty is understood in the school system, that children are taught not to blame themselves if there is no money for runners and no food for breakfast. Social workers, teachers, parents are sometimes stuck in the let's-not-rock-the-boat syndrome, let's not tread on anyone's toes. Let's not forget those who teach the teachers how to be teachers. Changes are needed. So please don't let this book just sit as a decoration on your bookshelf. Pass it on.

Please don't forget the children in this book.

If you are an adult and were an abused child, my heart goes out to you. Remember, it wasn't your fault.

———

It's so very hard to say this is the end. The phone rings. I meet someone who I just can't leave out of the book, and I open the journal again. I really should stop. Except to tell you that I was asked to be a guest as a writer at a run that children from two private schools were doing to raise money for Operation Eyesight. There I sat in that auditorium with about 450 children, some dressed in their red uniforms, others in navy.

Friendly, noisy, sweet-faced kids, who were not poor, who had good runners and adequate money in the family for nutrition. They picked their noses, scratched their heads, acted out, just like any other children that I've seen. They were all just children, because a child is just a child.

## Interviews with Children

### Kyle
*Kyle, age four. His family lives below the poverty line.*

I'm not poor. Just my mom doesn't get a lot of money, not from anything. She's not rich.

*What would you like to buy if you had money?*

A basketball and hoop, a big truck for my friend — he's not grown up yet. Some juicy pears.

*What kind of food would you buy?*

Celery, milk, some cereal, Cheerios, chocolate milk, some ice cream, and some of that pink stuff with the white stuff on it. When I'm grown up, I will buy ice cream all the time.

*Where will you get the money?*

I don't know how you get it.

### Ashley
*Ashley, age eight. Her family lives below the poverty line.*

*What does being poor mean?*

You can't buy food. You don't have a place to live. You can't buy a Nintendo. You can't have nice clothes .... You can't go to the movies .... You can't do what you want to do.

*What changes would you like to make if you had the power?*

I don't know, but the bank should give people money.

### Veronica
*Veronica, age 11. Her family lives way below the poverty line.*

Poor means not to have any money and no home. They might not feel all that well, especially when people bug them about it. They would probably feel very sad and stuff. If they had a home, they would probably go to their home and just sit there by themselves, probably. Poor kids sometimes they might just play by themselves because no one wants to play with them. They probably get pretty lonely.

*Why do people become poor?*

I guess it's just because they didn't finish school and stuff. They quit really early. Then they didn't get jobs. They just gave up I guess. I'm going into Grade 6. I hope to be a business woman. I'll keep in school and I'll get my degree.

Me and my sister used to have this book, sort of a catalogue, we would flip through and we'd have different coloured pens and say, "that's mine, that's mine, that's mine," pretend that we had lots of money and then we would go and buy them.

*How do you think poor children feel when they are in school?*

They probably feel pretty sad because lots of kids pick on them, I guess. They probably get beat up and stuff.

If I was the boss of everything, I would make it so that there was no such thing as money. If you don't have any money then you can't get anything and stuff. I would like it if people … they could just go into a store and say, can I please get whatever, and then they could get it. Right now there is such a thing as money and everybody has money, and you have to have money. If you don't have money, then you can't get food and stuff. I would make it so that there wasn't any money. Then you wouldn't have to starve or go without certain clothes and stuff. They would have cows and stuff and they would trade stuff. Like two loaves of bread for some milk and stuff like that.

*If I told you there was enough money to join any class that you wanted to join, what would you want to take?*

If I could join any club or anything like that, I would want to join … I used to want to play the piano, but now I want to learn how to … paint and stuff, and draw. Gymnastics, you know like how they twirl around on that board thing? And also swimming, I want to learn how to swim really good. You know how they dance on TV, like the music videos? I would like to learn how to do some of that.

*If you were a queen, what would you do?*

If I were a queen I would get my workers to build all sorts of houses for everybody. I would make it so that everybody can live in my kingdom. Anybody who wanted to live there could live there.

I'll tell you a sorta sad story. Once upon a time there was a little girl and she lived with her mother and her grandma. And she knew a girl who only lived where she lived in the summer, and she knew a boy who only lived there in the winter, and so she only had a few friends. She would play with the girl every summer, and they would go swimming and stuff, and then in the winter her and the boy would make snowmen and stuff. They would also have snowball fights. Then one day her grandma died. They didn't have very much money, so they didn't have a very good funeral. But they did have a funeral for her. They had a casket and it was closed because it was too sad. Everybody brang flowers and stuff. And the girl and the boy came too because they knew the grandma very well. And then one summer day the two little girls thought that they saw her grandma. And the grandma came down and reached out to the girl and gave her a big hug and then the grandma went back up to heaven and the little girl knew for sure that her grandmother loved her. The End.

## Paul

*Paul, age 16. I've known Paul since he was three years old. He and his family have always lived way below the poverty line.*

*Why are people poor?*

It's hard to say. There's too many people, there's not enough food to go around. I don't know, it's the way the world is. It's hard. I don't know, it's life. There's lots of charity, but charities got limits too, right? Everything's got a limit to it. There's more people than there is charity, you know. It's hard. At school once they called me Welfare Pauley. I got into a fight with another kid in my class. It wasn't too serious, the fight, but it was basically standing up for myself.

Solutions? Better living conditions is one thing. There's still a lot of old hotels down here. The more low-cost housing, I guess, the better for a lot of people, you know. Hotels are not safe. People are getting killed all the time. You gotta second thought on everything, you know, while you're walking down the street, anything can happen, anything's possible, you know? You can die any time.

If I'd had more money as a kid, it's hard to say what I would've used it on. Probably do what a lot of other people do, share it a bit. I would have changed a lot of things in my life. I would have made sure I would have had a house to live in as long as I'm on this planet, and the family and stuff. I would have taken a course for a recording engineer.

*Do you think you still have a chance of doing that?*

Oh yeah, but I've got to save up the money, it's quite a bit. I'm not in school. Yeah, I finished in Grade 8. I plan to go back eventually. Yeah, yeah, I quit because I just couldn't stand the hassle from the counsellors and stuff, you know. They were picking on me because I was a kid with the less money. They figured, they accused me of being on drugs and all kind of things which I was not.

I was about seven when I first knew I was poor. Basically, the way everything felt around me, you know. Not having a lot of money, a lot of the kids have a lot more than you have. You just got to put up with it, you know? That's what I did. Yeah.

I've lived in quite a few places in my life, between the age I am now and when I was really young. Even when I was first born we moved a couple of times between that and the time I was three years old. That's how it's been. I didn't pay a lot of attention to the fact of moving; that's something I never thought a lot about, but you get used to it after awhile, you know. Changing schools and moving to other places. It's hard to get to know new people, you know. All the new kids, you gotta find out who you want to be friends with and who you don't, who's gonna be a real friend to you and who's not.

I've lived in one house where I felt unsafe, in the Mount Pleasant area. There's a lot going on there, just a bad neighbourhood basically.

My plans for the future are to take the recording course, take both levels of that and eventually, when I get the money together, open up my own studio.

*How will you get the money together?*

Like I said, I'm gonna try to get a job. The only thing you can really get is McDonald's. Minimum wage usually, five-fifty to six bucks. That's all it is. It's quite low. I don't know if it has a medicare plan or dental. I don't think so. I had a job before, helping out a friend with his paper route and that. It was not too bad, was kind of fun, and now I'm a musician right now. I'm employed as a musician. I play mainly rock and blues and stuff like that ....

(I spoke with Paul again in September.)

*What's been happening over the summer?*

I went for three vacations, a couple close by. My grandfather died this summer, and a lot of bad luck. Still looking for a job. I do volunteer work. I'm still looking for a full-time job.

*Would you think about going back to school?*

No, I don't think so.

*Have your goals changed?*

My goals now? Well, there's a few new ones. I want to get into a new group, like a new band: I'm not in a band at this time. I want to pull it together and start playing clubs and that ... you know? Get some money together that way.

*What do you think your chances are of making it in the music world?*

Very slim. There's too much competition. It's very competitive, you know.

*What is the job scene like out there for you?*

For most people my age it's mostly Burger King or McDonald's. I think student wage is maybe six dollars an hour. It's not a lot, but it's passable, I guess. I've just filled out an application, but I haven't taken it back in yet.

*That's not what you really want to do, is it?*

No. I want to be a musician, record producer, recording engineer, songwriter ... that's what I'm already doing. I'm a songwriter and a musician now, but I want to do that for a living. I want to be a recording engineer. It would be great, but it costs money. I'm not too sure if I could get a grant. It could be possible.

I'm looking towards the future, I don't think about the past too much anymore. Well, at this point it looks like it's gonna happen. The present is rough.

*How do you manage to stay off drugs when you are around them all the time?*

I just never wanted to do that. I'm scared of it, that's why. The fear of it. If I would've done that, I realize what I could have lost. I could have lost everything that I have.

*How did you manage to say no when you were offered drugs?*

You just gotta be forceful about it. Sometimes it comes to the point when you have to tell them, tell them straight. It comes to a point when you might get into a fight over it, but I still say no, no. You gotta stick to your guns.

(A month later I saw Paul again. He said he was playing guitar in a group out in Coquitlam.)

## Exercises

1.  How do children understand poverty? In answering this question consider the following sub-questions:
    a)   What are the factors children understand in poverty?
    b)   What factors do children in this text not understand?
    c)   How are embarrassment, stigma, and poverty connected?
    d)   How are authority and trust issues evident in poverty?
    e)   How are children's dreams affected by poverty?
2.  What social factors come into play in poverty? E.g., child abuse, homelessness, "runaways," "single mothers," social stigma. How do these factors interconnect?
3.  What are the societal, economic, and governmental/political policies and practices that produce or fail to address poverty?
4.  How are schools, teachers, and other children a part of the realization of poverty in children's lives?
5.  How are "labels" harmful? E.g., "single mother, "welfare family"?
6.  How are health, drugs, abuse, and malnutrition issues in poverty?

## Chapter 27

# The Poor Fare
# Worst in Schools

**Alanna Mitchell**

### Better-off Children End Up in Gifted Programs; Low-Income Ones, in Remedial Classes

Canada's poorest children are more than three times as likely as the richest children to be in remedial education classes, Statistics Canada says.

And the richest pupils are almost twice as likely to be in gifted classes as the poorest, says the most comprehensive and the first representative national study conducted on the issue.

The poorest children are also twice as likely as all pupils to repeat a grade, according to figures published yesterday from Statscan's long-term survey.

The findings speak of what has become almost an unmentionable in Canadian society: an entrenched class system. And they point to the possibility that Canada's large and growing proportion of poverty-stricken children could create an underclass, with all the social chaos that suggests.

"We're in a circle of not allowing people to climb out of a lower echelon in society," said Joan Grusec, professor of psychology at the University of Toronto. "As a psychologist, I say someone's got to worry about those kids. Someone's got to do something for them."

The findings call into question whether Canada's educational system can actually accomplish its goal of being an equalizer.

They also raise a philosophical issue: Is it better to have an education system where everyone strives for academic success, or to adopt a more European model of respecting people who are good at other things and training them appropriately.

"Our ideology tells us we are a democratic, egalitarian, free society that is basically classless," said Ellen Gee, chairwoman of sociology and anthropology at Simon Fraser University in Burnaby, B.C. "The reality is that there are different opportunities."

Statscan's report, she said, "shows how this gets perpetuated."

The figures are stark. When pupils aged four to eleven are ranked according to socioeconomic group, children in the bottom fifth are much more likely than any others to be in remedial education.

The findings are based on interviews with the teachers and principals of about 7,000 pupils in 1994 and 1995 and on some math tests the children wrote.

(The determination of socioeconomic group was based on family income and the jobs and education of the parents.) Seventeen percent of those from the lowest fifth were in remedial education, compared with 5 percent of the highest fifth. The pattern reverses for pupils in gifted classes: 9 percent of the highest fifth were getting the advanced teaching compared with 5 percent of the lowest fifth.

Teachers were much more likely to rate children from the richest families at the top of their classes than those from the poorest: In fact, 40 percent of the richest children were rated as top readers compared with 16 percent of the poorest. The pattern was the same for writing, composition, and mathematics.

Richer children were also more likely to score higher on a math test: 28 percent of the top fifth scored highly compared with 14 percent of the bottom fifth. The results of children in the other socioeconomic groups ranged between those of the rich and the poor.

"We know poverty is a huge disadvantaging force in our society," said Susan McDaniel, a sociologist at the University of Alberta in Edmonton. "We also know it's getting worse."

Patrice de Broucker, of Statscan's Centre for Education Statistics, said that while the findings show that the wealthier children tend to be higher achievers, they also show that a child's fate is not sealed by the parents' socioeconomic status. He pointed to the fact that 5 percent of the children in the lowest socioeconomic group were in gifted programs.

"There still is no clear determinism," he said.

As well, he said, because this is a longitudinal study, it will follow the children for years. That means the study ought to be able to determine whether the remedial help eventually puts the poorer children on a level playing field with richer ones.

"It may show that schools are taking care of the most disadvantaged of society," he said.

To Carolyn Yewchuk, a professor of educational psychology at the University of Alberta and a Canadian delegate to the World Council of Gifted and Talented Children, the findings raise questions about whether Canada's education system is headed in the right direction.

"We still have this idea that every child can get through school and go to university," she said. "That's just not possible …. We are trying to equalize everything at the top end. But not everyone can be a neurosurgeon."

It's no secret why poorer children fare worse in school. For one thing, said Alan Mirabelli of the Vanier Institute of the Family, the parents in such families may have to work many more hours — and at less convenient times — than the parents in wealthier families. They may not have the skills or the time to read to children, tell them stories, or introduce them to music.

The poorer children may go to school hungry, be dealing with abusive parents, miss more school because of illness or be getting too little sleep. None of that predisposes them to academic excellence.

"The question from society's point of view is: How do you break that cycle?" Mr. Mirabelli said.

"Children in poverty tend to have proven academic needs," said Marie Pierce, executive director of the Canadian School Boards Association, one of the groups that requested the inclusion of education in the study.

She said the study underscores the need for extra resources and early intervention to assist those who do not arrive at school as ready and able as those from wealthier families.

"It points to the need to look at all variables" that bear on student success, she said, adding that future survey results should give schools a sharper idea of what works. For example, do remedial programs make a difference for students?

# Chapter 28

# The Organic
# Goode Simulation

## Bill Bigelow
## Norm Diamond

This activity is about power. Set in an imaginary society, it poses students a challenge: Can you overcome divisions and unite to create needed changes? If so, what circumstances encouraged this unity? If not, why not? Unfortunately, these days many students are cynical about their capacity to work together — for a better school, a better community, a better society. Without confronting that cynicism, students run the risk of dismissing much of the history from which they could draw hope for the future. This lesson lets them experience some of the pressures that lead workers to organize. Depending on what happens in class, students either glimpse the possibility of organizing and practice overcoming cynicism, or gain an experience out of which their attitudes can be directly discussed. It's also a lot of fun.

*Grade Level:*
Middle school to adult.

*Materials Needed:*
One large machine-like object, e.g., a TV or an overhead projector.

*Time Required:*
One class period (at least 45 minutes) to "play," and time for a follow-up discussion.

*Procedure:*

1. Close the door and pull the blinds in the classroom. Tell students to imagine that we are going to have to live in this classroom for the rest of our lives (many groans). Explain that there is no soil for farming but we are in luck because we have a machine that produces food — organic goodies. Correct yourself, and point out that actually you own the machine. Put the projector or whatever machine you've selected in the front of the classroom.

2. Tell students that you need people to work for you producing organic goodies. Workers will receive money to buy enough food to live on — those not working will find it hard to survive. Ask for volunteers who want to work, eat, and survive. (On those occasions when additional coercion is necessary, we tell students that to receive credit for the activity they must not starve.) Choose only half the class as workers. The other half will be unemployed. Sit the two on opposite sides of the room, one group facing the other.

3. Now explain the economics of your society. Put the "Organic Goodie Economy" chart (see below) on the board. (You might want to have the chart up earlier, covered with a map or a screen.)

   Explain that five organic goodies a day are necessary to survive in a fairly healthy manner. Those receiving less, the non-workers, will gradually get sick and starve. Go over the chart with students: Each worker *produces* eleven (11) goodies a day. All workers are paid $6 a day. A goodie costs $1. One dollar is deducted from the pay of each worker to make small welfare payments to the unemployed. So, after taxes, a worker can buy five goodies a day, enough to survive. Explain that as the owner, you of course deserve more because it's your machine, and without your machine everyone would starve.

4. Show the unemployed that, as the chart indicates, they only receive $2 a day in welfare payments. This means they can only buy two goodies a day — they are slowly starving to death. They desperately need work.

5. Make sure each student understands his/her position. Now the "game" begins. Your goal is to increase your profits — that's all you're after. The way you can do this is through cutting

---

**Organic Goodie Economy**

Production = 11 x number of workers

Per Day

|  | Workers | Unemployed | Owner |
|---|---|---|---|
| Wages | $6 x no. workers | Nothing | Nothing |
| Taxes | -$1 x no. workers | +$2 x no. unemployed | -$1 x no. unemployed (see note) |
| Consumption | 5 Organic Goodies x no. workers | 2 x no. unemployed | 6 Organic Goodies |
| Surplus | Nothing | Nothing | 4 x no. workers, minus 6 for daily consumption |

*Example:* If there were 10 workers and 10 unemployed, a total of 110 goodies would be produced. After taxes, the workers would be able to consume 50. From welfare payments, the unemployed would consume 20, leaving a total of 40 for the owner - 34 after consuming his or her six. *Note:* Workers' and owner's tax needs to provide $2 to each unemployed person (taxes paid in Goodies).

---

wages. *Note:* No money or goodies are actually exchanged. We generally begin by telling students to imagine that a number of weeks have elapsed and then ask members of each group how they have been eating, how they're feeling. (By the way, everyone could be employed to produce goodies — eleven a day, as mentioned — but we don't tell that to students unless they ask.)

6. There is no "correct" order in which to proceed, but here are some techniques that have worked for us:

   • Ask which of the unemployed people wants to work. Offer someone $5.50 a day — less than other workers but more than the $2 they're getting now in welfare payments. After you have a taker, go to the workers and ask who is willing to accept $5.50. Fire the first person who refuses to accept the lower wage and send him or her across the room to sit with the unemployed. Hire the unemployed person who was willing to accept the lower wage. Continue this procedure, trying to drive down wages.

- Occasionally you might ask workers to repeat after you, "I am a happy worker." Fire those who refuse and hire someone who is unemployed.
- We often make derogatory comments about the "welfare bums" and invite workers to do the same. (Later we can talk about why the people were on welfare, and who was the real bum.)
- Anyone who mentions "union" or striking or anything disruptive should be fired immediately. Get all workers to sign "yellow dog" contracts promising never to join a union as long as they work for you.
- Sometimes we hire a foreperson (a spy), for a little more money, who will turn in "subversive" workers. Occasionally we whisper something in a worker's ear, to encourage suspicion and division among workers. Someone usually threatens to take over the machine. When this happens we hire a police officer or two to protect it. We explain that she or he is here to protect "all our property equally, not just my machine." Having someone physically protect the machine also alerts students to the fact that they could take it over.
- It's important to keep workers and unemployed from uniting to strike, or worse, to take control of your machine. You can offer privileges to people to prevent them from seeing their common interests — differential wages, shorter work days, perhaps even profit sharing.
- If they are successful in uniting and stopping production, you have a couple of options:
  1. You can wait them out, indicating your surplus, and how quickly they will starve (use the chart to remind them how much you have left over everyday); or
  2. Give in to their wage demands and a little later raise the price of organic goodies. After all, you can justify your need for more income to meet your higher costs.

- Sometimes we announce that every three minutes an
    unemployed person will die of starvation. This
    emphasizes to the entire class that should they fail to
    act there will be consequences.

7. The game is unpredictable, and a range of things has happened
    while playing it. What *always* happens, however, is that people
    try to get organized. The game ends when students have had
    ample opportunity to get together — successfully or otherwise.
    Participants may be totally demoralized or they may have taken
    over the machine and decided to run it collectively.

8. For homework, we ask students to write on the experience.
    Questions might include: What did you personally do to try to
    stop my efforts to divide people? How effective were you? Were
    there actions you considered, but didn't take? Why not? If we
    were to do this simulation again, what different actions would
    you take?

Additional discussion and/or writing questions include:

- What methods did I use to try to keep people from getting together
    to oppose me? When was I successful? When unsuccessful?
- At which points were you most successful in getting together?
    When were you least successful?
- What kept you from immediately calling a meeting and
    demanding equal treatment, or simply walking over to the
    machine and taking it over? Here we try to get at students'
    preconceptions about people's capacity to stick together. Did
    they think that efforts to unite all workers and unemployed
    would eventually be betrayed? Why? We want to explore with
    students what in their lives would leave them hopeful or
    skeptical. Have they had experiences that convinced them that
    people could unite and act together for important goals?
- As the owner, what kind of attitudes would I want you to have
    about your ability to work together as a unified group? What
    attitude would I want you to have about property rights? About
    respect for authority?
- As a follow-up activity, sometimes we ask students to think of a
    time in their lives when they were able to work successfully

with others toward a common objective. We ask them to write this up as a story. We then share our stories in class and take notes on the circumstances that allow people to unite — creating what we call a "collective text," the wisdom we can draw from each other's lives.

Does all this sound too complicated? It's not. A number of teachers have told us, "I didn't want to do that activity because I wasn't sure I could remember everything, and I didn't know if it would work." As they discover: It works.

# Chapter 29

# Challenging
# Class Bias

## Toronto Board of Education
## (compiled and revised by Terezia Zoric)

### THE "ISMs": WHAT ARE THEY?

**Objectives**
- To define the words racism, sexism, classism, and ageism.
- To understand how prejudice, when reinforced by institutional power, becomes an "ism."

**Materials**
- A large "ISM Chart," copies of "Worksheet: Find the ISM," one for every two students.

**Implementation**
Explain to the students that when prejudice and stereotypes are practised by people with more power than others or by institutions, like schools, families, government, business, their effect is very great. Also, prejudice and stereotypes become more powerful when imbedded in cultural attitudes and values. In these cases, people or institutions practice discrimination — they treat people or groups of people differently because of their age, race, sex, or class. The practice of such discrimination is summarized by using an "ism" word.

Post the ISM Chart and discuss each "ism" separately. (Change the key words on the chart as appropriate.) In discussing the "isms" and the examples, explain that because norms and procedures of institutions or prevailing attitudes and values in society reinforce "isms," they are much more powerful than prejudice and stereotypes. In addition, examples of "isms" are harder to spot because they are often "hidden" in institutions. Explain that victims of "isms" subtly learn that they are not as good as or important as others, whereas those who benefit from the "isms" learn that they are normal, right, or important.

Have students work in heterogeneous pairs. Give each pair a copy of the Worksheet. One person reads the first situation aloud. Together they decide on answers and one person writes them in. They continue this procedure with other situations, deciding together who will read and write. Join as a class for discussion.

### To Review

*Prejudice* is an unfavourable *opinion* about a person or group of people not based on knowledge.

A *stereotype* is a *generalization* about a group of people not based on fact. *Isms* are prejudice and stereotypes enforced by people with more power than others, by institutions, and by cultural attitudes and values.

PREJUDICE + POWER = ISMS

### Worksheet: Find the "ISM"

1. Jobs are divided in the Wright family. Susan must do the dishes and vacuum the rug. She doesn't like these jobs! Peter's jobs are to mow the lawn and weed the garden. Peter likes getting exercise while doing his jobs. Susan would like to have some of Peter's jobs, but her parents say she must learn "women's work."

   Susan probably feels _____
   Peter might feel _____
   The Wright parents encourage _____

2. Laverne did a survey of her school library books. She found that most characters over 60 were described as old, ill, or helpless. Laverne's own grandparents are active and alert.

Laverne probably feels _____
Her grandparents might feel _____
Children's book publishing companies reinforce _____

3. Ralph's father works in a factory. He is a hard worker and hardly ever misses a day of work. He makes $8 an hour, or $320 a week. Ralph is an excellent student and would like to become a doctor. His family can't afford it. Even scholarships can't cover the $75,000 or more needed to get medical training.

   Ralph probably feels _____
   Colleges and medical schools support _____

4. Myra and Dwayne are excited because today they are going to the store to buy a board game. They walk up and down the aisles and notice that there is only one black child on any of the game boxes.

   If Myra and Dwayne are black they might feel _____
   If they are white they might feel _____
   Toy companies reinforce _____

## ISM CHART

People are seen and treated differently because of (1)_____ .
(2)_____ is/are viewed as better or more important than others and has/have more power in society. In our society those people are (3)_____ . Values and practices of institutions (schools, families, churches, media, etc.) support these inequalities.

*Key Words: (Fill in according to "ism" being discussed)*
    A: Racism
- 1) skin colour
- 2) one race
- 3) whites

    B: Sexism
- 1) being male or female
- 2) one sex
- 3) males

| C: Classism | 1) | the amount of money a person/family has |
| | 2) | some classes |
| | 3) | upper- and middle-class |
| D: Ageism | 1) | age |
| | 2) | certain ages |
| | 3) | adults (not elderly) |

### Examples

**Racism.** Jean walks through her school and notices there is only one picture of a black, Asian-American, or Latino person on the bulletin boards. The school bulletin boards show racism.

**Sexism.** Laurie wants to be on the soccer team. Applications were only given to boys. Laurie calls the recreation department and she is told girls aren't allowed on the boys' team and that there is no team for girls. The recreation department reinforces sexism.

**Classism.** Dominic looks through his social studies book and realizes that most of the people who are described as "important" are people with prestige and money. Few working-class or poor people are emphasized, even though their hard work built the nation. The textbook company encourages classism.

**Ageism.** For a school project, Lamar did a study of television shows and found that only three percent of the characters were over 60 years old, even though in real life in this country over 15 percent of the people are over 60. Lamar concluded that the television industry reinforces ageism.

# Chapter 30

# Students at Risk

## Njoki Nathani Wane

I can hear your low whispers
I have seen that silent gaze so many times
I can read your mind
What am I supposed to do?
Scream at the top of my voice to let the world know,
Know that I am a poor and marginalized student at risk?

I know the pressure is mounting for me to leave.
I do not want to leave
I want to make something out of myself
But I guess I have to leave because I have been failing all my courses
Why can't anyone see my bleeding heart?
My broken dreams? My dried up tears?
I thought the schools were for all of us
I thought there was something like, yes, like equal opportunity for
    all

Mrs. T sent me out of class the other day because I was sleeping
    during her history class
How could I tell her I slept because my history was excluded from
    her teaching and that my years of waiting weighted heavily on
    me?

How could I tell her I was left out, absent from her examples,
classroom textbooks, pictures, and discussion?

Mr. C shouted at me for "disturbing" his math class.
Little did he know I was explaining to others the concepts in
probability theory?
Mr. C has never acknowledged my good grades and even blames me
for "copying" from other students when it is all my work

I do not want to leave school
But I am forced to leave
Can't you see I want to make something out of myself?
I know I am getting tired, tired of my "silent screams"
My physical and emotional bruises hurt
I need help
I know there is someone out there who can help students at risk
Yes, I am talking to all of you
Yes, I am talking on behalf of all of us.
The students at risk.

# Epilogue

# Epilogue

What is education? What is meaningful education? For whom? How do we ensure that education promotes growth in a positive direction? This project has been a journey of discovery, learning, re-examination, and rethinking of what is equity in relation to school and society. It has enabled us to see the multiple connections between the two institutions that influence lives of young people. It has been an opportunity for us to question some of the epistimologies that we as educators employ in our everyday teaching practices. It has enabled us to reconsider the multiple layers of oppression that work together through these institutions. For example, gender is not viewed in isolation but can be seen to be layered with race, class, and sexuality, these biases working together to act on people through institutional structures. Each bias should not be privileged over the others. Each should be interrogated in its appropriate context. So questions of race should not overshadow sexuality. All need equal importance in the discussion. But they also cannot be isolated from the others as they work together. So, for example, when one uses only a race/sex model it is very narrow in its assumptions. But when we see the multiple biases working together then it is easier to see the magnitude of equity issues.

This project enabled us to reflect and ponder the inequities in our educational systems which are undergoing tremendous change. Some of these changes impact the lives of students in positive directions, increasing awareness of equity issues. But these changes are not widespread nor universal and some of them can have a numbing effect or reduce awareness of equity. This text works to counter these negative effects and to address situations where equity work is needed.

In working with students who are learning about equity the issue often arises as to what is the difference between equity and equality. Students need to ponder what an equality paradigm entails and how this is very different from an orientation to equity. An equality paradigm focuses attention on maintaining equal experiences for all students regardless of their backgrounds. An equity focus creates equivalent experiences for all students, taking into account their various locations. The equality focus can be seen to reproduce bias by maintaining instutional structures that perpetuate in-built biases. An equity focus avoids this pitfall by taking into account learners' backgrounds, such as their histories and social locations. For example, an equality focus would treat all students, despite different class backgrounds, as equal, thus reproducing bias against students of certain backgrounds. An equity focus takes into consideration the diverse backgrounds that students bring with them into the classroom and provides experiences that will enrich this diversity and address pre-existing gaps. In such a context, students of affluent backgrounds might gain experiences and understandings of those of other backgrounds, enabling them to re-examine their own positions.

In many instances we have encountered educators, students, and members of the general public who emphasize that they do not see colour or that they are colour blind. Those who purport not to see colour negate the presence of diversity in their classrooms and in society. By acknowledging a student's colour their presence is affirmed. But when colour is negated, student identity is also negated.

There is a common assumption that equity issues are only applicable to schools or educators with diverse backgrounds. This project has demonstrated that equity issues are for *all* schools whether students have diverse backgrounds or a school that is a monoculture. All students, even from monocultures, are in a diverse society and will encounter students who have been exposed to equity issues. To not provide these students knowledge of equity issues and experiences in re-examining society is to not prepare students to work in a complex society.

Equity in education should not be for specific courses or for specific educators but should be embraced by all educators and should be reflected in teaching pedagogy as well as resources. Our text is brought together for a specific course but opens the way for equity to be applied in all areas of education. Our text also indicates that equity does not stop at the end of a school year or semester but is an ongoing process all year round.

Every year educational training institutions produce thousands of teachers who may not be aware of interconnections of school and society or may have only limited awareness. Their narratives indicate that the biases of society are reproduced in school environments, in multiple ways, including institutional structures. It is to these new teachers that this text is particularly focused, but more experienced teachers who wish to increase their knowledge of equity issues will also find this text helpful. It is our hope that through this text, educators will begin a dialogue about equity and the multiple biases in society that are reflected in school systems.

# Appendix

# Discussing the Film
## For Angela

In regard to this film consider the following questions:

1.  What are the stereotypes of Aboriginal peoples presented here? How are these stereotypes produced/reinforced in society? How do these function to limit the lives of Native people?
2.  How do these stereotypes function in interactions between Native/ non-Native people?
3.  In the introduction, the narrator and main character says:

> What makes a good story? I've asked myself that question a lot lately — trying to see my world through the eyes of a journalist. But it's an ordinary world. Be objective. Be removed. Build a wall around your feelings so you can see the story — get the facts. Sometimes seeing isn't that simple. A lot of things are in the shadows. Maybe I'm looking for something I can't see. Maybe it's something in the shadows. No I don't want to look in the shadows!

4.  Later in the story the journalism professor says:

> These are crap. If you want to be journalists then please tell me I'm wrong. I'll tell you right now in the real world these

reports would have lost you your jobs. O.K. I want a new report, a new story in my office 9 a.m. tomorrow morning. And when I say a story I mean a new story, not what you did the last time. It's a new story and new rules. You lose 5% for every minute you are late. After 9:05 I won't even take it. This my friends is the real world.

5. How is objectifying in the portrayal of journalism part of stereotyping? How is media also a part of this production? Whose knowledge is portrayed in media? Discuss this media portrayal of a teacher/instructor? What stereotypes of education does it take up?

6. What resistance to dominant stereotypes and practices do the characters, the interviewees (after the film), and this film take part in?

7. At the end of the film the narrator says: "When I learn to say what I am and what I know and look without fear into the shadows, then my world and my daughters world can be different." Discuss how this leaves the responsibility for change of society in the individual work of Native people. Write another narrator comment that speaks to (1) changing institutions, and (2) responsibility of all.

# Discussing the Film
# *Woman in the Shadow*

In examining this film, it is helpful to think about erasure when this story talks about loss.

1. Whose identities have been erased? By what policies/practices?
2. How are Aboriginal people today struggling against this erasure?
3. How is the word "Indian" used in the film? By whom? When, how, and by whom is "Native" used?

## Questions to consider after the film
1. For you, what was going on in the film?
2. How did the film make you feel?
3. Did this film relate to something that you have seen or experienced in your life?
4. Did the language, camera angles, sequencing, etc. affect your reactions?
5. Whose opinions are represented here? Who benefits from these portrayals?

## Clarification Questions
1. What is colonialism? Examples of Colonialism: practice of governor not writing about his "country wife" and saying that her Indian name and identity are not known.

2.  The film suggests the "final defeat of the Métis Nation." Does this film suggest they were defeated?
3.  How are the Métis sash as well as bannock mix symbols of the Métis Nation portrayed, historically and now?
4.  Did the people in this story "choose to deny who they were" or were they given a real choice?

You may wish to develop a further set of questions for use of this film based on your viewing and your guidelines.

## Additional Questions

You might include questions about student reactions to scenes when they shuffle their feet, talk, laugh, or cough, etc. These reactions may show discomfort or resistance so are important to discuss. For example, you may include a question like: I noticed when _____ was going on in the film, you seemed to have something to say. What was going on for you at that point?

Following this film you may wish to look at images of Native people provided in posters by the Native Role Model Program, Kanawake, Quebec, which show diverse images of Native peoples who do not fit the stereotypes. You may wish to consider how these non-stereotypic images help students see Native people as diverse and help students counter the images so pervasive in many medias.

## Further Questions for Discussion
## of representations and stereotypes

1.  What is the importance of a historical perspective when including materials on non-mainstream or non-dominant groups into the curriculum?
2.  What considerations and care need to be taken in planning and facilitating these units?
3.  What are the implications of visual stereotypes and preferred meanings for using images and texts about different groups in the pedagogy?
4.  How are the Doxtator and Slapin et al. pieces and the posters interrupting mainstream stereotypes?

How are the films *Women in the Shadow* and *For Angela* interrupting or "talking back" to authoritative knowledge or mainstream stereotypes?

# Recommendations
# for Further Reading
# and
# Bibliography

# Recommendations for further Reading

## PART 1

Cameron, L.M. (1998). A practitioner's reflections. *Orbit*, 28(4), 10–15.

## PART 2

Aronowitz, S., and H.A. Giroux, H.A. (1988). Schooling, culture, and literacy in the age of broken dreams: A review of Bloom and Hirsch. *Harvard Educational Review*, 58(2), 172–194.

hooks, bell (1994). Writing autobiography. In M. Blair and S. Holland with S. Sheldon, *Identity and diversity: Gender and the experience of education*, Buckingham, UK: The Open University.

## PARTS 3 AND 4

Chase, F. (1978). What can we do? In T. Aoki, J. Dahlie, and W. Werner (eds.) *Canadian ethnicity: The politics of meaning*, Vancouver, BC: Centre for the Study of Curriculum and Instruction, University of British Columbia.

Dei, G. (1993). The challenges of antiracist education in Canada. *Canadian Ethnic Studies*, 25, 36–51.

Frankenberg, R. (1993). Growing up white: Feminism, racism and the social geography of childhood. *Feminist Review*, 45, 51–84.

Orenstein, P. (1994). Split loyalties: Homegirls vs. schoolgirls. In *Schoolgirls: Young women, self-esteem, and the confidence gap*, New York: Bantam Doubleday Dell Publishing Group.

Razack, S. (1995). The perils of talking about culture: Schooling research on south and east Asian. *Race, Gender and Class*, 2(3), 67–82.

Rymer, J., and I. Alladin (1996). Strategies for an antiracist education. In I. Alladin (ed.) *Racism in Canadian schools*, Toronto: Harcourt Brace and Company.

Toronto Board of Education (1994). Using film and video for anti-racist education. In *S.T.A.R.S. Equity Advisory Kit* (draft), Toronto: Toronto Board of Education.

## Part 5

Randhawa, B.S. (1995). Gender differences in academic achievement: A closer look at mathematics. *Alberta Journal of Educational Research*, 37(3), 241–257. In L.W. Roberts and R.A. Clifton (1995). *Crosscurrents: Contemporary Canadian educational issues*, Toronto: Nelson Canada.

## Part 6

Kaw, E. (1994). "Opening" faces: The politics of cosmetic surgery and Asian American women. In N. Sault (ed.) *Many mirrors: Body image and social relations*, New Brunswick, NJ: Rutgers University Press.

Ontario Ministry of Education (no year). *Engendering equity: Transforming the curriculum: Put gender on the agenda* (draft), Ontario: Ontario Ministry of Education.

Streitmatter, J. (1994). Teacher interactions; Getting started towards gender. In *Gender equity in the classroom: Everyday teachers' beliefs and practices*, Albany, NY: State University of New York Press.

## Part 7

Eyre, L. (1997). Re-forming (hetero)sexuality education. In L. Roman and L. Eyre (eds.) *Dangerous territories*, New York: Routledge.

Toronto Board of Education (1994). *Activities from lesbian and gay studies course* (draft), Toronto: Toronto Board of Education.


## Part 8

Evans, M. (1991). Culture and class from A good school: Life at a girls' grammar school in the 1960s. In M. Blair and J. Holland with S. Sheldon, *Identity and diversity: Gender and the experience of education*, Buckingham, UK: The Open University.

Fever, F. (1994). Who cares? Memories of childhood in care. In M. Blair and J. Holland, with S. Sheldon, *Identity and diversity: Gender and the experience of education*, Buckingham, UK: The Open University.

Manning, M. and L. Baruth (1995). Selections from personal characteristics. In *Students at risk*, Boston: Allyn and Bacon.

Maylor, U. (1994). Identity, migration and education. In M. Blair and J. Holland with S. Sheldon, *Identity and diversity: Gender and the experience of education*, Buckingham, UK: The Open University.

Solomon, P. (1996). Creating an opportunity structure for blacks and other teachers of color. In K.S. Brathwaite and C.E. James, *Educating African Canadians*, Toronto: James Lorimer and Company.


## Recommended Readings in *Rethinking Our Classrooms*

Bigelow, B., L. Christensen, S. Karp, B. Miner, and B. Peterson (eds.) (1994). *Rethinking our classrooms: Teaching for equity and justice*, Milwaukee, WI: Rethinking Schools.

### Part 1
Christensen, L. Building community from chaos, 50–55.
Kohl, H.I. Won't learn from you! Confronting student resistance, 134–135.

### Part 2
Christensen, L. Discipline: No quick fix, 56–57.
———Whose standard? Teaching standard English, 142–145.
Meier, T. Why standardized tests are bad, 171–175.
Miller, K. Tapping into feelings of fairness, 44–48.
Kohl, J. The politics of children's literature: What's wrong with the Rosa Parks Myth, 137–140.

Peterson, B. The challenge of classroom discipline, 34–35.

## Part 3 and 4

Bigelow, B., L. and Christensen. Videos with a conscience, 187–188.
The Council of Interracial Books for Children. 10 quick ways to analyze children's books, 14–15.
Schniedewind, N., E. and Davidson. Black lies/white lies, 75.

## Part 6

The need for districtwide changes, 104.
Stein, N., and L. Sjostrom. Flirting vs. sexual harassment: Teaching the difference, 106–107.

## Part 8

Hersh, S., and B. Peterson. Poverty and world resources, 92–93.
Math, equity, and economics, 94–95.

# Bibliography

## Part 1

Collins, M.N. (1995). Why I teach. In G. Taylor and T. Runté (eds.) *Thinking about teaching: An introduction,* Toronto: Harcourt Brace.

Ford, L., and L.B. Ford (1994). Our schools our selves: The story of a new teacher. *Orbit,* 25(4), 21–22.

Grant, C.A., and K.M. Ziechner (1995). On becoming a reflective teacher. In G. Taylor and T. Runté (eds.) *Thinking about teaching: An introduction,* Toronto: Harcourt Brace.

## Part 2

Allen, A. (1996). "I don't want to read this": Students' responses to illustrations of black characters in children's picture books. In K.S. Brathwaite and C.E. James (eds.) *Educating African Canadians,* Toronto: James Lorimer and Company.

Aoki, T. (1978). On being and becoming a teacher in Alberta. In T.A. Aoki, J. Dahlie, and W. Werner (eds.) *Canadian ethnicity: The politics of meaning,* Vancouver, BC: Centre for the Study of Curriculum and Instruction, University of British Columbia.

Levin, B., and J. Young (1994). Making sense of public schooling. In *Understanding Canadian schools: An introduction to educational administration*, Toronto: Harcourt Brace.

## Part 3

Hall, S. (1997). Section 1.1 Heroes or villains?; Section 4: Stereotyping as signifying practice; Section 4.1 Representation, difference and power. In S. Hall (ed.) *Representation: Cultural representations and signifying practices*, London: Sage Books.

Kivel, P. (1995). I'm not white; I'm not racist. In *Uprooting racism: How white people can work for racial justice*, Gabriola Island, BC: New Society Publishers.

McIntosh, P. (1990). White privilege: Unpacking the invisible knapsack. *Independent School*, Winter, 31–36.

Short, G. (1999). Antiracist education and moral behavior: Lessons from the Holocaust. *Journal of Moral Education*, 28(1), 49–62.

Tatum, B.D. (1992). Talking about race, learning about racism: The application of racial identity development theory in the classroom. *Harvard Educational Review*, 62(1), 1–24.

## Part 4

Doxtator, D. (1992). Chapter 1: The idea of Indianness; Chapter 6: Once upon a time: The role of Indians in history. In *Fluffs and feathers: An exhibit on the symbols of Indianness: A resource guide*, Brantford, ON: Woodland Cultural Centre.

Slapin, B., D. Seale, and R. Gonzales (1992). *How to tell the difference: A guide for evaluating children's books for anti-Indian bias*, No place: Author.

TVOntario. (1993). *Anti-racist education (selected readings and resources)* including B. Thomas, Principles of anti-racist education; N. Allingham, Guidelines for using film and videos on racism; Guidelines for the Selection of anti-racist materials, Toronto: Ontario Educational Communications Authority.

## Part 5

Bravo, E., and L. Miller (1994). What can teachers do about sexual harassment? In B. Bigelow, L. Christensen, S. Karp, B. Miner, and B. Peterson (eds.)

*Rethinking our classrooms: Teaching for equity and justice*, Milwaukee, WI: Rethinking Schools.

Coulter, P.R. (1996). Gender equity and schooling: Linking research and policy. *Canadian Journal of Education*, 21(4), 433–452.

Goldstein, T. (1998) Working towards equity. *Orbit*, 29(1), 14–16.

Hanrahan, M. (1987). Producing the female reserve labour force: Women and schooling. In T. Wotherspoon (ed.) *The political economy of Canadian schooling*, Toronto: Methuen.

Orenstein, P. (1994). Unbalanced equations: Girls, math, and the confidence gap; You can say "I think" in there; Too cute to be competent. In *Schoolgirls: Young women, self-esteem, and the confidence gap*, New York: Bantam Doubleday Dell Publishing Group.

Toronto Board of Education. (1994). Challenging Sexism. In *S.T.A.R.S. Equity Advisory Kit* (draft), Toronto: Toronto Board of Education.

## Part 6

Iseke-Barnes, J. (1999). Readings of cultural narratives of diet, technology, and schooling in multimedia stories. *Discourse: Studies in the Cultural Politics of Education*, 20(3), 409–426.

Wolf, Naomi. (1990). The beauty myth. In *The beauty myth*, Toronto: Vintage-Random House.

## Part 7

Gordon, L. (1994). What do we say when we hear "faggot?" In B. Bigelow, L. Christensen, S. Karp, B. Miner, and B. Peterson, *Rethinking our classrooms: Teaching for equity and justice*, Milwaukee, WI: Rethinking Schools.

Mac an Ghaíll, M. (1994). "(In)visibility: Race, sexuality and masculinity in the school context," from *Challenging lesbian and gay inequalities in education*, Buckingham, UK: Open University Press. In M. Blair, and J. Holland, with S. Sheldon, *Identity and diversity: Gender and the experience of education*, Buckingham, UK: The Open University.

Toronto Board of Education. (1977). *Safely out: Activities for challenging homophobia in schools*, including L. Chesley, D. MacAulay, and J. Ristock, Definitions of terms related to sexual orientation; V. Russell, Debunking myths; Gay Activists Alliance; V. Russell, and T. McCaskell, Homophobia in elementary schools: 4 Scenarios, Toronto: Toronto Board of Education.

# Part 8

Baxter, S. (1993). Journal; Interview with children. In S. Baxter, *A Child is Not a Toy*, Vancouver, B.C.: New Star Books.

Bigelow, B., and N. Diamond (1994). The organic goodie simulation. In B. Bigelow, L. Christensen, S. Karp, B. Miner, and B. Peterson, *Rethinking our classrooms: Teaching for equity and justice*, Milwaukee, WI: Rethinking Schools.

Toronto Board of Education (1997). *Challenging class bias* (draft), Toronto: Toronto Board of Education.

Mitchell, A. (1997). The poor fare worst in schools. *The Globe and Mail*, April 18, A1, A9.

Wane, N.N. (2000). Students at risk. *Canadian Woman Studies*, 19(4), 109.

# Appendix

Prouty, D. (Writer and Co-director), and N.T. Botkin (Director). (1993). *For Angela* [video]. (Available from the National Film Board of Canada, Montreal, QC).

Welsh, C. (Writer and Producer), N. Bailey (Director), and S. Johansson (Producer for Studio D). (1991). *Women in the shadows*. (Available from Studio D of the National Film Board of Canada, Montreal, QC and Direction Film Toronto, ON).